Human-Harmonized Information Technology, Volume 1

Toyoaki Nishida
Editor

Human-Harmonized Information Technology, Volume 1

Vertical Impact

 Springer

Editor
Toyoaki Nishida
Graduate School of Informatics
Kyoto University
Kyoto
Japan

ISBN 978-4-431-55865-1   ISBN 978-4-431-55867-5   (eBook)
DOI 10.1007/978-4-431-55867-5

Library of Congress Control Number: 2015954988

Springer Tokyo Heidelberg New York Dordrecht London

Printed on acid-free paper

Springer Japan KK is part of Springer Science+Business Media (www.springer.com)

Dedicated to the late Prof. Yoh'ichi Tohkura

Forewords

The Japan Science and Technology Agency (JST) is a major organization in Japan to promote science and technology policies and to provide research funds to researchers mainly in academia in order to support innovative science and technology. CREST is one of the funding programs promoted by JST, and in the field of Information and Communications Technologies, eight research areas are ongoing, one of which is "Creation of Human-Harmonized Information Technology for Convivial Society." Under the Research Supervisor, Prof. Toyoaki Nishida, who took over from the late Prof. Yoh'ichi Tohkura, 17 projects have been initiated. I have served as a research advisor for two different areas, one of which is this area. There are 17 highly advanced projects selected in the area. I noted as an advisor that the important point of projects in this area is to focus on the technologies for "convivial society." There have been several element technologies studied up to now such as virtual reality, augmented reality, robotics, sensing technologies, and so on. These technologies have been rapidly progressing, but in order to realize a convivial society, these element technologies should be combined and harmonized based on the requirements for convivial societies. The chapters in this publication can contribute to the creation of new theories, new architecture, new systems, and the invention of advanced applications to provide convivial societies. Such societies are required not only in the 2020s and 2030s, but in the 2040s, when "singularity of artificial intelligence" is envisaged to be a reality.

Tomonori Aoyama
Professor Emeritus, The University of Tokyo
Visiting Professor, Keio University

A harmonization between human beings and machines is becoming a more important function in daily life. The human-harmonized information technology that can understand a human's internal intentions will be able to realize healthy and cultured living and good preparation for an aged society. Some interesting themes of the human–machine harmonization have been explored by Prof. Tohkura and researchers in a CREST project. Chapters appearing in this book bring fascinating results not only to the harmonized society but also to Cyber Physical Systems and the Internet of Things.

Kazuo Asakawa
Fujitsu Laboratories, Ltd.

When the late Yoh'ichi Tohkura, Ph.D., started a field of research with the theme of harmony between human beings and the information environment, "information circulation" was emphasized as a key word that must never be forgotten. It not only referred to the processing of information but also pointed out the importance of feedback of the processed results to human beings. It expresses the idea that we should consider comprehensively the nature of the information environment being created, including "how" is "what feedback" given and whether the results will be useful at all. This book is the first to discuss the information circulation from three perspectives—with regard to people, information, and machines. The research findings introduced here serve as a persuasive guide to the design of our information society.

Eisaku Maeda
Vice President, Head of NTT Communication Science Laboratories

Technological singularity is widely considered as an Artificial Intelligence disaster triggered by highly advanced information technology. This idea of an exclusive relationship between human beings and machines is fascinating and seems to be a relationship inspired by the old story of Frankenstein's monster. The concept of human–machine harmonization, advocated by Prof. Tohkura, considers both human beings and machines as the necessary parts of the "information circulatory system" in human-harmonized information technology. This book predicts the future appearance of technological singularity that would not exclude humans; it will create a harmonious relationship between humans and machines in the information circulatory system. In the future, humanity will have its embodiment harmonized between humans and machines.

Taro Maeda
Professor, Graduate School of Information Science and Technology, Osaka
University/Center for Information and Neural Networks, NICT

This book guides the reader through cutting-edge research trends anticipating the way in which humans will live their lives in the rich information environments of the near future, receiving intellectual assistance while they work, study, eat, and have fun. The book's chapters cover a wide range of topics, but the reader may find that they come together under a coherent idea of looking ahead into the future. The entirety of this book is related to a research field of JST CREST, one of the most prestigious research grant schemes in Japan. This fact alone, however, does not fully account for the impression the book strikes on its readers. I am fond of the late Prof. Tohkura's stance in which a JST CREST research area should virtually function as a national research institute, with the research supervisor acting as its director. This was undoubtedly his role as the first research supervisor of the "Creation of Human-Harmonized Information Technology for Convivial Society" research area. From the beginning, he clearly showed his views regarding the definition of a convivial society, as well as how human-harmonized information technologies should be in such societies. In this regard, he emphasized that an information environment should enhance humans' intellectual capabilities. He showed his strong and talented leadership and excellent discernment while selecting all the research directors, who are responsible for each of the chapters in this book now with the prominent research outcomes. Moreover, he, as well as his successor, Prof. Nishida, continuously encouraged the research directors to not only pursue their original research objectives, but also to actively seek the opportunity to discuss and collaborate in joint research projects with other colleagues, in particular those working in this research area. I can say that those stances resulted in great success. I am sure the reader will enjoy going through every chapter.

Yôiti Suzuki

Professor, Research Institute of Electrical Communication, Tohoku University

Japan is becoming a super-aged society ahead of the rest of the world, and with it, the number of persons who have cognitive disabilities is sharply increasing. Moreover, persons who have developed visual or auditory function disorders or communication disorders in their youth must keep living in a society while burdened with a major handicap. Information technology (IT) compensates for weaknesses in human information processing, and the hope has been that IT will serve as a tool to assist those with language and/or communication disorders. While it is said that current artificial intelligence (AI) has functions that exceed human potential, we must wonder if it has become a technology that is beneficial to everyone. There is also the chance that globalization of useful IT will even lead to the homogenization of human thoughts and sensitiveness.

This project does not simply aim for IT that exceeds human ability for intelligence, but explores the underlying potential and diverse functions of humans while examining what IT should be, such as AI, for harnessing the potential and diverse functions of humans. Through my own research I have experienced how the underlying potential and diverse functions of humans can often surface for the first time after persons develop a physical disability. Persons who have developed language and/or communication disorders will try to converse through gestures or tactile means, while elderly persons who have developed cognitive impairments will increasingly try to convey something through facial expressions and gestures. However, that is insufficient to properly communicate with others and leads to social isolation, and society has yet to come up with a good approach for how to assist these people.

Fortunately, the researchers of the themes in this project have taken on the challenge of elucidating information on the processing function that lies deep within the brain; not just "intelligence", but also "emotion" and "consciousness" that lie in the background of intelligence. Furthermore, several of the themes feature highly creative approaches, such as discovering the possibilities of humans from new perspectives and helping to revive the aesthetic sense and spiritual cry that lie deep within the brain during the course of evolution. I believe that these approaches will contribute greatly to revealing and fostering human creativity, which are major goals of the project.

This book summarizes the results to date of this project. For example, it describes IT that grasps meanings conveyed by tactile means or movements in addition to words, whereby a computer answers using expressions with universal understanding. Persons with cognitive impairments and those with language and/or communication disorders have been waiting for this technology, which will become highly useful as a tool to promote their social participation. Additionally, research that reveals and fosters human creativity could give rise to various arts, such as new and yet familiar-sounding music that crosses racial and ethnic boundaries. This will give the joy of creativity to humans and give new purpose to living. This book describes how AI and IT should be developed, so that humans can truly understand each other and share the joy of creativity, and describes many hints and approaches for realizing this.

Professor Yoh'ichi Tohkura, the program officer for this project until 2014, was a friend of mine for more than 40 years. We shared the same dream of creating IT that is truly useful to humans, the kind described in this book. I hope that those of you who also wish to realize the same dream will enjoy this book.

Tohru Ifukube
Professor Emeritus, Institute of Gerontology, The University of Tokyo

Preface

The late Prof. Yoh'ichi Tohkura envisioned an information era in which information is used to achieve harmony for cultivating human and social potential, and proposed the idea of human-harmonized information technology. The vision was so fascinating that the Japan Science and Technology Agency (JST) decided to launch a EUR 40 million JST-CREST research area in FY2009 to substantiate a basic core of his grand idea in 8 years. Participated in by 17 research teams, the project has been actively working on building the human-harmonized information technology for significantly activating the inner power of individuals and the society for evolving creative life, and not just trying to passively follow their intentions. Although it was a profound sorrow that Prof. Tohkura passed away in December 2013 after intensively fostering the project in its infancy, the project kept growing after that tragedy and started to bear fruit.

This book is the first of two volumes that describe the major outcomes obtained from the JST-CREST research area on the creation of human-harmonized information technology for a convivial society, as delineated above. The challenge I tackled to assemble this book centered on uncovering not just hidden trails but also trunk highways, the untold philosophy, to restore the strategy of technical development toward a convivial society. To put it another way, I wanted to redraw a big picture that would tell why we need to develop a new technology for transforming the ongoing technical society into a convivial society, and moreover, exactly what difference and contribution we have been attempting to bring about by our human-harmonized information technology.

After nearly a couple of years of discussions, we have found that the idea of the human and social potential beautifully explains everything. Even though the current development of artificial intelligence would eventually release us from labors either physical or informational, the individuals and society will need to find new styles and ways of living for wellness in the new technology world. It is quite probable that we may have to overcome a great deal of suffering to reestablish a conciliation with technology, as the nature of our life and society to be brought about in a new AI-geared technology might be drastically different from the conventional one we have been familiar with, and the change might be much faster and overwhelming than we might have thought. It is evident that people will need to find a nontraditional style of self-actualization and society will aspire to a new principle of endorsing harmony.

Human potential is the power of an individual that enables her or him to actively sustain an endeavor to achieve a goal in maintaining a social relationship with other people. It involves vision, activity, sustainability, empathy, ethics, humor, and aesthetic sense. Social potential is the power that a society of people possesses as a whole. It encompasses generosity, supportiveness, conviviality, diversity, connectedness, and innovativeness. We believe that human and social potentials complement each other to enable conviviality, and that Prof. Tohkura focused on human perception to explore the research into the human-harmonized information technology on the road toward the convivial society. The framework of the human-harmonized information technology centers on understanding and enhancing cognitive dynamics resulting in the interaction between pathos based on embodied perception and logos based on modern civilization.

First, we have been shedding light on high-level but often tacit sensations in the search for better scientific understanding and technological support. For example, we have found that a sensation of presence results from complex dynamics over multiple sensations and tactile information—for instance, a feeling of hugging plays a critical role in convincing us of a presence. We have identified some tacit nonverbal cues that help people a lot in dealing with interpersonal relationships. We have also found that overtrust may result from an unconscious dependence on tacit cues.

Second, we have been developing artificial systems that can recognize the world in the way humans do. These new artifacts are useful in building a common ground in human–artifact symbiosis, which may make human–artifact interaction both proficient and reliable. The haptic sensation is a relatively new area of research. Some research teams in our research area have worked on not only high-performance recognition and production but also on integrating haptic sensation techniques in a multi-modal interaction environment.

Third, we have worked on design and dissemination. Design is a key to applying technology to produce satisfaction in society. Design encompasses activities of inventing social activities to composing a solution to achieve a desired goal by combining existing solutions and negotiating with the users for a consensus possibly with compromises in return for benefits. We have exploited the state-of-the-art technology to design novel services ranging from information display to a life-long infrastructure for food. Disseminating a tool is an important contribution from research based on computer science. Dissemination has many aspects in common with design, as tools need to be designed generically so they can fit into many application scenes.

Finally, we placed much emphasis on longitudinal large-scale interactive display at public places such as the National Museum of Emerging Science and Innovation (Miraikan) as well as long-term sustained field trials, where we can not only reach out to a large number of people with a broad background but also learn directly or indirectly from discussions on the spot where the technology is displayed. In this book, each contribution lays much weight on discussing the philosophy, concepts, and the implications underlying the project. The first volume, with the subtitle *Vertical Impact*, includes the nine works resulting from the projects launched in 2009–2010, while the second, with the subtitle *Horizontal Expansion*, the eight works from those launched in 2010–2011. Overall, the first concentrates more on basic perception, while the second more on compositional aspects.

Kyoto   Toyoaki Nishida
August 2015

Contents

Chapter 1
Introduction to Human-Harmonized Information Technology

Toyoaki Nishida

Abstract The JST-CREST research area on the creation of human-harmonized information technology for a convivial society aims for the establishment of basic technologies to achieve harmony between human beings and the information environment by integrating element technologies encompassing real-space communication, human interfaces, and media processing. It promotes a trans-disciplinary approach featuring (1) recognition and comprehension of human behaviors and real-space contexts by utilizing sensor networks and ubiquitous computing, (2) technologies for facilitating man-machine communication by utilizing robots and ubiquitous networks, and (3) content technologies for analyzing, mining, integrating, and structuring multimedia data including those in text, voice, music, and images. It ranges from scientific research on cognitive aspects of human-harmonized information processes to social implementation that may lead to breakthroughs in the harmonious interactions of human and information environments. This chapter presents the underlying philosophy, background, core concepts, and major results obtained from the first half of projects that were selected to pursue new findings in this research area.

Keywords Changing world · Computer and communication technology · Convivial society · Human and social potential · Human-harmonized information technology

1.1 Prologue

The Japan Science and Technology Agency (JST) is one of the core institutions sponsored by the Japanese government and it is responsible for the implementation

T. Nishida (✉)
JST-CREST Research Area on Creation of Human-Harmonized Information
Technology for Convivial Society, Kyoto University, Kyoto Japan/Research Supervisor,
Tokyo, Japan
e-mail: nishida@i.kyoto-u.ac.jp

© Springer Japan 2016
T. Nishida (ed.), *Human-Harmonized Information Technology, Volume 1*,
DOI 10.1007/978-4-431-55867-5_1

1

of science and technology policy in Japan.[1] As well as other grants, JST provides researchers with three types of competitive funds: those for strategic basic research programs, those for research and development programs focused on technology transfer, and those for global activities. The total amount of competitive funds from JST for FY2014 was slightly more than 700 million Euro.[2] About two thirds of these funds were provided to Strategic Basic Research Programs where our Core Research for Evolutionary Science and Technology (CREST) and 10 other programs were incorporated. CREST is a funding program for network-based (team-based) research that has given rise to outstanding results that are believed to lead to scientific and technological innovation. Thirty seven research areas consisting of 431 research teams were active in FY2014. Eight research areas were in green innovation, eleven were in life innovation, nine were in nano-technology and materials, and nine were in ICT.

Our research area is funded under the title of "creation of human-harmonized information technology for a convivial society.[3]" It was founded by the late Professor Yoh'ichi Tohkura and launched in FY 2009 to address strategic objectives to create a basic technology that enables an information environment that is in harmony with people. We propose a focus on perceptual information processing to harmonically interface between the human and information environment. The three main features of our program are:

- Recognition and comprehension of human behaviors and real-space contexts by utilizing sensor networks and ubiquitous computing,
- Technologies for facilitating man-machine communication by utilizing robots and ubiquitous networks, and
- Content technologies that are related to analyzing, mining, integrating, and structuring multi-media information processing.

Seventeen research teams were chosen from FY2009 to 2011: eight in the first year, five in the second, and four in the third as a result of peer reviews that followed applications that were received in response to calls for proposals each year. Each research team was funded for slightly more than 5 years. This chapter encompasses the entire scope of our research area and reports the results that were obtained by eight research teams that were launched in the first year together with another one that was launched in the second year and upgraded to an exploratory research for advanced technology office (ERATO) project from FY2014.

I will first discuss the impact that rapid progress in technology may eventually bring about in our daily lives and society in the long run in the rest of this chapter and point out vulnerabilities in humanity and society, as these comprise the background to and motivation for our research area. I will then introduce the concept of human-harmonic information technology as a means of enhancing human and social potential that is threatened by the surge in social change accelerated by technology. Finally,

---

[1] http://www.jst.go.jp/EN/index.html.

[2] Based on the exchange rate: 1 EUR = 130 JPN.

[3] http://www.jst.go.jp/kisoken/crest/en/research_area/ongoing/areah21-1.html.

I will overview the results obtained from the first group of research teams, discuss future perspectives, and conclude this chapter.

1.2   Changing World

The grand idea of human-harmonic information technology originated from Professor Tohkura's impressive conjecture that concerned the five-staged shift in roles of information in human society (Fig. 1.1). The first two stages were hunter-gatherer and agricultural societies. Information was used for survival in these stages. Just like other creatures, humans needed to find cues from the environment to survive by finding food while avoiding potential dangers. Unlike other creatures, humans invented a means for communication not just with allies but also with descendants beyond generations by handing down stories with spoken languages. The expression and preservation of thoughts in written language is far more stable and endowed mankind to evolve with memes or cultural genes that were orders of magnitudes faster than biological genes. It allowed mankind to significantly increase the capability and stability of producing food, which was first accomplished by hunting and then by agriculture.

The social structure in these two stages might be characterized as one that was supported by human intelligence, as schematically outlined in Fig. 1.2, where major

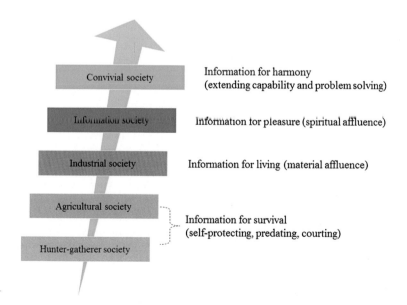

Fig. 1.1 Professor Tohkura's grand conjecture concerning the five-staged shift in roles of information in human society

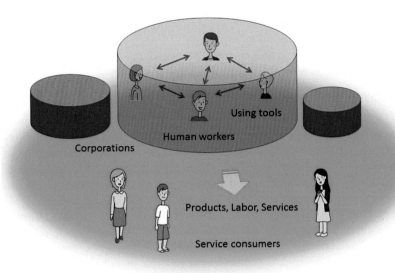

Fig. 1.2 The human society was supported by humans. © 2015, Toyoaki Nishida and At, Inc. Reproduced with permission

communications and decision making in corporations were supported by humans who conducted physical tasks. Printing technology contributed a great deal to preserve information and communicate it beyond generations and geographic distances.

Mankind exhibited enormous interest in improving the productivity of energy, materials, and machinery at lower cost and with less labor, which allowed us to witness the emergence of an industrial society in which energy, materials, and machinery enhanced one another to accelerate increases in productivity. The movable-printing technology that Gutenberg invented in the 15th century contributed to the rapid and reliable dissemination of knowledge that was required for production. Information was used by people to maintain and improve productivity. People were gradually freed from the burden of the heavy physical tasks that were involved in agriculture and hunting. The information tasks imposed on people were not greatly alleviated until the emergence of electrical and electronic engineering where electricity was used to represent signals by converting them into electronic representations for storage, transmission, and reproduction. The creation of new jobs allowed workers to become involved in contract-based work that released them from their previous destiny. Although the notion of automation was introduced, the logic for automation was tenuous when logic was mechanically implemented. The critical role of people shifted to information tasks, the control of artifacts using their capabilities for perception and cognition, and the design of novel products and services. This brought about the notion of employment, which in turn added another role to information, i.e., information for living.

Meanwhile, the structure of communication and decision making did not change much from the scheme in Fig. 1.2, even though the advent of electronics and electronic engineering and the modern transportation system significantly improved the efficiency of communication.

We witnessed the birth of digital computers in the last century. This reflected a trend in mathematics to formalize the idea of computation as mathematics. This idea was brought to fruition through electronic engineering. The invention of digital computers and networks rapidly penetrated into human society, having transformed it into an information society. The theoretical foundation for information and communication technology originated from the idea of a universal computing machine. This now called the universal Turing machine, which Alan Turing proposed in 1936, that for any recursive function, f, one can always program the universal Turing machine so it may calculate f. This is a super innovation as it suggests that if somebody builds a universal Turing machine, U, through some physical means such as electronic circuits, U can compute any recursive function "simply" by symbolically describing it, e.g., as a punched paper tape, and one does not need to reconstruct the whole electronic circuit for computing a given function. In fact, the idea of a universal Turing machine was substantiated by von Neumann and other innovators around 1945, and since then, technical improvements to digital computers have been exponentially taking place.

Another innovation in information and communication technology was the rapid development of digital networks that interconnected computers. The Internet rapidly reached world-wide, after the period of academic use that followed the military experimental stage and the invention of a hypertext mark-up language (HTML), its interpreters known as browsers, and the introduction of powerful search engines in the 1990s. Thus, there were 1.02 billion Internet users around the globe in 2005, which has kept growing at about 12.4% per year, until it reached 2.92 billion in 2014. This is expected to reach 5.5 billion by 2025 according to Cisco.[4]

The exponential growth of computer and communication technology reached a point at the end of the last century that convinced people that digital computers and networks constituted the most important part of our infrastructure that controlled energy and materials, as has been summarized in Table 1.1.

Many people now came to think of computers as new tools [21]. In fact, huge numbers of computer tools and systems were deployed to support human life. Although the tasks conducted by them were rather simple repetitive tasks, they potentially involved tremendous amounts of computation and complex logic. Both computers and networks became quite inexpensive compared with their performance at the beginning of this century while digital computers and networks were very slow and programming was quite expensive and non-dependable in the early days. Significant portions of basic software as well as data became open and free so many people could participate in activities to build ever new values on top of the new information and communication infrastructure.

It not only provided efficient and reliable transmission of information and computing, but it also gradually took over information tasks that had been conventionally imposed on people to support other people. The scheme presented in Fig. 1.2 was

---

[4]http://newsroom.cisco.com/press-release-content?type=webcontent\&articleId=888280.

Table 1.1 The rough history of the development of information and communication technology

Year	Epoch
1936	Turing Machine
1947	von Neumann Computer
1948	Information Theory, by C. Shannon and W. Weaver
1948	Cybernetics by N. Wiener
1957	FORTRAN by J. Backus
1961	Mathematical theory of Packet Networks by L. Kleinrock
1963	Interactive Computer Graphics by I. Sutherland
1968	Mouse and Bitmap display for oN Line System (NLS) by D.C. Engelbart
1969	ARPA-net
1970	ALOHAnet
1970	Relational Database Theory by E.F. Codd
1972	Theory of NP-completeness by S. Cook and R. Karp
Mid 1970s	Alto Machine by A. Kay and A. Goldberg
1976	Ethernet
1979	Spreadsheet Program Visicalc by D. Bricklin
1982	TCP/IP Protocol by B. Kahn and V. Cerf
Mid 1980s	First Wireless Tag Products
1987	UUNET started the Commercial UUCP Network Connection Service
1988	Internet worm (Morris Worm)
1989	World Wide Web by T. Berners-Lee
1989	The number of hosts on the Internet has exceeded 100,000
1992	The number of hosts on the Internet has exceeded 1,000,000
1994	Shopping malls on the Internet
1994	W3C was founded by T. Berners-Lee
1997	Google Search
1998	XML1.0 (eXtensible Markup Language) by W3C
1998	PayPal
2001	Wikipedia
2003	Skype/iTunes store
2004	Facebook
2005	YouTube/Google Earth
2006	Twitter
2007	Google Street View

Adapted from [19]

transformed into the one in Fig. 1.3, where increasingly more complex and intelligent tasks were delegated to computers that could serve as apprentices to human experts and not just as tools.

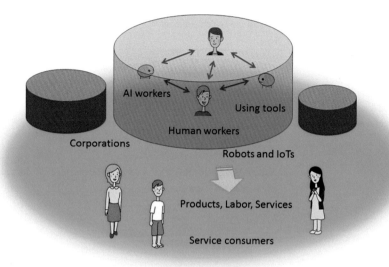

Fig. 1.3 The human society was supported by human-AI hybrid teams. © 2015, Toyoaki Nishida and At, Inc. Reproduced with permission

Significant portions of information tasks in corporations became replaced by computers that were able to perform these tasks both efficiently, reliably, and incessantly at low cost. As a result, people have been increasingly released from the laborious duties of repetition of simple information and have shifted into higher levels that require more abstract forms of intelligence, such as aesthetic sense, intuition, wisdom, or high-risk, high-return investments. People have simultaneously come to believe that essential value consists in information that may mean a ticket to pleasure.

The exponential growth in computer and communication technology did not stop or even slow down and still kept growing in the new century. It gave rise to an information explosion or the big data phenomenon. Many aspects of human life started to be featured or described as data.

The machine learning and data mining technologies that have been developed in artificial intelligence have been widely utilized to derive useful information from data to provide better services. The more data that are available results in the emergence of more intelligent machines, which in turn produces more data for further intelligent machines. In fact, this trend can be seen in the history of the development of ICT and AI technologies, which are roughly listed in Table 1.2.

It is evident that although AI technology was initially meant just to address a new academic challenge due to limitations in the scale and power of computers and available data, it became socially influential around 2010. It is now believed that AI has the potential to address the value of information and significantly amplify it. The synergy between big data and intelligent machines may eventually bring about an intelligence explosion.

Table 1.2 The rough history of AI technology development

Year	Epoch
1952–62	Checker program by A. Samuel
1956	Dartmouth Conference
1961	Symbolic Integration program SAINT by J. Slagle
1962	Perceptron by F. Rosenblatt
1966	The ALPAC report against Machine Translation by R. Pierce
1967	Formula Manipulation System Macsyma by J. Moses
1967	Dendral for Mass Spectrum Analysis by E. Feigenbaum
1971	Natural Language Dialogue System SHRDLU, by T. Winograd
1973	Combinatorial Explosion problem pointed out in The Lighthill report
1974	MYCIN by T. Shortliffe
Mid 1970s	Prial Sketch and Visual Perceptron by D. Marr
1976	Automated Mathematician (AM) by D. Lenat
1979	Autonomous Vehicle Stanford Cart by H. Moravec
1982	Fifth Generation Computer Project
1984	The CYC Project by D. Lenat
Mid 1980s	Back-propagation algorithm was widely used
1985	the Cybernetic Artist Aaron by H. Cohen
1986	Subsumption Architecture by R. Brooks
1989	An Autonomous Vehicle ALVINN by D. Pomerleau
1990	Genetic Programming by J.R. Koza
Early 1990s	TD-Gammon by G. Tesauro
Mid 1990s	Data Mining Technology
1997	DeepBlue defeated the World Chess Champion G. Kasparov
1997	The First Robocup by H. Kitano
1999	Robot pets became commercially available
2000	Honda Asimo
2004	The Mars Exploration Rovers (Spirit & Opportunity)
2010	Google Driverless Car/Kinect
2011	IBM Watson Jeopardy defeated two of the greatest champions
2012	Siri

Adapted from [19]

However, a couple of problems may arise [20] on the dark side. The first problem is technology abuse: new technologies can be applied to illegal or malicious activities. The second is responsibility flaws: the more complex artifacts become, the less likely it is that humans can place them under control, i.e., neither the product maker nor the owner of a complex artifact may take full responsibility for an artifact, if it is fairly complex.

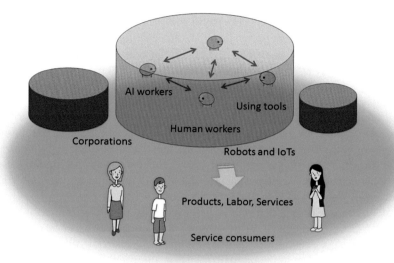

Fig. 1.4 The human society was supported by artificial intelligence. © 2015, Toyoaki Nishida and At, Inc. Reproduced with permission

1.3 Toward a Convivial Society

As many authors have discussed in the discourse of the latter half of the chessboard arguments, it will not take long until such exponential growth will rapidly change the social structure. AI will be able to outperform people so long as the criteria are clearly defined [3, 5]. Even very high-level information tasks that previously required a very abstract form of intelligence will be conducted by intelligent autonomous agents and the ratio of autonomous agents against humans in corporations will increase to infinity, which will result in the scheme of an AI-supported society illustrated in Fig. 1.4.

1.3.1 Brightness and Darkness in AI-Supported Society

The AI-supported society involves AI that is heavily used to mediate between people and services [20]. Social interactions may be accomplished hierarchically. The role of social interactions at low levels is to dynamically allocate computational resources to achieve maximal utility by taking into account fairness under priority settings. Social interactions at higher levels may be for more abstract social interactions including information sharing, collaboration, negotiation, contract making, coalition, and arbitration. Social interactions may be designed at the sociological level to negotiate conflicting intentions. Philosophers such as Thomas Hobbes discussed the negotiation between individuals and the government as a social contract problem of arbitration of conflicting benefits in a world governed by natural laws [16]. Apparently, positions such as "each person is to have an equal right to the most extensive basic liberty compatible with a similar liberty of others" and "social and economic inequalities are to be arranged so that they are both (a) reasonably expected to be to everybody's advantage, and (b) attached to positions and offices open to all" proposed as part of a theory of justice by Rawls [22] should be respected. However, these positions should only be taken as desiderata, and not as rigorous rules that are approximately implemented into artifacts and artificial societies. Such a best effort attitude is significant in the Internet age in the sense that providers only promise to make best efforts to offer good services and customers have to get used to these efforts. The technology for AI-mediated social interaction might resolve problems with technology abuse and responsibility flaws.

In addition, the AI-supported society will eventually even release humans from information tasks. Even though various people will continuously take care of corporate businesses, AI will automatically make the optimal decisions to run corporations to support mankind. AI-corporations will range from the infrastructure to highly intellectual tasks such as education or care-giving, due to its reliability, cost, and nice personalized interfaces. The less people that are required to run corporations, the fewer costs they will require. The total cost of supporting mankind will eventually be significantly reduced. Although some people will still work even harder than today in the AI-supported society, it will not be because they have to support themselves or their family or do it for some inescapable reasons, but because they want to achieve some accomplishments that they probably set up voluntarily as a goal to satisfy their dreams. The elderly and small children will be able to gain autonomy with the full support of intelligent physical assistants. The notion of profession will remain not as someone who is paid who has high-level and often licensed skills, but as a highly motivated and skilled person often with an implicit or explicit mission statement, such as someone who can release mankind from pain or entertain people to make them happy. In other words, professions as an obligation or a means of earning money will decrease, while those that require self-motivation will increase. The question is whether AI-supported society will be nice to people. Is that bad?

However, AI-supported society might bring about new problems. The first is a crisis in morality; as AI-assistants handle most social conflicts, people might become ignorant about ethics and humanity. Carr points out that we have started handing off moral decisions to computers [7]. Another problem is overdependence on artifacts: [20] as a result of AI being introduced, society might assume the infallibility of artifacts without rationale and people might use artifacts without a balanced sense of judgment. AI might bring about infirmity to individuals and society at the human level; as AI can do better than professional people who have respected expertise, human society may encounter significant social changes, and as a result, people might prefer AI to people, as has been pointed out by Turkle [27]. We need to overcome these problems until we reach the convivial society introduced by Professor Tohkura where information is used for harmony and empathy between humans and technology [18] is achieved so people and technology can know each other, feel each other, and share emotions and morals.

1.3.2 Transition to a Convivial Society

The transition phase from an information society to a convivial society might be painful. It involves such issues as *end of work* [8, 23] and *race against the machine* [4]. They are essentially caused by the conflicts between new and old regimes. Although change is welcome, human society does not seem to be prepared for any significant change to the AI-supported society. Among others, the end of work issue may cause the most serious concern, as work is not just a means of earning money, but also fulfills a more essential desire: self-actualization [17]. Even though one may find AI-supported human society suitable, s/he cannot necessarily adapt to her/his economical life to that shift. AI might become fairly creative, in the sense that it can even make important scientific discoveries. As a result, most people might eventually lose not just their jobs but also the opportunity for self-actualization, so long as employers want cheaper and better employees who can accomplish specified jobs. Although some jobs, such as those that require individual responsibility or symbolic ones that can only be done by a small number of people, e.g., top human players, will remain dedicated to humans, they are extremely competitive, as was described in Ando's enlightening book [2]. Although this is fair, it is not easy for people as they are not familiar with that kind of lifestyle.

People need to find other areas of self-actualization. It is extremely difficult to establish creativity at a level that other people can admire and recognize. People might lose the confidence, self-efficacy, and even self-esteem that originate from their skills and expertise in the conventional regime. Such desperation might lead to a loss of identity. People may give up on retaining identity by finding something that others cannot do. Even human autonomy might be lost; if people look for a better choice, they had better follow decisions made by AI. As Carr pointed out [7], excessive automation might alienate humans from activities, which are the source of humanity. He argues that this happens even today by referring to an article published in the Economist in 2012 that pointed out that "for most people, the servant (i.e., the smart phone) has become the master (of the owner)"

We need to completely design and implement the social regime for the transition to be successful, ranging from lifestyles to working styles and the redistribution of wealth. It is often quite difficult to destroy the social structure with which we have been familiar, particularly under circumstances where the outcome is not completely clear and not everybody may agree on the aspects of transition, though not the transition itself. Second, we need to change ourselves to match the new social regime. Even though people understand that work shift [9] is inevitable, it might not be easy at all for many people to change their work habits and void the expertise they have fostered during their lifetimes.

We will need to revamp the relationship between humans and technology, not just by inventing human-friendly technology, but also by making technology explore new forms of perception, activity, and creativity. This may suggest that human nature might be significantly influenced by technology and some virtues mankind has harnessed in history might be lost or at least threatened as a result. We need to teach computers about ourselves and our society, as computers as a metaphor for apprentices should be transformed into computers as a metaphor for partners in the transition phase. This includes numerous things, from commonsense to highly professional knowledge and skills. Even though teaching may be fun and meaningful to a majority of people, what is waiting for them after the transition will be rather difficult. As AI workers will undertake simple tasks, people need to be more creative than before, or engage in tasks only humans can do, e.g., those involved in evaluating other people or taking a certain amount of risk and responsibility to defy unpredictable challenges. This is pretty harsh, as the success ratio will be much lower than before. The success ratio might follow a power law rather than a normal distribution where people may become happy if they can be within the scope of being significantly over average. People understand effective traditional practices, such as diligence, to achieve success. In contrast, those virtues may not always be effective in achieving a very high degree of creativity, such as becoming a superstar. Indeed, no fixed paths seem to exist to achieve success in an information society [28].

The use of technology to increase empathy in society will be necessary to lead to the idea of the convivial society proposed by Professor Tohkura within a broader context. This is an approach to designing a good relationship between human society and technology by coping with the threat to humanity and human society both at the transitional stage that we will have to go through and the asymptotic stage that we will eventually witness, and that will therefore be enhanced through adequate means. I believe that the notions of human and social potential exist at the center.

1.3.3 Human and Social Potential

Issues on the transition to a convivial society are summarized in Fig. 1.5. It has been argued that human society will have to resolve numerous difficulties in the transition phase to the convivial society. We will have to make serious efforts on enhancing our own wisdom and resilience to build a new social regime and reach the convivial society in which humans and technology are in harmony.

We consider human and social potential to be a central issue. Human potential is the power of an individual that enables her/him to actively sustain an endeavor to achieve a goal in maintaining a social relationship with other people. It involves vision, activity, sustainability, empathy, ethics, humor, and aesthetic sense. Vision permits one to initiate a long-term coherent activity. It involves setting up a goal if it is considered important and meaningful even though it is painful and risky. Activity implies a decision of changing thought into actions when faced with numerous difficulties. Sustainability relies on a strong will to adhere to a plan when various kinds of unexpected events and failures occur. Great wisdom is needed from time to time to revise the initial plan on time, and whenever necessary. Empathy is the ability to reflect on the thoughts and emotions of other people and regard them as if they had happened to oneself. Ethics regulates one's intentions and activities to pay a great deal of respect to other people as well as following ethical principles. As a

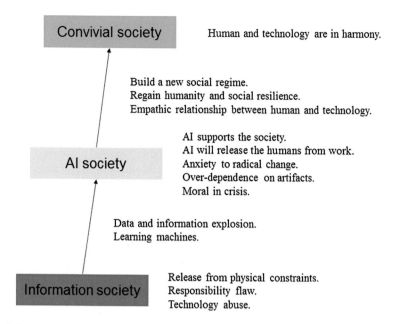

Fig. 1.5 Issues in the Transition to the Convivial Society. © 2015, Toyoaki Nishida and At, Inc. Reproduced with permission

result, one may sacrifice oneself to help others and refrain from taking advantage of the weakness of others. A sense of humor may be used to entertain oneself or other people by turning otherwise ridiculous or even negative events into a cheerful story. An aesthetic sense is about the creation and appreciation of beauty, which may make our lives pleasant and lovely. Although human potential is considered to be innate to individuals, it might be under threat due to rapid, unpredictable, and overwhelming torrents in the transition phase. People may forget or even lose the virtue of human potential under such difficulties.

Social potential is the power that a society of people possesses as a whole. It encompasses generosity, supportivity, conviviality, diversity, connectedness, and innovativeness. Generosity maximally alleviates the degree of potential penalty in failure to encourage members to address difficult challenges. Supportivity not only actually helps members engage in various challenges but also provides them with a feeling that their activities are being supported by society. Diversity encourages members to be different to increase the success of both society as a whole and individual members. Connectedness provides participants with the feeling of being connected to help one another to overcome difficulties and provokes the synergistic effect of sharing pleasure. Innovativeness is a shared attitude of individuals who aim at innovations as a whole society.

Human and social potentials complement each other to enable creativity. Human potential allows individuals to explore, set up, and sustain meaningful goals and efforts to achieve them. Even if the path is filled with difficulties and pains that have resulted from failure, human potential serves as a source of encouraging individuals not to give up. Social potential legitimately supports creativity. The more creative a society is trying to be, the lower the success ratio that results from this. Thus, a creative society tends to reward successful people more, is generous when failures occur, and promotes collaboration.

Among others, I believe that play and game are the center to human and social potential. As is suggested by "homo ludens" [10], play, defined as "a voluntary activity or occupation executed within certain fixed limits of time and place, according to rules freely accepted but absolutely binding, having its aim in itself and accompanied by a feeling of tension, joy, and the consciousness that it is 'different' from 'ordinary" life,[5]" is essential to humanity in the sense that "play is older than culture." Caillois [6] elaborated on the idea, shifting the focus from play, defined as an activity which is essentially free, separate, uncertain, unproductive, governed by rules and make-believe, to game which is classified into four categories: agon (competition), alea (chance), mimicry (simulation), and ilinx (vertigo). We have good reason to believe both play and game are closely related to the creativity of individuals and conviviality of a society in the AI-supported society.

1.3.4   Roadmap for Enhancing Human and Social Potential

A roadmap for enhancing human and social potential (Fig. 1.6) may consist of multiple levels, ranging from philosophy to technology.

The top level constitutes a manifesto from the viewpoints of ethics and humanities. It should promote the development and use of technology to enhance human and social potential, where the technology should be designed to encourage active participation for creativity in a technology-supported society, and not to deactivate people. The convivial society needs to be discussed in depth, and consensus in this society should be democratically formulated. Among others, the end of work issue should be discussed from the viewpoint of ethics and humanities until a global consensus is obtained. The potential difficulty and pain in the transition phase to it need to be addressed. Even though spontaneous painstaking for innovation might be encouraged, people should not be compelled to accept pain.

The strategy level should pave the road for the convivial society so that each sector in the society may smoothly depart from the conventional social and economic regime without excessively suffering from difficulties. Coping with work shift might be among the most critical issues and a maximally effective strategy for this needs to be formulated and shared. A practical strategy for incrementally taking advantage of advanced technology and embedding it into society needs to be figured out to formulate an empathic relationship between technology and mankind. People with

---

[5]p. 28 in [10].

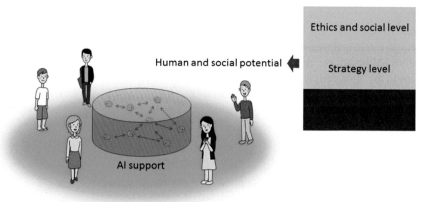

Fig. 1.6 Roadmap to the Convivial Society

great expertise in the conventional paradigm should be respected and protected in the transition phase.

New technical challenges need to be identified at the technology level to create the transition and achieve the convivial society. Scenarios regarding how new technologies contribute to enhancing human and social potential need to be made explicit and shared. Human harmonized information technology, to be presented in the rest of this chapter, is focused on to enhance human perception of the convivial society.

1.4 Human-Harmonized Information Technology

The JST-CREST research area on creation of human-harmonized information technology for the convivial society was established in 2009 to address the imbalance between humans and technology, which may hinder rather than help the creativity of humans through fast and overwhelming technological developments. We placed particular emphasis on innovative theory and technology to achieve an innovative perceptual information environment in harmony with people not just to adapt to them but also to cultivate spontaneous activities to enable creativity and establish an empathic relationship between humans and technology. Our program features recognition and comprehension of human behaviors and real-space contexts by utilizing sensor networks and ubiquitous computing, technologies for facilitating man-machine communication by utilizing robots and ubiquitous networks, and content technologies related to analyzing, mining, integrating and structuring multi-media information processing.

We focus on innovative approaches in human-harmonized sensations by encompassing analysis and modeling and computational realization and applications. Our scope not only includes basic computational sensations such as audio-visual information processing that has a long history of research and tactile and haptic information processing that is relatively new, but it also strives for novel computational sensations such as a sense of presence and distrust/mistrust, which have been rarely addressed before. Although we encouraged each team to span from basic research to applications in the open calls for proposals and in fact placed equal emphasis on technology deployment and social implementation as well as basic research and technical development, we gave greater priority to innovative proposals that might lead to deep insights into research topics.

1.4.1 Organization of Research Teams in Research Area

We selected 17 teams for funding out of the 223 proposals we received over 3 years from 2009–2011, as listed in Table 1.3. We promoted collaboration among different teams after the selection so that they could not only help but also stimulate one another to achieve more challenging innovations. In this volume, we assemble the first nine teams which were already concluded, we will report the forthcoming results from the remaining eight teams in the succeeding volume. This volume is with the subtitle "Vertical Impact" as it is the first impact that spans from the foundation not only to application but also to social implementation, whereas the second volume will be with the subtitle "Horizontal Expansion" as it will demonstrate the breadth of the scope.

Chapter 2 describes the results obtained from a project entitled "studies on cellphone-type tele-operated androids transmitting human presence" conducted by Ishiguro [11]. Ishiguro's team addressed a new communication medium for transmitting human presence and developed a series of new tele-operated androids. Telenoid, among others, was designed to allow the user to transmit her/his presence to a distant location by using the Telenoid so that a conversation partner in the location could talk to the Telenoid as if it were the user herself/himself. A significant reduction in the cortisol levels was found for participants who had conversations with huggable devices, such as the Telenoid, in an experimental evaluation.

Chapter 3 reports the results from a project entitled "modeling and detecting overtrust from behavior signals" led by Takeda [26]. Based on large signal corpora, Takeda's team investigated the mathematical modeling of human behaviors by mapping the behaviors onto two discrete-continuous hybrid systems, i.e., a cognition-decision process and a decision-action process. This research involved building a behavioral model that could relate the human internal state and observed behavioral signals. The results from the research were applied to detecting over-reliance in an automated driving system.

Chapter 4 explains what was obtained from a project entitled "life log infrastructure for food" led by Aizawa [1]. Although food is one of the most important and regularly consumed factors in our daily lives, it has rarely been viewed as an object of information processing. Aizawa's team developed an infrastructure for life logs, with an emphasis on food and food-related activities in our daily lives. It allowed

Table 1.3 Teams of the JST-CREST research area on creation of human-harmonized information technology for Convivial Society

Year	ID	Team
2009	P1	Life Log Infrastructure for Food (PI: Kiyoharu Aizawa)
	P2	Dynamic Information Space based on High-speed Sensor Technology (PI: Masatoshi Ishikawa)
	P3	Developing a communication environment by decoding and controlling implicit interpersonal information (PI: Makio Kashino)
	P4	Smart seminar room based on multi-modal recognition of verbal and non-verbal information (PI: Tatsuya Kawahara)
	P5	Elucidation of perceptual illusion and development of secse-centered human interface (PI: Yasuharu Koike)
	P6	Sensing and controlling human gaze in daily living space for human-harmonized information environments (PI: Yoichi Sato)
	P7	Modeling and detecting overtrust from behavior signals (PI: Kazuya Takeda)
	P8	Construction and Utilization of Human-harmonized "Tangible" Information Environment (PI: Susumu Tachi)
2010	P9	Studies on cellphone-type teleoperated androids transmitting human presence (PI: Hiroshi Ishiguro)
	P10	[a]Development of a sound field sharing system for creating and exchanging music (PI: Shiro Ise)
	P11	[a]Enabling a mobile social robot to adapt to a public space in a city (PI: Takayuki Kanda)
	P12	[a]Development of Fundamental Technologies for Innovative Use of Character/Document Media and Their Application to Creating Human Harmonized Information Environment (PI: Koichi Kise)
	P13	[a]Behavior Understanding based on Intention-Gait Model (PI: Yasushi Yagi)
2011	P14	[a]Building a Similarity-aware Information Environment for a Content-Symbiotic Society (PI: Masataka Goto)
	P15	[a]Pedagogical Machine: Developmental cognitive science approach to create teaching/teachable machines (PI: Kazuo Hiraki)
	P16	[a]User Generated Dialogue Systems: uDialogue (PI: Keiichi Tokuda)
	P17	[a]Harmonized Inter-Personal Display Based on Position and Direction Control (PI: Takeshi Naemura)

[a]: in volume 2

them to investigate the capture, analysis, visualization, and interfacing of multimedia logs of food and related experiences. They drew on this data collection to investigate potential community discovery, support for communications, standardization of life log data, and privacy control issues. Healthcare was addressed as an application.

Chapter 5 presents the results obtained from a project entitled "dynamic information space based on high-speed sensor technology" by Ishikawa [12]. A new information space was constructed in this project that allowed humans to identify phenomena that exceeded the limitations of human senses. Crucial to this effort were: perfect detection of underlying dynamics and a new model of sensory-motor integration drawn from work with a kilohertz-rate sensor and display technologies. As the sampling rate within the information space is matched with the dynamics of the physical world, humans are able to deterministically predict the attributes of the surrounding, rapidly-evolving environment. This leads to a new type of interaction, where the learning rate and capacity of our recognition system are augmented.

Chapter 6 overviews the outcome from a project entitled "construction and utilization of a human-harmonized 'tangible' information environment" that was led by Tachi [25]. The aim of Tachi's project was to construct an intelligent information environment that was both visible and tangible, where real-space communication, a human-machine interface, and media processing were integrated. Tachi's team created a human-harmonized "tangible information environment" to attain this end that allowed human beings to obtain and understand haptic information in real space, to transmit the thus-obtained haptic space, and to actively interact with other people using the transmitted haptic space. The tangible environment enables telecommunication, tele-experience, and pseudo-experience with the sensation of working as though one were in a natural environment. It also enables humans to engage in creative activities such as design and creation as though they were in a real environment.

Chapter 7 presents the work by Yasuharu Koike on his project [15] entitled "elucidation of perceptual illusion and development of a sense-centered human interface." Koike's team shed light on replicating physically plausible information by providing a real sensation of presence in tele-existence. Koike's team proposed the concept of a sense-centered human interface as a technique of producing haptic sensations without the use of haptic devices. The concept was achieved through pseudo-haptics, which is a technique of simulating haptic sensations by using visual feedback. Its applications include Touch-Centric interaction embodiment eXploratorium (TCieX), surgery robots, and power-assist robots.

Chapter 8 describes the results from a project entitled "sensing and controlling human gaze in daily living space for human-harmonized information environments" by Sato [24]. The main goal of this project was to develop novel technologies for sensing and controlling human gaze non-invasively in daily living space. Such technologies are the key to achieving human-harmonized information environments that can provide us with various kinds of support more effectively without distracting us from our other activities. Sato's team developed gaze estimation techniques to attain this goal, which required none or very limited calibration efforts by exploiting various cues such as the spontaneous attraction of people's visual attention to visual stimuli. Sato's team took two approaches to shifting gazes to required locations in a non-disturbing and natural way to attain gaze control: subtle modulation of visual stimuli based on visual saliency models, and non-verbal gestures in human-robot interactions.

Chapter 9 gives an overview of a project entitled "smart Posterboard: multimodal sensing and analysis of poster conversations", which was led by Kawahara [14]. A smart posterboard was developed in this project that employed multiple sensing devices to record poster conversations, so the user could review who came to the poster and what kind of questions or comments he/she made. Conversation analysis combines speech and image processing such as head tracking, speech enhancement, and speaker diarization (identification of who spoke when information was obtained in a multi-party conversation). High-level indexing of interest and the comprehension level of the audience was accomplished based on their multi-modal behaviors during the conversation.

Chapter 10 discusses the insights obtained from a project entitled "developing a communication environment by decoding and controlling implicit interpersonal information" that was led by Kashino [13]. The team studied smooth and effective interpersonal communication that strongly depended on implicit, non-symbolic information that emerged from the interaction between partners (implicit interpersonal information: IIPI). Kashino's team developed new methods to improve the quality of communication by decoding IIPI from brain activities, physiological responses, and body movements, and by controlling IIPI by using sensorimotor stimulation and non-invasive brain stimulation.

1.4.2 Structured Overview of First Outcome

I combined the results into a big picture because a structural description of the results from each team is given in succeeding chapters and here discuss how they contributed to achieving human-harmonized information technology. Table 1.4 provides us with a bird's eye view of the entire contribution.

1.4.2.1 Basic Research Level

We obtained basic conceptualizations and scientific findings for human-harmonized information technology, which encompasses human perception and cognition at the basic research level.

Ishiguro's team introduced *sonzai* to represent human presence or existence and *sonzaikan* to represent a feeling of presence in the challenge to transmit human presence [11]. They argued that although *sonzai* is used to refer to an objective presence, *sonzaikan* is only present when its presence is recognized by a person. Thus, recognition is crucial for one to perceive *sonzaikan*, and at least two modalities are needed. The idea of using minimal modalities to induce *sonzaikan* brought about the idea of *sonzaikan* media from minimal design that combines auditory and tactile sensations. They proposed to examine changes in cortisol hormones to measure the effect of interaction with *sonzaikan* media on the human neuroendocrine system.

Table 1.4 A Bird's Eye view of the human-harmonized information technology in this volume

Category and features

Basic

- *Sonzai* and *sonzaikan*: cognitive model of sense of presence [11]
- Cognitive model of excessive trust [26]
- Implicit interpersonal information in communication [13]
- Haptic primary color model [25]
- Conceptual model of sense-centered human interface based on illusions in perceived heaviness [15]
- Multi-modal corpus for poster conversation [14]

Platform

- Smart Posterboard for archiving poster conversation [14]
- Technology for sensing and controlling human gaze in daily living space [24]
- Tangible information environment encompassing haptic information display (Gravity Grabber, TACHTILE Toolkit, a vision-based thermal sensor that uses themosensitive paint and camera), Telexistence avatar robot system: TELESARV, RPT-based full-parallax autostereoscopic 3D: RePro3D, and an autostereoscopic display for seamless interaction with the real environment mixed together: HaptoMIRAGE [25]
- Dynamic information space based on integrated high-speed 3D vision for insensible dynamics sensing, high-speed resistor network proximity sensor array for detecting nearby object, noncontact low-latency haptic feedback, and high-speed display of visual information [12]

Application

- FoodLog Web with image processing for food-balance estimation and FoodLog app for assisting food recording by image retrieval [1]
- A suite of *sonzaikan* media: Telenoid, Hugvie, and Elfoid [11]

Social implementation

- Field studies with FoodLog Web and app [1]
- Field studies on *sonzaikan* media: eldery care and education support [11]

Takeda's team worked on a cognitive model of excessive trust in human cognition and behaviors in (semi-) automated system environments, which was aimed at achieving accompanying intelligence that could assist the user in how to behave in complex environments [26]. They used piecewise auto- regressive systems with exogenous input (PWARX) models to express decision/action situations to complement them to adapt to new data and consistently identify the models. They used their method to build an integrated model of gaze and vehicle operational behavior and demonstrated that it was effective in detecting risky lane changes.

Kashino's group studied implicit interpersonal information (IIPI) that is considered to enable people to enable smooth and effective interpersonal communication. Their findings consists in the four lines of research: (1) decoding mental states, such as saliency, familiarity, and preference from micro-saccade and change in pupil diameter; (2) identification of the cause of impaired communication in high-functioning autism spectrum disorder (ASD); (3) the development of the methods for improving the quality of communication by controlling IIPI and/or neural processes involved in he processing of IIPI; and (4) elucidation of neural mechanisms involved in the processing of IIPI.

Based on studies on how information is mapped between the physical, physiological, and psychological spaces, Tachi's team has proposed a haptic primary color model that can serve as the foundation for designing a haptic information display to recreate cutaneous sensation [25].

Koike's team addressed the conceptualization and perceptual foundation for a sense-centered human interface [15]. Koike's team investigated the illusion in perceived heaviness induced by the time offset between visual and haptic contact. They found that an object was perceived to be heavier when force was applied earlier than visual contact and perceived to be lighter when it was applied later. They also found that an illusion became smaller after participants had been conditioned to the time offset. Furthermore, they introduced two indices, i.e., the point of subjective simultaneity (PSS) and the point of subjective equality (PSE) to quantitatively measure the subjective evaluation of timing and weight perception. In addition, they conducted an fMRI experiment to estimate the representation of motion in the brain. Their results conformed with previous results that have been reported so far. They are currently working on applying their insights to touch-centric interaction embodiment exploratorium (TCieX), which is a surgery robot augmented with a sensor-centered human interface, and power assist robots.

Kawahara's team studied a multi-modal corpus that was obtained with the Smart Posterboard they developed and gained some useful insights into the prediction of turn-taking, speaker dialization, hot spot detection, and the prediction of interest and comprehension levels by analyzing multi-modal conversations. Eye-gaze information was generally found useful in predicting turn-taking and in improving speaker dialization. It was found that about 70 % of next speakers in turn-taking events could be predicted by combining eye-gaze objects, joint eye-gaze events, duration, and backchannels. Multi-modal speaker dialization was achieved by integrating eye gazes and acoustic information. This indicated that eye-gaze information was useful for dialization in noisy environments. Hot spots were not necessarily associated with laughter but consistently and meaningfully with reactive tokens and specific prosodic patterns. It was found that interest levels could be predicted by using the occurrence of questions and prominent tokens and comprehension levels could be estimated from question types.

1.4.2.2 Platform Research Level

We obtained generic computation schemes and systems that could serve as a platform for building human-harmonized information systems at the platform research level.

Ishikawa's team developed four technologies: high-speed 3D vision for insensible dynamics sensing, a high-speed resistor network proximity sensor array for detecting nearby objects, noncontact low-latency haptic feedback, and a high-speed display of visual information toward achieving a dynamic information space that could harmonize a human perception system, a recognition system, and a motor system [12]. The first technology allowed them to capture depth images containing 512×512 pixels in real time at 500 fps on a high-frame-rate (HFR) camera-projector system. Time division multiplex 3-D structured-light measurements were implemented on the HFR camera-projector system to acquire complete 3-D information with minimal occlusion using multiple camera-projector modules. The second technology brought into being a high-speed proximity sensor array to simultaneously detect azimuth and elevation. The main features of the proposed dome-shaped sensor included rapid responsiveness and simpler wiring, while maintaining a $360°$ sensing range and detection from the sensor's sides to the top. The third technology was based on an airborne ultrasound tactile display (AUTD). A freely extendable phased array system allowed them to construct an array of a 576×454.2 mm^2 aperture. The system was able to produce highly localized vibrotactile sensations on human skin 600 mm away from the device with a focal intensity of 74mN, and programmable vibrotactile sensations of 2 kHz and 320-level quantization. The fourth technology consisted of a high-frame-rate LED display, smart LED tiles (SLTs), and aerial imaging by using retro-reflection (AIRR). The high-frame-rate LED display was driven by an LED video processor that distributed an input image into image data for the tiled LED units. Spatiotemporal coding was used to transmit HFR images to a conventional digital video interface. The SLTs integrated a microcontroller, sensors, a wireless module, and battery within the size of an LED panel. The SLTs were used to build a wireless sensor network to share sensed information even when the smart tiles were moved. AIRR was achieved by using retro-reflected material to create images from an HFR LED panel (960 fps). Ishikawa's group demonstrated how a system for dynamic information space could be developed by using these four technologies. Their demonstration included an AR typing interface for mobile devices and a high-speed gaze controller for high-speed computer-human interactions, as well as more integrated systems such as a VibroTracker, which is a vibrotactile sensor for tracking objects, and an AIRR Tablet, which is a floating display with a high-speed gesture user interface.

Tachi's team developed a rather comprehensive suite of platforms for a tangible information environment [25]. They developed a number of haptic information displays. Gravity Grabber can present normal and tangential forces on a fingertip. The TACHTILE Toolkit is an introductory haptic toolkit for disseminating haptic technologies as the third medium in the field of art, design, and education. A vision-based thermal sensor uses themosensitive paint and a camera. Thermosensitive paint is used to measure thermal changes on the surface of the haptic sensor for telexistence, as it changes its color according to thermal changes. The telexistence avatar robot system, TELESAR V, is a telexistence master-slave robot system that can provide the experience of an extended "body schema" to permit the user to maintain an up-to-date representation in space of the positions of her or his various body parts. Retro-reflective Projection Technology (RPT)-based full-parallax autostereoscopic 3D (RePro3D) can generate vertical and horizontal motion parallax, allowing the user to view a 3D image without having to use special glasses when she or he looks at the screen through a half-mirror. RePro3D may be combined with Gravity Grabber to produce tactile interaction with a video image, e.g., a virtual character. An autostereoscopic display called HaptoMIRAGE can produce a 3D image in mid-air with a wide angle of view of 180°, which allows up to three users to observe the same image from different viewpoints.

Sato's team developed a suite of techniques for sensing and controlling human gazes not only in a laboratory environment but also in a living life space. They introduced and implemented three key ideas for gaze sensing: (1) an appearance-based gaze sensing method with adaptive linear regression (ALR) that could make an optimal selection of a sparse set of training samples for gaze estimation, (2) a new approach to the auto-calibration of gaze sensing from a user's natural viewing behavior that was predicted with a computational model of visual saliency, and (3) user-independent single-shot gaze estimation. They studied two methods of guiding the human gaze: (1) a subtle modulation of visual stimuli based on visual saliency models (e.g., modulation of intensity or color contrast) and (2) the use of a robot's nonverbal behaviors in human-robot interaction.

Kawahara's team developed a Smart Posterboard system that could record the conversations and related behaviors of participants during a poster session. The current version consists of a large liquid-crystal display (LCD) screen that can serve as a digital poster and attached sensors that include a 19-channel microphone array on the top, six cameras, and two Kinect sensors. It allowed them to build a multi-modal corpus for detailed quantitative analysis.

1.4.2.3 Application Level

Application depends on a story that can be shared between the society and the technology. It is quite challenging to spin a story that is not only technologically novel and feasible but also beneficial from the viewpoints of society and business. In our research area, Ishiguro's team succeeded in developing a suite of *sonzaikan* media, consisting of Telenoid, Hugvie, and Elfoid. Telenoid was created as a test-bed based on the minimal design of a human. Hugvie was a human-shaped cushion phone. Human-likeness in visual and tactile information was emphasized in Telenoid's design to facilitate human-robot and mediated inter-human interactions. Hugvie focused on a human voice and a human-like touch. Elfoid was a hand-held version of Telenoid. The cellular phone version could connect to a public cellular phone network and was designed to provoke stronger *sonzaikan* than normal cellular phones. The underlying technologies included motion generation through speech information and motion generation and emotional expression through visual stimuli. Aizawa's team developed FoodLog Web and app. FoodLog Web is a system that not only allows the user to create a food log simply by shooting a photograph of what they have eaten but also applies image processing to analyze the uploaded photograph to generate food balance information to enable food assessment [1]. Foodlog app runs on smart phones to allow the use of photographs as a means of easily adding textual descriptions. Work by other teams is in progress whose outcome will be reported in Volume 2 of this book.

1.4.2.4 Social Implementation and Field Study

Long-term public installation plays a critical role in social implementation. It is far more than that many citizens come to touch and feel state-of-the-art technology; interaction with a large number of people brings about honest and frank criticisms of the technology from which researchers can gain plenty of invaluable insights about the future research. In the case of our research area, we have encouraged the PIs to host a long-term exhibition at the National Museum of Emerging Science and Innovation (Miraikan)[6] which attracts about a million of visitors per year. So far, four teams from our research area, those led by Naemura,Ishiguro, Tachi, and Yagi, respectively, have hosted or are hosting along-term exhibition directly or indirectly related to their research theme in this research area for around a half year or more (Fig. 1.7).

The first exhibition by Naemura's team had been mounted for 164 days from July 3rd, 2013 to January 13th, 2014. It was entitled "the studio—extend your real world—.[7]" It demonstrated display design in the mixed reality environment (Fig. 1.7a) and attracted about 130,000 visitors. During the exhibition period, numerous open events, such as introductory talks, workshops, laboratory events have been organized. The second exhibition by Ishiguro's team has been sustained for over an year since June 25th, 2014. The exhibition[8] keeps asking each visitor a question what is human, through the interaction with Androids and a Telenoid (Fig. 1.7b). The estimated number of visitors is more than 500,000. Over a ten thousand visitors have actually experienced communication through Hugvie or other androids. Over 1500 media reports were published by the end of February 2015. The third exhibition by Tachi's team had been open under the title "touch the world, feel the future", from October 22nd, 2014 to June 15th, 2014.[9] It allowed the visitors to feel the world through a sense of touch (Fig. 1.7b). Around 140,000 people had visited in the first half of the entire exhibition period. The fourth by Yagi's team started on July 15th, 2015.[10] It is about behavior understanding based on an intention-gait model. The exhibition will be held until April 11th, 2016. Progress report will be given in Volume 2 of this book.

There are a couple of teams that have gone farther. Ishiguro's team conducted numerous field studies on *sonzaikan* media [11]. The acceptability of Telenoid was first estimated. Then, elderly care with Telenoid, cultural differences toward Telenoid, and educational support with Telenoid were investigated in field studies. Fourteen organizations were using the FoodLogWeb API that was provided by Aizawa's team when this article was written [1]. A joint project with a nonprofit organization called Table for Two (TFT) is ongoing, which provides a unique program called "calorie

---

[6]http://www.miraikan.jst.go.jp/en/.

[7]http://miraikan.jp/medialab/en/12.html.

[8]https://www.miraikan.jst.go.jp/en/exhibition/future/robot/android.html.

[9]http://miraikan.jp/medialab/en/14.html.

[10]http://www.miraikan.jst.go.jp/en/exhibition/future/digital/medialabo.html.

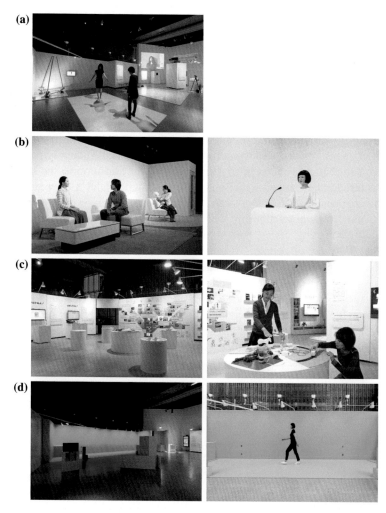

Fig. 1.7 Technology exhibitions at the National Museum of Emerging Science and Innovation (Miraikan). Reproduced with the courtesy and permission of Miraikan. **a** Laboratory for new media 12th exhibition "The Studio—Extend Your Real World—". **b** Robot world "Android: What is Human?" **c** Laboratory for new media 14th exhibition 'Touch the World, Feel the Future'. **d** Laboratory for new media's 15th exhibition "Let's Walk! The first step for innovation"

transfer" to support school lunches for children in five African countries so that eating healthy meals may help needy children in underdeveloped countries.

1.5 Conclusion

This chapter overviewed the JST-CREST research area on the creation of human-harmonized information technology for a convivial society. I emphasized changing world phenomena as a background and characterized our research area as a challenge to develop key technology for the convivial society in which humans and technology are in harmony. I referred to late Professor Tohkura's grand conjecture concerning the five-staged role shift in information in society, and pointed out that we are at the stage of an information society and are moving toward an AI-supported society. I have argued that a key idea in making a successful transition to the convivial society is through human and social potential. Human potential is the power of an individual that enables her or him to actively sustain an endeavor to achieve a goal in maintaining a social relationship with other people. It involves vision, activity, sustainability, empathy, ethics, humor, and aesthetic sense. Social potential is the power that a society of people possesses as a whole. It encompasses generosity, supportivity, conviviality, diversity, connectedness, and innovativeness. We believe that our research area contributes to building a technology for enhancing human and social potential. The outcome from the first group encompasses a suite of topics ranging from the foundation to social implementation, covering novel subjects such as implicit interpersonal information, sense-centered human interfaces, excessive trusts, and sense of presence (*sonzaikan*). The applications include FoodLog and a suite of *sonzaikan* media that has been socially implemented through field trials.

References

1. K. Aizawa, FoodLog: multimedia food recording tools for diverse applications (2016). (in this volume)
2. T. Ando, *Losing Battle After Battle* (The University of Tokyo Press, 2001). (in Japanese)
3. Nick Bostrom, *Superintelligence: Paths, Dangers Strategies* (Oxford University Press, Oxford, 2014)
4. E. Brynjolfsson, A. McAfee, *Race Against the Machine* (Digital Frontier Press, Lexington, MA, 2011)
5. E. Brynjolfsson, A. McAfee, *The Second Machine Age* (W. W. Norton & Company, New York, 2014)
6. R. Caillois, *Les jeux et les hommes: Le masque et le vertige*. Gallimard, 1958. (translated by Meyer Barash and printed from The Free Press of Glencoe, Inc. in 1961)
7. N. Carr, *The Glass Cage: Automation and Us* (W. W. Norton & Company, 2014)
8. T. Cowen, *Average is Over: Powering America beyond the Age of the Great Stagnation* (Dutton, 2013)
9. L. Gratton, *The Shift: The Future of Work is Already Here* (Harper Collins Pub., 2011)
10. J. Huizinga, *Homo Ludens: A Study of the Play Element in Culture* (Beacon Press, New York, 1955). (Originally published in 1938)
11. H. Ishiguro, Transmitting human presence through portable teleoperated androids—a minimal design approach (2016). (in this volume)
12. M. Ishikawa, I. Ishii, Y. Sakaguchi, M. Shimojo, H. Shinoda, H. Yamamoto, T. Komuro, H. Oku, Y. Nakajima, Y. Watanabe, Dynamic information space based on high-speed sensor technology (2016). (in this volume)

13. M. Kashino, S. Shimojo, K. Watanabe, Critical roles of implicit interpersonal information in communication (2016). (in this volume)
14. T. Kawahara, Smart Posterboard: Multi-modal sensing and analysis of poster conversations (2016). (in this volume)
15. Y. Koike, Elucidation of perceptual illusion and development of sense-centered human interface (2016) (in this volume)
16. C.B. Macpherson. *The Political Theory of Possessive Individualism—Hobbes to Locke* (Oxford University Press, 1962)
17. A.H. Maslow, *Motivation and Personality* (Addison-Wesley Educational Publishers Inc., 1954)
18. T. Nishida, Toward mutual dependency between empathy and technology. AI SOC **28**(3), 277–287 (2013)
19. T. Nishida, Information and communication technology for augmenting human and society potential: The role of artificial intelligence. J. Inf. Process. Manage. **57**(8), 517–530 (2014). (in Japanese)
20. T. Nishida, R. Nishida, Socializing artifacts as a half mirror of the mind. AI SOC **21**(4), 549–566 (2007)
21. D.A. Norman, *The Invisible Computer: Why Good Products Can Fail, the Personal Computer Is So Complex, and Information Appliances Are the Solution* (The MIT Press, 1998)
22. J. Rawls. *A Theory of Justice* (Oxford University Press, 1999)
23. J. Rifkin, *The End of Work, The Decline of the Global Labor Force and the Dawn of the Post-Market Era* (G. P. Putnams Sons, 1995)
24. Y. Sato, Y. Sugano, A. Sugimoto, Y. Kuno, H. Koike, Sensing and controlling human gaze in daily living space for human-harmonized information environments (2016). (in this volume)
25. S. Tachi, Haptic media: construction and utilization of haptic virtual reality and haptic telexistence (2016). (in this volume)
26. K. Takeda, Modeling and detecting exceesive trust from behavior signals: overview of research project and results (2016). (in this volume)
27. Sherry Turkle, *Alone Together: Why we expect more from technology and less from each other* (Basic Books, New York, 2011)
28. E. Zhunda, *Youtube Millionaire—Every Million view Channel Secrets Revealed (English Edition)* (Edgar Zhunda, 2015)

Chapter 2
Transmitting Human Presence Through Portable Teleoperated Androids: A Minimal Design Approach

Hiroshi Ishiguro

Abstract In this article, results from the JST/CREST project "Studies on cellphone-type teleoperated androids transmitting human presence" are described. The goal of this project is to develop new robotic communication devices that can provide a strong feeling of human presence, called "sonzaikan", by distance and to clarify the principles of human nature behind this. We took a synthetic approach, exploring three bidirectional processes: system development, field studies, and evaluation. We first define *sonzaikan*, which forms the core concept of this study, and then in the following sections describe various implementations of *sonzaikan* media prototypes and supporting technologies, evaluations of *sonzaikan* media, and field studies using prototypes we developed. We discuss the results in detail and then conclude this article with a brief summary of our essential findings and a mention of future work.

Keywords Teleoperated android · Minimal design · Human presence · Robotic media · Telenoid · Elfoid · Hugvie

2.1 Introduction

In the past two decades, people have acquired countless new means for communication: cellphones, e-mail, online chat, social networking services, and so on. With such a plethora of communication media, along with progress in information technologies and devices such as the World Wide Web and smartphones, the modern human lifestyle has rapidly changed. We can now talk with others anywhere, anytime and can send and receive not just text or voice data but also images and movies to express our ideas and feelings in finer detail. Such changes have not only increased the bandwidth and relaxed the distance limitations of communicationthey have also changed how people communicate with each other. Although such technologies seemingly increase opportunities for social relationships, studies have shown that more and

H. Ishiguro (✉)
Advanced Telecommunications Research Institute International,
2-2 Hikaridai, Keihanna Science City, Kyoto 6190288, Japan
e-mail: ishiguro@sys.es.osaka-u.ac.jp

© Springer Japan 2016
T. Nishida (ed.), *Human-Harmonized Information Technology, Volume 1*,
DOI 10.1007/978-4-431-55867-5_2

more people feel socially isolated [1]. Our current technologies are failing to create a strong subjective feeling of being with others.

There are now various types of robots being developed and appearing on the market that are designed to work in our daily environment. Some robots can make simple conversation with people autonomously, while other cannot speak but are anthropomorphized by people who talk to them. Still others function as a mobile video chat system. Robots differ from other information devices in that they can physically interact with real world objects. Specifically, they can move around in the world in which we live, can carry things, and can touch people or be touched by them. One can feel a strong presence of the robot itself, and as such, when robots are used as communication devices, they may have advantages over current communication tools.

Recent studies in cognitive science have argued that an object is represented as the integration of multimodal information in the human brain [2, 3]. For example, one study showed that people more accurately and rapidly identify objects when they are defined by a combination of auditory and visual cues than when the same objects are defined by unimodal cues alone [4]. Ernst and Banks proposed maximum likelihood estimation as a general principle of human sensory integration both within and across modalities for robust perception [5, 6]. Interestingly, their model suggests that the variance in an integrated estimate is reduced and the robustness of perception is increased by combining and integrating sensory information not only from within but also across modalities. These studies imply that the integration of sensory cues across different modalities is an alternative approach to facilitate and improve object recognition other than the integration of rich information within a single modality. Besides, we are fine tuned to recognize and interact with other humans. Many functionalities in our brain are specialized toward perceiving and reacting to other people. From this viewpoint, humanlike robots may be a key component for realizing a revolutionary new style of communication that is in harmony with human nature, easy to use, and provides new meaning in communication.

The question then arises: how much in the way of humanlike characteristics must we reproduce on the media to create the feeling of a human presence? Eliminating elements that are not required to induce a feeling of human presence might enhance the feeling because only relevant verbal and non-verbal information for human perception would be presented. In addition, developing a humanlike robot with the essential elements to feel human presence would help us understand how we perceive each other and enable us to design a robot's internal mechanism suited to natural interactions with people.

In this article, results from the JST/CREST project "Studies on cellphone-type teleoperated androids transmitting human presence" are described. The goal of this project is to develop new robotic communication devices that can provide a strong feeling of human presence, called *sonzaikan*, by distance and to clarify the principles of human nature behind this. We took a synthetic approach, exploring three bidirectional processes system development, field studies, and evaluation (Fig. 2.1).

As a first step, we must construct an appropriate robotic medium to understand how people recognize humanlike robotic media created with a minimal design approach.

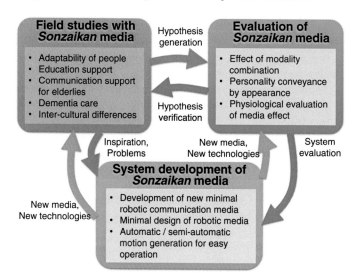

Fig. 2.1 Overview of JST/CREST project "Studies on cellphone-type teleoperated androids transmitting human presence." A synthetic approach using bidirectional processes including system development, field studies and evaluation is taken

In this process, existing findings in cognitive science and psychology stimulate discussion of possible elements to enhance *sonzaikan* since they provide detail on the impact of each cue in the sensory information relating to humans on human perception. We also need artistic intuition to design an entire system based on such elements.

Besides the design of a robotic medium, we need to develop new technologies to allow people to easily use them as an effective communication media. Normally, teleoperated robots require complex operation and their human interface aspects have rarely been examined, as they are currently used only in specialized areas such as large-scale construction or the exploration of hazard scenes. Besides, when creating communication media for daily use, the robotic body needs to be portable and compact, and only a limited space is available to embed the equipment (such as actuators) that make up a robotic medium. In light of these requirements, we need new means to implement the necessary functionalities for *sonzaikan* media.

After developing a new medium, it remains unclear how people will treat it because it provides new experiences for them. In this case, we must observe a variety of interactions between ordinary people and the medium in actual situations to generate and test several hypotheses. Field studies are essential to investigate which features of the medium contribute to *sonzaikan*. They also provide new ideas about media design and improvement. At the same time, experiments under controlled conditions must be conducted to verify the discovered hypotheses and to evaluate the media's effect. The verification and evaluation results are useful in terms of identifying possible applications and improving the media to enhance *sonzaikan*.

Once we identify the important features to enhance the feeling and the problems to be solved in the existing media through observation using case studies and evaluation of the media, the process focuses on system development. To this end, we develop new media with fewer features and new technologies to confirm and improve the effect of the features or to explore elements to enhance the feeling. We again observe the effect of the developed media using case studies and evaluate them through laboratory experiments.

In the following sections, we first describe the definition of *sonzaikan*, which forms the core concept of this study. In Sects. 2.3 and 2.4 we describe our implementation of *sonzaikan* media prototypes and their supporting technologies. Section 2.5 introduces studies evaluating *sonzaikan* media, and various field studies using the developed prototypes are described in Sect. 2.6. We then discuss the results and conclude the article with a brief summary of our essential findings and a mention of future work.

2.2   Presence, *sonzai*, and *sonzaikan*

In the past, we have run studies on android robots to create robots with humanlike presence and have developed several androids for this purpose. The most popular android we have developed is the Geminoid HI modeled on Ishiguro (the author), as shown in Fig. 2.2. The operator of the Geminoid HI talks with a visitor by watching the monitors. The operator's voice is sent to the android via the Internet and the operator's computer analyzes the voice and generates corresponding lip movements on the android. The computer also tracks the operator's face and head movements on the basis of images from a USB camera and synchronizes the android's face and head movements to the operator's. That is, the operator can see on the monitor the android moving the lips and head as the operator talks and moves and can make sure that he/she talks with a visitor by using the android body.

In our earlier experiments, we found that both visitor and operator can feel as if the android were a human. When Ishiguro operates the android modeled on himself, the visitor interacts with the android as if it were he. At the same time, Ishiguro,

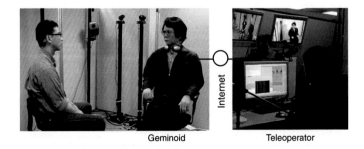

Geminoid   Teleoperator

Fig. 2.2 Geminoid™ HI: teleoperated android of an existing person

who is operating the android, feels the android body as his own body. We have studied a teleoperated android called the Geminoid for the purpose of developing a new information media that can transmit human presence to distant places [7, 8]. "Geminoid" means a twin or doppelganger whose presence is not separate from the operator.

The Geminoid is a robot system that transmits the operator's presence to distant places. In order to investigate and discuss the many interesting phenomena concerning this system, we need to start with a careful study of "presence." In Japanese, we have two terms, *sonzai* and *sonzaikan*, corresponding to "presence." *Sonzai* means "presence" or "existence" in English. There is no English word that perfectly matches the notion of *sonzaikan*, but as *sonzaikan* comprises *sonzai* and -*kan*, where -*kan* literally means "feeling", it might be translated as "a feeling of presence". However, this translation does not capture the precise meaning of the term.

The differences between *sonzai* and *sonzaikan* are subtle but substantial. *Sonzai* or presence of an object, say a human or a robot, implies the obvious or objective presence of the human or the robot, and many people can equally share its presence. Needless to say, it is difficult to theorize about presence per se, but we submit that whatever is present, e.g., Ishiguro the man or the Geminoid modeled on Ishiguro, many people share an awareness of the presence of them. For example, Ishiguro is considered to be present because anyone can see, hear, or touch him.

In contrast, *sonzaikan* is to feel *sonzai* or presence, and it differs from the obvious presence. An object may have *sonzaikan* even if we cannot see, hear, or touch it. That is, *sonzaikan* is the feeling of presence, and the relevant kind of feeling may not be sensory.

2.2.1 Hypotheses on Recognition and sonzaikan

In the Geminoid system, there are two types of *sonzaikan*: the *sonzaikan* visitors feel about the android and the *sonzaikan* operators feel through operating the android. These have some common features. Here, we focus on the first type, i.e., the feeling of a human presence in an android. Before proceeding, we need to consider what recognition is. For something to have *sonzaikan* (to a person) is for its presence to be recognized (by the person) in some sense. Therefore, we have to define "recognition" before considering *sonzaikan*.

Recognition is defined differently in different fields. For example, in psychology it is defined as consciousness of information that comes from the external world and is loaded with meaning, while in informatics it is usually defined as pattern recognition. This definition implies that recognition is to collect data about a particular target from various sensors. While bearing in mind the definitions in psychology and informatics, we propose an original and simpler definition: namely, recognition is to "represent information obtained through more than one modality". For example, we cannot recognize an orange as such merely on the basis of its shape. The recognition of an orange requires (at least) one more modality, typically smell. If we can perceive the smell of an object when we see its shape, then we can recognize it as an orange. Recognition of an object involves representing it in more than one modality and linking representations in different modalities with each other. We can apply this general idea of recognition to the specific recognition of human presence. We need to have at least two modalities to feel the reality of human presence or *sonzaikan*. Paradoxical as it may seem, robots or media can have *sonzaikan* if we can feel them in just two modalities.

2.2.2   The Minimum Design Requirements for Providing sonzaikan

When we interact with a person, we obtain via various sensors a variety of information related to his or her appearance, movement, voice, smell, and so on and recognize who it is by integrating this information. Then, how many sensors do we need? How many modalities do we need in order to recognize the person? To help with this inquiry, we developed the Telenoid, Hugvie and Elfoid, described in the following.

The Telenoid is different from the Geminoid in that its appearance and movement lack human likeness. The Telenoid was developed in the pursuit of the minimal design of a human being. It looks vaguely like a human, but we cannot tell its age or gender. The Hugvie is even more deprived of humanlike appearance, but even so, we can still feel *sonzaikan* when we are with a Hugvie. The modalities that the Telenoid can provide are much fewer than the Geminoid provides, but it still maintains a basic humanlike appearance, movement, and voice. In contrast, the Hugvie only provides human voice and humanlike touch.

The Hugvie is a human-shaped cushion designed to be used as a smartphone folder. There is a pocket for a smartphone on the head. Users talk while hugging it. That is, users can hear a human voice from the Hugvie and feel its humanlike surface by touch. The Hugvie is totally different from regular smartphones. When we use it, we have a feeling of holding the person who is speaking, even though he or she is nowhere near us. Our hypothesis is that we feel the *sonzaikan* of a human if we feel it through (at least) two modalities. Our earlier experiments with Hugvies contribute to verifying our hypothesis, at least to some extent.

Another interesting finding in our experiments is that we humans always fill in the lack of information with one or another positive interpretation when we feel *sonzaikan* in a limited number of modalities. When we use Telenoids or Hugvies, we identify the person who is speaking from the voice. However, identification by voice may fail. In such cases, we have some mental image of the speaker. If we hear an unknown but appealing voice from a Hugvie, we always imagine that the person speaking is attractive. We never have negative images. Similar effects have been confirmed in Telenoids. This may be why the elderly particularly like Telenoids (as discussed later).

We consider the Telenoid, Hugvie and Elfoid to be *"sonzaikan* media," meaning media that produce feelings of humanlike presence. *Sonzaikan* media are often more widely accepted than Geminoids that have a humanlike presence. Geminoids, perhaps because of their fixed and detailed appearance, limit one's imagination, whereas *sonzaikan* media, because they do not have such appearances, leave room for imagining its identity and coming up with positive interpretations thereof.

2.3 System Development of *Sonzaikan* Media

In this section, we introduce the development of three *sonzaikan* media, Telenoid, Hugvie, and Elfoid, based on the minimal design concept of *sonzaikan*.

People tend to attribute humanlike qualities to nonhuman objects to some extent, regardless of whether they resemble humans and whether they have intelligence [9, 10]. Based on this anthropomorphism tendency, researchers have demonstrated that people will treat even simple robots like a human in typical human-robot interactions. Matsumoto et al. developed Muu, which only has one eye, in a minimal design approach that eliminated the nonessential components and kept only the most fundamental functions for human-agent communication [11]. Osawa et al. demonstrated that attaching body parts to an object generates a virtual body image of it [12]. They also developed a ring-shaped robot called Pygmy with eyes and a mouth to anthropomorphize the user's hands [13]. They designed robot agents by focusing on the facial elements as the minimal parts of a human. Although they enhanced the user's feeling of being with socially interactive agents, their designs seem inappropriate to convey a human presence since their robots do not resemble humans. As a consequence, the interaction between users and robots is not the same as human-human interaction.

One option to enhance *sonzaikan* is to interact with a robot teleoperated by a person at a distant location. Many teleoperated robots have been developed to facilitate telecommunication. Some robots, which are utilized in elderly care [14], medical care [15], and group work [16], are equipped with a display monitor to project the teleoperator's image [17]. Others have a movable artificial head rather than a monitor for telecommunication [18, 19]. These robots have achieved some level of success in terms of enhancing *sonzaikan* because they convey teleoperator movements, voices, and images. However, these studies ignore the perception of interaction partners because they aim to provide telepresence for the teleoperators. We address the design issues in terms of the perception of the person who is facing the robots.

2.3.1 Telenoid

Telenoid was made as a test-bed in the pursuit of the minimal design of a human being [20]. The Telenoid robot is 70 cm long and weighs about 3 kg (Fig. 2.3). It has nine degrees of freedom (DoFs), most of which are assigned to control its eyes, mouth, and head with the rest devoted to its left and right hands.

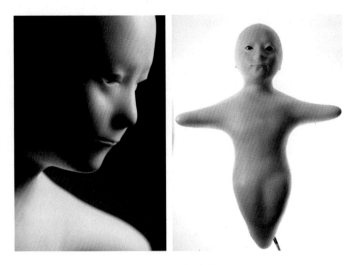

Fig. 2.3 Telenoid™. Photo copyright by Rosario Sorbello

Telenoid's design emphasizes its human likeness in visual and tactile information to facilitate both human-robot and mediated human-human interactions. To provide a contrast to existing androids such as Geminoid HI [8], we removed as many features less important for communication with a human as possible from Telenoid.

We designed Telenoid in three steps. First we identified the important features for communication with a human and eliminated non-neutral and less important ones. Psychology has shown that non-verbal information such as gaze behavior and bodily gestures plays a crucial role in communication [21, 22], so we considered not only voice but also a humanlike head and body to be important while eliminating non-neutral and less important features such as beards, hair, and eyebrows.

Second, we reevaluated whether the chosen features fit the design requirements by eliminating less important ones. We eliminated legs since we assume that a robotic medium and its partner do not move around. Although fingers are often used for hand gestures, especially pointing, in human communication [21], we eliminated hands and retained arms because pointing is possible if a robot has arms. Even though facial expressions provide fundamental information about emotions, we do not consider them in our current development because vocal information conveys a person's emotion to some extent [23].

Finally, we integrated the crucial features we chose. We kept the symmetry in Telenoid's face because a symmetrical face increases attractiveness [24]. Personality biases, including gender and age, cause problems because such personal information about virtual and robotic avatars affects both the teleoperator's attitude and the partner's to the avatar [25, 26]. To avoid this, we designed Telenoid's face and body in our current design as both ageless and sexually neutral.

Telenoid is covered with soft vinyl chloride. Its tactile quality resembles that of humans and it is much more robust and suitable for physical contact than silicon rubber (as was used for Geminoids). It enables people to feel that they are touching a person during such physical interactions as hugging.

We chose a teleoperation system to control Telenoid because this allows Telenoid to not only be used as a robotic avatar but also to pretend to be an autonomous agent by using a Wizard of Oz approach. We do not implement an autonomous system on Telenoid since our focus is how people react to its appearance and/or behavior, regardless of its behavioral robot architecture and the cognitive processes that might occur inside the robot. In the following experiments, we used Telenoid as a robotic avatar and participants were informed of the existence of a teleoperator behind it. The Telenoid teleoperation system conveys its teleoperator's movements and vocal information. We used the teleoperator's head movements and lip motions to produce these movements for Telenoid. The actual motor commands are computed by face-tracking and lip motion systems and sent to a server by TCP/IP. The teleoperator can also display such predefined behaviors as goodbyes or hugs using GUI buttons on the laptop screen. Some involuntary movements including breathing and blinking are generated automatically so that the interaction partner feels as if Telenoid is alive. The system is easy to use and carry: it requires only a single laptop with a Web camera.

According to our hypothesis that *sonzaikan* is enhanced when sensory information representing a human from at least two different modalities is presented, Telenoid provides rich information even though much information is eliminated since it presents visual, tactile, and audio information. This richness allows us to investigate the effect of possible combinations of modalities on *sonzaikan* in various interactions.

2.3.2 Hugvie

Observations from field studies with Telenoid have shown that physical contact with it, especially hugging, is a primary form of interaction and has a strong psychological impact on a wide age range of users. This implies that a combination of auditory and tactile sensations enhances *sonzaikan*, supporting our hypothesis that the feeling is enhanced when information is presented from at least two different modalities. On the basis of this finding, we developed a human-shaped cushion phone called Hugvie [27] (75 cm, 600 g) as a communication device that focuses on the hugging experience (Fig. 2.4). While Telenoid maintains a minimal humanlike appearance, movement, touch, and human voice, Hugvie focuses on just the human voice and humanlike touch. It is a soft cushion filled with polystyrene microbeads and is covered with spandex fiber, which is often used for microbead pillows. It resembles a person with open arms for a hug and enables us to bring the hug experience into telecommunication by putting a hands-free mobile phone inside a pocket in its head. Since the phone is in the pocket, people can call and talk while hugging Hugvie. As they converse with a distant partner, they become immersed in the vocal and tactile information since they almost do not see Hugvie while they are hugging it. This increases the feeling that they are actually hugging their distant conversation partner.

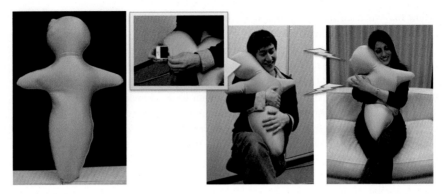

Fig. 2.4 Hugvie™. A user inserts his/her smartphone in a pocket at Hugvie's head and talks by hugging it

Preliminary studies with a Hugvie revealed that conversations with a female while hugging it stimulated the affections that heterosexual male users felt to her [27, 28].

2.3.3 Elfoid

Elfoid is a hand-held version of Telenoid [29]. Figure 2.5 shows a cellular phone version of Elfoid that can connect to a public cellular phone network and enables communication with other telephones. In addition to the cellular phone version, we have developed a Bluetooth version that has functionality similar to a Bluetooth headset for cellular phones.

Similar to Telenoid, Elfoid has a simplified human shape and is designed to transfer the speaker's voice and gestures using the cellphone network. Unlike Telenoid, Elfoid

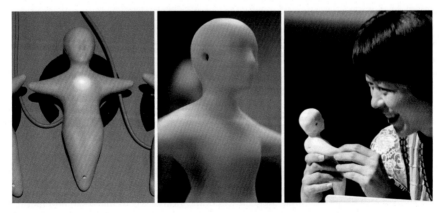

Fig. 2.5 Elfoid™. In contrast to cellphones, people use Elfoid by holding it in front of them and talking to others through it

is covered with urethane gel, which provides a soft, pleasant feeling on touching and holding it. Its functionality is further reduced from that of Telenoid, having a smaller size, fewer appearance features, and reduced embedded equipment. We assume Elfoid to be used as shown in Fig. 2.5, where the user is holding it in hand in front and talking to it. In this way, we expect people to feel stronger *sonzaikan* of others compared to usual cellular phone usage while maintaining the ubiquity of cellular phone, thus enabling people to use it anytime, anywhere.

2.3.4 Exploration of Human Form from Ancient Human Design

Although Telenoid, Hugvie, and Elfoid were designed with a minimal design approach, it remains unclear whether their components actually satisfy the minimal requirements to enhance *sonzaikan*. To explore this, we studied the minimal requirements of the human form by investigating the chronological development of Dogū, one of the most ancient examples of attempts to create an artificial human form [30]. The purpose of these small human/animal figures remains unknown, but they were probably meant to represent a human or to communicate with invisible spirits that take human form [31, 32]. We surveyed the development of Dogū and found that the torso, not the face, was considered the primary element for representing a human. Less attention was paid to the arms, legs, hair, and ears, all of which were represented very crudely. On the basis of these survey findings, we examined what kind of body representation is necessary to feel *sonzaikan* by using a conversation task consisting of one speaker and five hand-held avatars whose body forms are different. In the experiment, participants spoke to an experimenter through one of the avatars or the speaker in his/her hand about a topic provided by the experimenter. After the conversation, they rated the degree to which they felt the experimenter's presence on a five-point Likert scale from 0 (not at all) to 4 (very strongly) and then repeated conversations with different avatars on different topics. The experimental results showed that the forms for the torso and head enhance this feeling most significantly, while the arms and legs have less impact. This implies that Telenoid's appearance satisfies the requirements to feel *sonzaikan* and that we can eliminate more elements from it, such as arms and legs.

2.4 Technologies Behind *sonzaikan* Media

The development of a new medium requires new background technologies for the human interface as well as for the internal structures. In this section, we describe some of the technical studies that support our implementation of *sonzaikan* media.

2.4.1 Motion Generation Through Speech Information

In our field studies, we observed that people sometimes had difficulty communicating with Telenoid because the teleoperator's voice is not synchronized with Telenoid's movements when we generated its movements by vision-based head and lip tracking techniques, such as active appearance models. A problem with such image processing techniques is that their performance depends on good lighting conditions and image resolution. This is often crucial for applications in the real world. For example, our system failed to capture a teleoperator's movements in experiments at a shopping mall and at an elderly care facility because of poor lighting conditions. Therefore, complementary approaches are required that use information other than visual. A motion capture system achieves synchronization, but it is too expensive and complex for daily use. If the motions are reproduced from vocal information, synchronization can be easily maintained.

Ishi et al. generated lip motions based on the teleoperator's speech information. They transformed the formant spaces where vowel information is associated with lip shape in strong correlations between the two and demonstrated that the transformed space allows us to generate natural lip motions from the teleoperator's speech without any sensor system for motions [33]. They also analyzed the head motions associated with speech in human conversations and found a strong relationship between head motion and such dialogue acts as affirmative or negative reactions, the expression of emotions like surprise or unexpectedness, and turn-taking functions. On the basis of this finding, they constructed a model to generate head movements from teleoperator's dialogue acts and were able to improve the naturalness of robot head movements [34].

2.4.2 Motion Generation and Emotional Expression Through Visual Stimuli

In use cases with Telenoid, both young and elderly users pointed out that it was too heavy. Its weight (3 kg) is mostly due to the electric motors used as its actuators, although we did try to minimize them. To further reduce the weight, we need another implementation to produce its movements. This approach is especially useful to develop small, cheap, and portable robots because electric motors increase costs and reduce portability. If a robot can help users perceive the illusory motions of its limbs by light, sounds, or vibrations, it can support natural interaction without embedded actuators that move the limbs. Sakai et al. induced the illusion of motion with Elfoid by embedding blinking LEDs in its face [35]. After evaluating several possible patterns, we designed a blinking LED pattern to induce an illusory nodding motion, which is an important nonverbal expression in face-to-face communication. We demonstrated that Elfoid with illusory nodding motions eased participant frustrations more than with a random blinking pattern when participants grumbled at it.

This approach is a new way to achieve a portable robot avatar designed with minimal elements to enhance feelings of *sonzaikan*.

The idea of using blinking LED patterns for motion generation is also applicable to emotional expressions. Fujie et al. explored this possibility [36] by investigating which emotions are conveyed by blinking color patterns. Multi-color LEDs were embedded into Elfoid's face, its torso, and a spherical object. Eight color patterns (red, blue, green, yellow, purple, orange, blue-green, and yellow-green) were displayed with three different blinking patterns (continuous emission, emission at 0.1 s intervals, emission at 1.0 s intervals). Thirty-two participants saw all conditions randomly and evaluated each one with Plutchik's set of eight basic emotions (joy, acceptance, fear, surprise, sadness, disgust, anger, and anticipation) [37] on a six-point scale from 1 (not felt at all) to 6 (felt extremely strongly). While no conspicuous difference was observed between Elfoid and the spherical object with respect to red, blue, green, yellow, and yellow-green light, different impressions were created by purple, orange, and blue-green lights between Elfoid and the spherical object. With Elfoid, a purple light increased negative emotions, an orange light at the chest decreased anger, and a blue-green light increased fear. For both Elfoid and the spherical object, high-speed blinking increased surprise. Elfoid's humanlike appearance induces different emotions conveyed by color patterns compared to simply shaped objects.

2.5 Evaluation of *sonzaikan* Media

2.5.1 *Impact of Physical Embodiment on* sonzaikan

Although Telenoid's physical embodiment apparently conveys *sonzaikan*, it remains unclear which factors play an important role in enhancing that feeling. Tanaka et al. evaluated the impact of several key factors on *sonzaikan*, including physical presence, voice, body motion, and appearance [38, 39]. In their experiments, they controlled the factors with different communication media. Participants explained electronic devices for more than 1 min in the same room to a remote conversation partner through Telenoid, a static Telenoid, an audio speaker, a virtual avatar, a video chat system, or their partner. The partner gave vocal backchannel feedback with head nodding. In this conversation, each medium presented the information shown in Fig. 2.6. To evaluate the impact of the physical embodiment on *sonzaikan*, participants rated how realistically they felt they were with the partner on a nine-point Likert scale.

Results showed that the movements presented by the media enhanced *sonzaikan*. Interestingly, this effect was significantly stronger when a physical entity (an actual person or Telenoid) was presented than when a teleoperator's image or a virtual avatar was projected on a display monitor or only the partner's voice was presented. Telenoid's score was significantly lower than the score of the actual person. On

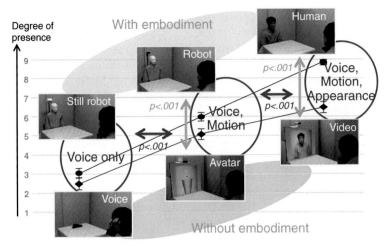

Fig. 2.6 Effect of physical embodiment. Combination of elements were compared to check their contribution to presence transmission

the other hand, its scores nearly equaled those of the video chat system, although it provides less visual information than video chat systems. These results indicate that Telenoid's humanlike physical presence enhances *sonzaikan* in comparison with vocal information and displayed visual images. Also, *sonzaikan* is more enhanced when Telenoid moves.

2.5.2 Personality Conveyance

Since Telenoid has a humanlike appearance that consists of the important components to represent a human, people can easily recognize it as a teleoperator, unlike other robots whose appearance greatly differs from that of the teleoperator. Kuwamura et al. verified that Telenoid can convey the teleoperator's personality, hypothesizing that teleoperated robots whose appearances differ from humans distort the teleoperator's personality more than those that resemble humans because such appearances make different impressions on the teleoperator [40]. Participants conversed with a teleoperator who talked through one of three physical entities with different appearances (Telenoid, a stuffed-bear robot, and a video chat system) in three different face-to-face conversations: free talk, teleoperator's self-introduction, and interviews by the teleoperator.

The teleoperator's personality was measured by the Japanese Big Five personality test, a 60-item questionnaire that represents five personality parameters (extraversion, neuroticism, openness to experience, agreeableness, and conscientiousness) that was translated from the Adjective Check List [41, 42]. We evaluated the distortion effect with the consistency of the answers to questions from each parameter in the measurement. We found that if a physical medium's appearance differs from that of the teleoperator, the answers to questions related to each parameter cause inconsistencies because some questions in each parameter are answered on the basis of impressions of the medium's appearance while others are answered on the basis of those of the teleoperator. The stuffed-bear medium had poor consistency on extraversion in the interview situation and on agreeableness in the self-introduction situation. Such poor consistency was not observed for Telenoid or in the video chat cases. This indicates that the personality transmitted through the stuffed-bear robot was distorted under certain situations, while Telenoid conveyed the teleoperator's personality to a similar extent to what a video chat system can convey. Although we did not directly compare Telenoid with its teleoperator, the results imply that Telenoid can maintain the teleoperator's *sonzaikan*.

2.5.3 Changes in Impression Toward Others

In another study, we examined whether the act of using *sonzaikan* media through can enhance positive feelings toward others [27]. Hugvie was designed so that its users could naturally hug the device in order to listen to their conversation partner's voice. In most cultures, social morals strongly discourage hugging strangers; if you are hugging someone, you are in close relationship with that person, sometimes an intimate relationship. However, using Hugvie, you are naturally led to perform the act of hugging even when you are talking with a stranger. Does this act of hugging change your impression toward the stranger?

In 1974, Dutton and Aron showed that one's affections are sometimes mistakenly evoked [43]. In their experiment, male participants were interviewed either on a fear-arousing suspension bridge or a non-fear-arousing bridge. The participants showed stronger response in the fear-arousing situation, but only when they were interviewed by a female. From these results, Dutton et al. concluded that misattribution of arousal happened to those participants; that is, their raise in tension and heartbeat change due to the fearful situation were mistakenly perceived as due to the attractiveness of the interviewer, which led to a stronger positive impression toward the female. Nishimura et al. showed that similar changes can be induced by controlling the frequency of the heartbeat-like vibration provided to participants [44].

In the experiment, we focused on hugging behavior through media among young people and found that using Hugvie enhances the feeling of being together and being loved compared to a Bluetooth headset. All participants were male university students and were told to interact with the other participant, which was actually a recorded female voice played by the experimenter, and watch a movie together while connected by the media. After the interaction, participants answered a questionnaire and were briefly interviewed. We used a "Loved-Liked scale," a passive version of a questionnaire, to measure positive impression toward others, specifically, participants' impression on how the people on the other side thought about themselves.

We found significant differences in both loved and liked scales: when using Hugvie, people tended to feel that they are more liked/loved by others than when using a normal headset.

We also found that participants with Hugvie were more impressed by a movie scene where a boy says, "I love you." This is a scene in which one typically feels rather embarrassed even if watching alone, and even more so when watching it with someone else nearby. This seems to indicate that using Hugvie provided participants with a much stronger and realistic feeling of their conversation partner's presence.

2.5.4 Physiological Measures

Even though the results from the above studies seem to suggest that *sonzaikan* media has a strong effect on people, it remains unclear whether the usage of such media can produce physiological responses as observed in real human interactions, or sometimes even stronger responses than toward other people. To address this issue, we investigated whether endocrine changes are observed following a brief conversation through a huggable communication device [45]. This approach enables us to quantitatively evaluate the physiological effects of the mediated touch without relying on subjective reports of affective states.

We hypothesized that communication with a remote person by giving a hug to a physical device would be sufficient to influence the human neuroendocrine system. To test this idea, we examined the changes in cortisol hormone, which is a reliable bio marker of psychological illnesses [46], before and after participants engaged in a human-human conversation mediated by a huggable communication device. We focused on the cortisol hormone because stress relief is one of the most critical issues in providing social support to facilitate recovery from many types of mental and physical illness [47]. Considering the potential applications of communication media for social support, the impact of the media on stress relief is highly relevant.

In the present study, participants had a conversation with a stranger while hugging a Hugvie (Hug group). In a control group, participants went through the same procedure but used a mobile phone instead of Hugvie (Phone group). To assess the neuroendocrine responses to the social interaction with the communication media, we measured cortisol levels before and after the conversation session. We collected the cortisol levels both from the blood and salivary samples since they can be dissociated due to differences in their regulatory mechanisms [46]. We predicted that physical contact with the huggable device would reduce the cortisol levels at a greater rate than the control group in which participants had conversations on a mobile phone without physical contact. We also evaluated the effect of physical contact on subjective psychological states with a post-session questionnaire that assessed positive effect, negative effect, and calmness.

Results showed that hugging the communication medium reduced the cortisol levels in both saliva and blood. These results, which support our hypothesis that physical contact with communication media can produce an effect even at the endocrine level, suggest that physical contact with such a medium might be effectively used for mental stress relief. To the best of our knowledge, this is the first study that demonstrates an endocrine effect from physical contact with a communication medium.

We also found a reduction of the cortisol levels in both the blood and saliva samples and a positive correlation between the changes in salivary and blood cortisol. This indicates that we can use salivary cortisol, which can be more easily handled than blood cortisol, to evaluate the effect of physical touch with communication media. We expect salivary cortisol to be a promising new measure to assess the effects of physical touch with communication media that have previously been evaluated only with behavioral or psychological measures.

Our results provide us with two important implications. First, they suggest that communication media do not need to actively stimulate a person's skin to reduce cortisol levels. In previous research on interpersonal touching, active touching by others, such as stroking the arm and massaging, was primarily used as tactile stimuli [48–50]. Other studies used a combination of several types of inactive touch, such as holding hands and hugging, along with other factors (e.g., watching romantic videos) [51, 52]. There has been little investigation on the endocrine effect of single inactive touch, aside from one study that reported changes in the heart rate and blood pressure during gentle touches of the wrist [53]. Our results demonstrate that 15 min inactive touching with an inanimate object reduces the levels of stress hormone.

Second, our results indicate that communication media can be used as research tools to investigate the positive effects of physical touch independently of the touching situation and the person doing the touching. The effects of interpersonal touch on physiological responses are affected by how people are touched and by whom [54]. For example, while positive physiological changes are induced by a hug with a friend or family member, such changes do not occur for a hug with a stranger of the opposite sex because it could be taken as sexually offensive. By contrast, our present study shows that hugging an inanimate object reduces cortisol even during conversations with a stranger of the opposite sex. This suggests that communication media allow us to separate the actual effects of physical contact from the effect of intimate relationships in interpersonal touching, which could induce multiple effects.

The ability to reduce cortisol levels seems suitable for improving the quality of intimate social interaction in which trust and bonding are crucial. For example, remote counseling services are widely used to improve patients' psychological states and mental health. The quality of communication with therapists, typically conducted with telephones, the Internet, or videophones, may be enhanced by huggable devices [55].

2.6 Field Studies with *sonzaikan* Media

We brought Telenoid into public places, elderly care facilities, and an elementary school to observe how people react to its appearance and/or behavior and what information substantially enhances *sonzaikan*. In this section, we first report ordinary people's responses to Telenoid in such public places as a shopping mall and then describe the responses of seniors in one-to-one conversations with Telenoid in elderly care facilities to investigate their impressions. We also compare interaction responses with Telenoid between Japan and Denmark to examine cultural differences. Finally, we report on Telenoid's effectiveness at representing a remote person's presence in a group setting.

2.6.1 Acceptability from People

Since Telenoid is a new robotic medium, it is unclear to what extent it makes people feel *sonzaikan*. Ogawa et al. observed how people responded to it through a demonstration at a shopping mall [20]. Seventy-five people, many of whom were in their 20s, had 5 min conversations with an experimenter through Telenoid. After the conversations, we asked whether Telenoid was better than a telephone for talking to a remote person. More than 70 % felt that Telenoid outperformed the telephone. They were also asked for their impressions of Telenoid. About 36 % admitted that it was strange at first glance. However, about 73 % said that their attitudes became more positive after hugging it. These tendencies were also observed for elderly people. At an open house at Advanced Telecommunications Research Institute International in Kyoto, 47 elderly people had 5 min conversations with Telenoid and were also asked whether Telenoid was better than a telephone, with 66.6 % preferring Telenoid and 88.8 % giving positive comments. Interestingly, all of the elderly users hugged it immediately after they got it. These results show that ordinary people generally accept Telenoid, although some had a cautious first impression. Physical contact with Telenoid might be a primary component to enhance *sonzaikan* because hugging it made the users' attitudes more positive.

2.6.2 Elderly Care with sonzaikan Media

The fact that elderly people are attracted to Telenoid suggests possible applications to elderly care. Yamazaki et al. used Telenoid at a residential care facility to observe the reactions of elderly people to it [56]. The participants were ten elderly women with dementia (mean age, 86.6 years), including mildly demented patients who could live independently with supervision and patients with moderate to severe dementia who had difficulty communicating with others.

Each participant had a relaxed, 20 min conversation about her health, hobbies, or family with Telenoid, which was teleoperated by the experimenters or the chief caretaker at the facility (Fig. 2.7, left). The caretaker reported that the overall reactions of participants were quite positive. We also observed that they frequently interacted with Telenoid by talking to and touching it. The verbal and non-verbal responses of nine of the ten participants to Telenoid were positive from the very start. The

Fig. 2.7 Elderlies interacting with Telenoid in Japan (*left*) and in Denmark (*right*)

patients with mild dementia were especially responsive in verbal interactions. At first glance, almost every senior reacted positively to interaction with it, often making such comments as "You are really cute." Generally, attachment to Telenoid increased when they held it. Although the participants with severe dementia had difficulty maintaining verbal communication, they intermittently caressed its back and arms and slowly interacted with it. Interestingly, some participants asked it questions like, "May I hold you?" Although they might speak to it, such asking behavior is not typical for interaction with a doll, implying that the participants treated Telenoid more like a human. In fact, some seemed to confuse Telenoid with a child; one woman said, "You look about five years old" when the teleoperator asked the woman to guess its age. Perhaps its appearance, which was designed with fewer human elements, provides enough information to enhance *sonzaikan*.

2.6.3 Cultural Differences in Responses Toward Telenoid

Although it has been shown that elderly people accept Telenoid, is this attitude specific to Japan? In a field experiment in Denmark, Telenoid was introduced into care centers and the homes of elderly persons to investigate cultural attitudes to it [57]. In one case, we observed 2-hour free conversations between Telenoid and two participants who were living alone in houses attached to care facilities: a healthy 92-year-old and a 75-year-old with mild Alzheimer's disease. In both cases, Telenoid was set up in the relaxing environment of a living room (Fig. 2.7, right). Telenoid was teleoperated by experimenters, nursing students, or the patient's friends. The conversation topics included health, hobbies, family, and a cooperative map game.

As observed in Japan, Telenoid elicited positive responses and behaviors from both participants, who actively talked with it and engaged in conversations from the beginning. For example, the healthy participant entertained Telenoid by playing the piano and singing. The participant with mild Alzheimer's basically remained quieter and calmer, but he did talk about his interests. Both participants engaged in physical contact, such as touching, holding, hugging, imitating, and kissing. Our observations indicate that both physical contact with Telenoid and its appearance might play an important role in enhancing *sonzaikan* across cultures, although investigation with more participants from various age groups and cultural backgrounds is required.

2.6.4   *Education Support with* sonzaikan *Media*

While the above studies focused on adults, Yamazaki et al. introduced Telenoid into an elementary classroom's group activities to observe how children dealt with and adapted to it [58]. A class consisting of 28 children participated in the experiment in a typical Japanese classroom. They were divided into six groups of four or five students to discuss scenarios for a four-frame cartoon. One member of each group teleoperated Telenoid from a small room next to the classroom during the group discussions. We qualitatively assessed the effect of Telenoid by comparing the group work with or without its intervention on the basis of recorded dialogues, the recorded children behaviors, and post-interviews (Fig. 2.8).

We observed each group's changing structure in the interaction among the children and the Telenoid controlled by a group member. Before Telenoid was introduced, the children's participation in discussions was limited because they were dominated by a member who had been assigned as the leader; other members performed tasks irrelevant to the group task (partial participation). After Telenoid was introduced, however, all of the children started to negotiate with the operator, who became a newcomer to the group, since they were attracted to the novel tool. However, once group work began, they realized Telenoid's limited function to cooperate with them

Fig. 2.8 Group-work in elementary school with Telenoid. One of the students is joining the class through Telenoid

and so began to work together to help the operator (cohesion and negotiation). Once Telenoid was accepted as a member of the group with the help of the others, the operator also made valuable contributions to the group. She began to take on the role of coordinator because she was able to keep an objective eye on the behaviors and roles of the others. Interestingly, as discussion continued, some of the children said that Telenoid seemed to be the operator herself. In other words, they felt the operator's presence (full participation). These observations indicate that Telenoid can maintain a classmate's *sonzaikan* due to its physical embodiment. They also demonstrate Telenoid's usefulness for facilitating group work.

In another study, Hugvie was used in school to help increase the concentration of students [59]. This was based on the idea that the stress reduction and human presence enhancement effect of Hugvie would allow younger students, especially first graders, to better concentrate on listening to their teacher. Children this age have not yet learned that listening to others is a very active process and is critical for learning and memory [60]. Despite the importance of listening, many young students have a problem with it; they walk around the classroom, chat with friends, and exhibit other restless/disobedient behaviors during class. The inability to concentrate in class causes many problems for children, especially those in the lower grades of elementary school, because it lowers academic performance in later life. Hugvie can relieve this problem by encouraging children to pay more attention in class.

In this study, we introduced Hugvie into a storytelling context to 33 preschool children who will soon start elementary school. They were given Hugvies and instructed how to use them. Two volunteers told them stories that were illustrated with picture cards.

Somewhat surprisingly, no child walked around the room or chatted with friends during the talking stories of the volunteers. Figure 2.9a shows a typical scene during storytelling. Although we had worried that some children might play with their Hugvies, all of the children calmly listened to the volunteers in both storytellings. About two thirds listened to the volunteer voices from their Hugvies, while the rest used them like cushions. Many children preferred to listen to the storytellers through the Hugvies. Children at the back of the room seemed to listen to the volunteers' voices from Hugvies without any complaints, even though they had difficulty seeing the picture cards. Hugvie seemed to help children continue to pay attention even from the back of the room.

In contrast, while not using Hugvie, the attention of the children in the back of the room shifted to other things, even as the children in the front continued to focus on the volunteers. Some children in the back walked around the room and others started playing with their friends (Fig. 2.9b). This might be because the volunteers sometimes concentrated on themselves without addressing the children. However, since more of the children who showed restless behavior were observed in the back of the room than in the front, perhaps the children in the back had less feeling that the volunteers were talking to them due to the distance.

These results demonstrate that Hugvie has the potential to help children maintain their attention to listening to others by reducing their stress and strengthening the feeling that a storyteller is close. Our observation of storytelling to children supports

Fig. 2.9 **a** Storytelling with Hugvie and **b** paper-cutout activity without Hugvie

such potential, suggesting that Hugvie is a useful tool to relieve the educational problem caused by children who show restless and disobedient behavior during class. We believe that concentration on listening can improve learning and memory performances, as suggested in a listening model [61]. We also believe that Hugvie's effect is useful for children with such developmental disorders as attention deficit and hyperactivity disorder (ADHD), who typically have difficulty maintaining attention in class. We have begun applying our system for storytelling to such special-needs children.

2.7 Discussion

Our field studies showed that ordinary people easily accepted Telenoid and enjoyed talking with it. Their positive impressions seemed enhanced when they hugged it. Studies at a shopping mall and elderly care facilities showed that seniors also quickly accepted Telenoid and actively talked to it. These results highlight the possible contributions of its appearance, movements, voice, and touch for enhancing *sonzaikan*. The combination of humanlike touch and a human voice seems especially important. This finding supports our hypothesis and inspired us to develop Hugvie. Although Hugvie shows sufficient effect to change human attitude, further studies are required in terms of its shape. For example, if it had a normal cushion shape instead of a humanlike shape, would the same results hold? Would a user still have the feeling of hugging a distant conversation partner in such a case? We will address these questions in future work.

Our observations in an elementary school revealed that introducing Telenoid into group activities changed the group's structure. Its physical embodiment and its movements captivated the children and helped them accept Telenoid as their classmate. Consequently, their distant classmate became more integrated into the group's activities. These results indicate that a medium designed with our approach has enough human information to convey a teleoperator's personality and to encourage involvement in group activities, even though it provides much less information than Geminoids.

Some of our field work findings were evaluated in controlled experiments. Telenoid's physical presence and motions created greater *sonzaikan* feelings than virtual avatar systems and an audio speaker. Its humanlike appearance conveyed a teleoperator's personality with less distortion than a non-humanlike appearance. Therefore, its physical embodiment and motion features provide significant effects of this feeling. Our results confirmed that Telenoid has advantages over existing media in terms of its enhancement of *sonzaikan* and personality conveyance. However, its appearance can be simplified because experimental results based on the findings from ancient human Dogū forms imply that a simpler human appearance has the same effect as Telenoid. It is also worth investigating whether *sonzaikan* provided by Telenoid and a simpler robot is comparable with that by Geminoid and whether they can induce natural responses from people as Geminoid can. Even though in our field studies we found that tactile interaction was observed as a primary factor, no investigation has evaluated the effect of physical contact with the media on this feeling. We have to verify the effect in controlled experiments.

2.8 Conclusion

In this paper, we proposed a minimal human design approach to explore the minimum requirements to enhance the feeling of a human presence, or *sonzaikan*, and gave an overview of our work with Telenoid, which was developed using minimal human design. Since developed communication media always provide new experiences for people, careful observations in exploratory studies are necessary to identify the primary factors to achieve *sonzaikan* as well as evaluation in control conditions and system development. These three processes, system development, field study, and system evaluation, must be repeated to explore the minimal requirements to enhance such feelings of a human presence. From field studies with Telenoid, we found that its physical embodiment and physical contact with it are crucial factors to experience the *sonzaikan* feeling. In controlled experiments, we verified some of our findings, which helped us develop a new medium and improved technologies to enhance the feeling. We also discussed some potential advantages of our approach. The lack of information might not be a disadvantage because it promotes positive social interaction.

We developed a simple but effective communication media for Hugvie based only on the minimal design approach (not on existing approaches) to telepresence media that reproduced the original modalities. Beyond the existing communication media, this approach will also usher in a new fashion of *sonzaikan* media that might, for example, make us feel another person's presence only by auditory and tactile information. We expect that this approach will improve social support systems in our future highly networked societies and help us understand how we recognize a human and how we design an autonomous system that can naturally interact with ordinary people.

Several technical challenges related to problems found in the field work and the evaluation results were addressed. Motion generation from vocal information [34] was easily synchronized between voice and motion, which is often a problem during teleoperation, without a large sensor system such as a motion capture system. The design of motion and emotional expressions with blinking light patterns [35, 36] is a new idea to achieve high portability. Although these methods show effective performance in certain telecommunication aspects, evaluating their effects on *sonzaikan* must be conducted in the future since they have not yet been assessed in this context.

Even though several issues of behavior generation were addressed, less attention has been paid to the development of recognition systems. To enhance *sonzaikan*, the teleoperator and conversation partner states must be extracted as precisely as possible. However, we have to avoid devoting too much computation to recognizing them since this prevents real-time conversation. Image processing forces a system to spend excessive computational loads. Cloud computing is a possible solution to reduce the computational load. We plan to design an effective facial recognition system by exploiting cloud computational resources.

In *sonzaikan* evaluations, many different subjective measures were used. We have to develop a unified measure for future evaluations. For example, we will integrate several measures of telepresence, social presence, and copresence that were used to evaluate the virtual agents [62]. In addition, physiological evaluations, including changes in brain activity and hormonal activities, must be conducted not only to evaluate *sonzaikan* but also to show how feeling *sonzaikan* affects our mental and physical health. We have already started addressing this issue in an investigation of the stress release of Hugvie with hormonal tests [45].

At the time we started the series of studies described here, we were not completely sure what exactly is entailed by transferring human presence to a remote operator. Through the development of *sonzaikan* devices and several basic studies, our ideas on *sonzaikan* have become much more clear and we were able to build a hypothesis on essential elements for *sonzaikan* transfer. First, as described in Sect. 2.2, we clarified our idea in terms of presence, *sonzai* and *sonzaikan*. *Sonzai* denotes explicit status as being human or robot as commonly accepted by many people. We can assume something exists when many people share a common belief on its status. In contrast, *sonzaikan* denotes the feeling that something is present. While being present or not is clear and explicit, there are degrees of *sonzaikan*, from strong to weak. In an extreme case, we can feel the *sonzaikan* of an entity even if it is not visible.

On the basis of these definitions, we composed a hypothesis on the principles embedded in us for establishing the *sonzaikan* of others. That is, the *sonzaikan* of people requires at least two unique modalities of human likeliness. Mere voice transfer is not sufficient; the transfer of an additional modality, such as vision (humanlike appearance or motion) or humanlike tactile sensation, is required. In the studies described here, we have been investigating the minimum necessary modality to represent human *sonzaikan*. Field tests using the developed *sonzaikan* devices, namely Telenoid and Hugvie, seem to support our hypothesis. In most cases, the teleoperated robotic media exhibited a strong and significant effect, sometimes even stronger than interacting with people face to face. Such results are supported not only in Japan but also in European countries, especially in Denmark, and the development of real-world application such as in care facilities has already started. Through investigation, both in basic studies and in practical usage of our robotic media, we aim to establish a firm design guideline for developing further advanced *sonzaikan* media and new forms of human communication.

Acknowledgments This project has been a collaborative work between several researchers from Advanced Telecommunications Research Institute International (ATR), Osaka University, and Tottori University. As principle investigator, I, Hiroshi Ishiguro, deeply appreciate the active collaborative work of everyone in the project. Dr. Shuichi Nishio at ATR took the initiative with the Telenoid field tests in Denmark and Japan. In addition, he helped me to summarize this report. Dr. Takashi Minato at ATR developed various versions of Telenoid and Elfoid. Dr. Carlos T. Ishi developed the software system that generates lip and head movements from the operator's voice. Dr. Hidenobu Sumioka took the initiative with the Hugvie studies in elementary schools. Dr. Ryuji Yamazaki at ATR contributed to the field tests with Telenoid in Denmark. Prof. Hideyuki Nakanishi at Osaka University took the initiative with the psychological studies with Telenoid. Prof. Kazumasa Tanaka at Osaka University worked with Prof. Hideyuki Nakanishi and contributed to the psychological studies. Prof. Aya Nakae at Osaka University worked with Dr. Hidenobu Sumioka on the hormone tests with Hugvie. Prof. Yoshio Iwai at Tottori University developed the vision system of Telenoid. Prof. Hiroki Yoshimura and Prof. Maiya Hori worked with Prof. Yoshio Iwai on the vision system. In addition to these researchers, our students at ATR, Osaka University, and Tottori University made contributions that are much appreciated. This project has been very successful and has obtained a good reputation, especially in Japan and Denmark. We could not have made this achievement without the efforts of all these collaborators. This work has been supported by JST/CREST.

References

1. M. McPherson, L. Smith-Lovin, M.E. Brashears, Social isolation in america: changes in core discussion networks over two decades. Am. Sociol. Rev. **71**(3), 353–375 (2006)
2. M.O. Ernst, H.H. Bulthoff, Merging the senses into a robust percept. Trends Cogn. Sci. **8**(4), 162–169 (2004)
3. L. Shams, R. Kim, Crossmodal influences on visual perception. Phys. Life Rev. **7**(3), 269–284 (2010)
4. M.H. Giard, F. Peronnet, Auditory-visual integration during multimodal object recognition in humans: a behavioral and electrophysiological study. J. Cognitive Neurosci. **11**(5), 473–490 (1999)
5. M.O. Ernst, M.S. Banks, Humans integrate visual and haptic information in a statistically optimal fashion. Nature **415**(6870), 429–433 (2002)

6. J.M. Hillis, M.O. Ernst, M.S. Banks, M.S. Landy, Combining sensory information: mandatory fusion within, but not between, senses. Science **298**(5598), 1627–1630 (2002)
7. H. Ishiguro, S. Nishio, Building artificial humans to understand humans. J. Artif. Organs **10**(3), 133–142 (2007). doi:10.1007/s10047-007-0381-4
8. S. Nishio, H. Ishiguro, N. Hagita, Geminoid: Teleoperated android of an existing person. in *Humanoid Robots: New Developments* ed. by A.C. de Pina Filho (I-Tech Education and Publishing, Vienna, Austria, 2007) pp. 343–352
9. B.R. Duffy, Anthropomorphism and the social robot. Robot. Auton. Syst. **42**(3), 177–190 (2003)
10. B. Reeves, C. Nass, *The Media Equation* (Cambridge university press, Cambridge, 1996)
11. N. Matsumoto, H. Fujii, M. Okada, Minimal design for human-agent communication. J. AROB **10**(1), 49–54 (2006)
12. H. Osawa, J. Mukai, M. Imai, Anthropomorphization framework for human-object communication. J. Adv. Comp. Intell. Intell. Inform. **11**(8), 1007–1014 (2007)
13. M. Ogata, Y. Sugiura, H. Osawa, M. Imai, in *Proceedings of the Asia Pacific Conference on Computer Human Interaction*. Pygmy: a ring-shaped robotic device that promotes the presence of an agent on human hand (2012), pp. 85–92
14. J.M. Beer, L. Takayama, in *Proceedings of the International Conference on Human-robot Interaction*, Mobile remote presence systems for older adults: acceptance, benefits, and concerns, pp. 19–26 (2011)
15. P. Thacker, Physician-robot makes the rounds. JAMA: J. Am. Med. Assoc. **293**(2), 150–150 (2005)
16. M. Lee, L. Takayama, in *Proceedings of the Conference on Human Factors in Computing Systems*. Now, i have a body: uses and social norms for mobile remote presence in the workplace, pp. 33–42 (2011)
17. E. Paulos, J. Canny, in *Proceedings of the SIGCHI Conference on Human Factors in Computing Systems*. Prop: personal roving presence (1998), pp. 296–303
18. T. Kashiwabara, H. Osawa, K. Shinozawa, M. Imai, in *Proceedings of the ACM SIGCHI Conference on Human Factors in Computer Systems*, Teroos: a wearable avatar to enhance joint activities, pp. 2001–2004 (2012)
19. Y. Tsumaki, Y. Fujita, A. Kasai, C. Sato, D. Nenchev, M. Uchiyama, in *Proceedings of the International Workshop on Robot and Human Interactive Communication*. Telecommunicator: a novel robot system for human communications, pp. 35 – 40, (2002). doi:10.1109/ROMAN. 2002.1045594
20. K. Ogawa, S. Nishio, K. Koda, G. Balistreri, T. Watanabe, H. Ishiguro, Exploring the natural reaction of young and aged person with telenoid in a real world. J. Adv. Comput. Intell. Intell. Inform. **15**(5), 592–597 (2011)
21. A. Kendon, Do gestures communicate? a review. Res. Lang. Soc. Interact. **27**(3), 175–200 (1994)
22. A. Mehrabian, *Silent messages* (Wadsworth Pub, Belmont, California, 1971)
23. K.R. Scherer, Vocal communication of emotion: a review of research paradigms. Speech Commun. **40**(1–2), 227–256 (2003). doi:10.1016/S0167-6393(02)00084-5
24. D.I. Perrett, D. Burt, I.S. Penton-Voak, K.J. Lee, D.A. Rowland, R. Edwards, Symmetry and human facial attractiveness. Evol. Human Behav. **20**(5), 295–307 (1999). doi:10.1016/S1090-5138(99)00014-8
25. I. Straub, S. Nishio, H. Ishiguro, in *IEEE International Symposium on Robot and Human Interactive Communication*. Incorporated identity in interaction with a teleoperated android robot: a case study, Viareggio, Italy, pp. 139–144, (2010). doi:10.1109/ROMAN.2010.5598695
26. N. Yee, J. Bailenson, The proteus effect: the effect of transformed self-representation on behavior. Hum. Commun. Res. **33**, 271–290 (2007)
27. K. Kuwamura, K. Sakai, T. Minato, S. Nishio, H. Ishiguro, in *IEEE International Symposium on Robot and Human Interactive Communication*. Hugvie: a medium that fosters love (Gyeongju, Korea, 2013) pp. 70–75, doi:10.1109/ROMAN.2013.6628533

28. J. Nakanishi, K. Kuwamura, T. Minato, S. Nishio, H. Ishiguro, in *the First International Conference on Human-Agent Interaction*. Evoking affection for a communication partner by a robotic communication medium, (Hokkaido University, Sapporo, Japan, 2013), pp. III–1–4
29. T. Minato, H. Sumioka, S. Nishio, H. Ishiguro, in *the RO-MAN 2012 workshop on social robotic telepresence*. Studying the influence of handheld robotic media on social communications, (France, Paris, 2012), pp. 15–16
30. H. Sumioka, K. Koda, S. Nishio, T. Minato, H. Ishiguro, in *IEEE International Symposium on Robot and Human Interactive Communication*. Revisiting ancient design of human form for communication avatar: design considerations from chronological development of dogu, Gyeongju, Korea, pp. 726–731, (2013a). doi:10.1109/ROMAN.2013.6628399
31. S. Kaner, D. Bailey (2009) The power of Dogū: Ceramic figures from ancient Japan
32. MIHO Museum (ed.) Dogu, a Cosmos (Hatori Press, 2012)
33. C.T. Ishi, C. Liu, H. Ishiguro, N. Hagita, Speech-driven lip motion generation for tele-operated humanoid robots, *Processing of the the International Conference on Audio-Visual Speech* (Volterra, Italy, 2011), pp. 131–135
34. C. Liu, C.T. Ishi, H. Ishiguro, N. Hagita (2013) Generation of nodding, head tilting and gazing for human-robot speech interaction. Int. J. Humanoid Rob. **10**(1), 1350,009(1–19) (2013), doi:10.1142/S0219843613500096
35. K. Sakai, H. Sumioka, T. Minato, S. Nishio, H. Ishiguro, Motion design of interactive small humanoid robot with visual illusion. Int. J. Innovative Comput. Inf. Control **9**(12), 4725–4736 (2013)
36. Y. Fujie, M. Hori, H. Yoshimura, Y. Iwai, in *Proceedings of the HRI2013 Workshop on Design of Humanlikeness in HRI from uncanny valley to minimal design*, Emotion transmission by color effects for a teleoperated mobile communication robot, pp. 19–25 (2013)
37. R. Plutchik, *Emotion: A Psychoevolutionary Synthesis* (Harper and Row, New York 1980)
38. K. Tanaka, H. Nakanishi, H. Ishiguro, *Appearance, Motion, and Embodiment: Unpacking Avatars by Fine-Grained Communication Analysis* (Practice and Experience, Concurrency and Computation, 2015a). doi:10.1002/cpe.3442
39. K. Tanaka, H. Nakanishi, H. Ishiguro, Physical embodiment can produce robot operator's pseudo presence. Frontiers in ICT **2**(8), (2015). doi:10.3389/fict.2015.00008
40. K. Kuwamura, T. Minato, S. Nishio, H. Ishiguro, Personality distortion in communication through teleoperated robots, *IEEE Int. Symp. Robot Hum. Interact. Commun.* (France, Paris, 2012), pp. 49–54
41. H. Gough, A. Heilbrun, The adjective check list manual (Consulting Psychologists Press, Palo Alto, 1983)
42. S. Wada, Construction of the Big Five Scales of personality trait terms and concurrent validity with NPI. Jpn. J. Psychol. **67**(1), 61–67 (1996). in Japanese
43. D.G. Dutton, A.P. Aron, Some evidence for heightened sexual attraction under conditions of high anxiety. J. Pers. SoC Psychol. **30**(4), 510–517 (1974). doi:10.1037/h0037031
44. N. Nishimura, A. Ishi, M. Sato, S. Fukushima, H. Kajimoto, in *CHI '12 Extended Abstracts on Human Factors in Computing Systems*. Facilitation of affection by tactile feedback of false heratbeat, pp. 2321–2326 (2012). doi:10.1145/2212776.2223796
45. H. Sumioka, A. Nakae, R. Kanai, H. Ishiguro, Huggable communication medium decreases cortisol levels. Sci. Rep. **3**(3034), (2013b). doi:10.1038/srep03034
46. D.H. Hellhammer, S. Wust, B.M. Kudielka, Salivary cortisol as a biomarker in stress research. Psychoneuroendocrinology **34**(2), 163–171 (2009)
47. S. Cohen, Social relationships and health. Am. Psychol. **59**, 676684 (2004)
48. B. Ditzen, I.D. Neumann, G. Bodenmann, B. von Dawans, R.A. Turner, U. Ehlert, M. Heinrichs, Effects of different kinds of couple interaction on cortisol and heart rate responses to stress in women. Psychoneuroendocrinology **32**(5), 565–574 (2007)
49. T. Field, M. Hernandez-Reif, M. Diego, S. Schanberg, C. Kuhn, Cortisol decreases and serotonin and dopamine increase following massage therapy. Int. J. Neurosci. **115**(10), 1397–1413 (2005)

50. J. Holt-Lunstad, W.A. Birmingham, K.C. Light, Influence of a "warm touch" support enhancement intervention among married couples on ambulatory blood pressure, oxytocin, alpha amylase, and cortisol. Psychosom. Med. **70**(9), 976–985 (2008)
51. K.M. Grewen, S.S. Girdler, J. Amico, K.C. Light, Effects of partner support on resting oxytocin, cortisol, norepinephrine, and blood pressure before and after warm partner contact. Psychosom. Med. **67**(4), 531–538 (2005)
52. K.C. Light, K.M. Grewen, J.A. Amico, More frequent partner hugs and higher oxytocin levels are linked to lower blood pressure and heart rate in premenopausal women. Biol. Psychol. **69**(1), 5–21 (2005). doi:10.1016/j.biopsycho.2004.11.002. Current Trends in Women's Health Research
53. J.L. Edens, K.T. Larkin, J.L. Abel, The effect of social support and physical touch on cardiovascular reactions to mental stress. J. Psychosom. Res. **36**(4), 371–381 (1992)
54. W.J. Nilsen, S.R. Vrana, Some touching situations: the relationship between gender and contextual variables in cardiovascular responses to human touch. Ann. Behav. Med. **20**(4), 270–276 (1998)
55. P.E. Bee, P. Bower, K. Lovell, S. Gilbody, D. Richards, L. Gask, P. Roach, Psychotherapy mediated by remote communication technologies: a meta-analytic review. BMC Psychiatry **8**, 60 (2008)
56. R. Yamazaki, S. Nishio, K. Ogawa, H. Ishiguro, Teleoperated android as an embodied communication medium: a case study with demented elderlies in a care facility, *IEEE Int. Symp. Robot Human Interact. Commun.* (France, Paris, 2012), pp. 1066–1071
57. R. Yamazaki, S. Nishio, H. Ishiguro, M. Nørskov, N. Ishiguro, G. Balistreri, Acceptability of a teleoperated android by senior citizens in Danish society: a case study on the application of an embodied communication medium to home care. Int. J. Soc. Robot. **6**(3), 429–442 (2014). doi:10.1007/s12369-014-0247-x
58. R. Yamazaki, S. Nishio, K. Ogawa, K. Matsumura, T. Minato, H. Ishiguro, T. Fujinami, M. Nishikawa, Promoting socialization of schoolchildren using a teleoperated android: an interaction study. Int. J. Humanoid Rob. **10**(1), 1350,007(1–25) (2013), doi:10.1142/S0219843613500072
59. J. Nakanishi, H. Sumioka, M. Shiomi, D. Nakamichi, K. Sakai, H. Ishiguro, in *Proceedings of the Second International Conference on Human-agent Interaction*. Huggable communication medium encourages listening to others, pp. 249–252 (2014). doi:10.1145/2658861.2658934
60. A.D. Wolvin, *Listening and Human Communication in the 21st Century* (Wiley Online Library, 2010)
61. A. Wolvin, C. Coakley, *Listening*. (McGraw Hill, New York, 1996)
62. K. Nowak, in *Presence 2001 4th Annual International Workshop*. Defining and differentiating copresence, social presence and presence as transportation (2001)

Chapter 3
Modeling and Detecting Excessive Trust from Behavior Signals: Overview of Research Project and Results

Kazuya Takeda

Abstract An approach which would allow us to better understand behavioral states inherent in observed behaviors is proposed, based on the development of a mathematical representation of driving behaviors signals using our large driving behavior signal corpus. In particular, the project is aimed at developing technologies for preventing excessive trust in users of automated systems. Misuse/disuse of automation is introduced as a cognitive model of excessive trust, and methods of quantitative measurement are devised. PWARX and GMM models are proposed to represent discrete and continuous information in the cognition/decision/action process. We also develop a method of modeling visual behavior aiming at understanding environmental awareness while driving. We showed the effectiveness of the model experimentally through risky lane change detection. Finally, we show the effectiveness of the method to quantify excessive trust based on developed technology.

Keywords Behavior signal processing · Driving behavior · Misuse/disuse of automation systems · GMM · PWARX model · Visual behavior · Excessive trust in automation systems · Telephone fraud

3.1 Overview of Research Project

The objective of this research was to develop an approach which would allow us to better understand behavioral states inherent in observed behaviors. This was achieved through mathematical modeling of human behavior using large scale signal corpora to integrate data modeling and physical/cognitive modeling. This research also aimed to establish practical detection techniques which could be applied to detecting excessive trust in automated systems in order to prevent negative outcomes, such as bank transfer fraud and traffic accidents.

K. Takeda (✉)
Nagoya University, Furo-cho, Chikusa-ku, Nagoya 464-8601, Japan
e-mail: kazuya.takeda@nagoya-u.jp

© Springer Japan 2016
T. Nishida (ed.), *Human-Harmonized Information Technology, Volume 1*,
DOI 10.1007/978-4-431-55867-5_3

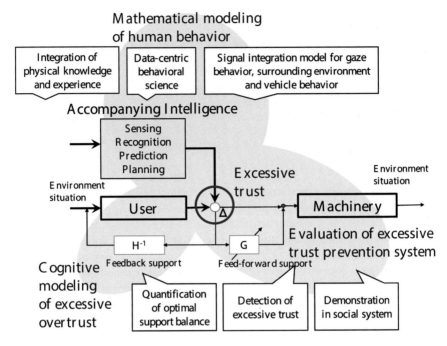

Fig. 3.1 Project overview

Figure 3.1 illustrates the scope of the technologies involved in this project. The central objective of the project was to construct an Accompanying Intelligence which could assist users of automated and semi-automated systems by controlling their interactions. This accompanying intelligence needs to be able to understand human behavior in terms of how and what this person likes to do, in addition to conventional artificial intelligence functions, i.e., environmental awareness, planning and operation. In order to understand human behavior, it is necessary to mathematically model these behaviors. Although we are aware that excessive trust is the result of over acceptance of positive support, even when the users goal conflicts with the intention of the accompanying intelligence, quantitative measurement of this phenomenon is difficult, creating a need for research into cognitive modeling of excessive trust. Moreover, technologies used to detect excessive trust need to be tested under realistic conditions.

In this chapter, we discuss our research project and our results from three perspectives, as described below:

Section 3.2: Mathematical modeling of human behavior.
Section 3.3: Cognitive modeling of excessive trust.
Section 3.4: Evaluation of technologies which detect excessive trust.
Section 3.5: Detecting excessive trust in telephone fraud calls.

3.2 Mathematical Modeling of Human Behaviors

3.2.1 *Large Scale Behavior Signal Corpora*

With the coming acquisition and distribution of big data, behavior signal corpora will become crucial elements of real world research into human behavior. This research project is part of this data-centric understanding of human behavior, which we seek to lead by constructing a large corpus of behavior signals recorded in real world environments. We also wish to develop methods for collecting behavior signals in real world environments, as well as tag labeling methods for acquired data, and to make this data available to the public for research purposes.

In particular, we have been collecting multi-sensor vehicle driving behavior signals continuously for more than ten years. Using a vehicle equipped with a variety of sensors, e.g., sound, video, kinematics and driver physiology, we have collected data from over 1,000 real world drivers (Fig. 3.2). In addition, in connection with this study, we have collected driving behavior data during 1,000 highway driving passing (overtaking) events, since this represents a typical situation in which excessive trust

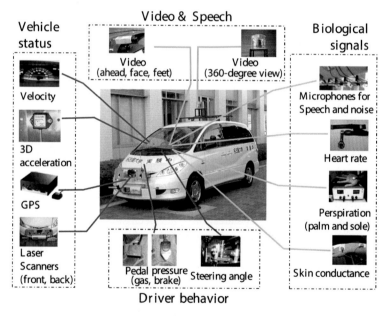

Fig. 3.2 Test vehicle equipped with a variety of sensors. Our test vehicle is equipped with various kinds of sensors for collecting driving behavior and biological data from drivers, as well as data on peripheral vehicles. As part of our passing behavior study, we recruited five instructors from a driving school and five ordinary drivers, and had each driver drive a circular route which contained expressways twice. For our project to model excessive trust, we collected data from more than forty passing events for each driver, for a total of about 1,000 lane change events

Fig. 3.3 Labeling of gaze direction. We labeled driver gaze direction with tags, using the lane change driving data mentioned above. A gaze direction labeling tool was developed which can classify gaze direction into one of 10 categories based on video images of drivers faces. We used the collected driving data and gaze label data to successfully model the relationship between driver gaze behavior and driving behavior

in an automated system may occur. We developed tags for driver gaze behavior during passing events (Fig. 3.3) and subjective risk scores were assigned to each passing event by five driving safety evaluators, based on collected video footage.

3.2.2 Mathematical Modeling of Human Behavior

In order to achieve a symbiotic relationship between human beings and automated systems, we first need to describe human behavior in relation to such a system mathematically, as a sequence of motions. Although machine control theory has traditionally been used to describe human behavior as a sequence of motions, methods which can handle a wide variety of non-deterministic human behaviors, which result from a range of human internal states, have not been sufficiently developed, and methods of identifying control parameters have also not become clear. In this project, we attempt to boldly use information technology to describe human behavior as a sequence of motions, and to develop data-centric, dynamic methods of constructing human behavior models.

To achieve this, we focus on Piece-Wise ARX models (PWARX) and Gaussian Mixture Models (GMM), powerful mathematical models which can be used for representing the dynamics of human behavior. The technical details of applying these models to driver behavior modeling are described in [1, 2]. These two models are mathematically equivalent to each other when squared error is used as the optimization criteria. Thus, we aim to improve both models developmentally from a complementary viewpoint, and then evaluate them with experiments using a test vehicle. By using mathematical behavior models, we can predict unique driving behavior associated with a particular driver, which makes it possible to optimize vehicle control for an individual driver. For example, the subjective risk level from the surrounding environment felt by a driver can be estimated using a behavior model, which can then be used as an evaluation criterion in path planning problems.

In one of our previous studies, we confirmed the stability of such a human-in-the-loop system through an experiment using a small electric vehicle equipped with a longitudinal driving assistance system, which was controlled using the same type of individualized path planning method described above [3].

PWARX Modeling In our project, PieceWise Auto Regressive systems with eXogenous input models (PWARX) are primarily used as a mathematical expression of decision/action situations, but the original model has two problems:

1. It cannot simultaneously classify and estimate piecewise auto regressive systems;
2. It is not robust to probabilistic variability in training data.

Therefore, we needed to improve the original model by incorporating probabilistic elements into the piece-wise ARX model. For the purpose of extracting human identity and behavioral characteristics from large volumes of data, we employed a probabilistic approach and proposed a Probability Weighted ARX (PrARX) model, which also includes a parameter estimation method [2, 4, 5].

Gaussian Mixture Modeling The technical merit of GMM formulation compared to PWARX is its compatibility with data-centric approaches, e.g., adaptation to new data and/or consistent model identification. In order to complement PWARX implementation in this project, we developed two adaptations for GMMs for application with driving behavior signals. For the model adaptation problem, we developed a Maximum A posteriori Probability (MAP) adaptation of distribution weight to correspond to mode distribution while driving, e.g., frequent stops during city driving versus uninterrupted driving on highways [6]. A non-parametric Bayesian approach was also implemented to estimate the optimal model structure (number of distributions) for a given set of training data. This approach has proven to be very effective when building robust models using data collected under real world conditions. Also, it then becomes possible to automatically determine which model structure to employ to correspond to changes in the environment. As a consequence, the range of models which can be applied is expanded.

Hitherto, it has been common, when we want to describe a driver's behavior, to consider the driver as a signal source or as a controller who can decide outputs based on external environmental input information. However, there are also situations in which the impact of environmental information is primary, in which drivers respond according to their own risk evaluation function (i.e., each driver's unique interpretation of the situational risk level). Therefore, if we can estimate how a driver's behavior is controlled by these risk evaluation functions, it becomes possible to construct a robust driver model. Based on this observation, we studied collision avoidance maneuvers and examined driver risk perception of local environments as the evaluation function of a path decision problem, and attempted to estimate the evaluation function.

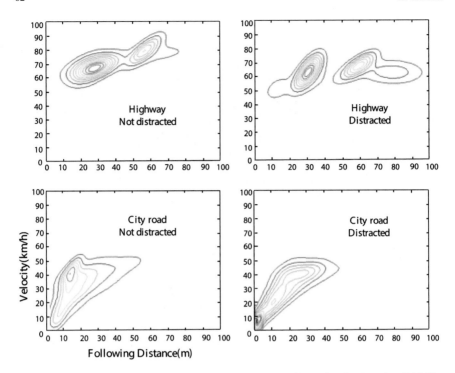

Fig. 3.4 GMM driver models trained by non-parametric Bayesian estimation based on Dirichlet process. Each GMM represents a probabilistic function of the vehicle velocity under the given following distance for each individual driver

By investigating adaptation of a non-parametric Bayesian method using the Dirichlet process, the number of Gaussians of each GMM can be determined. It also becomes possible to automatically decide which model structure to employ, corresponding to changes in the environment. Figure 3.4 shows the distributed structure of the trained driver model. It can be confirmed that the optimal number of Gaussians has been selected, and that optimal shapes have been trained.

3.2.3 Integrating Visual Behavior into the Mathematical Driver Behavior Model

By considering human behavior as a holistic system of cognition, decision and action, we can attempt to model the process from cognition to decision as the process that converts consecutive signals from the outside world into a sequence of discrete internal states. Thus, we can formulate this as a conventional pattern recognition problem. As a result of this process, we discovered a new approach to constructing driver behavior models, which considers the driver's internal state, by modeling the mutual relationship between environmental changes, gaze behavior and driving behavior. Using large amounts of driving behavior signals from our corpus, we have investigated the proposed modeling method, which integrates driver gaze behavior (cognition of the environmental situation) and operational behavior (decision making and vehicle operation), and the effectiveness of our model was verified [7–9].

3.2.4 Analysis of Gaze Behavior in Relation to Environmental Change

Drivers internal states are influenced by external stimulation, and actions in response to this stimulation are manifest as reactions. Therefore, there should be a correlation between gaze behavior and changes in the driving environment. By characterizing the relationship between signals associated with gaze behavior and environmental change, we can detect differences in a driver's internal state, such as concentration or distraction, for example Fig. 3.5.

When considering passing cars as external stimulation, it was confirmed that drivers in a normal operating state (concentrating on the surrounding environment)

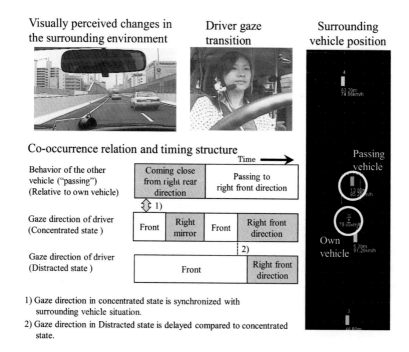

Fig. 3.5 Analysis of internal driver state based on synchronicity of changes in driving situation and gaze behavior. In order to understand the relationship between changes in the driving situation and gaze behavior, we analyzed differences in driving situations in which drivers exhibited either concentration or distraction (such as searching for music while driving) using a large-scale data corpora

reacted more quickly to changes in the environment than distracted drivers (who were searching for music using a speech recognition interface). This was indicated by the visual fixation of focused drivers on surrounding vehicles, resulting in a significant difference in response time of about 500 ms. Utilizing this difference between focused and distracted driving, we employed maximum a posteriori probability estimation based on a Naive Bayes method, and achieved an improvement in the precision of detection of a driver's internal state of approximately 20 % in comparison to a driver state identification method used in previous studies, namely anterior fixation gaze ratio [10, 11]. In addition, based on principal component analysis of gaze direction, it was also confirmed that gaze shifting patterns are synchronized with surrounding driving situations when drivers are in a state of concentration, but that gaze shift patterns are not in synchronization when drivers are distracted. On average, gaze movement in response to passing vehicles is delayed when drivers are distracted. These differences in gaze movement can be used to improve the accuracy of inattentive driving detection [12].

3.2.5 Integrated Model of Gaze and Vehicle Operation Behavior

We then focused on lane change scenes in which both gaze behavior and vehicle operation behavior were crucial for safety, and evaluated the effectiveness of modeling the correlation between gaze behavior and vehicle operation behavior signals by attempting to detect risky lane changes. Our driving signal corpus of 1,000 lane changes was used for this experiment.

The correlation between signals was modeled using a Hidden Markov Model (HMM) which had 3–5 states, each of which was characterized by a multivariable, discrete symbol distribution, i.e., gaze direction, pedal operation, longitudinal and lateral acceleration, etc. Each variable was coded into 4–10 discrete symbols, as shown in Fig. 3.6. Two different HMMs were trained using two sets of training data, i.e., the 5 % safest and 5 % riskiest lane change events, and were labeled Safe HMM and Risky HMM, respectively.

Based on the likelihood ratio between the probabilities calculated using the Safe and Risky HMM models, experiments to detect risky lane change events were performed. Figure 3.7 shows the results of these experiments. As shown in the figure, by integrating visual and operational behaviors we were able to improve risky lane change detection accuracy by 10 %, achieving 90 % accuracy with a false positive rate of 20 % [7–9]. Using this approach, the degree of correlation between driver concentration and driving operation can be quantified using a combination of visual and driving behavior signals. The technology developed here will be utilized for detecting excessive trust in Sect. 3.4.

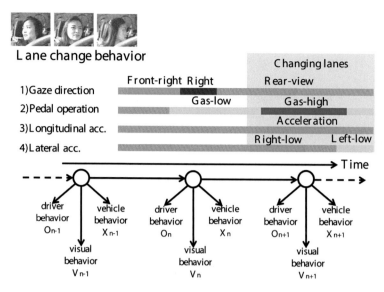

Fig. 3.6 Integrative modeling of gaze behavior and vehicle operation behavior. Integrative cognitive behavior modeling was used to describe the cognitive state of a driver, in relation to both the surrounding environment and to the driver's gaze behavior, in a mathematical and integrative manner. In this model, gaze behavior and driving behavior are represented as a time series of discrete events, based on a Hidden Markov model. It was confirmed that dangerous vehicle operation behavior can be detected with a high degree of accuracy and also that an HMM can characterize safe and risky lane changes

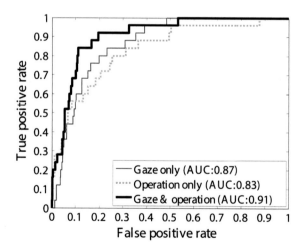

Fig. 3.7 Detection results for risky driving using the integrated model. This figure shows the improvement in the risky driving detection rate achieved using the proposed integrated model, confirming that the proposed integration of driver gaze and behavior data greatly improved detection accuracy, compared with models using only gaze or only driving behavior. Thus, the degree of driver concentration can be quantified using gaze direction, vehicle behavior and driver operation behavior

3.3 Cognitive Model of Excessive Trust

3.3.1 Misuse/Disuse of Automated Systems

In this project, excessive trust is defined based on misuse/disuse of automated systems. As shown in Fig. 3.8, misuse/disuse of a system is a function of the relative performance of the automated system compared to the performance of manual operation by the user. When an automated system is not used, even though its performance is superior to that achieved during manual operation, the automated system is *disused*. When an automated system is used, even though its performance is inferior to that achieved during manual operation, the automated system is *misused*. As part of this study, we developed a method of quantitatively analyzing the misuse/disuse of automated systems using a 3D plane, as shown in Fig. 3.9. The decision whether or not to use an automated system is made based on reliance on the system, which does not exactly correspond with the actual capabilities of either the automated system (C_a) or performance during manual operation (C_m). Therefore, in general, the discrepancy between use of the automated system and its actual capabilities can be measured by observing how much the user misuses or disuses the system (Fig. 3.10).

3.3.2 Measuring Misuse/Disuse

The basic scenario used to measure misuse/disuse of the system can be described as follows. The subject performs a line tracing task with the help of an automated drafting system. The subject can use either auto or manual mode for performing the task, but the accuracy of both the automated system and the manual drawing system are manipulated so that they do not work properly sometimes. If the subject uses the assistance system effectively, the frequency of usage is expected to approach the frequency of accurate functioning of the system. When a subject uses the automated system much less frequently than its frequency of accuracy, the user is considered to have a tendency to disuse the system. Results are characterized using a three

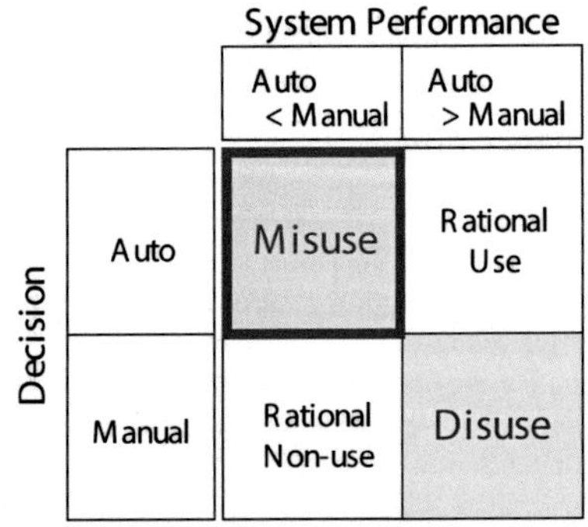

Fig. 3.8 Misuse/disuse of automated systems

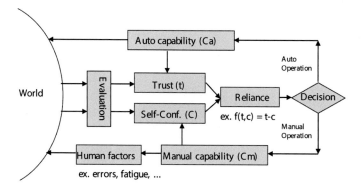

Fig. 3.9 Cognitive model of user switching between manual operation and an automated system, based on Gao and Lee [13]

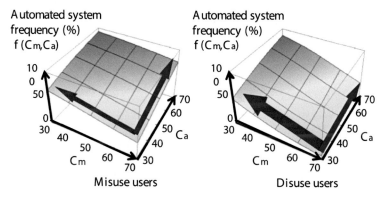

Misuse users   Disuse users

Fig. 3.10 Characterization of misuse/disuse. The tendency to misuse/disuse an automated system can be characterized by changes in the frequency of using an automated system compared to manual operation, taking into account the given capacities of both the automated system C_a and manual operation C_m, i.e., $f(C_m, C_a)$. It was found that operators who disuse automated systems are more sensitive to changes in manual performance, based on the observation that the slope of C_m $(\partial f / \partial C_m)$ is larger than that of C_a

dimensional plane consisting of the frequency of auto-mode usage, user satisfaction with auto system functioning and user satisfaction with the results of manual drawing. In order to control manual performance, the system is designed to also behave incorrectly at the same given frequency even when in manual mode. Therefore, we can measure the misuse/disuse tendency as a function of both automatic and manual drawing. This basic experiment was performed using 200 subjects and the effectiveness of the scenario was confirmed [14].

As shown in Fig. 3.11, this experiment can be implemented using different platforms, including a real vehicle, a driving simulator, or a simple PC gaming interface.

This misuse/disuse testing framework can be used to quantify the degree of excessive trust in an automated system. The results of this experiment clearly showed that, compared with subjects who have a tendency to misuse the automated system,

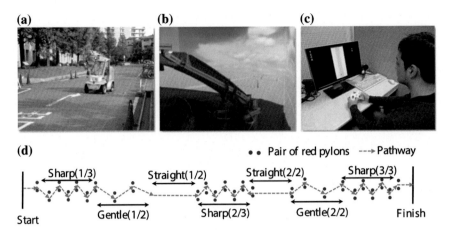

Fig. 3.11 Multi-platform test environments. Test conditions, which included multiple platforms with different degrees of abstraction, included a real vehicle, a driving simulator and a video game. The experimental scenario was common to all of the systems, and all of the systems used a similar driving course. By using such a multi-platform test, it is possible to discuss the consistency of behavior across different systems. **a** Real car (real system). **b** DS (virtual system). **c** Game (laboratory system)

subjects who disused the system were unable to evaluate the capabilities of the system properly. Disusers were more sensitive to changes in functioning capability when making decisions [15–17]. In addition, by modeling misuse/disuse tendencies with the proposed integrated cognitive architecture (ACT-R), we were able to confirm our hypothesis [18, 19].

3.4 Study Measuring Overreliance on an Automated Driving System

We then conducted a simulator study to quantify the degree of driver overreliance on an automated driving system by modeling the consistency of driver decision making and driver gaze behavior during automated driving [20].

3.4.1 Definition of Over-Reliance

Figure 3.12 shows our hypothetical model of driver over-reliance on an automated driving system. We assumed that a driver is more dependent on the automated system if he or she was less sensitive to the risk level of the surrounding environment when making decisions during automated driving compared to conventional driving.

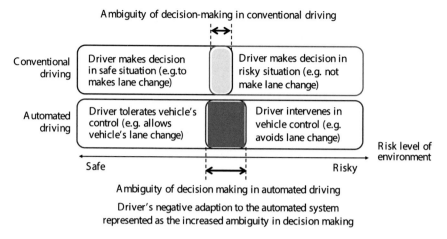

Fig. 3.12 Degree of driver over-reliance on an automated system as represented by the gap in decision making ambiguity between conventional and automated driving

In other words, over-reliance on a system can be represented by a decrease in the consistency of a decision making threshold during automated driving as compared to during conventional driving.

3.4.2 Experimental Conditions

3.4.2.1 Visual Behavior Based Situational Awareness

We focused on an automated driving system which requires drivers to monitor the surrounding environment and vehicle behavior in order to be ready to take control of the vehicle during critical situations. Since drivers are not required to operate the gas or brake pedals or steering wheel during automated driving, the degree of driver over-reliance on the automated system needs to be detected by observing behavior other than vehicle operation. In this study, we focused on using driver gaze behavior during lane changes to measure situational awareness. We analyzed the gaze behavior of fifteen drivers and observed their decision making process when changing lanes during conventional and automated driving.

3.4.2.2 Traffic Scenario

Fifteen subjects drove on a simulated, straight highway consisting of two lanes of traffic moving in the same direction using a driving simulator (Fig. 3.13). Each subject drove under conventional and automated driving conditions. They each made

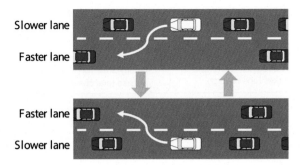

Fig. 3.13 Traffic scenario used in the driving simulator. Drivers under time pressure make lane changes into the faster moving lane. Then the faster moving lane gradually becomes congested and turns into the slower moving lane, and drivers move back into their original lane. The speed of the traffic flow alternates iteratively between lanes

approximately 40 lane changes, both to the left and to the right, under each condition. Subjects were instructed to reach their destination as quickly as possible while driving close to the speed limit, by passing other vehicles ahead of them by making lane changes, if possible.

During automated driving, subjects could take their feet off the gas and brake pedals and their hands off the steering wheel, but were instructed to continue monitoring the roadway so that they could take control of the vehicle at any time, such as when automated control of the vehicle becomes risky. They could intervene in control of the vehicle by operating the pedals or steering wheel themselves if they felt there was any danger.

3.4.3 Estimation of Driver's Risk Tolerance When Making Decisions

We represented the driver's risk tolerance when making decisions as a two-dimensional surface, estimated using logistic regression. Figure 3.14 shows an example of the surface obtained for a sample driver. The driver's lane change decisions during conventional and automated driving are shown in the graphs on the left and right, respectively. Each dot in the graph shows the result of the driver's decision whether or not to make a lane change, according to the risk level of the surrounding environment. We can see the round and triangular dots on the graph overlapped more widely during automated driving than during conventional driving, and that the decision surface became more uniform during automated driving, indicating that the decision-making threshold became more ambiguous.

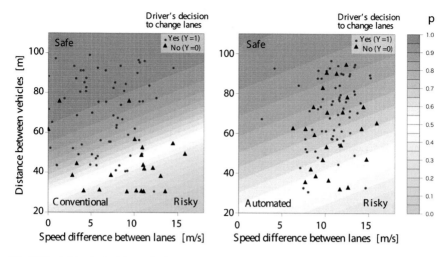

Fig. 3.14 A driver's decisions whether or not to make lane changes based on the risk level of the surrounding environment with probability surface, derived using logistic regression (*Left* Conventional driving. *Right* Automated driving)

3.4.4 Gaze Behavior During Lane Changes

Driver gaze direction was classified into one of five directions using the driver's gaze coordinates on the screen of the simulator. Figure 3.15 shows an example of the gaze behavior of a driver during lane changes. The figure shows the relative frequencies of the five gaze directions accumulated at each point in time during right lane changes. The top and bottom graphs correspond to conventional and automated driving, respectively. We analyzed gaze direction for 20, 10 s before and 10 s after the beginning of each lane change.

We can see from Fig. 3.15 that the proportion of the driver's gaze directed in front of the vehicle decreased significantly during automated driving. The driver also looked to the right or into the right rear-view mirror more often when the vehicle was making automated right lane changes than when the driver made manual right lane changes. He also looked more to the left or into the left rear-view mirror when the vehicle was making automated left lane changes than when he made manual left lane changes.

3.4.5 Detection of Excessive Trust by Analyzing Relationship Between Driver Decision Making and Gaze Behavior

Figure 3.16 shows the relationship between increased inconsistency in decision making and deviation in gaze behavior during automated and conventional driving. The horizontal axis represents increasing inconsistency in a driver's decision to make a lane change during automated driving as compared with inconsistency during conventional driving. The vertical axis shows the deviation in driver gaze behavior during automated driving from gaze behavior during conventional driving. We can observe some correlations between these parameters. For example, this figure shows that drivers who showed a larger deviation in consistency between automated and conventional driving also tended to be less sensitive to risk factors in the surrounding environment. This data also confirms that driver over-reliance on an automated driving system could be detecting by monitoring the deviation in driver gaze behavior between automated and conventional driving.

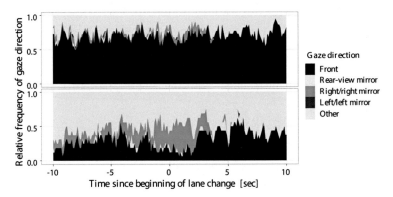

Fig. 3.15 Driver gaze behavior during right lane change (*Top* Conventional driving. *Bottom* Automated driving)

Fig. 3.16 Deviation in gaze behavior between automated and conventional driving in relation to increased inconsistency in lane change behavior

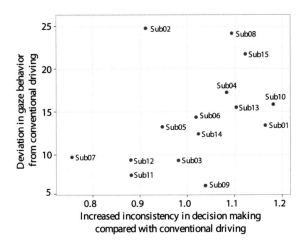

3.5 Detecting Excessive Trust in Telephone Fraud Calls

This method of detecting excessive trust is applicable to other problems as well. For example, "Ore-Ore" ("It's me") telephone fraud has become a serious problem in Japan. Victims receive a telephone call from a fraudster who pretends to be a family member—a grandson, for example—who is in some kind of trouble. Eventually, the victim begins to believe the fraudster (i.e., develops excessive trust in the situation)—the "grandson" really is about to be arrested if the missing company funds are not recovered, so the victim transfers a large sum of money to him in order to save him. These kinds of crimes are successful due to excessive trust in the reality of the faked urgent situation, as well excessive trust in the fraudster. In order to prevent this kind of fraud, we applied a different type of behavior model from the one used in driver modeling. We theorized that the conversational behavior of victims during fraud calls may change in two ways, namely, vocabulary and speech quality. Therefore, we used keyword spotting technology and developed a speech quality measurement technique that characterizes physical changes in the vocal cords, i.e., stiffness. To measure these physical changes, we used Power Difference in Sub-band Spectrum (PDSS) to measure the harmonic structure of vocal cord vibration, a measurement technique originally developed for speaker recognition [21]. As shown in Fig. 3.17, stressed utterances recorded during simulated fraud call situations lack the regularity of harmonic structure in the higher frequency band which occurs in unstressed speech.

We conducted a field test of our "Ore-Ore fraud" detection system which combined the above mentioned speech quality measure and keyword spotting technologies to count special words such as "transfer", "police" and "lawsuit", used during fraud-related conversations. With the help of the Okayama Prefectural Police and a bank, we evaluated the performance of our system in a real-world field test. During the field test there were no reported cases of telephone fraud scams in Okayama Prefecture, when, on average, there are 4–8 cases per month, an obvious, pronounced effect. Although we could not precisely confirm the effectiveness of the detection system, we could confirm that there were no false cases of fraud detection during the experiment.

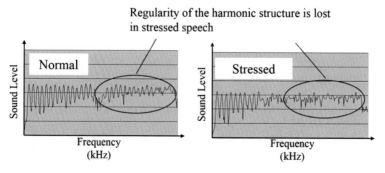

Fig. 3.17 Spectral characteristics of vocal cord vibration in normal and stressed utterances. The observed irregularity in the high frequency region can be quantified using PDSS

3.6 Conclusion and Details of Ongoing Project

The purpose of this project was to develop an approach which would allow us to better understand behavioral states inherent in observed behaviors. In order to develop a mathematical model of driving behavior we developed two models, a PWARX and a GMM model. Furthermore, we extended the basic formulation of these models in order to improve their robustness and to make them more adaptable to new environments. Fully utilizing our large driving behavior signal corpus, we also analyzed and modeled the visual behavior of drivers during lane changes. We confirmed the effectiveness of the visual behavior model through experimental evaluation involving the detection of risky lane changes. Finally, in order to quantify excessive trust in automated systems, we conducted a simulator study which compared driver gaze behavior during lane changes during conventional and automated driving, and our experimental results showed that drivers who exhibited greater deviation in gaze behavior tended to be over-reliant on the automated driving system.

The driver behavior modeling technologies developed during this research will have a big impact on the safety and energy efficiency of intelligent vehicles. Our research on behavior during semi-automated (mixed-mode) driving is very important, particularly during the early stages of the commercialization of automated driving technologies. Nevertheless, since the achievements of these projects have only been verified under simulated or limited experimental conditions, the robustness of these technologies will need to be tested and improved in real-world situations. In 2014, the Ministry of International Trade and Industry of Japan (MITI) began a research project on next generation advanced driving assistance systems, in order to develop advanced safety technologies utilizing big data and mathematical driver models. The project focuses on building large signal corpora that contain a sufficient number of accidents/events, and then building a safe driver model using these corpora. The approach developed in the current research project is also used as the fundamental method of modeling driving behavior in the MITI project. The biggest challenge the MITI project faces is verifying how any developed technologies will scale up to incorporate big data that will include almost every possible real-world driving situation. To achieve that goal, the authors are studying technologies that can subdivide traffic situations into meaningful chunks, and generate huge but discrete representations of actual driving situations.

References

1. P. Angkititrakul, C. Miyajima, K. Takeda, Stochastic mixture modeling of driving behavior during car following. J. Inf. Commun. Convergence Eng. **11**(2), 95–102 (2013)
2. H. Okuda, N. Ikami, T. Suzuki, Y. Tazaki, K. Takeda, Modeling and analysis of driving behavior based on a probability-weighted ARX model. IEEE Trans. Intell. Transport. Syst. **14**(1), 98–112 (2013)
3. H. Okuda, X. Guo, Y. Tazaki, T. Suzuki, B. Levedahl, Model predictive driver assistance control for cooperative cruise based on hybrid system driver model, in *Proceedings of American Control Conference* (2014)

4. K. Maeda, E. Konaka, H. Okuda, T. Suzuki, Hierarchical modeling of obstacle avoidance and steering behavior, in *World Congress on Intelligent Transport Systems and Services* (2012)
5. H. Okuda, Y. Kondo, Y. Tazaki, T. Suzuki, S. Tanaka, T. Owada, Evaluation of decision-making ability in car driving while operating interior devices based on probability-weighted ARX models, in *World Congress on Intelligent Transport Systems and Services, AP-00054,* pp. 1–8 (2012)
6. P. Angkititrakul, C. Miyajima, K. Takeda, Modeling and adaptation of stochastic driver-behavior model with application to car following, in *Proceedings of IEEE Intelligent Vehicles Symposium (IV2011)* (2011)
7. M. Mori, C. Miyajima, T. Hirayama, N. Kitaoka, K. Takeda, Integrated modeling of driver gaze and vehicle operation behavior to estimate risk level of lane change maneuvers, in *Proceedings of IEEE Conference on Intelligent Transportation Systems (ITSC2013)*, pp. 2020–2025 (2013)
8. M. Mori, C. Miyajima, T. Hirayama, N. Kitaoka, K. Takeda, Modeling driver gaze and vehicle operation patterns to estimate long-term risk levels of driving behavior, in *Proceedings of Workshop on Digital Signal Processing for In-Vehicle Systems 2013)* (2013)
9. M. Mori, C. Miyajima, T. Hirayama, N. Kitaoka, K. Takeda, Use of driver gaze information for detecting risky lane changes, in *Proceedings of RISP International Workshop on Nonlinear Circuits, Communications and Signal Processing (NCSP14)* (2014)
10. T. Hirayama, K. Mase, K. Takeda, Analysis of temporal relationships between eye gaze and peripheral vehicle behavior for detecting driver distraction. Int. J. Veh. Technol. **2013**, 8 (2013)
11. M. Mori, C. Miyajima, P. Angkititrakul, T. Hirayama, Y. Li, N. Kitaoka, K. Takeda, Measuring driver awareness based on correlation between gaze behavior and risks of surrounding vehicles, in *Proceedings of IEEE Conference on Intelligent Transportation Systems (ITSC2012)*, pp. 644–947 (2012)
12. T. Hirayama, S. Sato, K. Mase, C. Miyajima, K. Takeda, Analysis of peripheral vehicular behavior in drivers gaze transition: differences between drivers neutral and cognitive distraction states, in *Proceedings of IEEE Intelligent Transportation Systems Conference* (2014)
13. J. Gao , J.D. Lee, Extending the decision field theory to model operators' reliance on automation in supervisory control situations, IEEE Trans. Syst. Man Cybern. B Cybern., **36**(5), pp. 943–959 (2006)
14. A. Maehigashi, K. Miwa, H. Terai, K. Kojima, J. Morita, Experimental investigation of calibration and resolution in human-automation system interaction. IEICE Trans. Fund. **E96-A**, 1625–1636 (2013)
15. A. Maehigashi, K. Miwa, H. Terai, K. Kojima, J. Morita, Y. Hayashi, Experimental investigation of misuse and disuse in using automation system, in *Proceedings of HCI International* (2011)
16. A. Maehigashi, K. Miwa, H. Terai, K. Kojima, J. Morita, Selection strategy of effort control. allocation of function to manual operator or automation system, in *Proceedings of Conference of the Cognitive Science Society* (CogSci2011), pp. 1977–1982 (2011)
17. Y. Mizuno, K. Kondo, T. Nishino, N. Kitaoka, K. Takeda, Fast source separation based on selection of effective temporal frames, in *Proceedings of European Signal Processing Conference (EUSIPCO2012)* (2012)
18. J. Morita, K. Miwa, A. Maehigashi, H. Terai, K. Kojima, F. Ritter, Modeling human-automation interaction in a unified cognitive architecture, in *20th Behavior Representation in Modeling & Simulation (BRIMS) Conference*, March 21–24, 2011, pp. 148–153
19. J. Morita, K. Miwa, A. Maehigashi, H. Terai, A. Kojima, F. Ritter, Modeling decision making on the use of automation, in *Proceedings of Conference of the Cognitive Science Society (CogSci2011)*, pp. 1971–1976 (2011)
20. C. Miyajima, S. Yamazaki, T. Bando, K. Hitomi, H. Terai, T. Hirayama, M. Egawa, T. Suzuki, K. Takeda, Analyzing driver gaze behavior and consistency of decision making during automated driving, in *IEEE Intelligent Vehicles Symposium*, June 2015
21. S. Hayakawa, K. Takeda, F. Itakura, *Speaker Identification Using Harmonic Structure of LP-residual Spectrum (Audio and Video-based Biometric Person Authentication)* (Springer, Berlin Heidelberg, 1999), pp. 253–260

Chapter 4
FoodLog: Multimedia Food Recording Tools for Diverse Applications

Kiyoharu Aizawa

Abstract Our daily food is an emerging target for multimedia research community. Health care field is paying considerable attention on dietary control, which requires that individuals record what they eat. We developed and made publicly available multimedia applications, that are, FoodLog, multimedia food recording tools that allow users to take photos of their meals and to produce food records. We developed two kinds of tools: One is FoodLog Web and the other is FoodLog app used by smartphones. In both systems, image processing techniques are incorporated. For example, in case of FoodLog app, unlike conventional smartphone-based food recording tools, it allows users to employ meal photos to help them to input textual descriptions based on image retrieval. We summarize the outline of FoodLog, its deployment in diverse applications including health care, and analysis of data captured by a year-long operation of FoodLog app.

Keywords Food log · Food record · Dietary assessment · Image processing · Multimedia

4.1 Importance of Food Recording

Food is an emerging issue for multimedia technology. It is indispensable in our daily life. It is also deeply related to many different matters such as healthcare, nutrition, diet, cooking, recipes, restaurants, social interaction, food marketing, food production, agriculture and culture etc. In this project, we investigated capture, processing and utilization of multimedia data of our daily food, with the objective of improving the health and quality of our life in a practical way. Our technology can be related to various applications as well. In our project, which was supported by the JST CREST project (from October 2011 to March 2015), we created "FoodLog: a multimedia

K. Aizawa (✉)
The University of Tokyo, 7-3-1 Hongo, Bunkyo, Tokyo 113-8656, Japan
e-mail: aizawa@hal.t.u-tokyo.ac.jp

© Springer Japan 2016

T. Nishida (ed.), *Human-Harmonized Information Technology, Volume 1*,
DOI 10.1007/978-4-431-55867-5_4

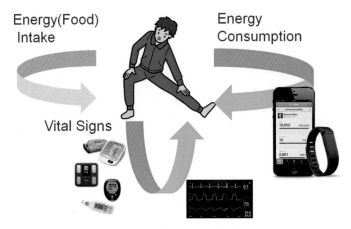

Fig. 4.1 Progress of healthcare technology. Food intake is the one which most needs IT innovation

food recording tool", which is a novel method to record our daily food intake primarily for healthcare purposes. In addition to healthcare, it has diverse applications. As far as we know, FoodLog is the only food recording service available for the public that makes use of image processing techniques.

Food recording is an important issue for healthcare. Healthcare requires the monitoring of three factors as shown in Fig. 4.1: energy consumption (i.e. activity), vital signs (i.e. blood pressure etc.), and energy intake (i.e. food). Energy consumption monitoring is easy by using the widely available wearable activity meters. Vital signs can be also measured by household instruments which are also available. However, recording food intake in most cases follows the traditional method, which depends on human memory, and manually complete forms to remember what was eaten. Manually recording detailed information about meals is a tedious task, and it is difficult for people to adhere to the process for a long time. Thus, there is a strong demand for information technology to help people record their food intake [1].

In this chapter, we would like to present FoodLog: multimedia food recording tools primarily for healthcare applications. Differing from conventional food recording tools, FoodLog tools make full use of images of foods. There are two types: FoodLog Web [2] and FoodLog app [3]. The former is the one we made earlier before smartphones have become widely available, and the latter is our later outcome. Both are made open to public use. We will describe the outline of each of them and some applications. FoodLog was initially created in our university research project. Later, in parallel to our project, a startup company foo.log Inc. takes care of its management and contributes to developing new services, while we, in the university, continue to work on various research issues of data analysis and new possibilities related to FoodLog.

4.2 Related Works: "Food" Is an Emerging Issue for Information Technology

Food is merging as the object of works in information processing as shown in the multiple workshops. For example, meetings such as "Workshop on Multimedia for Cooking and Eating Activities", "Computer Cooking Contest (in the field of AI)", and "Workshop on Multimedia Assisted Dietary Management" are open in 2015 [4]. In addition, giant IT companies such as IBM and Google recently announced their efforts in food-related developments.

Most of the previous work on the image processing of food images has focused mainly on recognition of meals or food items. Joutou and Yanai [5] investigated recognition of the meal associated with a food image from among 50 selected meals. They estimated the meal with an accuracy of up to 61.30 %. Their approach involved a bag-of-features (BoF) model, color histograms and Gabor texture features as the image features and multiple kernel learning as the machine-learning method. Zhu et al. [6] estimated the amount of food that a person had eaten. They used photographs of the food and the plates both before and after the meal. When taking the photographs, they used a white dish on a black and white checkerboard. They identified 19 food items in a small dataset of 63 images and the accuracy was between 84.5 and 95.8 %, depending on the amount of training data used within the dataset. Wu and Yang [7] estimated the calorie content of a limited set of fast-food menus. They used the matching of SIFT features and Web-based calorie data for fast food. The estimation accuracy was between 40 and 73 %. Yang et al. [8] proposed a method for identifying fast-food items. They used pairs of pixels and their local features. The accuracy was up to 28 %. Bosch et al. [9] evaluated various global and local image features for food classification. The number of images in the dataset was limited to 179 images in total, and they found color features contributed most and local features such as SIFT were also efficient. Kawano developed FoodCam, a smartphone implementation of food image recognition composed of GrabCut segmentation and linear SVM. They built a dataset of food images, that is EUC-Food 101 which consists of 101 food classes with app. 100 images per class, to evaluate the recognition performance, and obtained 79 % classification rate for top 5 category candidates [10]. Bossard et al. applied a random forest algorithm to mine descriminative superpixels of food images and applied SVM for classification [11]. For the evaluation, they built a food image dataset, Food-101 containing 101 classes of foods with 1000 images per class collected from a social media. Very recently, following the significant advance of Deep Learning, CNNs have been applied to food images as well. Bossard reported CNN showed better performance compared to their proposal [11]. Kagaya et al. investigated the parameters of CNN, compared them against existing techniques based on SVM, and showed CNN outperform them [12].

Apart from recognition of food images, Kitamura et al. [13] presented our previous system for detecting food images and estimating food balance [14] i.e., the categorization of food into grains, vegetables, meat/fish/beans, fruit and milk products. The system extracted image features such as colors, circles and scale-invariant feature transform (SIFT) features from each image, and analyzed them using either support vector machines (SVMs) or AdaBoost. The performance with respect to food-image detection was 92 % and food-balance estimation had an average error of 0.69 SVs in each category per image. Miyazaki et al. [15] presented calorie content estimation based on visual similarity, in which the food photograph is visually searched using low-level features in a food-photograph dataset with calorie values and the higher-ranked candidates are used in a regression to produce the estimation. The average estimation error of their method was 140 kcal per image. In general, previous works all used general datasets and did not consider any statistical bias that depends on a specific person. Aizawa et al. [16] presented that the estimation was made more accurate by personalization by making use of personal dietary tendencies in image analysis. Ogawa et al. [17] and Aizawa et al. [18] developed a smartphone based food recording tool that assists users by visual search of a food domain interactively specified on the touch screen.

From application system point of view, a few systems were proposed which can be potentially applied to food recording. For example, in TADA project, a mobile based system was proposed, which includes food image recognition function mentioned above [6]. A crowd sourcing, Platemate [19], was designed for food recording using food images in such a way that tasks for food region segmentation, labeling food region and nutrition value counting were separated. However, none of those systems have been utilized in real situation. On the other hand, our FoodLog tools have been used by general public users. FoodLog web has been open since 2009, and FoodLog app since 2013.

In the following, we would like to summarize our works in making practical food recording tools, FoodLog: FoodLog web and FoodLog app. We made both tools available to general public. FoodLog app, a smartphone based tool has been accepted by a number of people, and the number of food records exceeds one million after one year operation. We found the data acquired by users are largely diverse and the number of food classes surprisingly huge. We also describe our work investigating the diverse nature of the data.

4.3   FoodLog Web with Image Processing for Food-Balance Estimation

To make it easy to keep a record of one's meals using photos, we first developed the FoodLog web-based system [13, 16]. In this system users create a food log simply by taking a photo of what they eat, using their mobile phone or smartphone, and uploading the photo to the server. In addition to displaying the uploaded photos, FoodLog performs image processing analyses on the photos to generate food-balance information. FoodLog is the world's only website open to the public that offers these features. Food-balance is a simple way to assess a meal by classifying food into five categories, namely staple foods (e.g.: grains), main dishes (e.g.: meat/fish/beans), side dishes (e.g.: vegetables), dairy products, or fruits.

Fig. 4.2 FoodLog web: the user uploads his/her photos, the images are analyzed and they are arranged into food diary with estimation of food balance

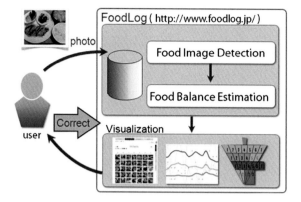

The following is an overview of the six main functions currently offered by the FoodLog website (see Fig. 4.2).

(1) FoodLog makes recording meals as simple as possible.

A user takes a photo of a meal with a digital camera, mobile phone, or smartphone and uploads the photo. Users can upload photos directly to FoodLog or using a photo-sharing website such as Flickr. After linking the accounts, if necessary, FoodLog imports the photos and creates the food log.

(2) An image processing engine analyzes the content of the meals.

The image processing engine determines whether the picture is a food image. If so, it processes the image to determine what food types appear in the picture and how they fit into the dietary balance. It then estimates the dietary balance values. Dietary balance is a simple way to assess a meal by classifying food into one of five categories, namely staple foods (e.g., grains), main dishes (e.g., meat/fish/beans), side dishes (e.g., vegetables), dairy products, or fruit. Figure 4.3 (top) shows the monthly calendar view of the food photos and an example of a result of details of the estimation of food balance (bottom).

(3) FoodLog displays the photos and presents an analysis of the results in visual form.

The system displays the information recorded in various formats. Users can view their food log in calendar format, as a list of meal times or as photos of meals appearing on a map if the photos provide location data. They can also view the results of a dietary balance analysis in graphical form.

(4) Users can interactively correct data.

Because the analysis offered by the image-processing function may not be 100 % accurate, the software lets users correct the results as necessary.

(5) Users can label tags for search.

A user can add a description of a meal (such as the name of the dish) and then later conduct a search using these keywords.

(6) Users can share their logs.

Users can view pictures of meals from other users if permission has been given.

Fig. 4.3 FoodLog web. Calendar view (*top*) and the result of food balance estimation for the food (*bottom*)

Food images largely vary between users because of not only the food content itself, but also the imaging environment (camera and illumination). The food image content is very distinct among people. Accordingly, the processing of food log images has to be personalized. The personalization is an important nature of multimedia food data processing [16].

Although FoodLog was designed as a self-monitoring tool, it can also enable third parties such as dietitians, nurses, and doctors to monitor their clients. A health insurance organization uses FoodLog to monitor and instruct a group of its clients. For such usage, the browser is customized so that the dietitian can give comment feedback to the patient.

4.4 Image Analysis of FoodLog Web

4.4.1 Overview of Existing System

Both food-image detection and food-balance estimation were performed via image analysis. Supervised learning based on multiple image features was used.

The food-image detection uses SVM with the common image features except block features described below. Using the image features, SVM is applied to classify the image into the binary classes, namely, "food" or "nonfood".

In the estimation of the food balance, the quantities of five dietary components, based on the Japanese Food Balance Guide [14] (Fig. 4.4), are estimated. It classifies food into five categories, namely grains, vegetables, meat/fish/beans, fruit and dairy

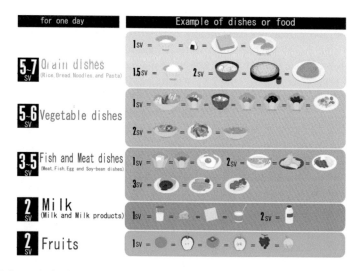

Fig. 4.4 Japanese food-balance guide [14]

products. It assesses a meal by the value of SVs in each category. The SV unit enables ordinary people to assess their food intake easily, giving a reasonable description of the volume of each food category. For example, as shown in Fig. 4.4, food balance is used in general as a discrete value for simplicity. The value varies by the volume and content of the food. For example, if the food image contains a cup of rice, a dish of salad, a dish of baked fish, it is evaluated as 1 SV in grain, 1 SV in vegetable, and 2 SVs in meat/fish/beans categories. The specification has guidelines on how many SVs in each category should be consumed per day. An ordinary person is recommended to take in a day 5–7 SVs in grain, 5–6 SVs in vegetable, 3–5 SVs in meat/fish/beans, 2 SVs in milk/dairy and 2 SVs in fruit categories. FoodLog users can compare their daily consumption with these guidelines to keep track of and improve their dietary balance. Because each category in general has several or a few levels of SVs, the estimation of food balance can be considered a classification problem. The level will be called a "class" below. Unlike the general classification problem, we evaluate the results by average distance between classes of the actual and the estimated SVs, which corresponds to the mean errors of the estimation.

The food-balance estimation has two major components. The first component is an analysis of blocks of the image using image features, that is, assigning each block into one of the six labels including the five categories and "nonfood". The second component is the analysis of the whole image using image features and the histogram of the labels (block features) made by the block-wise analysis. The image is standardized into 320×240 pixels during preprocessing, the size of each block is 16×16, and as a result, there are 300 blocks in the image.

Image features such as colors and BoF of local features were chosen. These features are widely used. Colors and textures are considered important for food images. Bosch et al. [9] also showed that colors and local features are most effective in food recognition. In addition, we also used a circle feature, which possibly reflects round objects such as plates in the images.

All of the above features were finally merged into a 552-dimensional feature vector. Different AdaBoost classifiers were formed for each food category. Finally, SVs of each food category of the image were estimated by classifying the vector into one of several or a few classes by AdaBoost. Regarding the performance of the current deterministic approach, the accuracy of food-image detection is over 90 %, and the average error in food-balance estimation is 0.69 SVs. The error of food-balance estimation is measured by the average absolute difference between the classes; for example, the estimation error would be 1 SV if the image of 2 SVs of grain would be estimated as 1 SV.

The automatic estimation is not always correct, and the user can adjust the estimation if needed.

4.4.2 Improving Estimation by Using Personal Dietary Tendencies

Estimation relying on photograph-only seems unnecessarily limited because we know that dietary habits are richly diverse. We can imagine that food images of each individual reflect personal dietary tendencies to some extent because of individual preferences. For example, Fig. 4.5 shows sets of images uploaded by three FoodLog users labeled A, B and C. There are significant visual differences for these different users. Therefore, we decided to improve the accuracy of food-balance estimation by making use of personal dietary tendencies that differ from the estimation made by the global model.

We introduce a Bayesian framework in place of the deterministic approach in order to make use of personal dietary tendencies improve the estimation. The Bayesian framework facilitates incrementally updating the estimator using the correction. Specifically, likelihood, prior distribution and mealtime categories are taken into account.

The extension of this Bayesian approach to food-balance estimation involves the following equation.

$$P(\theta_i | F^N, c_j) = \frac{P(F^N | \theta_i, c_j) P(\theta_i | c_j)}{P(F^N | c_j)} \tag{4.1}$$

Here, each c_j indicates one of the five categories of food balance (grains, vegetables, meat/fish/beans, fruit and dairy products), F^N is the N-dimensional feature vector extracted from the image and θ_i indicates the class corresponding to the SV being estimated. Grain, meat/fish/beans and vegetables have four classes each, with fruit and dairy products having two classes each. $P(F^N | \theta_i, c_j)$ is called the likelihood, and $P(\theta_i | c_j)$ is the prior probability. Mealtime, such as breakfast, lunch and dinner, is also taken into account by defining five categories for each meal time. Expression (4.2) can be used for Bayesian estimation because the right-side denominator $P(F^N | c_j)$ of expression (4.1) is invariant with respect to the class θ_i.

$$P(\theta_i | F^N, c_j) \propto P(F^N | \theta_i, c_j) P(\theta_i | c_j) \tag{4.2}$$

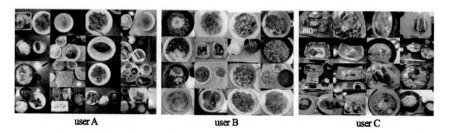

user A   user B   user C

Fig. 4.5 Differences between user images

Fig. 4.6 Mean absolute errors when using all three factors: personal trends, prior probabilities and mealtime categories. The average error for the five food groups is significantly improved from 0.69 to 0.28 SVs

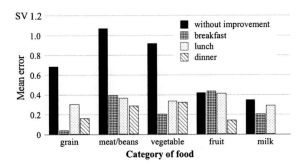

The prior probability can be calculated simply by using statistical information, whereas the likelihood requires an approximation because it is not easy to evaluate directly. A global Bayesian estimation model is created using the data from many users. To adapt the global model to a specific user, the Bayesian estimation model should be updated by corrections made by the user. Please see the details in [16].

In the experiment to investigate food-balance estimation, we used the 616 food images from 79 users of FoodLog to create the general model, and 497 images for the test from two users (215 from user A, and 282 from user B). The results shown in this section are the average of results for the two users, there being no significant

By incorporating likelihoods, prior probabilities and mealtime categories together to the food-balance estimation, the average error was found to improve significantly, from 0.69 SVs to 0.28 SVs, as shown in Fig. 4.6. In the figure, the results for three major categories, namely grains, meat/beans and vegetables, are greatly improved by using the three factors.

4.5 FoodLog App: Assistance of Food Recording by Image Retrieval

In the second phase of our project, we built a FoodLog app that runs on smartphones with connection to cloud storage [17, 18]. Differing from FoodLog Web, which only contains images and food balance evaluation, we aimed at including more detailed description (meal name and volume) of food in a similar way to the traditional food recording methodology. Using a food nutrition database, the meal name and volume of food are sufficient to compute the nutritional content such as energy (calorie). Although the description result follows the traditional method, we make use of multimedia technology to assist users. Screen shots are shown in Fig. 4.7.

FoodLog app allows users to use photos of meals to help them input textual descriptions based on image retrieval. It has two modes for the input of names for food items: a text-based mode and an image-assisted mode as shown in Fig. 4.8.

The text mode is the baseline method in the system and the image mode assists users to input textual descriptions via image retrieval. In the text-based mode, the

Fig. 4.7 Screen shots of FoodLog app. Calender views (*top*) and detailed views (*bottom*). In the calender view, the food domains cut out from the images are shown. In the detailed view, the textual descriptions are shown for the image, and tags of calories displayed for food domains

food name and portion size are required inputs. Part of the name is sufficient as an input because partial match searching is enabled. A default common database is searched when part of the name of the dish is entered as text. A personal database based on the user's history is also searched simultaneously. Both of the search results are displayed as a list. The user can select from the list and select the portion size. Free text input is also available if no items are found in the databases.

We developed the image-assisted mode to make these interactions simpler and more intuitive using an image retrieval technique. The system is operated as follows.

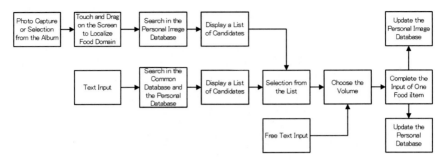

Fig. 4.8 Flowchart of food recording with FoodLog

Fig. 4.9 Image assisted
mode of FoodLog app.
A user takes a photo and
specifies a food domain
(*left*), and visual search in a
personal database results
in top 20 candidates

(1) Take a photo of a meal.
(2) Specify the food domain by touching the screen and adjust the size.
    of the domain (Fig. 4.9 left). A visual similarity search in the personal image
    database is performed by the smartphone, and the top 20 results are shown as a
    list (Fig. 4.9 right).
(3) Choose the appropriate food from the list and adjust its portion size.
    The specified food domain is then registered in the personal image database for
    the next search. The visual search process was sufficiently fast because the time
    required to search was much less than 1 second. Since FoodLog makes use of a
    user's personal database, the precision of top 20 candidates is sufficiently high.

Provided that the food can be identified in the candidate list, the user operations
are simply touch, adjust, and select. However, if the target food is completely new
or the visual search results do not contain the appropriate food, the user employs the
text-based mode to specify the food domain.

4.6 FoodLog App: Accuracy of Food Image Retrieval

Regarding the visual search of the image retrieval, FoodLog app currently makes use of food image data only in his/her personal use history (personal database). Then, at the beginning of the use, FoodLog app functions as a text based baseline system. As the user uses FoodLog app, he/she grows the amount of food images in the personal database. Since eating is habitual, it is often we have the same food again in a short interval. The next time the user has the same meal as the one already recorded, FoodLog can likely assist the user by image retrieval. The current visual search makes use of color-based image feature, that is, a spatial pyramid of color feature. Food contents are very diverse among users and the imaging conditions such as lighting are diverse as well. The use of personal data helps keeping accuracy higher in the retrieval.

Figure 4.10 shows evaluations of its precision of the personalized visual search. The precision of the retrieval is sufficiently high. We made a dataset of three different users' food records which were obtained from their three month long use. 1/4 of the data were chosen for the test, and the evaluation was repeated 5 times. The number of unique food items was different among the three. User A, User B and User C had 461, 165 and 501 different food items, respectively. Figure 4.10 shows top 5, top 10 and top 20 precision for the three users. Top 20 precision was higher than 80 % for all the three: For User B, it was higher than 94 %.

As described above, the cold start, that is, the user has to start with a text only system, is one of the limitations of the current system. In order to improve the cold start problem, the use of huge number of images uploaded by many different users would be beneficial. Considering the state of the art of image recognition, making

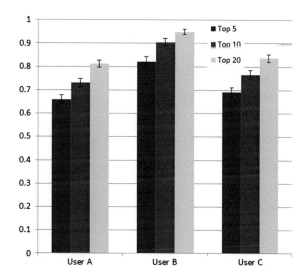

Fig. 4.10 Precision of image retrieval for a dataset of three different users of their three month long use

use of deep features would make visual search accurate [12]. However, there are a lot of problems in making use of the huge data from many users before applying the new methodology. We are currently in the process of these improvements.

4.7   User Studies of FoodLog App: Is the Image Assistance Beneficial?

We investigated if the novel function of FoodLog app (image-assisted mode) benefits users. We compared two food recording tools: One is FoodLog app with image assistance, and the other is a food recording tool with text input only, which was the baseline of FoodLog app [18]. Hereafter, FoodLog app, and FoodLog with text input only are abbreviated as FL-I and FL-T, respectively. Eighteen university students were recruited for the one month long experiments. The students were not familiar with the FoodLog application. They used the tools in their daily lives. They were divided into two groups, one group started using FL-I, and the other FL-T. After two weeks, the FL-I group started using FL-T for another two weeks. At the same time, the FL-T group switched to the FL-I system for another two weeks. In total, each group used the Foodlog systems for one month.

Figure 4.11 shows the result of their subjective evaluation in terms of ease of use (A1), fun (A2), frequency of browsing (A3), and intention to continue using the system (A4). The subjective evaluation showed significant differences in the responses to questions (A2), (A3), and (A4) for FL-I and FL-T. The remarkable difference in question (A2) indicated that all of the participants had fun when using FL-I. The responses to question (A3) showed that the participants browsed their food records more frequently with FL-I than FL-T. The responses to question (A4) showed that the participants were more positive about their intention to continue using FL-I than FL-T. The difference in ease of use (A1) was not significant. Regarding (A1),

Fig. 4.11 Subjective evaluation results, showing the average scores for: ease of use (*A1*), fun (*A2*), frequency of browsing (*A3*), and intention to continue use (*A4*)

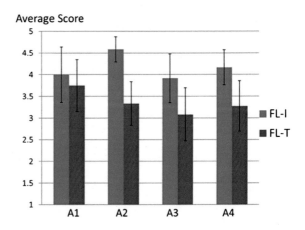

according to the comments written in the questionnaires, a few participants who scored text input higher reported that they felt unpleasant when they missed taking meal photos, and they might have needed more time to get used to it.

In summary, the image assistance is beneficial for the user to keep food records. At the same time, there is a need to improve the user interface. This result is very encouraging for further improvements.

4.8 Analysis of FoodLog Data

FoodLog app was launched in July 2013 in the Apple's AppStore and in October of the same year in Google's Play Store. Since then, food recording data has been continuously accumulated. At the end of the first year's operation (July 2014), the number of food records (textual description) exceeded one million. We started the investigation of the food records using the one year long data. What was surprising to us was that within one million food names, we found approximately 70,000 unique food names. Our default food database has approximately 2,000 names. There were so many new food names, registered or customized, that we found it overwhelmingly difficult to calculate even simple statistics because of the variation of the food names.

Because of this fact, we summarized food names to represent food categories [20]. In order to create such food category representatives, each food name was decomposed into words, which were then grouped with similar group of names of entire FoodLog data. A word graph was made for the group and the minimum path found was used as the representative. The abstract level of the representatives is controlled by changing the size of the group. Figure 4.12 shows the frequency of the representatives when the number of them is approximately 15,000. As it is possible to see, the frequency follows a very steep power law. Only 500 representatives (indicated by the dotted line) are enough to cover 80 % of the entire data.

Fig. 4.12 Frequency versus food category representatives

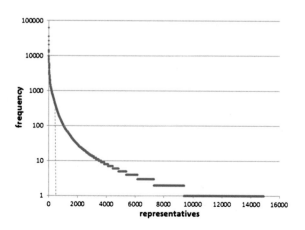

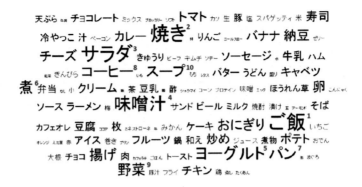

Top 10 frequent representatives:
1.rice(ご飯), 2.grilled(焼き), 3.salad(サラダ), 4.miso soup(味噌汁),
5.yogurt(ヨーグルト), 6.simmered(煮), 7.bread(パン),
8.coffee(コーヒー), 9.vegetable(野菜), and 10.soup(スープ)

Fig. 4.13 The top 100 frequent representatives of FoodLog data: the larger the font size, the higher the frequency. The top 10 frequent representatives are shown at the *bottom*

Figure 4.13 shows top 100 food category representatives extracted from the entire FoodLog data. In the figure, the top 10 frequent representatives are numbered. They are rice, grilled, salad, miso soup, yogurt, simmered, bread, coffee, vegetable, and soup. See the bottom of Fig. 4.13 for their correspondence to Japanese words. Note that "grilled" and "simmered" are familiar words related to cooking methodsthey appeared because of the decomposition of the food names.

4.9 Development and Applications

FoodLog Web and FoodLog app share their database, and the data uploaded by FoodLog app can be seen in FoodLog Web interface, too. The database plays the role of platform for various extended applications as shown in Fig. 4.14.

Currently, Web API is provided to 29 organizations and 14 of them are in use of either real services or limited experiments. For example, we have a collaboration with the hospital of the University of Tokyo, where they focus on self-management of health for diabetic patients. Three factors are used by them: vital signs, exercises, and food intake [21]. Vital sign and exercises are recorded by home instruments and wearable devices, and the data is uploaded to their servers. FoodLog included in their interface works for food recording. Proper comments are informed to the patients based on these records. The system is being evaluated in the hospital.

Donation associated with food logging [22] is another interesting example of its application which creates new value for FoodLog through a joint project with a nonprofit organization called Table for Two (TFT). TFT provides a unique program

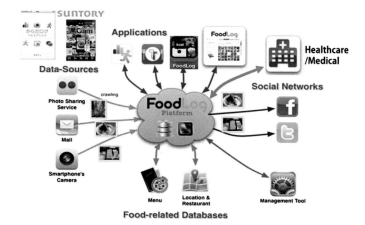

Fig. 4.14 Development of FoodLog. FoodLog platform is applied to various applications

called "calorie transfer" to support school lunches for children in five African countries. TFT partners with hundreds of corporate cafeterias, university dining halls, and restaurants, and offers a healthy, set of TFT menu items. Whenever a diner orders one of these items, 20 yen of his/her payment is donated to TFT, where one school lunch costs 20 yen. In developed countries, where overeating and obesity are serious problems, the TFT program offers healthy menus and it encourages people to make healthy choices. As a result, eating more healthily helps children in need in underdeveloped countries. The system we developed through joint efforts by FoodLog and TFT is now available free of charge as an iPhone app (called the TFT app) based on the FoodLog platform [23]. The concept of the system is drawn in Fig. 4.15. Its main features are as follows.

(1) The TFT app runs on a smartphone. The user can simply take a photo and upload it via the smartphone.
(2) As one of its basic functions, the app creates a food log similar to that created by FoodLog, enabling users to keep a meal diary to help manage their dietary balance. In addition to supporting dietary balance, it provides an estimation of the calorific content of the food [15].
(3) Each time a user uploads a meal photo, he/she clarify whether the meal is healthy or not.
(4) Each time a user declares a healthy meal and uploads the photo to FoodLog, this single upload generates a donation of one yen. Uploading 20 photos of healthy meals pays for one school lunch. At the end, the screen shows a photo of African children and a "Thank you" message.

The only thing users need to do is to upload photos of the healthy meals they eat. The actual donation money comes from contributions that companies make to TFT, not from the users themselves. Users can find value in accumulating meal photos by helping not only themselves, but also other people and society as a whole.

Fig. 4.15 An application of FoodLog for reducing international imbalances in food intake, with photos of healthy food being transformed into donations

The donations are more than simple cash donations because they are generated by people's decisions to eat healthy meals. The system of donations therefore works both ways. In what might sound like an overstatement, the system encourages people who might overeat to become healthier while providing meals for children in impoverished countries. The contributions of the companies that make donations are also twofold: they not only support food for the children overseas, but also promote healthy eating at home.

4.10   Conclusion

In this chapter, we summarized our research project on multimedia FoodLog. Food-Log is a specific application, but it is possible to generate new applications from the existing logs. For user of FoodLog tools, the value lies in personal enjoyment, in managing their health, or in making a social contribution, depending on how they choose to use it. Being able to generate such additional applications may be a key factor in encouraging users to change their lifestyles.

There are still a lot of topics untouched. The huge accumulating food data is excellent source for data analysis. Finding knowledge in the data will leads to far wider applications of food related services. Food is so essential in our daily life.

References

1. F.E. Thompson, A.F. Subar, C.M. Loria, J.L. Reedy, T. Baranowski, Need for technological innovation in dietary assessment. J. Am. Diet. Assoc. **110**(1), 4851 (2010)
2. FoodLog Web. http://www.foodlog.jp/en/
3. FoodLog app. http://app.foodlog.jp
4. CEA2015. http://www.mm.media.kyoto-u.ac.jp/CEA2015/CCC2015; http://ccc2015.loria.fr/MADiMa2015; http://madima.org
5. T. Joutou, K. Yanai, in *IEEE ICIP*. A food image recognition system with multiple kernel learning, pp. 285–288 (2009)
6. F. Zhu, M. Bosch, I. Woo, S.-Y. Kim, C.J. Boushey, D.S. Ebert, E.J. Delp, The use of mobile devices in aiding dietary assessment and evaluation. IEEE J. Sel. Top. Sign. Process. **4**(4), 756–766 (2010)
7. W. Wu, J. Yang, in *IEEE ICME*, Fast food recognition from videos of eating for calorie estimation, pp. 1210–1213 (2009)
8. S. Yang, M. Chen, D. Pomerleau, R. Sukthankar, in *IEEE CVPR*. Food recognition using statistics of pairwise local features, pp. 2249–2256 (2010)
9. M. Bosch, F. Zhu, N. Khanna, C.J. Boushey, E. Delp, in *IEEE ICIP*. Combining global and local features for food identification in dietary assessment, pp. 1789–1792 (2011)
10. Y. Kawano, K. Yanai, FoodCam: a real-time food recognition system on a smartphone. Multimedia Tools Appl. **74**(14), 5263–5287 (2015)
11. L. Bossard, M.Guillaumin, L. Van Gool, Food-101—mining discriminative components with random forests, European Conference on Computer Vision (2014)
12. H. Kagaya, K. Aizawa, M. Ogawa, Food detection and recognition using convolutional neural network. ACM Multimedia **2014**, 1085–1088 (2014)
13. K. Kitamura, T. Yamasaki, K. Aizawa, Food log by analyzing food images, ACM Multimedia, pp. 999–1000 (2008)
14. Ministry of Agriculture, Forestry and Fisheries of Japan, Food Balance Guide. http://www.maff.go.jp/j/balance_guide/ (in Japanese)
15. T. Miyazaki, G.C. de Silva, K. Aizawa, in *IEEE ISM*. Image-based calorie content estimation for dietary assessment, pp. 363–368 (2011)
16. K. Aizawa, Y. Maruyama, H. Li, C. Morikawa, Food balance estimation by using personal dietary tendencies in a multimedia food log. IEEE Trans. Multimedia **15**(8), 2176–2185 (2013)
17. M. Ogawa, Y. Sato, K. Aizawa, Foo.Log.Inc—Counting Calories with Your Camera (2011). www.health2con.com/tv/foo-log-inc-tools-andtrackers
18. K. Aizawa, M. Ogawa et al., Comparative study of the routine daily usability of foodlog: a smartphone-based food recording tool assisted by image retrieval. J. Diabetes Sci. Technol. **8**, 203–208 (2014)
19. J. Noronha, E. Hysen, H. Zhang, K.Z. Gajos, in *ACM UIST*. PlateMate: crowdsourcing nutrition analysis from food photographs, pp. 1–12 (2011)
20. S. Amano, K. Aizawa, M. Ogawa, Food category representatives: extracting categories from meal names in food recordings and recipe data. IEEE Multimedia Big Data 48–55 (2015)
21. K. Waki, K. Aizawa et al., Dialbetics with a multimedia food recording tool, foodlog: smartphone-based self-management for type 2 diabetes. J. Diabetes Sci. Technol. **9**(3), 534–540 (2015)
22. K. Aizawa, Multimedia foodlog: diverse applications from self-monitoring to social contributions. ITE Trans. Media Technol. Appl. **1**(3), 214–219 (2013)
23. TFT. http://jp.tablefor2.org/project/app.html

Chapter 5
Dynamic Information Space Based on High-Speed Sensor Technology

Masatoshi Ishikawa, Idaku Ishii, Yutaka Sakaguchi, Makoto Shimojo, Hiroyuki Shinoda, Hirotsugu Yamamoto, Takashi Komuro, Hiromasa Oku, Yutaka Nakajima and Yoshihiro Watanabe

Abstract The purpose of this research is to realize a dynamic information space harmonizing human perception system, recognition system, and motor system. Toward this purpose, our key technology is high-speed sensor technology and display technology focusing on vision and haptic sense which performs at the order of kHz. Based on these technologies, our information space can obtain the dynamics of humans and objects in perfect condition and displays information at high speed. As subsystems for our goal, we have newly developed four important elemental

M. Ishikawa (✉) · H. Shinoda · Y. Watanabe
The University of Tokyo, Tokyo, Japan
e-mail: Masatoshi_Ishikawa@ipc.i.u-tokyo.ac.jp

H. Shinoda
e-mail: Hiroyuki_Shinoda@k.u-tokyo.ac.jp

Y. Watanabe
e-mail: Yoshihiro_Watanabe@ipc.i.u-tokyo.ac.jp

I. Ishii
Hiroshima University, Hiroshima, Japan
e-mail: iishii@robotics.hiroshima-u.ac.jp

Y. Sakaguchi · M. Shimojo · Y. Nakajima
University of Electro-Communications, Tokyo, Japan
e-mail: sakaguchi@is.uec.ac.jp

M. Shimojo
e-mail: shimojo@mce.uec.ac.jp

Y. Nakajima
e-mail: nakajima@hi.is.uec.ac.jp

H. Yamamoto
Utsunomiya University, Tochigi, Japan
e-mail: hirotsugu_yamamoto@cc.utsunomiya-u.ac.jp

T. Komuro
Saitama University, Saitama, Japan
e-mail: komuro@mail.saitama-u.ac.jp

H. Oku
Gunma University, Gunma, Japan
e-mail: h.oku@gunma-u.ac.jp

© Springer Japan 2016
T. Nishida (ed.), *Human-Harmonized Information Technology, Volume 1*,
DOI 10.1007/978-4-431-55867-5_5

technologies including high-speed 3D vision toward insensible dynamics sensing, high-speed resistor network proximity sensor array for detecting nearby object, non-contact low-latency haptic feedback, and high-speed display of visual information for information sharing and operation in real space. Also, in order to achieve the coordinated interaction between individual humans and this information space, we have conducted the research about the human perceptual and motor functions for coordinated interaction with high-speed information environment. In addition, we have developed various application systems based on the concept of dynamic information space by integrating the subsystems.

Keywords High-speed vision · Proximity sensor · Airborne Ultrasound Tactile Display (AUTD) · High-speed LED display · Human interface · Dynamic information environment

5.1 Introduction

In this research, we aim at realizing a dynamic information space harmonizing human perception system, recognition system, and motor system. Toward this goal, we focus on the acquisition of the human and object dynamics perfectly in a information space and the high-speed display whose performance is dramatically improved. Integrating these functions, the platform of the new information space become possible to be built.

However, the conventional visual information sensing and display at video rate (30 Hz, for example) does not have enough performance for the dynamics involved in the high-speed human/object motion. Similarly, the sensing and display technologies of the haptic information does not have enough speed. Also, haptic technologies have a limit requiring physical contact between device and target. In order to allow the high-speed dynamics in the information space, it is essentially required to achieve the non-contact and unrestricted sensing and display.

Therefore, we have developed four new technologies including high-speed 3D vision toward insensible dynamics sensing, high-speed resistor network proximity sensor array for detecting nearby object, noncontact low-latency haptic feedback, and high-speed display of visual information for information sharing and operation in real space.

On the other hand, information provided by the sensing and display exceeding the speed of human perceptual ability is difficult to be utilized for human. In order to overcome this limit, we have conducted the research about the human perceptual and motor functions for coordinated interaction with high-speed information environment. This allows us to realize the coordinated interaction between individual humans and this information space.

As a final goal, we have developed various types of dynamic information space, which are mainly for the computer-human interfaces, by integrating these technologies. This integrated system allows high-speed user interaction in a contactless manner without any constraints about the moving humans and targets.

5.2 High-Speed 3-D Vision Toward Insensible Dynamics Sensing

High-speed vision systems that can capture and process real-time imagery at hundreds or thousands of frames per second (FPS) are an important step toward the realization of harmonized dynamic information environments. These systems are powerful sensing tools for detecting "insensible dynamics," which the human eyes can only barely sense. To completely capture rapid human motion in three-dimensional (3-D) space with only minor occlusions, multiple depth images in different views must be simultaneously captured and processed at a high frame rate. In this section, we introduce structured-light high-speed 3-D vision systems that can capture and process depth images containing 512×512 pixels in real time, at 500 FPS on high-frame-rate (HFR) camera-projector systems.

Our structured-light high-speed 3-D vision system contains a 3-D module consisting of a high frame rate (HFR) camera head, an HFR projector, an IDP Express board [1], and a personal computer (PC) equipped with a GPU board. The 3-D module uses a Digital Light Processing (DLP) development kit projector for HFR projection, which is based on digital micromirror device (DMD) technology (Texas Instruments Inc., US), and a monochrome camera head (Photron Ltd., Japan). A system overview in which the DLP LightCommander 5500 is used as a projector is shown in Fig. 5.1. On a level surface 550 mm below the camera, depth information over a 484×484 mm square is captured as a 512×512 image.

The DLP LightCommander 5500 can project hundreds of 1024×768 binary patterns at 1000 FPS or greater. The IDP Express was designed to implement various image-processing algorithms, and to record images and features at a high frame rate onto PC memory. The camera head captures 8-bit gray-level 512×512 images at 2000 FPS. The IDP Express board has two camera inputs, along with a

Fig. 5.1 System overview

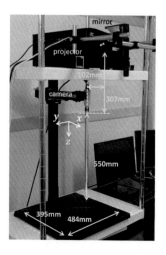

Fig. 5.2 Pipelining-output of depth images

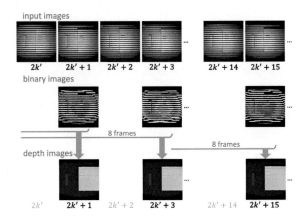

frame-straddling function and trigger I/Os for external synchronization. Two 512 × 512 images and their processed results can be mapped onto PC memory at 2000 FPS, via a Peripheral Component Interconnect Express (PCI-e) bus. The Tesla C1060 is a computer processor board based on the NVIDIA Tesla T10 GPU. It is capable of a processing performance of 933 Gflops/s, using 240 processor cores operating at 1.296 GHz and a bandwidth of 102 GB/s for its internal 4 GB memory. We use a PC with the following specifications: ASUSTeK P6T7 WS main board, Intel Core i7 3.20 GHz CPU, 3 GB RAM, two 16-lane PCI-e 2.0 buses. To compute depth images at a high frame rate with minimal synchronization errors, a motion-compensated structured-light algorithm [2], which is based on Inokuchi's method [3], was implemented; binary light patterns coded with an 8-bit gray code are projected at 1000 FPS, and the projected light patterns are captured at 1000 FPS. Depth image processing was accelerated using parallel processing with 512 blocks of 1 × 512 pixels on the GPU board; the total time is 1.81 ms, and depth image processing of 512 × 512 images can be conducted in real time at 500 FPS (Fig. 5.2).

Figure 5.3 shows the 3-D measurement results for a human hand moving periodically; (a) shows the experimental scenes captured using a standard camera, (b) shows the x, y, and z coordinates of the right hand, (c) depicts the depth images measured by our motion-compensated structured-light method with an 8-bit gray code using a 1000 FPS video (denoted by MCGC1K), (d) shows the 8-bit gray-code structured-light method without motion compensation [4] using a 1000 FPS video (GC1K), and (e) depicts 30 FPS video (GC30). The hand was moved horizontally in a circular orbit at a certain distance from the desk plane at a frequency of once per second. On the desk plane, a computer keyboard, books, and many 3-D objects were placed as background objects, and the left hand was kept stationary. In Fig. 5.3b, the centroid position of the right hand, which was computed by subtracting the background from the MCGC1K depth images, was periodically changed at a rate of once per second. Compared with the MCGC1K and GC1K depth images, the GC30 depth images were incorrect; this occurred because synchronization errors generated by 3-D measurements of moving objects (using different frames) increase when the frame interval is increased.

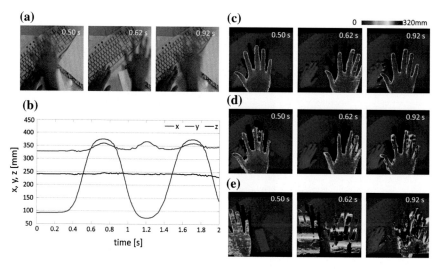

Fig. 5.3 3-D measurement of a moving human hand. **a** Experimental scenes, **b** xyz coordinate values, **c** depth images (MCGC1K), **d** depth images (CGC1K), **e** depth images (GC30)

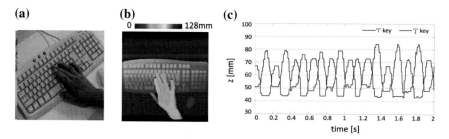

Fig. 5.4 3-D measurement of finger-tapping on a computer keyboard. **a** Experimental scenes, **b** depth image, **c** temporal images of tapped keys

Synchronization errors were significantly minimized by introducing an HFR camera-projector system. Compared with the GC1K depth images, the MCGC1K depth images show that the 3-D shape of the human hand was accurately measured with minimal synchronization errors when the hand was moving. Figure 5.4 shows (a) the experimental scene, (b) the MCGC1K depth image, and (c) the depth information of the "j" key and "i" key, when the forefinger of the right hand taps the "j" key and its middle finger taps the "i" key alternatively at a 5 Hz frequency. Our 3-D vision system can detect high-speed finger motions, and the timing of each key tapping, to detect the input content.

By adding an RGB projector to expand the HFR camera-projector system, pixel-wise projection mapping can be conducted onto time-varied 3-D scenes. Infrared (IR) light patterns projected from an IR HFR projector are simultaneously captured and processed for depth image calculation, and the RGB light patterns are interactively generated and projected from the RGB projector onto the 3-D scene. The IR and RGB

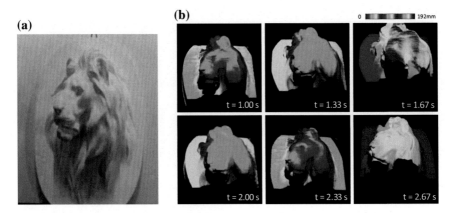

Fig. 5.5 Pixel-wise projection mapping results for a moving lion relief. **a** Plaster lion relief, **b** color-mapped scenes

projectors have the same projection fields. A camera head with an IR wavelength filter can capture only IR light patterns for the 3-D structured-light measurement when the RGB light patterns are projected for enhanced tasks. Figure 5.5 shows the experimental scenes captured using a standard camera, when depth-based color mapping with a cyclic jet color map was conducted onto a 10 cm-deep plaster lion relief (for sensitive and distinct depth visualization). The relief was moved with periodic up-and-down motions and slight rotations by a human hand. It can be seen that the white-surface relief was enhanced by pixel-wise projection mapping with a cyclic jet color map, which can directly visualize its detailed height information for human eyes. Such projection mapping techniques based on high-speed 3-D vision will extend augmented reality (AR)-based applications for dynamic human computer interactions.

To conduct complete 3-D information acquisition with minimal occlusion using multiple camera-projector modules, time division multiplex 3-D structured-light measurement was implemented on an HFR camera-projector system. The timings of light pattern projection and image capture are straddled using a short time delay; this enables each camera-projector system to simultaneously obtain 3-D information in its view field without crosstalk between light patterns projected from different camera-projector systems. Figure 5.6 shows a prototype system for time division multiplex 3-D structured-light measurements; it is composed of two opposing HFR camera-projector modules, an IDP Express board, and a PC equipped with a Tesla C1060 GPU board. The camera-projector module consists of an HFR projector of 854×480 pixels (DLP LightCrafter 4500; Texas Instruments Inc., US) and an HFR color camera head of 512×512 pixels (Photron Ltd., Japan). In the present implementation, both camera-projector modules are operated with 0.5 ms-exposure image capture and 0.7 ms-duration light pattern projection at 500 FPS, whereas the two modules are straddled with a 1-ms time delay. The state of each module is alternatively switched at 1 ms intervals, to reduce interference from the light-patterns pro-

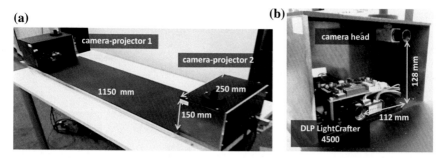

Fig. 5.6 Time division multiplex HFR camera-projector system. **a** Experimental setting, **b** camera-projector module

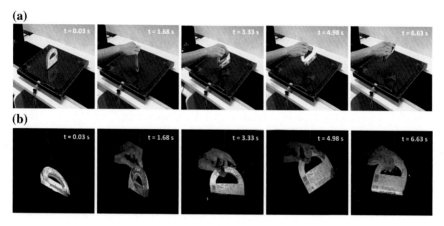

Fig. 5.7 Experimental results when a color-patterned object is moved by a human hand. **a** Experimental scenes, **b** texture-mapped 3-D scenec

jected by the other module. Accelerated by parallel processing on the GPU board, the 512×512 pixel depth and color RGB images are computed in 1.43 ms for each camera input; both the left- and right-side-view depth images can be simultaneously processed at 250 FPS on our time division multiplex HFR camera-projector system. Figure 5.7 shows (a) the experimental scenes and (b) the synthesized 3-D scenes when a color-patterned tape box was moved by a human hand. The 3-D scenes that are texture-mapped with color images are synthesized using the left- and right-side-view depth images, and displayed using the OpenGL environment. It can be seen that both sides of the 3-D shapes of the color-patterned tape box and human hand were displayed with minimal occlusion in real time when the human hand was rapidly moving.

To enlarge the view fields in 3-D structured-light measurement, which would facilitate more accurate 3-D image acquisitions, the number of camera-projector modules can be increased by connecting many 3-D structured-light measurement systems with short time delays via a TCP-IP network. This extension can be conducted without decreasing the acquisition rate of depth images; however, the exposure time used

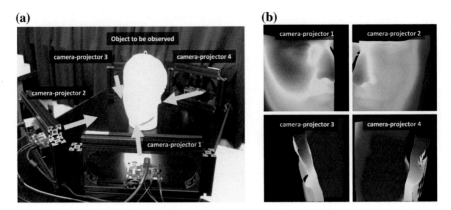

Fig. 5.8 3-D structured-light measurement using four HFR camera-projector modules. aExperimental setting, **b** measured depth images

for image capturing and the duration time used for light pattern projection should both be reduced, in inverse proportion to the number of camera-projector modules. Figure 5.8 shows (a) the experimental setting and (b) the measured depth images from different view angles, when a planar head sculpture was observed using four HFR camera-projector modules. Synchronizing the four camera-projector modules with 0.5, 1.0, and 1.5 ms time delays, the four different-view-angle depth images were simultaneously computed at 250 FPS with no crosstalk from light patterns projected from different angles.

Such a structured-light 3-D vision system using HFR camera-projector modules allows the simultaneous detection and localization of dynamic behaviors. It enables complete 3-D information acquisition with minimal occlusion for human-computer interactions; standard cameras operating at dozens of FPS are generally unable to perform such acquisitions. High-speed 3-D vision technology will play a role as one of the most important dynamic sensing technologies in next-generation dynamic information environments.

5.3 High-Speed Resistor Network Proximity Sensor Array for Detecting Nearby Object

This research focuses on the development of high-speed proximity sensor array that excels at close-range sensing from contact to several tens of centimeters. The sensor uses a photo-reflector comprising a light-emitting diode (LED) and a photo-transistor as its detection element. Photo-transistors capture reflected infrared light from the LED, and the position of a proximal object is inferred according to the photo-current distribution. A primary feature of this sensor is that object position inference can be performed using analog computation by a resistor network circuit [5]. Serially reading the response levels of individual photosensitive elements, as in the case of a general-purpose CCD image, requires complex wiring due to the number of elements and the size of the unit. Moreover, data acquisition and processing times are long. On the other hand, when using proposed sensor, high-speed response (less than 1 ms) and simple wiring requirements are retained, even when the number of elements is increased to accommodate the form of the installation surface. This is an important consideration for application to a complex shape, such as a grip designed to fit the human hand.

5.3.1 Sensor Design and Detection Principles

We refer to the developed azimuth and elevation proximity detector as a dome-shape sensor. The dome-shape sensor is formed from two sensor ring (Fig. 5.9) [6]. Each of the two ring can obtain one-dimensional positional coordinates. Azimuth is determined by orthogonally aligning each sensor's coordinate axis. Each ring can also measure the distance to target objects. Elevation is determined by placing rings in two layers in the height direction, and performing distance detection with each.

This section describes the one-dimensional resistor network proximity sensor array (RNPS), which is the most fundamental part of the dome-shape sensor. Figure 5.9 shows the overview and the circuit structure. The one-dimensional RNSP consists of a resistor network. The resistor network is formed from $n - 1$ internal resistors $r_i (i = 1 \sim n - 1)$ between the photo-reflectors, and an external resistors R_0 that connect the terminals on both ends V_{S1}, V_{S2} and a negative supply $V^{[-]}$. Light from an infrared LED reflects off of objects proximal to the sensor, and is collected in the photo-transistor. This causes photocurrent distribution that corresponds to the distribution of reflected light at the phototransistor surface. When a photocurrent I_i occurs at the ith element, the currents flowing between terminals V_{S1} and V_{S2} are described as follows:

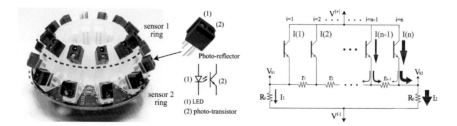

Fig. 5.9 *Left* The dome-shape sensor is formed from two ring of one-dimensional resistor network proximity sensor array (RNPS). The rings are placed in two layers in the height direction. *Right* Circuit diagram of the one-dimensional RNPS: When a photo current occurs at the element, the currents diverges and flows to the negative supply $V^{[-]}$ [6]

$$I_{i1} = \frac{\sum_{k=i}^{n-1} r_k + R_0}{\sum_{k=1}^{n-1} r_k + 2R_0} I_i, \quad I_{i2} = \frac{\sum_{k=1}^{i-1} r_k + R_0}{\sum_{k=1}^{n-1} r_k + 2R_0} I_i \tag{5.1}$$

The difference between the currents flowing to terminals V_{S1} and V_{S2} is therefore

$$I_{i1} - I_{i2} = \frac{\sum_{k=i}^{n-1} r_k - \sum_{k=0}^{i-1} r_k}{\sum_{k=1}^{n-1} r_k + 2R_0} I_i \tag{5.2}$$

The numerator in Eq. (5.2) is the product of the resistance at each element from the center of the serially connected resistor network with the current flowing through it, and represents the one-dimensional moment of the current at the center. When a photocurrent arises in the each element, the photocurrents will therefore flow together, and the following equations will hold:

$$\sum_{i=1}^{n-1} (I_{i1} - I_{i2}) = \sum_{i=1}^{n-1} I_i \frac{\sum_{k=i}^{n-1} r_k - \sum_{k=1}^{i-1} r_k}{\sum_{k=1}^{n-1} r_k + 2R_0} = \frac{V_{S1} - V_{S2}}{R_0} \tag{5.3}$$

$$\sum_{i=1}^{n-1} I_i = I_{all} = \frac{V_{S1} + V_{S2} - 2V^{[-]}}{R_0} \tag{5.4}$$

Removing the one-dimensional moment calculated by Eq. (5.3) from the overall current I_{all} calculated by Eq. (5.4) allows identification of the photocurrent distribution's central point. To improve ease-of-use, Eq. (5.5) is used on the one-dimensional RNPS output to normalize the center point to the range $[-1, 1]$.

$$x_c = - \left(1 + \frac{2R_0}{\sum_{i=1}^{n-1} r_i} \right) \left(\frac{V_{S1} - V_{S2}}{V_{S1} + V_{S2} - 2V^{[-]}} \right) \tag{5.5}$$

When the amount of reflected light gathered by the phototransistor changes according to the distance between the sensor and the proximal object, the total current through the resistor network also changes. This allows estimation of the approximate distance to the object by using Eq. (5.4) to obtain the total current through the resistor network.

5.3.1.1 Azimuth Detection

The azimuthal orientation of the object is detected by deriving cosine and sine values from the one-dimensional RNPS output. Figure 5.10a shows the circular arrangement of the sensor elements of the one-dimensional RNPS. The internal resistors in the

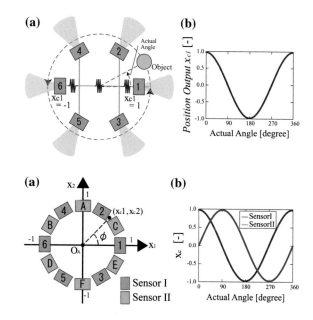

Fig. 5.10 Structure and output of the circular one-dimensional RNPS: The positioning output forms a cosine wave for an object at the outer sensor periphery by the circular arrangement of the sensor elements and the internal resistors set [6]. **a** Structure of sensor 1, **b** output of sensor 1

Fig. 5.11 Detection principle of azimuth: The orthogonally orienting two circular sensor allows derivation of the cosine and sine value of the object's azimuth from these positioning output [6]. **a** Structure of sensor, **b** output of sensor

proximity sensors are set so that positioning output forms a cosine wave when an object goes around the sensor, as shown in Fig. 5.10b. In the case where six elements are used (Fig. 5.10), the ratios of internal sensors will be 1:2:1 in proportion to real-space positions. Two such circular one-dimensional RNPS are used, and are respectively called sensor I and sensor II. As Fig. 5.11 shows, orthogonally orienting these sensors creates a 90° phase shift between them, allowing derivation of the sine value of the object's azimuth from the positioning output. The positioning output (x_{c1}, x_{c2}) obtained by the respective sensors and Eq. (5.6) can therefore uniquely determine the object's azimuth ϕ.

$$
\phi = \begin{cases}
\frac{\pi}{2}\,\mathrm{sgn}(x_{c2}) & x_{c1} = 0 \\[2mm]
\arctan\left(\dfrac{x_{c2}}{x_{c1}}\right) & x_{c1} > 0 \\[2mm]
\pi\,\mathrm{sgn}(x_{c2}) + \arctan\left(\dfrac{x_{c2}}{x_{c1}}\right) & x_{c1} < 0
\end{cases}
\tag{5.6}
$$

5.3.1.2 Elevation Detection

The two circular one-dimensional RNPS provide two distance outputs I_{all}, which are used to detect elevation without compromising the azimuth detection characteristics. The two circular RNPS are placed as shown in Fig. 5.12a. Because changes in elevation will change the distance to each of the sensors, the photocurrent flowing

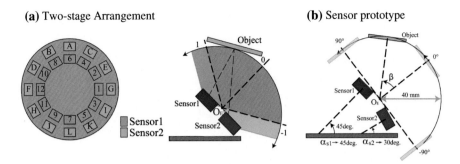

Fig. 5.12 Detection principle of elevation: **a** The two circular sensors are placed in two layers in the height direction. The changes in elevation will change the distance to each of the sensors. **b** Overview of simulation operation for determining element tilts: The angle at which the normalized elevation output is 0 is taken as 0°, and a 90 mm square object was moved through the space between −90° and 90° with respect to the origin of the elevation angle O_E [6]

through sensors 1 and 2 will also change. Specifically, taking the distance output of the two circular RNPS as I_{all1}, I_{all2} allows use of Eq. (5.7) to find the elevation output θ, normalized to the range $[-1, 1]$.

$$\theta = \frac{I_{all1} - I_{all2}}{I_{all1} + I_{all2}} \qquad (5.7)$$

The normalized elevation output will be +1 if only sensor 1 is responding, −1 if only sensor 2 is responding, and continuously varying in the range $-1 < \theta < 1$ in the case where both sensors are responding. In this method, the range at which elevation can be detected depends on the tilt and positioning of the two circular RNPS. This allows the detection range to be set according to the intended purpose of the dome-shape sensor.

5.3.2 Prototyping and Experiments

5.3.2.1 Sensor Prototype

When designing a dome-shape sensor, it is possible to adjust element tilt and positioning according to the intended application. Here we developed equipment for the purpose of tracking a human hand. We identified the following design requirements:

- The elevation detection range must include the space to the sides and above the dome-shape sensor.
- The sensor must be shaped to fit a human hand, based on a circular form with approximately 65 mm diameter.

- Detected objects would primarily be human palms, and thus an approximate planar square of $90 \times 90 \, \text{mm}^2$.

We varied the tilt of the elements in sensors 1 and 2 (α_{s1}, α_{s2}, respectively), and determined the element positioning best suited to our basic circular form. Because it would be difficult to create and test prototype sensors with a variety of tilt combinations, we used a RNPS detection simulator developed in our lab.

As a result of the simulations, Fig. 5.12b shows the side view of the dome-shape sensor prototype. Twelve elements were evenly spaced along the dome sensor's periphery.

5.3.2.2 Detection Characteristics

(1) Azimuth Detection Characteristics

In this section, we examine the azimuth detection characteristic by an experiment with the prototyped dome-shape sensor. The distance between the sensor and the object was 30–60 mm.

Figure 5.13a shows the results of the experiment.

The figure indicates that the azimuth output of the sensor increased monotonically with increasing azimuth of the object.

(2) Elevation Detection Characteristics

Figure 5.13b indicates that the absolute value of elevation output near 0° or 90° increases with increasing distance.

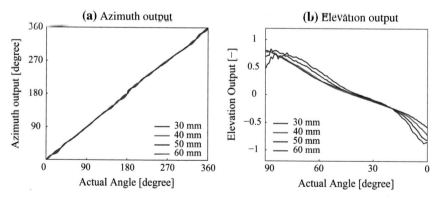

Fig. 5.13 a Experimental results with changing the distance of 30–60 mm. Detection is possible over the entire 360° range. Detection error was within approximately ±5°. **b** Elevation output of the experimental results with changing the distance of 30–60 mm

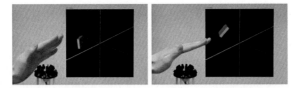

Fig. 5.14 Human-machine interface usage of the dome-shape sensor: The sensor with the rapid response features can be applied to non-contact human interface applications. This photo shows a detected palm position [6]

The elevation output difference due to distance change decreases with decreasing distance between the sensor and the object. Thus, incorporating the dome-shape sensor into the grip will allow tracking of hands by using the result in proximity as target.

5.3.3 Conclusion

The present study developed a high-speed proximity sensor array for simultaneous detection of azimuth and elevation. The features of the proposed dome-shape sensor include rapid responsiveness and simpler wiring, while maintaining a 360° sensing range and detection from sensor sides to top. The rapid response features of the method can be applied to noncontact human interface applications (Fig. 5.14). In future research, we plan to create more practical dome-shape sensors with wider detection range on the same principle, and investigate potential applications.

5.4 Noncontact Low-Latency Haptic Feedback

One of the key components of the Dynamic Information Space is a haptic display without constraining users' behavior. Haptics would be an indispensable modality in the computational support of human dynamic motion though it is still in an early stage of the applications. In order to indicate the motion direction, notify the motion timing, and comprehend the circumstance in fast human motions, haptics would be a promising modality to transmit such information with acceptable delays as realtime feedbacks. A problem in haptic feedbacks had been physical stimulation to human skins. If the device is a bulky mechanical system installed on the ground or a table, the workspace is limited to a narrow area around the device. It is also difficult to receive passive stimulation in free motions using such mechanical systems. Therefore, the recent technological main stream is to develop small and lightweight haptic devices wearable or installed in a mobile device. Based on the recent technological achievement, haptics is beginning to find wide ranging applications as computer interface.

However, the problem that still remains is the area to receive haptic stimulation is limited and localized in practical scenes. It is not straightforward to stimulate various body parts to support the motions. And it is also a problem that such devices should be worn in advance before haptic feedbacks are necessary, which cannot be supposed in some applications.

With this background, we developed a noncontact tactile display that produces tactile sensation using ultrasound traveling in the air [7]. Airborne Ultrasound Tactile Display (AUTD) was first proposed by the authors and demonstrated with a small ultrasound phased array [8, 9]. In this project, we extended this to a large aperture phased array to widen the workspace. In the following subsection, we describe the system design to realize such large aperture and effective tactile display. The total system combined with sensors and visual displays will be described in the later section.

5.4.1   Remote Vibrotactile Sensation Produced with Airborne Ultrasound

There are some options to generate tactile sensations in noncontact manners. Air flow produced by a propeller or jet nozzle would be a feasible method to stimulate the human skin remotely. Very strong infrared would induce temperature elevation when it is radiated on the skin. The features of ultrasound stimulation are:

1. A small spot comparable to the sound wavelength can be selectively stimulated. The distance from the sound source can be as large as the aperture of the phased array keeping the convergence,
2. Low frequency ultrasound ~40 kHz can propagate a long distance (with −1 dB/m at 40 kHz),
3. Ultrasound amplitude can be modulated at a frequency as high as 1 kHz. The force produced by the ultrasound radiation pressure on the skin can be controlled with 1 kHz bandwidth.

Though the maximum pressure would be limited to 100 mN practically and a large aperture ultrasound transducer array is necessary, the above features are desirable for non-constrained high speed tactile feedback. A problem in principle is that time delay by the sound velocity is inevitable. For 340 m/s sound velocity, the stimulation delay is as large as 3 ms/m. But for many applications, this delay would be acceptable.

The key physical phenomena called radiation pressure is a nonlinear acoustic phenomenon, to convert the alternating sound pressure amplitude into static pressure on the reflection surface. The details are described below.

5.4.1.1 Acoustic Radiation Pressure

Physics showed sound waves are accompanied with radiation pressure proportional to the energy density of the sound [10]. Since ultrasound with a short wavelength can be localized in a small area, it can create a concentrated radiation pressure on a skin. The radiation pressure applied to the surface reflecting an ultrasound is given as

$$P = \frac{\alpha p^2}{\rho c^2} \tag{5.8}$$

where p [Pa] denotes the effective value of sound pressure, c [m/s] the sound velocity in the medium, ρ [kg/m^3] the density of the medium, and α a coefficient determined by the reflectance. When ultrasound propagates in the air and blocked off by liquid or solid, almost all of the ultrasound is reflected on the boundary and in this case α becomes 2 in vertical incidence. Following this equation, we can control temporal profiles of radiation pressure by amplitude modulation of ultrasound pressure. The attenuation of ultrasound propagation in the air depends on its frequency. The attenuation rate of 40 kHz ultrasound in air is about 1 dB/m, while the frequency is much higher than the highest frequency that human can feel as vibrotactile stimulation ($\sim$1 kHz) [11].

5.4.1.2 Controlling Radiation Pressure

The Airborne Ultrasound Tactile Display (AUTD) in this project is an ultrasound transducer array with 10 mm period [8, 9]. By setting a proper phase shift on each transducer, the three-dimensional position of the focal point can be controlled. Let $\mathbf{r}_i$ be the position of the ith transducer among N transducers and $\mathbf{r}_F$ be the desirable focal position. The phase shift on i th transducer is calculated so that it compensates the phase delay through distance:

$$\theta_i = k|\mathbf{r}_i - \mathbf{r}_F|, \tag{5.9}$$

where k denotes the wavenumber. In the prototype, a 1.5-cm-diameter spot of radiation pressure can be formed around the array. The spot center can be moved in accuracy of 1 mm horizontally. Its position can be switched at a refreshing rate of over 2 kHz. The whole phase calculation can be done within 50 μs in the system, which is faster than 2 kHz.

The ultrasound amplitude is controlled with pulse width modulation. The pulse frequency is fixed to the transducer's resonant frequency $f = 40$ kHz and the amplitude is controlled with the pulse width d [s] as

$$p = p_0 \sin(\pi d / T) \tag{5.10}$$

Fig. 5.15 Airborne
ultrasound tactile display
with 3 by 3 units [7]. The
size of a unit is $19 \times 15\,\mathrm{cm}^2$

where $T = 1/f$, and p_0 denotes the maximal amplitude for $d/T = 1/2$ [9]. The
pulse width $d(t)$ is calculated so that the radiation pressure P becomes the target
value. It should be noticed that the radiation pressure P always has a positive value
(Fig. 5.15).

5.4.2 Multi-unit Phased Array Scheme

In this project, we developed a freely extendable phased array system [7]. Extending
the phased array aperture size enlarges the workspace where focusing is ensured.
We design an AUTD unit of $19 \times 15\,\mathrm{cm}^2$ having a serial input port and three output
ports as shown in Fig. 5.16. Each unit has FPGAs that calculate each signal phase of
the transducer on it. The serial signal receiver is programmed in the Master FPGA.
Master FPGA receives the focal point position (x, y, z) and the amplitude p, and
transmit the information to the next unit. Since the signal delay between the neighbor
units is sufficiently small ($\leq 50\,\mathrm{ns}$), multiple units can be connected freely. Since it
has three output ports, $1 + 3 + 3^2 + 3^3 + 3^4 = 121$ units can be connected within
200ns delay.

Each AUTD unit must know its position in the global coordinates and its own
posture in advance. This information is at first sent to the Master FPGA of each
AUTD unit. Since all the focal information sent is in the global coordinates, the
Master FPGAs convert it to their own local coordinates, which the Slave FPGAs
receive. Slave FPGAs calculate the phase delays and generate all driving signals on
transducers according to the focal position and the amplitude.

The duty cycle of 40 kHz pulse $d(t)$ can be quantized up to 640 levels. As the
result, the radiation pressure $P(t)$ is quantized up to 320 levels. The current system
can switch the duty cycle fast enough to generate vibrotactile sensation with the
temporal resolution of 0.5 ms (2 kHz).

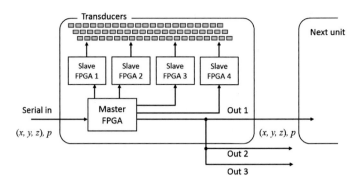

Fig. 5.16 System architecture of an AUTD unit

5.4.3 Experiments

We fabricated a phased array composed of 3×3 units as shown in Fig. 5.15 and measured the spatial distribution of generated ultrasound amplitude, in order to confirm ultrasound focusing. The 9-unit AUTD was mounted on an aluminum cabinet so that the transducer surface faced the ground, parallel to the ground. A standard microphone (B&K Type 4138) with a pre-amplifier (B&K Type 2670) was mounted on the 3D stage, with the xy-plane parallel to the AUTD. The xy-coordinates corresponded to the lattice of transducers and the z-axis was vertical to the AUTD surface. The recorded voltage was amplified with a power amplifier (B&K Type 5935). We used the reference sound source that provides 94 dB sine wave of 1 kHz for the mapping of the recorded voltage to sound pressure. The frequency characteristic of the whole recording system was almost flat from 0 to 40 kHz. The total array size was $576 \times 454.2 \, \text{mm}^2$.

The focal point was set to $(0, 0, -600 \, \text{mm})$. We measured sound pressure near the focal point and estimated the produced radiation pressure from Eq. (5.8). The parameters were set as $c = 340 \, \text{m/s}$, $\rho = 1.18 \, \text{kg/m}^3$ and $\alpha = 2$. The left figure of Fig. 5.17 depicts the calculated radiation pressure distribution in the plane at $z = -600 \, \text{mm}$. High radiation pressure can be seen localized within the diameter of $10 \sim 15 \, \text{mm}$. The right figure of Fig. 5.17 shows a 1D distribution across the focal point along $(y, z) = (0, -600)$. Focusing is clearly observed.

5.4.4 Conclusion

A non-contact vibrotactile display with a wide workspace was developed and its performance was examined. The developed AUTD is extendable by connecting multiple ultrasound transducer units and we constructed an array of $576 \times 454.2 \, \text{mm}^2$ aperture. The system succeeded in producing highly localized vibrotactile sensations

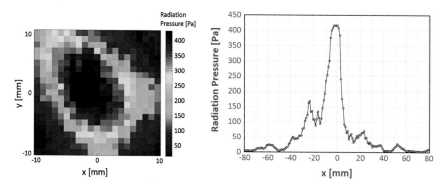

Fig. 5.17 Experimental results [7]. Distribution of acoustic radiation pressure measured at 60 cm from a 3 × 3 unit AUTD

on human skin 600 mm apart from the device. The focal intensity was experimentally demonstrated to be 74 mN. Temporal profiles of vibrotactile sensations were programmable with a sampling rate of 2 kHz and 320-level quantization.

5.5   High-Speed Display of Visual Information for Information Sharing and Operation in Real Space

Recent requirements for information displays include not only resolution but also frame rate and latency because interactive interfaces must show the responses without noticeable delay for users. Light emitting diode (LED) is a prospective light source for high-speed operations. Instantaneous operation of visual information in real space is considered to be one of the essentials for human-harmonized information technology. In this section, high-frame-rate and low-latency LED displays are described in Sects. 5.5.1 and 5.5.2. In Sect. 5.5.3, we describe aerial imaging technique that enables floating LED screen with wide viewing angle.

5.5.1   High-Frame-Rate LED Display

In current LED display systems, a large LED screen is constructed by tiling LED units. The control signals for LED units are given by an LED video processor, which distributes an input image into image data to tiled LED units. In order to transmit high-frame-rate (HFR) images via a current digital video interface, we introduced a spatiotemporal coding, as shown in Fig. 5.18. Four sub-fields pixel values are spatially arranged into quad pixels in a frame. The coded image signal is transmitted into the

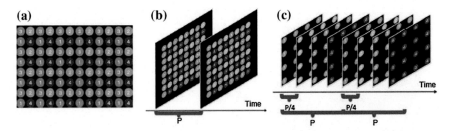

Fig. 5.18 a Composition of a coded image. **b** Spatiotemporally coded image signal is input into a video processor at an interval P (=8.3 ms for 120 Hz). **c** The spatiotemporal codes are decoded by the video processor. Sub-frames are re-freshed at the quadrupled rate (480 fps) of the input DVI signal

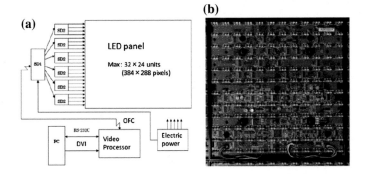

Fig. 5.19 a Composition of 480-fps LED display system. SD denotes signal distributor. OFC is an optical fiber cable. **b** A photograph of an LED unit

LED video processor at the refresh rate of the graphic card. When using 120 Hz DVI signal, the interval is 8.3 ms. The LED video processor decodes the spatial codes into temporal displayed images. The decoded image data are fed to each LED unit at the quadrupled frame rate of the input DVI signal. Thus, we have developed the HRF LED panel displays full-color (24-bits) images at 480 fps. Its maximum luminance is 5000 cd/m^2 [12] (Fig. 5.19).

The developed HFR LED panel was utilized for a kind of steganography, of which objective is to provide decoding fun of a hidden secret with a waving hand [13, 14], as shown in Fig. 5.20. The proposed method of displaying information is a kind of steganography technique with a novel way of decoding the hidden message. Such steganography can be enabled by LED's high speed of response time and high brightness that is enough to make afterimage.

In this experiment, a pair of coded images were alternatively shown on the LED panel. A text was embedded in black and white on a gray background image. A secret text was embedded into HFR images and represented at 240 fps. When the video image of the LED display was taken with camera at 60 fps, as shown in Fig. 5.21a, no text was perceived. A high-speed video (1200 fps) reveals flip-flop of the encoded

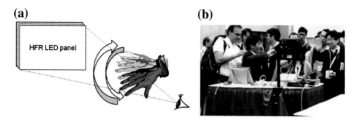

Fig. 5.20 **a** Schematic illustration of hand-waving steganography. By viewing the high-frame-rate LED panel, the viewer perceives the embedded information. **b** A photograph at an exhibition of hand-waving steganography

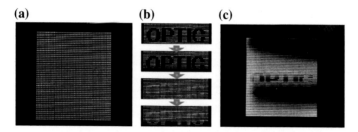

Fig. 5.21 **a** Schematic illustration of hand-waving steganography. By viewing the high-frame-rate LED panel, the viewer perceives the embedded information. **b** A photograph at an exhibition of hand-waving steganography

images, as shown in Fig. 5.21b. An example of viewed image through a waving hand is shown in Fig. 5.21c. Moving fingers blocked a portion of the flip-flop images and the hidden text was decoded. The position of the decoded portion was changed instantaneously because waving the hand was not synchronized to alternating the encoded images on the LED panel. However, after waving the hand in a certain time, the secret text was perceived. Viewers enjoy decoding with waving their hands continuously until they read the text.

5.5.2 Smart LED Tile

For the applications for visualization of sensory outputs, such as visualization of sound, acceleration, and rotation, it is necessary to reduce the total latency. We have originally designed and developed a new LED display module that integrate the sensors and display devices, named smart LED tile (SLT) [15].

Architecture of SLT is shown in Fig. 5.22. SLT integrates a microcontroller, sensors, a wireless module, and battery within the size of an LED panel, as shown in Fig. 5.23. We have designed all the circuit boards of which size is smaller than the LED panel (5 cm × 5 cm). It is possible to put the smart LED tiles face to face. The wireless network communication is based on ZigBee standard. SLT shows sensed

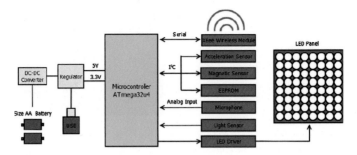

Fig. 5.22 Smart LED architecture that integrates LED panel, LED driver, sensors, a processor, a wireless communication module, and battery

(a)   **(b)**

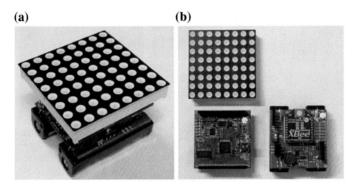

Fig. 5.23 **a** Smart LED tile and **b** its electronic boards and LED panel

information instantly and automously without any assistance with a host PC. SLT builds a wireless sensor network to share sensed information even when the smart tiles are moved. This feature is a solution for addressing and communication problems for a large LED screen with real-time sensor inputs.

Visualization of the acceleration vector of a smart LED tile has been conducted. Acceleration vector is mapped onto the RGB color space. The color is changed depending on the direction and the value of the acceleration. Experimental results are shown in Fig. 5.24. It is confirmed that changes of the acceleration are shown instantly on the LED panel when a smart LED tile is waved in front of a camera.

5.5.3 Aerial Imaging by Retro-Reflection (AIRR)

Aerial and transparent display is a prospective technique for digital signage to provide sensation to viewers. We propose aerial imaging by retro-reflection (AIRR) [16, 17]. Its principle is shown in Fig. 5.25a. Light rays that are reflected on the beam splitter impinge the retro-reflective material. After the retro-reflection, the lights travel reversely toward the light source. About a half of the retro-reflected

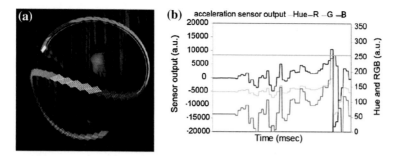

Fig. 5.24 **a** Visualization of acceleration by use of a smart LED tile. **b** Acceleration sensor outputs and converted color shown on the smart LED tile

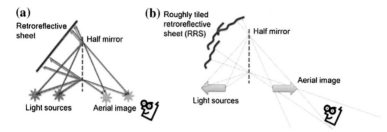

Fig. 5.25 **a** Principle of aerial imaging by retro-reflection (AIRR). **b** Aerial image is independent from the curvature of the retro-reflectors

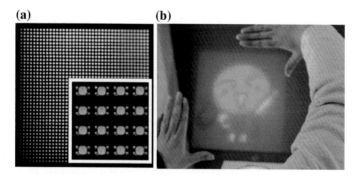

Fig. 5.26 **a** A photograph of 960-fps LED panel. The *inset* is a close-up of the LED panel. **b** Aerial image of the LED panel formed between hands

lights are transmitted through the beam splitter and form aerial image of the light sources. The basic setups were used for inverting pseudoscopic images in holographic display [18]. As shown in Fig. 5.25b, the image position does not depend on the position and curvature of the retro-reflective fabric.

Experimental results are shown in Fig. 5.26. HFR (960 fps) LED panel [19] was used for the light sources. Aerial image is floating between the hands. Note that the black regions between LED lamps (about 3 mm), shown in the inset of Fig. 5.26a, are filled in the aerial image.

5.6 Human Perceptual and Motor Functions for Coordinated Interaction with High-Speed Information Environment

It is essential to understand the nature of human sensori-motor system in order to achieve the coordinated interaction between individual humans and information environment. In this research project, we have dealt with three research topics related to this issue: (1) Effective error feedback timing for visuo-motor adaptation, (2) Prediction of human action based on spatio-temporal structure of human body movement (i.e., motor synergy), and (3) Nature of human visual perception for high-speed stimulus presentation. Below, we describe the first and third topics in detail.

5.6.1 Effective Error Feedback Timing for Visuo-Motor Adaptation

One of the human astonishing abilities is sensori-motor learning/adaptation: Humans can flexibly update internal memory so as to achieve a given task in a changing environment. In shooting a ball to a visual target, for example, people can readily modify the throwing action according to the ball weight. When the visual environment is distorted by a wedge prism or virtual reality devices, moreover, the shooting error gradually decreases and people correctly shoot the target after a few dozen trials. Such flexible ability plays a significant role when humans act in new information environments.

How does our brain acquire the information required for regaining task performance? For prism adaptation in a shooting or reaching task, visual information of the endpoint is essential because the adaptation hardly proceeds if the endpoint cannot be seen. The endpoint error calculated from visual information drives the adaptation. Here, in addition to spatial (or position) information, the timing of information feedback is also significant. Specifically, Kitazawa et al. [20] demonstrated that prism adaptation was slowed when the visual feedback was delayed: If visual presentation of the endpoint was delayed for more than 50 ms, the magnitude of adaptation diminished significantly. This effect has been replicated by recent studies [21, 22]. These findings suggest that human brain may accept error signals most effectively when they are synchronized with the end of reaching movements. In other words, temporal association between the motor action and its sensory consequence is an essential factor in visuo-motor learning [22].

In a shooting task, a ball reaches a target some time after it leaves the shooter's hand, meaning that the timing of the task-end (i.e., ball impact) is dissociated from that of motor execution (i.e., body movement). Here, an interesting question arises whether error feedback should be linked to *task-end* or *movement-end* (Fig. 5.27a, b). Considering that the motor adaptation is the mechanism for maintaining task per-

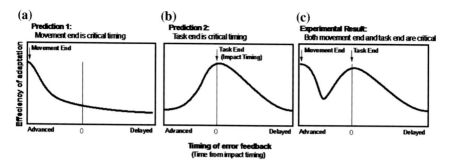

Fig. 5.27 Effect of error feedback timing on visuo-motor adaptation

formance, the timing of task-end, rather than movement-end, may be critical for accepting feedback information.

To answer the above question, we conducted a behavioral experiment using a virtual shooting task: Subjects were asked to control their wrist movements to shoot a target on a screen by moving a cursor as accurately as possible. A visual shift was implemented by displacing the ball trajectory on the screen. The time from the throwing action to impact was fixed to 600 ms, independent of the wrist movement speed. The timing of visual feedback of the impact location was manipulated as an experimental condition. The amount of visual feedback delay/advance was chosen from nine values: −500, −300, −200, −100, 0, 100, 200, 300, and 500 ms, where negative values mean that the task feedback was brought in advance of the ball impact and positive values mean the delayed feedback. We also prepared a condition that the impact timing was indicated by an additional timing cue so as to examine the effect of certainty of the impact timing. The magnitude of adaptation was measured by the amount of aftereffect estimated from the adaptation curve.

First of all, the visual shift introduced in our virtual shooting environment resulted in a learning curve similar to those reported for prism adaptation experiments. This confirmed that our experimental environment was meaningful.

The result shows that the amount of aftereffect varied depending on the timing of feedback. The aftereffect was large under the −500 ms condition (that is, when feedback was given just after movement-end) and decreased under the −300 ms condition. It then increased again and peaked broadly across the 0–500 ms feedback delay range (i.e., around task-end). When the feedback was delayed 1000 ms, the aftereffect decreased again. The effect of feedback delay was statistically significant. A similar pattern of results was obtained when the impact timing was indicated by an additional timing cue.

These results demonstrate that the efficiency of visuo-motor adaptation varied depending on the timing of error feedback, and increased around movement-end and task-end. This tendency was consistently observed irrespective of the time between movement-end and task-end, and regardless of whether a timing cue signaled task-end. Therefore, the present result indicates that the timing of error feedback significantly affected the efficiency of visuo-motor adaptation, and that efficiency was enhanced both around movement-end and task-end (Fig. 5.27c).

Finally, we would like to discuss the mechanism underlying the acceptance of error information in visuo-motor adaptation. At least three ways are possible in which the brain determines the timing of error acceptance: (1) locked to the time of motor command generation; (2) specified by the sensory information accompanying movement-end or task-end; or (3) predicted within the brain. As we discussed in our journal paper in detail [23], however, we consider that no single mechanism determines the timing of error acceptance. Therefore, we speculate that multiple error acceptance mechanisms must be involved in visuo-motor adaptation.

5.6.2 Human Perception for High-Speed Visual Presentation

We investigated the nature of human visual perception for flicker stimuli using a high-speed video projector. The point is that we used flicker stimulus with a wide range of frequencies which could not be presented with conventional video displays (including CRT and LC displays). In another study, we examined the perception of a high-speed moving object. A high-speed projector improves the temporal resolution of stimulus presentation, which brings temporally dense visual information: Moving stimuli can be presented more continuously and smoothly compared with the conventional display devices.

It is broadly accepted that people could not detect the temporal change in luminance of a flickering stimulus if its frequency is higher than 50–60 Hz. This threshold frequency is called "critical fusion frequency (CFF)". CFF has a quite important role in visual device. For example, the refresh rate of visual displays has been determined to be higher than CFF. People cannot distinguish two above-CFF flickering stimuli with equal subjective luminance if they are presented simultaneously at different locations. Recently, however, it has been reported that when the stimuli are presented sequentially at the same position, a transient "twinkle" can be perceived around the moment of their changeover [24]. We name this phenomenon "transient twinkle perception (TTP)," and examined its nature by a psychophysical experiment (Fig. 5.28a, b).

Significance of this phenomenon is that it suggests that human visual system can deal with the above-CFF visual stimuli. Recent progress in device technology has brought us new display devices with high refresh rates. Investigation of nature of our visual system for high-speed visual presentation is important for examining the merits and demerits of such novel devices.

On the other hand, this phenomenon is suggestive for understanding the computational process of our visual system. What mechanism causes TTP? A simple hypothesis is that perceptual luminance is determined by the temporal moving average of the physical luminance of the stimuli. In the present study, we examined whether this hypothesis can explain the TTP phenomenon using a computational model (boxes in Fig. 5.28a, b).

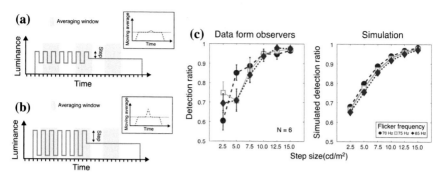

Fig. 5.28 Transient twinkle perception (TTP) [25]

In the psychophysical experiments, we adopted a high-speed video pro-jector (DLP) for presenting high-speed visual stimuli. In the experiment, ring-shaped stimuli having a sinusoidal luminance profile were presented on a uniform background ($50\,cd/m^2$). Subjects were asked to discriminate TTP condition (sequential presentation of stationary and flickering stimuli) from no TTP condition (stationary stimulus only) by temporal 2-AFC. Flicker frequency was set to 70, 75, or 85 Hz in one experiment (using CRT), and to 100, 150, 200, 250, or 300 Hz in the other experiment (using DLP).

Subjects could discriminate TTP from no TTP conditions while the flicker frequency was no more than 200 Hz. In addition, correct rates were decreased as the amplitude of the flicker stimulus was smaller. This means that our visual system can detect the transient luminance change above CFF, but such detection requires a sufficient luminance difference between flickering and stationary stimuli [25].

We built a computational model for explaining these experimental findings. Our model consists of two processing stages, moving average and nonlinear transformation. In order to normalize the output of moving average, we calculated the relative deviation of the moving average from the long-term mean (DMR). Next, we transformed the DMR into the probabilistic value by applying a non-linear function. The resultant probability corresponded to the ratio that the subjects perceived the transient twinkle. Parameter values of the model were optimized to fit the result of the psychophysical experiments.

The behavior of the computational model is quite similar to that of human subjects (Fig. 5.28c). In addition, this model successfully replicated the result of another psychophysical experiment where the temporal deviation of moving average was induced by temporal perturbation to the stimuli. These results suggest that TTP may be basically brought by the short-term luminance averaging mechanism in the visual system, and that the larger luminance difference results in the larger temporal deviation from the long-term luminance mean which causes TTP. In other words, the perception of transient twinkles is determined by whether or not the amount of temporally averaged luminance around the transition exceeds a certain threshold.

As for the perception of a moving object, we have examined several topics; below, we briefly report the result on the misperception of position of a moving object.

It has been known that position of a moving object is often misperceived. Especially, the distance between the endpoints (or the length of motion path) of a reciprocally moving object tends to be perceived shorter than the veridical distance. However, it has been reported that this "perceptual shrinkage" hardly occurs if the object moves in one-way and /or at high speed [26]. In the present study, we tested this using a high-speed video projector which can present moving stimuli with a refresh rate of 500 Hz, much higher than the previous experiments. We measured the perceptual bias at the onset and offset positions of an one-way (12.8°) moving object at a speed faster than 30 deg/s. Different from the previous reports [26], perceptual shrinkage was observed also in the high-speed one-way motion: The onset position was perceived shifted toward the direction of motion while the offset position was perceived shifted backward. The amount of the shift was larger at the onset position than those at the offset position.

Therefore, the present study demonstrates that the high-speed and one-way motion could distort the perceptual position of a moving object, using high-speed visual presentation. This result supports the model that the perceptual position is represented by the spatiotemporal positional averaging and trajectory detection mechanism, even in the high-speed condition, again implying that the simple averaging mechanism may be the fundamental signal processing of our visual system [27].

In summary, we examined the characteristics of visual system for high-speed visual information in the present study. We have obtained several other findings related to visual motion perception, including position perception and trajectory prediction of a moving object. These results were obtained by means of utilizing a high-speed video projector whose refresh rate was much higher than the conventional video devices. In this sense, the high-speed visual technology can be a novel tool for investigating the mechanism of human visual system. Together, it implies that novel visual devices have possibilities to extract human potential abilities and to realize more sophisticated coordination between humans and information environments.

5.7 Development of the Systems for Dynamic Information Space

5.7.1 High-Speed and Non-contact Interfaces for Human Support

With the progress of hardware and image processing technologies, camera-based user interfaces are becoming familiar. For example, a gesture interface in which users can remotely control devices is realized by recognizing human hand motions from images captured by a camera. Augmented reality (AR) technology is also attracting attention, which fuses real space and virtual space by overlaying computer graphics (CG) on images captured by a camera.

However, user interface systems using a camera/cameras have a problem of input-output delay (latency). Even in conventional input interfaces such as a mouse, delay of image drawing and displaying sometimes affects their operability. When a camera is used, the delay due to the camera's low frame rate, transfer delay, and image processing delay are added, which often results in a system with low responsivity.

On the other hand, we are developing new user interface systems which realizes high responsivity by using a high frame rate camera instead of a standard camera. In this section, an example of such systems is shown.

5.7.1.1 AR Typing Interface for Mobile Devices

Mobile devices equipped with a touch panel, such as smartphones, have become widely used. One of the advantages of a smartphone is that it allows the user to do works anywhere that previously required a PC. However, the screen of a smartphone is small and there are users feeling that the device lack usability because of the small operating area on the surface. This problem is particularly annoying in character entry.

To solve this problem, we have proposed an interface that allows a user to type on a virtual keyboard with his/her multiple fingers in the space behind a mobile device. This interface overlays a virtual keyboard and the user's hand on real images captured by a camera, and recognizes user's hand motions using optical flow information. We named this interface *AR typing interface* as it uses AR technology, which overlays CG on real images from a camera.

We constructed a PC-based experimantal system instead of using a real mobile device to evaluate the usability of the proposed interface. The system consists of a 4.3-in. display, a small high-frame-rate camera, and a PC. The image size and the frame rate of the camera is 320 × 240 pixels and 112 fps, respectively. Figure 5.29 shows an appcarance of the system.

Fig. 5.29 The appearance of the experimental system [28]. A small high-frame-rate camera (112 fps @ 320 × 240 pixels) is attached to the back of a small (4.3 in.) display. A virtual keyboard is overlaid on real images captured by the camera. A user can operate the keyboard with his/her hand in the space behind the device

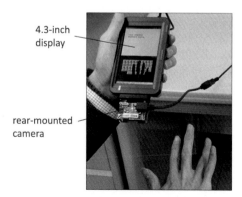

4.3-inch display

rear-mounted camera

captured image   hand region   shrunk convex hull   optical flow

Fig. 5.30 The process to calculate optical flow [28]. A hand region is extracted by using skin color information. Optical flow is calculated in the hand region outside the shrunk convex hull of the hand region and above the centroid of the hand region

The system uses optical flow information to recognize typing action. To reduce computational cost, optical flow is calculated only in the regions around fingertips. The process is shown in Fig. 5.30. First, a hand region is extracted from a camera image by using skin color information. Then, the convex hull of the hand region is extracted and shrunk. Optical flow is calculated in the hand region outside the shrunk convex hull and above the centroid of the hand region.

After calculating optical flow, moving regions are detected by thresholding the flow magnitudes. The regions are separated by labelling and the average of the flow magnitudes in each region is calculated. The region with the maximum average magnitude is regarded as a key pressing region and its centroid is used as the pressed position.

When the whole hand is moving, almost all fingertip regions are regarded as moving regions. In such a case, the system does not perform key pressing action recognition.

Using this simple algorithm, fast typing recognition with a processing time of 8.33 ms (about 120 fps) is realized.

By using the recognition method above, we developed a keyboard typing application named *AR-keyboard*. A virtual keyboard is overlaid on captured images, and the user's hand image is also overlaid on the keyboard. By doing so, it is possible for users to perform key typing with the sense that there were a real keyboard under the user's hand. When a key pressing action is detected, the key on the keyboard at the pressed position is typed. A user can operate AR-keyboard not only in the air but at any space behind the display such as on the desk and on his/her knees.

Figure 5.31 shows the screenshot of AR-keyboard and sequential images of key typing. Multiple fingers are used for typing and multi-finger typing is realized. Also, high responsivity is realized by performing fast image processing with a high frame rate of 120 fps, which enables users to perform comfortable key typing with small delay.

Fig. 5.31 Screenshot of AR-keyboard and multi-finger typing images [28]. Multiple fingers are used for typing

5.7.2 High-Speed Gaze Controller for High-Speed Computer-Human Interaction

5.7.2.1 Introduction

Gesture recognition based on computer vision is one promising approach for Computer-Human Interaction (CHI), since computer vision can recognize the operator's gesture without any contact nor bindings. In particular, if high-speed vision system, that can acquire images typically at 1000 fps, is adopted as the computer vision, very quick and smooth interaction is able to be achieved.

Most computer vision is usually used with a fixed field of view (FOV). Thus the area of interaction is limited within the FOV of the vision system. And there also exists a trade-off between the interaction area and the image resolution of the target, such as a human hand or body. If the interaction area is set to be much larger than the target size, the ratio of the target size to the FOV becomes smaller. Thus the vision system has to recognize the target from the coarser image. This trade-off can be solved by a pan/tilt camera that can control their gaze by two-axis rotational mechanical platform, commonly used for the monitoring and security purposes. However, if the high-speed vision is mounted on the conventional pan/tilt platform, the slow steering speed becomes system bottleneck and limits the advantage of the high-speed vision.

A new type high-speed gaze controller was developed originally to solve this problem. The goal was set to achieve a high-speed pan/tilt camera with the ability to change its gaze direction extremely quickly comparable to the frame rate of the high-speed vision. Conventional mechanical approach is difficult to achieve this goal due to the large inertia of the vision system usually composed of a camera lens and a housing of an imager. Thus, a special optical component that can steer the direction of the vision system was developed, so that the mounted camera was able to change its gaze direction without any physical movement. The developed component was also able to steer the projection direction of a conventional projector. And this function

Fig. 5.32 Illustration of a
general pan/tilt camera (**a**),
and the high-speed gaze
controller (**b**)

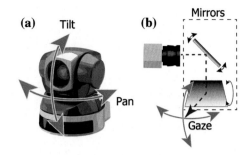

can realize a new projection mapping method on a dynamic object, including human
body and hand.

5.7.2.2 Saccade Mirror and 1 ms Auto Pan/Tilt (APT) Technology

To realize a high-speed gaze controller, it's important to eliminate moving mechanical
parts with large inertia. We focused on two-axis rotational mirrors for gaze control
as shown in Fig. 5.32b, because:

- The inertia of a mirror can be considerably reduced by adopting small size mirrors.
- Flat mirror is known as one of an ideal optical components because they have no
  chromatic aberration and can easily achieve high optical performance with precise
  flat shape.

However, direct coupling of two-axis rotational mirrors and a camera requires a
significant area of the mirror and reduces quick response ability.

To solve this problem, a pupil shift lens was inserted between the camera and
rotational mirrors. The pupil is a position that limits the incident rays to the camera,
which corresponds to the pinhole of the pinhole camera model. The pupil shift lens
can shift the pupil to another place in open space in front of the camera lens. Since
the ray bundle at pupil has the minimum cross-sectional area, even a small mirror
can reflect all the necessary incident ray. For the details, refer the reference [29].
This type new high-speed gaze controller was named "Saccade Mirror" [29].

The saccade mirror can be applied to a noble video shooting system for moving
objects by coupled with the high-speed vision system. It can capture the certain
moving target as if it stopped and was fixed at the center of the field of view, and
this technology was named "1 ms Auto Pan-Tilt (APT)" [30]. Figure 5.33 shows
the photograph of a prototype and system connection of the 1 ms APT (a), and
the captured image sequence with full high-definition size of a basket ball passed
between two persons. The thrown ball is almost always tracked at the center of the
FOV. Due to the high-speed response of the whole system, the 1 ms APT system had

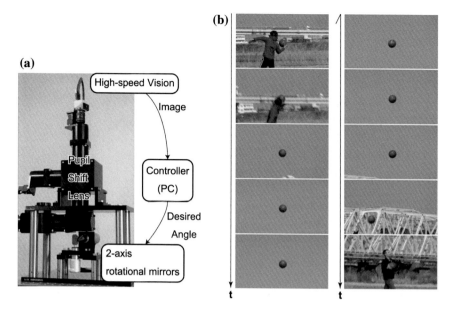

Fig. 5.33 Photograph of the prototype and schematic figure of the system connection (**a**), and captured image sequence while tracking a thrown basket ball (**b**)

also demonstrated the stable tracking of a high-speed table tennis ball in rally, and a quickly rolling yoyo [31, 32].

5.7.2.3   Lumipen: Active Projection Mapping on Dynamic Objects

The saccade mirror was explained as a gaze controller in above. However, if a projector is mounted on the saccade mirror instead of a camera, the saccade mirror can also control the projecting direction. Due to the principle of reversibility of light rays, the structure of the projector is very similar to the structure of the camera. Only the direction of the light ray is inverse. And this is the reason that the saccade mirror can work with projectors.

If the projection direction is always kept at the center of a moving object based on the 1 ms APT technology, the projected image would appear on the object as if it is printed on its surface. Because the conventional projectors have considerable timing delay ($\sim$100 ms) from the input of an image signal and the projection of the image, this delay makes it very difficult for the conventional projectors to fit the projection image position onto the object position precisely, and there exists the position shift between the object and projected image when the target is moving. The saccade mirror has much shorter delay of $\sim$3.5 ms and make it possible to project the given image precisely on the surface of the moving object.

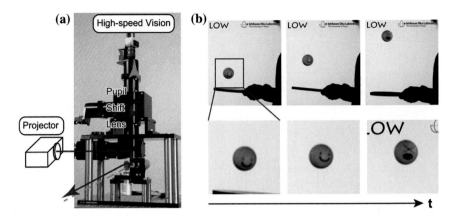

Fig. 5.34 Schematic figure of the system connection (**a**), and the projected image sequence on a lifting table tennis ball (**b**). A facial expression image was stably superimposed on the surface of quickly moving ball

This active projection technology was named "Lumipen" [33, 34]. Figure 5.34a shows a configuration of the Lumipen system. The projector is mounted on the saccade mirror sharing the optical axis with the high-speed vision so that the both instruments share the field of view/projection. Stable tracking control enables the projector always project an image on the surface of the target object. Figure 5.34b shows the projected image sequence on the lifting table tennis ball. The facial expression was always projected on the bouncing ball.

5.7.3 Integrated Systems

5.7.3.1 Concept and Related Systems

We have designed various types of the information space integrating high-speed sensing technology, high-speed display technology and human model.

As one of the promising conceptual architecture, "Invoked Computing" is proposed [35]. Direct interaction with everyday objects augmented with artificial affordances is clearly a very efficient approach leveraging natural human interaction capabilities. Hence the idea of conceiving ubiquitous computing as an invisible world can be "condensed" on real objects. Ubiquitous computing field actually is described as an "enchanted village" in which people discover hidden affordances in everyday objects. In "Invoked Computing", we explore the reverse scenario: a ubiquitous intelligence capable of discovering affordances suggested or represented symbolically by human beings (as actions and scenarios involving objects and drawings). We propose the following example: taking a banana and bringing it closer to the ear. The

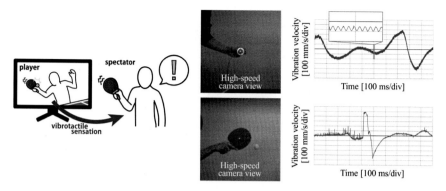

Fig. 5.35 VibroTracker: a vibrotactile sensor tracking objects [36]

gesture is clear enough: directional microphones and parametric speakers hidden in the room would make the banana function as a real handset on the spot.

Also, in order to enhance the experience in the information space, we newly have developed "VibroTracker" by integrating the "Saccade Mirror" and vibration meter [36]. For example, it is exciting merely to watch sports events, but simulating the haptic sensations experienced by a player would make spectating even more enjoyable. This is not peculiar to sports events. In addition to video and audio, the ability to relive the sensations experienced by others would also offer great entertainment value at temporal and spatial distances. The existing systems have some problems in measuring vibrations. A contact-type vibrometer deforms the original vibrations and is a burden to wear or carry. Even with a non-contact sensor like a microphone, it is difficult to measure slight vibrations of a fast-moving target against the surrounding noise. Our VibroTracker system solved these issues by using a laser Doppler vibrometer (LDV) and a high-speed optical gaze controller (Saccade Mirror), enabling users to relive the vibrotactile sensations experienced by others. Figure 5.35 shows the concept and the results of the developed system.

Moreover, we have developed a new type of wearable user interface involving high-speed vision technologies. The current trend towards smaller and smaller mobile devices may cause considerable difficulties in using them. Based on this background, we propose an interface called "Anywhere Surface Touch", which allows any flat or curved surface in a real environment to be used as an input area [37]. Figure 5.36 shows the developed system. The interface uses only a single small camera and a contact microphone to recognize several kinds of interaction between the fingers of the user and the surface. The system recognizes which fingers are interacting and in which direction the fingers are moving. Additionally, the fusion of vision and sound allows the system to distinguish the contact conditions between the fingers and the surface. Evaluation experiments showed that users became accustomed to our system quickly, soon being able to perform input operations on various surfaces.

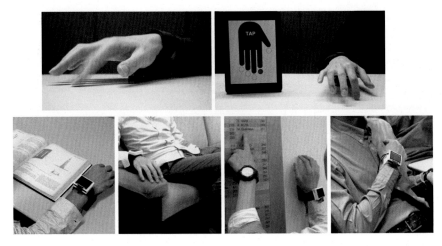

Fig. 5.36 Anywhere surface touch: utilizing any surface as an input area with a wearable device [37]

We also have developed two more systems which integrates the subsystems described in the previous sections.

5.7.3.2   Visual and Tactile Cues for High-Speed Interaction

This is a new system which integrates two subsystems. Figure 5.37 shows the developed system. One subsystem can extract a 3-dimensional position of a moving object every 2ms, and project pictures (e.g. a screen of a video game or a computer, a movie etc.) on the moving object at the same time, using two "1ms Auto Pan-Tilt" systems described in Sect. 5.7.2 which can track an object in 3-dimensional space without delay by high-speed vision and two rotational mirrors. Another subsystem can display tactile sensation on an object depending on its 3-dimensional position, especially a particular position on a palm of a hand, using "Airborne Ultrasound Tactile Display (AUTD)" described in Sect. 5.4. This time, we realized a demonstration that papers around us and our hands are transformed into a screen of a computer or a smartphone, and we can feel even tactile sensation. In a sense, this system can be regarded as a moving object version and a tactile sensation version of projection mapping technology.

This system recognizes our hands and objects existing in the environment at a high-speed beyond human's ability of recognition by high-speed image processing technology, and it is possible to use the system to display and input information without uncomfortable feelings such as a delay. Thus, this system shows that we can use an object as a tool for human interfaces even if the object is moving. While we aim to embed intelligent function into objects such as conventional computers and

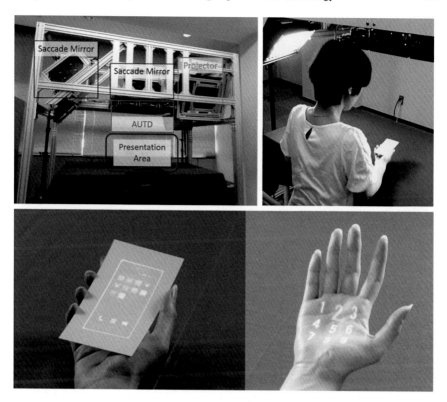

Fig. 5.37 Visual and tactile cues for high-speed interaction

smartphones, this system embeds information into existing environments and objects; it points the way toward future dramatic changes in our information environment.

5.7.3.3 AIRR Tablet: Floating Display with High-Speed Gesture UI

This system integrates high-speed and high-brightness floating display and high-speed 3D gesture recognition. For the aerial image, we use a display technology called AIRR technology described in Sect. 5.5.3 and the 3D high-speed hand tracking and gesture recognition [38] made it possible to manipulate the aerial image in high speed.

We believe that this will be the next generation of user-friendly 3D display technology. Previous methods to generate aerial image are based on lenses and mirror arrays. By using AIRR, much wider viewing angle is achieved. Furthermore, by using our newly developed LED display, bright image can be formed even under strong room lighting. In addition, the image can be viewed by multiple persons simultaneously (Fig. 5.38).

Fig. 5.38 AIRR Tablet: floating display with high-speed gesture UI

The high-speed 3D gesture recognition utilize super high-speed stereo cameras, which makes it possible to recognize gesture and track 3D position (500 fps) with extremely small latency. Not only the user can expand and rotate the floating screen, even if we perform extremely fast action such as punching it can still be detected. It can be said that high speed operation on floating image will become the next generation of information environment.

The system we integrated is called "AIRR Tablet" which recognizes hands or any other objects in high speed beyond human perception. We achieve input and output without any delay, and we show that we can turn the empty space into a large tablet. Unlike conventional computers and smartphones, we can perform operations without any physical collision. It enables high-speed 3D input and output.

References

1. I. Ishii, T. Tatebe, Q. Gu, Y. Moriue, T. Takaki, K. Tajima, 2000 fps real-time vision system with high-frame-rate video recording. *Proceedings IEEE International Conference on Robotics and Automation*, pp. 1536–1541 (2010)
2. Y. Liu, H. Gao, Q. Gu, T. Aoyama, T. Takaki, I. Ishii, High-frame-rate structured light 3-D vision for fast moving objects. J. Robot. Mechat. **26**(3), 311–320 (2014)
3. S. Inokuchi, K. Sato, F. Matsuda, Range imaging system for 3-D object recognition. *Proceedings Conference on Pattern Recognition*, pp. 806–808 (1984)
4. J. Chen, T. Yamamoto, T. Aoyama, T. Takaki, I. Ishii, Simultaneous projection mapping using high-frame-rate depth vision. *Proceedings of IEEE International Conference on Robotics and Automation*, pp. 4506–4511 (2014)

5. M. Shimojo, T. Araki, S.Teshigawara, A. Ming, M. Ishikawa, A net-structure tactile sensor covering free-form surface and ensuring high-speed response. *Proceedings of IEEE International Conference on Intelligent Robots and Systems*, pp. 670–675 (2007)

6. H. Arita, Y. Suzuki, H. Ogawa, K. Tobita, M. Shimojo, Hemispherical net-structure proximity sensor detecting azimuth and elevation for guide dog robot. *2013 IEEE/RSJ International Conference on Intelligent Robots and Systems*, pp. 653–658 (2013)

7. K. Hasegawa, H. Shinoda, Aerial display of vibrotactile sensation with high spatial-temporal resolution using Large-Aperture airborne ultrasound phased array. *Proceedings of IEEE World Haptics Conference 2013*, pp. 31–36 (Daejeon, Korea, 2013)

8. T. Iwamoto, M. Tatezono, H. Shinoda, Non-contact method for producing tactile sensation using airborne ultrasounders. *Haptics: Perception, Devices and Scenarios: 6th International Conference, Eurohaptics 2008 Proceedings* (*Lecture Notes in Computer Science*), pp. 504–513 (2008)

9. T. Hoshi, T. Masafumi, T. Iwamoto, H. Shinoda, Noncontact tactile display based on radiation pressure of airborne ultrasound. IEEE Trans. Haptics **3**(3), 155–165 (2010)

10. J. Awatani, Studies on acoustic radiation pressure. I (General considerations). J. Acoust. Soc. Am. **27**, 278–281 (1955)

11. P.J.J. Lamoreet, H. Muijser, C.J. Keemink, Envelope detection of amplitude-modulated high-frequency sinusoidal signals by skin mechanoreceptors. J. Acoust. Soc. Am. **79**, 1082–1085 (1986)

12. H. Yamamoto, M. Tsutsumi, K. Matsushita, R. Yamamoto, K. Kajimoto, S. Suyama, Development of high-frame-rate LED panel and its applications for stereoscopic 3D display. Proc. SPIE **7956**, 79560R (2011)

13. S. Farhan, S. Suyama, H. Yamamoto, Hand-waving decodable display by use of a high frame rate LED panel. *Proceedings of IDW '11*, vol. 3, pp. 1983–1986 (2011)

14. H. Yamamoto, K. Sato, S. Farhan, S. Suyama, Hand-waving steganography by use of a high-frame-rate LED Panel. *SID 2014 DIGEST*, pp. 915–917 (2014)

15. K. Sato, A. Tsuji, S. Suyama, H. Yamamoto, LED module integrated with microcontroller, sensors, and wireless communication. *Proceedings of the International Display Workshops* **20**, 1504–1507 (2013)

16. H. Yamamoto, S. Suyama, Aerial 3D LED display by use of retroreflective sheeting. Proc. SPIE **8648**, 86480Q (2013)

17. H. Yamamoto, Y. Tomiyama, S. Suyama, Floating aerial LED signage based on aerial imaging by retro-reflection (AIRR). Optics Express **22**(22), 26919–26924 (2014)

18. C.B. Burckhardt, R.J. Collier, E.T. Doherty, Formation and inversion of pseudoscopid images. Appl. Opt. **7**, 627–631 (1968)

19. T. Tokimoto, K. Sato, S. Suyama, H. Yamamoto, High-frame-rate LED display with pulse-width modulation by use of nonlinear clock. *Proceedings of 2013 IEEE 2nd Global Conference on Consumer Electronics*, pp. 83–84 (2013)

20. S. Kitazawa, T. Kohno, T. Uka, Effects of delayed visual information on the rate and amount of prism adaptation in the human. J. Neurosci. **15**, 7644–7652 (1995)

21. H. Tanaka, K. Homma, H. Imamizu, Physical delay but not subjective delay determines learning rate in prism adaptation. Exp. Brain Res. **208**, 257–268 (2011)

22. T. Honda, M. Hirashima, D. Nozaki, Adaptation to visual feedback delay influences visuomotor learning. PLoS ONE **7**, e37900 (2012)

23. T. Ishikawa, Y. Sakaguchi, Both movement-end and task-end are critical for error feedback in visuomotor adaptation: a behavioral experiment. PLoS ONE **8**, e55801 (2014)

24. S. Cheadle, A. Parton, H. Muller, M. Usher, Subliminal gamma flicker draws attention even in the absence of transition-flash cues. J. Neurophys. **105**, 827–833 (2011)

25. Y. Nakajima, Y. Sakaguchi. Abrupt transition between an above-CFF flicker and a stationary stimulus induces twinkle perception: evidence for high-speed visual mechanism for detecting luminance change. J. Vis. **13**, 311 (2013)

26. M. Sinico, G. Parovel, C. Casco, S. Anstis, Perceived shrinkage of motion paths. J. Exp. Psychol. Hum. Percept Perform. **35**, 948–957 (2009)

27. Y. Nakajima, Y. Sakaguchi, Perceptual shrinkage of motion path observed in one-way high-speed motion. *Proceedings 24th Annual Conference JNNS*, pp. 88–89 (2014)
28. M. Higuchi, T. Komuro, Multi-finger AR typing interface for mobile devices using high-speed hand motion recognition. *Extended Abstracts on ACM SIGCHI Conferene on Human Factors in Computing Systems* (*CHI 2015*), pp. 1235–1240 (2015)
29. K. Okumura, H. Oku, M. Ishikawa, High-speed gaze controller for millisecond-order Pan/tilt Camera. Proc. IEEE ICRA **2011**, 6186–6191 (2011)
30. K. Okumura, K. Yokoyama, H. Oku, M. Ishikawa, 1 ms auto Pan-Tilt–video shooting technology for objects in motion based on Saccade Mirror with background subtraction. Adv. Robot. **29**, 457–468 (2015)
31. YouTube, https://youtu.be/9Q_lcFZOgVo
32. YouTube, https://youtu.be/Of2suN6ijao
33. K. Okumura, H. Oku, M. Ishikawa, Acitve projection AR using high-speed optical axis control and appearance estimation algorithm. *Proceedings of IEEE ICME* (2013). doi:10.1109/ICME.2013.6607637
34. T. Sueishi, H. Oku, M. Ishikawa, Robust high-speed tracking against illumination changes for dynamic projection mapping. *Proceedings of IEEE VR2015*, pp. 97–104 (2015)
35. A. Zerroug, A. Cassinelli, M. Ishikawa, Invoked computing: spatial audio and video AR invoked through miming. *Proceedings of Virtual Reality International Conference* (2011)
36. L. Miyashita, Y. Zou, M. Ishikawa, VibroTracker: a vibrotactile sensor tracking objects. *SIGGRAPH 2013*, Emerging Technologies (2013)
37. T. Niikura, Y. Watanabe, M. Ishikawa, Anywhere surface touch: utilizing any surface as an input area. *The 5th Augmented Human International Conference* (2014)
38. M.S. Alvissalim, M. Yasui, C. Watanabe, M. Ishikawa, Immersive virtual 3D environment based on 499 fps hand gesture interface. *International Conference on Advanced Computer Science and Information Systems*, pp. 198–203 (2014)

Chapter 6
Haptic Media: Construction and Utilization of Haptic Virtual Reality and Haptic Telexistence

Susumu Tachi

Abstract This project aims to construct an information environment that is based on our proposed theory of haptic primary colors and is both visible and tangible. This environment will be one where communication in real space, human interfaces, and media processing are integrated. We have succeeded in transmitting fine haptic sensations, such as material texture and temperature, from an avatar robot's fingers to a human user's fingers by using a telexistence anthropomorphic robot dubbed TELESAR V. Other results of this research project include RePro3D, a full-parallax, autostereoscopic 3D (three-dimensional) display; TECHTILE Toolkit, a prototyping tool for the design and improvement of haptic media; and HaptoMIRAGE, a 180°-field-of-view autostereoscopic 3D display that up to three users can enjoy at the same time.

Keywords 3D · Autostereoscopy · Haptics · Haptic primary colors · Haptic editors · Virtual reality · VR · Augmented reality · AR · Retroreflective projection technology · RPT · Virtual shutter glasses · Teleconference · Videoconference · Teleoperation · Telepresence · Telexistence · TECHTILE Toolkit · RePro3D · TELESAR · HaptoMIRAGE

6.1 Introduction

The author and his team are trying to construct an intelligent haptic information environment that integrates communication in real space, human interfaces, and media processing [1, 2]. In other words, we seek to establish methods for collecting, understanding, and transmitting haptic information in real space and for displaying it to humans located at remote sites. Furthermore, we want to use an information space that feels like the natural space in which people move and act not only to make remote communication, remote experiences, and pseudo-experiences possible

S. Tachi (✉)
The University of Tokyo, Tokyo, Japan
e-mail: tachi@tachilab.org

© Springer Japan 2016
T. Nishida (ed.), *Human-Harmonized Information Technology, Volume 1*,
DOI 10.1007/978-4-431-55867-5_6

but also to build human-harmonized "haptic media" in which creative activities such as content design and production can take place in ways similar to the ways they currently do in the real world.

The information we acquire through real life gives us a holistic experience fully incorporating a variety of sensations and bodily motions—seeing, hearing, speaking, touching, smelling, tasting, moving, etc. However, the sensory modalities that can be transmitted in our information space are usually limited to the visual and auditory. Haptic information is rarely used in our daily lives' information space, except in the case of warnings or alerts such as cell-phone vibrations.

Generally, human haptic sensations can be categorized into cutaneous sensation (the sensing of pressure/force, vibration, pain, and temperature) and proprioception (kinesthetic sense—i.e., the sensing of position, movement, and weight/force). Haptic media providing both proprioception and cutaneous sensations would let users feel like they were touching distant people and objects and would let them "touch" artificial objects. Transmission of texture, mass, warmth, moisture, and other sensory information would expand the current passive information space, which comprises only images and sounds, to an active and human-harmonized information space where the user could extend his/her hand and feel the presence of an object that isn't really there.

A number of technologies have been developed to build a haptic information space, but they fail to provide a holistic experience because of two shortcomings:

1. The technologies can communicate only a select spectrum of haptic sensation because they use ad hoc methods based on an insufficient and still-primitive understanding of haptic sensation.
2. They offer only a narrow definition of haptic sensation, one that does not sufficiently incorporate visual/auditory sensation and bodily motion.

To establish foundation technologies for the "recording and analysis," "transmission," and "playback, synthesis, and display" of haptic information and to build technologies to fully transmit haptic sensation and bring haptic sensation to a level where it can be treated as information media, much like visual and auditory sensations, this research will:

1. expand upon the principle of haptic primary colors previously formulated by the author and his team, further elucidating the haptic sense mechanism in humans, and
2. establish a design method for haptic information combined with visual sensation and bodily movement.

Figure 6.1 shows the concept of haptic media comparable to visual media, which transmits and/or creates a realistic visible and tangible three-dimensional (3D) environment based on the haptic primary color theory.

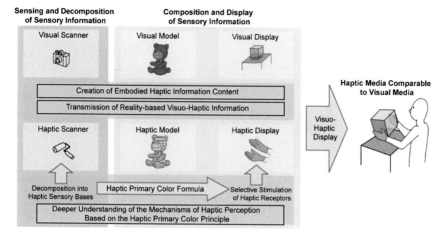

Fig. 6.1 Haptic media comparable to visual media [1]

6.2 Haptic Media Project

This research concerns the development of a "haptic information space," an information system that makes possible the simultaneous delivery of high-resolution haptic, visual, and auditory information. Figure 6.2 shows the outline of the project. The real world is sensed by a haptic scanner, and the scanned information is analyzed and decomposed using the formulation of haptic primary colors before being transmitted to distant places. It is also possible to store the scanned information, which can be retrieved and edited using haptic editors. Transmitted or retrieved information is synthesized using the formulation of haptic primary colors and is displayed to human users through a haptic display.

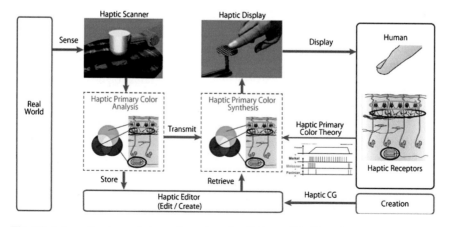

Fig. 6.2 Information transmission and creation of realistic tangible 3D environment [1]

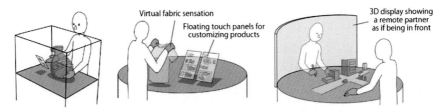

Fig. 6.3 Museum implementation (*left*), tangible product catalog (*middle*), and co-creation (*right*) [1]

Some possible applications of these systems would include implementation of the information content of museums and libraries, as well as training in the fields of medicine and space research. For example, visual and haptic data for a precious object in a museum's collection (that one is normally not allowed to touch) could be archived in a computer, and users could access the object via a studio-type information space that lets them experience touching the object with their own hands (see Fig. 6.3 left). These systems could also be used in daily life. For example, a shop could store visual and haptic information about all its products and produce a tangible catalog of its goods. The customer could customize the product on the spot and try it out prior to deciding on a purchase (Fig. 6.3 middle), or two people at distant locations could cooperate in creative activities (Fig. 6.3 right).

6.2.1 Haptic Device Design Based on Haptic Primary Colors

Our understanding of human perceptual mechanisms for processing visual and auditory information continues to progress through physiological and psychological research, and visual and auditory information measurement and design methods for human presentation based on principles of human sensory perception are already established. It is for this reason that cameras, televisions, audiovisual displays and other general-use devices that acquire, transmit, and display visual and auditory information have been designed and widely used. Similar progress, however, has not been made with regard to haptic information. There are no standard methods and/or devices acquiring, transmitting, and displaying haptic information that are comparable to those used with visual and auditory information. This research has as its goal the establishment of design methods for processing haptic sensory information in ways that are based on a better understanding of sensory mechanisms.

Broadly speaking, human haptic sensation can be divided into cutaneous sensation (pressure sense, vibration sense, thermal sense, and pain sense) and proprioception (kinesthetic sense, position sense, and movement sense). Cutaneous perception is created through a combination of nerve signals from several types of tactile receptors located below the surface of the skin.

If we consider each type of activated haptic receptor as a sensory base, we should in principle be able to express any given pattern of cutaneous sensation through the synthesis of the signals from these bases. For pressure and vibration there are four kinds of tactile receptors—Meissner's corpuscles, Merkel cells, Pacinian corpuscles, and Ruffini endings—each activated by a different stimulus or different combination of stimuli.

Because in color theory three colors are called the primary colors, we have called these haptic information bases the "haptic primary colors" and continued to investigate them. Using this concept of haptic primary colors as a foundation, our technical concern is the recreation of cutaneous sensation through signal delivery to each sensory base separately (i.e., by selectively stimulating tactile receptors). We offer selective stimulation of the Meissner's corpuscles and Merkel cells through electrical stimulation as one method for the reproduction of haptic primary colors. We have developed a cutaneous sense display capable of high spatial and temporal resolution, thereby demonstrating the efficacy of the formulation of haptic primary colors [3].

The development of force vector distribution sensor called "GelForce" has made possible the collection of real-world temporal and spatial haptic information. The haptic telexistence system has been devised by using these technologies in measurement and presentation. The system allows for long-distance transmission of haptic information through the use of a robotic hand with GelForce sensors embedded in its fingertips and a "master hand" with an electro-tactile display embedded in the fingertips. Haptic information about the objects gripped by the robotic hand is transmitted to the operator, who is therefore able to operate the robotic hand smoothly [4].

However, although it is already possible to recreate simple conditions like contact and pressure, it is not yet possible to create more detailed natural haptic sensations like the feel of metal and the texture of paper. Reproducing natural haptic sensations will require physical information collected from the real world to be "resolved" into haptic sensory bases and will require selective stimulation of each type of tactile receptor through composition of the nerve-firing patterns of human tactile receptors. To date, there have been virtually no examples of a conversion system for this decomposition and composition, and no effective methodologies have been established. This is one reason that previous haptic sensory research has been limited to individual tactile sensations.

In this investigation, we expand upon our principle of haptic primary colors. By adding cold receptors (free nerve endings), warmth receptors (free nerve endings), and pain receptors (free nerve endings) to the original four haptic sensory bases and reconsidering sensory activation as a temporal and spatial composition of seven sensory bases, we aim to attain a better understanding of the haptic primary colors formula for converting haptic information through decomposition and composition. In order to expand the current selective stimulation method from Meissner's corpuscles and Merkel cells to other sensory bases, we must first deepen our biological understanding of haptic receptors. And to develop a new method for selective stimulation, we need to better understand the nature of temporal and spatial perception of haptic sensation. We will formulate design principles for haptic sensors and tactile displays that better fulfill the formula of haptic primary colors, and we will develop transmission systems that can transmit natural haptic sensations.

6.2.2   Construction Method for Embodied Haptic Contents

The use of image editing software, three-dimensional CAD, computer graphics libraries like DirectX and OpenGL, and other information composing and editing technologies has resulted in an information environment where anyone can freely create visual information contents.

In this investigation we aim to develop fundamental technologies for the creation of haptic information contents and to integrate visual information contents into haptic information, thereby constructing a haptic information space. When one touches an object with his/her hand or fingers, the haptic information is barely sensed at all unless the hands and fingers are moved. The complete haptic information about the object is collected only when one moves his/her hands and fingers. In addition, the hand and finger haptic sensations for the same portion of the same object can differ depending on many factors, including the angle, speed, and pressure of the touch. The haptic sense differs greatly from the visual and auditory senses in that the haptic perception processes are mediated by bodily movement. Haptic sensations are thoroughly embodied perceptions. This creates a necessity, when expressing haptic information contents, to control the reproduced haptic information and respond in real time to a user's bodily movement throughout the information experience.

Kinesthetic sensation can be quantified and presented in real time by using physical simulation technologies, but it is not yet possible to simulate cutaneous sensation in real time. Using our understanding of human haptic perception, we are working to develop (1) technologies for a haptic scanner that can capture real-world haptic sensations (texture), (2) methods for mapping haptic sensory textures by using 3D computer graphics modeling, and (3) technologies that can be used to compose haptic sense information in response to arbitrary bodily movements based on the collected haptic sensory textures. We are also trying to establish a method for building haptic sensory contents with a sense of embodiment.

In this research we seek to compress motion-based haptic sense information, simplify haptic sense quantifications, and establish technologies for creating embodied haptic information contents (Fig. 6.4).

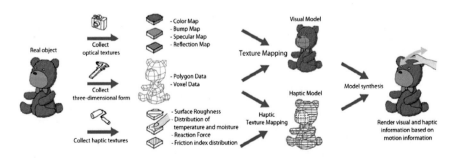

Fig. 6.4 Technologies for creation of embodied haptic information content [1]

6.2.3   Tangible Visuo-Haptic 3D Display

Touching an object as it is viewed is an absolutely essential element in experiencing the "reality" of the target object. It has been proven that if the user of an advanced stereoscopic display system cannot extend his/her hand and touch a stereoscopic image, he/she will lose cognizance of the "reality" of the target object and experience a sense of discomfort. There is thus a strong awareness that with the popularization of stereoscopic images it is necessary to fuse visual and haptic information. Since for the content offered by conventional visual displays the concept of direct "touch" is not considered, with them it is not possible to align the positional relationship between visual information and haptic information. If a head-mounted display (HMD) is used, presenting stereoscopic images within the grasp of the user is achievable; however, it is hard to say that a "human-harmonized 'tangible' information environment," which is the object of this study, is suited to such use since HMDs are isolated from the surrounding environment. Assuming that haptic information is available, the ability to provide 3D haptic information at the user's fingertips and the ability to move one's hands freely without a device at the location where information is provided are requisite conditions. In this study users are able to take and touch three-dimensional images as well as perform operations while perceiving autostereoscopic visual information using binocular parallax and motion parallax. In other words, a 3D visuo-haptic display that can provide "reality" to target objects is being developed (Fig. 6.5).

6.2.4   Construction and Verification of Embodied Tangible 3D System

6.2.4.1   Transmission of Realistic Tangible 3D Environment

The interim milestone for the present study was to construct, within a three-year target period, a haptic information transmission system. The system was supposed to transmit signals from a haptic sensor in real time and provide haptic sensations,

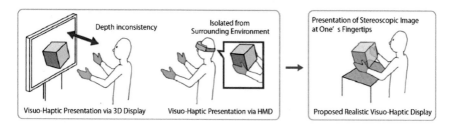

Fig. 6.5 From a conventional 3D visuo-haptic display to a 3D visuo-haptic display that presents reality [1]

Fig. 6.6 Creation of realistic
tangible 3D environment

Fig. 6.6 Creation of realistic
tangible 3D environment

including temperature sensations, to a haptic display in such a way that haptic sensations are integrated with visual sensations. We have succeeded in transmitting fine haptic sensations, such as material texture and temperature, from an avatar robot's fingers to a human user's fingers by using the experimentally constructed TELESAR V system.

6.2.4.2   Creation of Realistic Tangible 3D Environment

The final milestone of this study was to construct a tangible information environment system that presents integrated visual and haptic information. Visual as well as haptic models of real objects should be acquired and added to a database to produce content. RePro3D and HaptoMIRAGE have been invented to demonstrate the final milestone, and they have enabled information content to be "experienced" in situations that unite haptic senses, visual senses, and motion. These demonstrations have revealed that necessary and sufficient haptic information has been acquired, transmitted, and presented.

Future goals will be to verify and assess such complex haptic items as a sense of touching a fish as well as feeling water resistance, moistness, and slipperiness. Figure 6.6 shows such a future demonstration using a haptic aquarium.

6.3   Haptic Primary Colors

Humans do not perceive the world as it is. Different physical stimuli give rise to the same sensation in humans and are perceived as identical. A typical example of this fact is color perception in humans. Humans perceive light of different spectra as having the same color if the light has the same amount of red, green, and blue (RGB) spectral components. This is because the human retina typically contains

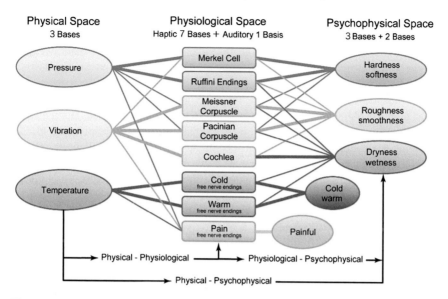

Fig. 6.7 Haptic primary color model [1]

three types of color receptors called cone cells or cones, each of which responds
to a different range of the color spectrum. Humans respond to light stimuli via 3-
dimensional sensations, which generally can be modeled as a mixture of red, blue,
and green—the three primary colors.

This many-to-one correspondence of elements in mapping from physical to psychophysical perceptual space is the key to virtual reality (VR) for humans. VR
produces the same effect as a real object for a human subject by presenting its virtual
entities with this many-to-one correspondence. We have proposed the hypothesis that
cutaneous sensation also has the same many-to-one correspondence from physical
to psychophysical perceptual space, via physiological space. We call this the "haptic
primary colors" [1]. As shown in Fig. 6.7, we define three spaces: physical space,
physiological space, and psychophysical or perception space. As shown in Fig. 6.7,
different physical stimuli give rise to the same sensation in humans and are perceived
as identical.

In physical space, human skin physically contacts an object, and the interaction
continues with time. Physical objects have several surface physical properties such
as surface roughness, surface friction, thermal characteristics, and surface elasticity.
We hypothesize that cutaneous phenomena can at each contact point of the skin be
resolved into three components—pressure/force $p(t)$, vibration $v(t)$, and temperature
$e(t)$—and objects with the same $p(t)$, $v(t)$, and $e(t)$ are perceived as the same even
if their physical properties are different.

We measure $p(t)$, $v(t)$, and $e(t)$ at each contact point with sensors that are presented on an avatar robot's hand. Then we transmit these pieces of information to the
human user who controls the avatar robot as his/her surrogate. We reproduce these

pieces of information at the user's hand via haptic displays of pressure/force, vibration, and temperature so that the human user has the sensation that he/she is touching the object as he/she moves his/her hand controlling the avatar robot's hand. We can also synthesize virtual cutaneous sensation by displaying computer-synthesized $p(t)$, $v(t)$, and $e(t)$ to human users through the haptic display.

This breakdown into pressure/force, vibration, and temperature in physical space is based on the human restriction of sensation in physiological space. Human skin has limited receptors, as is the case in the human retina. In physiological space, cutaneous perception is created through a combination of nerve signals from several types of tactile receptors located below the surface of the skin. If we consider each activated haptic receptor as a sensory base, we should be able to express any given pattern of cutaneous sensation through synthesis by using these bases.

Recall the four kinds of tactile receptors mentioned in Sect. 6.2.1: Merkel cells activated by pressure, Ruffini endings activated by tangential force, Meissner's corpuscles activated by low-frequency vibration, and Pacinian corpuscles activated by high-frequency vibration, respectively. Adding cold receptors (free nerve endings), warmth receptors (free nerve endings), and pain receptors (free nerve endings) to these four vibrotactile haptic sensory bases, we have seven sensory bases in physiological space. It is also possible to add the cochlea, to hear the sound associated with vibration, as one more basis. This is an auditory basis and can be considered cross-modal.

Since all the seven receptors are related only to pressure/force, vibration and temperature applied on the skin surface, these three components in physical space are enough to stimulate each of the seven receptors. This is the reason that in physical space we have three haptic primary colors: pressure/force, vibration, and temperature. Theoretically, by combining these three components we can produce any type of cutaneous sensation without the need for any "real" touching of an object.

6.4 Haptic Information Display

When we use the haptic primary colors as a foundation, a technical concern is the recreation of cutaneous sensation by designing a haptic information display [1]. There are two ways of designing a haptic information display: through the physical layer or through the physiological layer. The latter involves the delivery of the stimulus to each sensory base separately, i.e., the selective stimulation of tactile receptors. We have realized selective stimulation of the Meissner's corpuscles and Merkel cells through electrical stimulation as one method for the reproduction of haptic primary colors. We have developed a cutaneous sense display that is capable of high spatial and temporal resolution and have thereby demonstrated the efficacy of the haptic primary color theory [5, 6].

A force vector distribution sensor called "GelForce" has been developed for the quantification of pressure sense information [7]. It made possible the collection of real-world temporal and spatial haptic information and has been used, along with presentation technologies, in a haptic telexistence system [4]. The system allows for long-distance transmission of haptic information through the use of a robotic hand with GelForce sensors embedded in its fingertips, and a "master hand," worn by the human operator, with electro-tactile displays embedded in its fingertips. Haptic information about the objects gripped by the robotic hand is transmitted to the human operator, who is then able to operate the robotic hand smoothly.

However, although it is already possible to recreate simple conditions such as contact and pressure, it has not been possible to create more detailed natural haptic sensations, such as the feel of metal or the texture of paper, by direct stimulation of the physiological layer. To display texture information naturally, we are using physical-layer information such as force/pressure, vibration, and temperature instead of the physiological-layer information. We have made prototype devices that are able to display normal/tangential force, vibration, and temperature. These are described in Sects. 6.4.1, 6.4.2, and 6.4.3, respectively.

6.4.1 Normal/Tangential Force Display: Gravity Grabber

We have developed a wearable haptic display, called Gravity Grabber [8], that presents normal and tangential forces on a fingertip (Fig. 6.8). It has a pair of geared DC motors with rotary encoders (Maxon Motor Corp., RE10, 1.5 W, gear ratio = 1: 16) to activate a belt. The belt depresses and drags the palm side of a fingertip. As shown in Fig. 6.9, the motors work in a complementary manner to generate forces in two directions.

The most fundamental sensation of grasping is the normal force (vertical force). A Gravity Grabber reproduces this type of force sensation by driving the two motors in opposing directions to roll up the belt and generate a normal force (vertical force). The prototype device can generate a force of up to 6.5 N.

Fig. 6.8 Gravity grabber in use

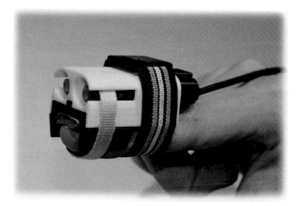

Fig. 6.9 Methods for generating vertical force (normal force) (*left*) and shearing force (tangential force) (*right*)

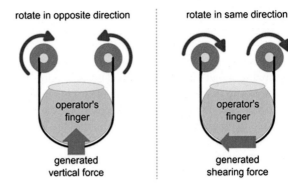

When we hold an object such as a bottle, we feel the shearing force between the bottle and our fingers; this feeling is important because it tells us not to drop the bottle. The tangential force needed to reproduce it is generated by driving the two motors in the same direction to roll up one end of the belt and to release the other end. In this way, the tangential force (shearing force) can also be presented by this device. The current prototype has a frequency range of 0–200 Hz. By combining the normal force and the tangential force applied to a fingerpad, we can display force vectors in any direction.

We have found that fingerpad deformation caused by the weight of an object can generate a reliable weight sensation even when the proprioceptive sensations on the wrist and arm are absent. This indicates that a simple ungrounded display for presenting virtual mass can be realized by reproducing the fingerpad deformation.

6.4.2 Vibration Sensor and Display: TECHTILE Toolkit

TECHTILE Toolkit [9] is an introductory haptic toolkit. Combining "TECHnology" with "tacTILE" perception/expression, it is intended to disseminate haptic technology as a third medium in the fields of art, design, and education. The new medium will extend conventional "multimedia," which currently comprise only visual and auditory information.

The current version of the toolkit (see Fig. 6.10) is composed of haptic recorders (microphones), haptic reactors (small voice-coil vibrators or Force Reactor vibrators), and a signal amplifier that is optimized to present not only the zone of audibility (20–20,000 Hz) but also low-frequency (1–20 Hz) vibrotactile sensation.

This toolkit is intuitive to use and can reduce development costs. It can deliver more highly realistic haptic sensations than many other conventional haptic devices. TECHTILE Toolkit uses the conventional method of auditory media. The sources of auditory sensation and tactile sensation are the same.

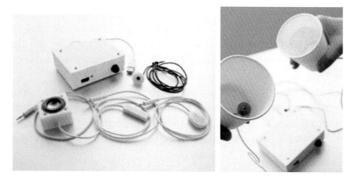

Fig. 6.10 TECHTILE Toolkit

The vibration of an object generates a sequence of vibrations of the air that is perceived as sound; conversely, if the object were touched directly, it would be perceived as a tactile sensation. The auditory sensation can be recorded as a sequence of sound waves that are easily editable and that can be shared on the Internet via services such as YouTube and via other content-sharing websites.

6.4.3 Thermal Sensor and Display

We have proposed a vision-based thermal sensor that uses thermosensitive paint and a camera. Thermosensitive paint changes its color when its temperature changes. We have used the thermosensitive paint to measure the thermal change on the surface of the haptic sensor for telexistence.

Figure 6.11 shows the configuration of the proposed vision-based thermal sensor [10]. This sensor consists of an elastic sheet with thermosensitive paint, a transparent elastic body, a camera, a heat source, and a light source. The thermosensitive paint is printed on the inside of the sensor surface so that its color changes corresponding to the thermal change on the sensor's surface. The camera detects the color of the thermosensitive paint and converts it to the temperature of the sensor's surface.

Fig. 6.11 Configuration of the proposed vision-based thermal sensor

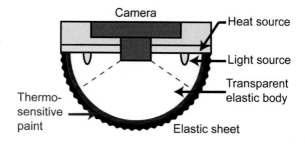

We ensure that the compliance of the elastic body is the same as that of a human fingertip, so the elastic body can mimic the deformation of human skin caused by contact. The heat source maintains the temperature of the sensor and that of the human fingertip at the same level. The temperature of the sensor surface is controlled to follow the temperature of the fingertip.

To convert color into temperature, we use the hue of the captured image. Note that the color of normal thermosensitive paint stops changing when the temperature changes by more than 5 °C or 10 °C. Therefore, to include the temperature measurement range of 15–45 °C, we must use several paints that have various temperature ranges.

The measured temperature is reproduced by Peltier actuators placed on the operator's fingertips.

6.5 Telexistence Avatar Robot System: TELESAR V

Telexistence [2] is a concept named for the general technology that enables a human being to have a real-time sensation of being at a place other than where he or she actually is and to interact with the remote environment that may be real, virtual, or a combination of both. It also refers to an advanced type of teleoperation system that enables an operator at the control to perform remote tasks dexterously with the feeling of being in a surrogate robot working in a remote environment. Telexistence in the real environment through a virtual environment is also possible [11, 12].

TELESAR V (TELExistence Surrogate Anthropomorphic Robot version V) [1, 13–16] is a telexistence master–slave robot system that was developed to realize the concept of telexistence. It was implemented with a high-speed, robust, full-upper-body mechanically unconstrained master cockpit and a 53-degree-of-freedom(DOF) anthropomorphic slave robot. The system provides an experience of our extended "body schema," which allows a human to maintain an up-to-date representation in space of the positions of his/her various body parts. Body schema can be used to understand the posture of the remote body and to perform actions with the belief that the remote body is the user's own body. With this experience, users can perform tasks dexterously and feel the robot's body as their own body through visual, auditory, and haptic sensations, which provide the most simple and fundamental experience of feeling that one is someone somewhere. The TELESAR V master–slave system can also transmit fine haptic sensations, such as the texture and temperature of a material, from an avatar robot's fingers to a human user's fingers.

As shown in Figs. 6.12 and 6.13, the TELESAR V system consists of a master (local) and a slave (remote). A 53-DOF dexterous robot with a 6-DOF torso, a 3-DOF head, 7-DOF arms, and 15-DOF hands was developed. The robot also has Full HD (1920 × 1080 pixels) cameras for capturing wide-angle stereovision, and stereo microphones are situated on the robot's ears for capturing audio information from the remote site. The operator's voice is transferred to the remote site and outputted through a small speaker installed in the robot's mouth area.

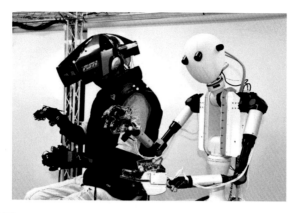

Fig. 6.12 TELESAR V master (*left*) and slave robot (*right*)

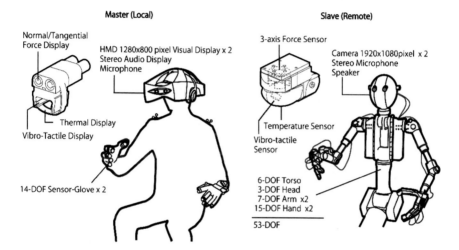

Fig. 6.13 TELESAR V system configuration

On the master side the operator's movements are captured with a motion capturing system (OptiTrack) and sent to the kinematic generator PC. Finger bending is captured to an accuracy of 14 DOF with the modified "5DT Data Glove 14."

6.5.1 Development of 53-DOF Human-Size Anthropomorphic Robot

As shown in Figs. 6.14 and 6.15, the TELESAR V slave robot consists of four main systems: a body, a head, arms, and hands. The body is a modified "Mitsubishi PA

Fig. 6.14 TELESAR V
slave robot

Fig. 6.15 Kinematic
configuration of
TELESAR V

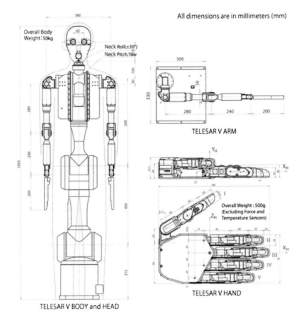

10-7C Industrial Robot Manipulator" placed upright. The first six joints of the manipulator arm are used as the torso, and the final joint with separately attached DC motors is used as the 3-DOF (roll, pitch, and yaw) head.

Custom-designed 7-DOF human-size anthropomorphic robotic arms are fixed between body joints 6 and 7 so that the robot resembles a human-sized dexterous robot. To increase the level of dexterity of the slave robot's arms, they were designed with joints (with limited angles) similar to those of human arms. However, we have included a position-based electrical limit overriding the mechanical limit to provide extra safety in case of a joint-angle overshoots.

The arm joints are driven by 12 V DC motors, and the first three joints (J1, J2, and J3) use harmonic drive gears to keep backlash and vibration low while providing the necessary torque. The hands are custom-designed human-sized anthropomorphic robotic hands with a number of joints similar to that in real human hands. The robotic fingers of each hand are driven by 15 individual DC motors, and dynamically coupled wires and a pulley-driven mechanism connect the remaining joints that are not directly attached to a motor. All of the DC motors are connected to standard DC motor drivers, and a combination of optical encoder output potentiometer readings is used as position measurements. Furthermore, voltage and current are monitored at each motor, and the torque at the motor shaft is calculated. Communication between the motor drivers and the PC is carried out through a PCI-Express ×1 bus.

6.5.2 Development of Wide-Angle HD Stereovision System

To capture Full HD video from the robot, we used as each of the robot's eyes a CMOS camera head (model: TOSHIBA IK-HK1H) and a wide-angle lens (model: FUJINON TF4DA-8) configuration. Two cameras were installed 65 mm apart and parallel to each other. To provide a HD wide-angle stereovision sensation to the operator, a HD (1280 × 800 pixels) wide-angle head-mounted display (HMD) was developed. To provide a wide–angle view while maintaining a small footprint, we used a 5.6-in. LCD display (model: HV056WX1-100) and increased the length of the optical path by using a special lens arrangement. The HMD has two parallel virtual projection planes located 1 m from both eyeballs, to present stereoscopic vision independently between the eyes, thus enabling the operator to sense the distance correctly [11]. A knob is provided at the front of the HMD so that the operator can adjust the convergence angle of the left and right eyes for clear stereovision.

With the above specifications, we were able to produce a wide-angle field of view for each eye (61° horizontally and 40° vertically). In addition, two cameras were installed on the front of the HMD. This is useful when the operator needs to change his/her vision to the video see-through mode (see Figs. 6.16 and 6.17).

Fig. 6.16 Telexistence head-mounted display with see-through videocameras

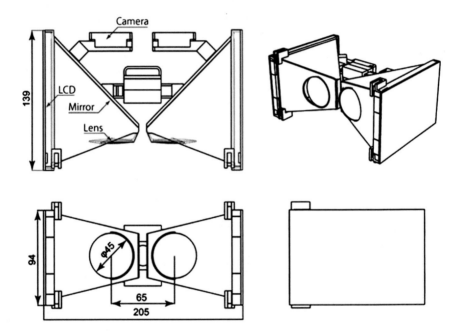

Fig. 6.17 Telexistence head-mounted display assembly view

6.5.3 Development of Thermal and Haptic Transmission System

As shown in Fig. 6.18, the haptic transmission system consists of three parts: a haptic scanner, a haptic display, and a processing block. When the haptic scanner touches an

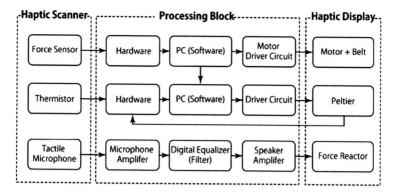

Fig. 6.18 Haptic system configuration

object, it obtains haptic information such as contact force, vibration, and temperature. The haptic display provides haptic stimuli on the user's finger to reproduce the haptic information obtained by the haptic scanner. The processing block connects the haptic scanner with the haptic display and converts the obtained physical data into data that include the physiological haptic perception reproduced by the haptic display. The details of the mechanisms for scanning and displaying are described below [17].

First, a force sensor inside the haptic scanner measures the vector force when the haptic scanner touches an object. Then two motor-belt mechanisms in the haptic display reproduce the vector force on the operator's fingertips. The processing block controls the electrical current of each motor to provide torques based on the measured force. As a result, the mechanism reproduces the force sensation when the haptic scanner touches the object.

A microphone in the haptic scanner records the sound generated on its surface when the haptic scanner is in contact with an object. Then a force reactor in the haptic display plays the transmitted sound as a vibration. This vibration provides a high-frequency haptic sensation, so the information should be transmitted without delay. The processing block therefore transfers the sound signals by using amplifiers and an equalizer.

A thermistor sensor in the haptic scanner measures the surface temperature of the object. The measured temperature is reproduced by Peltier actuators placed on the operator's fingertips. The processing block generates control signals for the Peltier actuators, and the generation of each signal is based on a PID control loop with feedback from a thermistor located on the Peltier actuator.

Figures 6.19 and 6.20 show the structures of the haptic scanner and the haptic display. Figure 6.21 shows the left hand of the TELESAR V robot with the haptic scanners and shows the haptic displays set in the modified 5DT Data Glove 14.

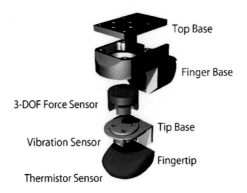

Fig. 6.19 Structure of haptic scanner

Fig. 6.20 Structure of haptic display

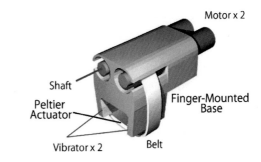

Fig. 6.21 Slave hand with haptic scanners (*left*) and master hand with haptic displays (*right*)

Figure 6.22 shows TELESAR V performing various tasks: picking up sticks, transferring small balls from one cup to another cup, producing Japanese calligraphy, playing Japanese chess (shogi), and feeling the texture of a cloth.

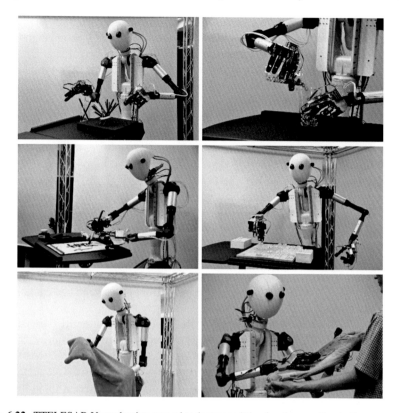

Fig. 6.22 TTELESAR V conducting several tasks transmitting haptic sensation to the user

6.6 RePro3D: Full-Parallax Autostereoscopic 3D Based on Retroreflective Projection Technology (RPT)

Autostereoscopic 3D creates 3D images based on the human binocular perception of 3D depth without requiring the viewer to use special headgear or glasses. Most common stereoscopic displays are based on the binocular stereo concept, but binocular-stereo-based displays without motion parallax cannot render an accurate image and cannot create images that provide different perspectives of the same object or scene from different points of view. Motion parallax plays an important role in the manner in which humans perceive 3D shapes. Multiview autostereoscopic 3D provides the perception of left–right motion parallax, and full-parallax autostereoscopic 3D provides the perception of both left–right motion parallax and up–down motion parallax. Full-parallax 3D, which provides different perspectives according to the viewing direction, is not only useful for motion parallax for a single viewer but is also necessary for simultaneously displaying stereoscopic images to a large number of people.

Most conventional multiview or full-parallax autostereoscopic3D systems are based either on the parallax barrier method or on the integral photography (IP) method. In the parallax barrier method, a barrier with a number of slits is placed in front of an image source so that a different pixel is seen from different viewing angles. However, the parallax barrier method is not capable of generating vertical parallax and thus cannot provide full-parallax autostereoscopic 3D. Thus, IP is the most appropriate method of realizing full-parallax autostereoscopic 3D. In the IP method a light field is reproduced by placing an array of microlenses in front of an image source, and the number of viewpoints can easily be increased depending on the resolution of the image source. However, because the resolution of the 3D image from a viewpoint depends on the number of lenses per unit area, the lenses must be sufficiently small to have the necessary resolution. Thus only relatively crude implementations have been produced using today's technology.

Moreover, for the user to view the displayed object as a real object, full-parallax autostereoscopic 3D alone is not sufficient. The object's image should not be displayed on a screen but superimposed in real space. That is, a full-parallax autostereoscopic 3D image must be produced as an aerial image (i.e., one floating in the air). However, conventional IP produces 3D images in front of a screen and cannot produce aerial images.

Figure 6.23 shows the basic principle of RePro3D, which is the RPT-based full-parallax autostereoscopic 3D display method [18, 19]. When images from a projector array are projected onto a retroreflector, light is reflected only in the direction of each projection lens. Images from the projector array are projected onto the retroreflector. When users look at the screen through a half-mirror, they can see, without the use of glasses, a 3D image that has motion parallax. RePro3D can generate vertical and horizontal motion parallax. An identical number of viewpoints are created on either side of the axis of symmetry of the half-mirror. The resolution of the image from each viewpoint depends on the projector resolution, and the number of viewpoints is equal to the number of projectors. It is therefore easy to improve the image resolution. It

Fig. 6.23 Basic principle of RePro3D, consisting of a projector array, a half-mirror, and a retroreflector

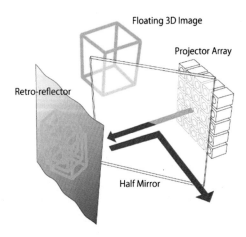

is also easy to produce a full-parallax autostereoscopic 3D image as an aerial image because RePro3D inherently uses a half-mirror.

When a large number of projectors are arranged in a matrix, a 3D image can be viewed from multiple viewpoints. To realize smooth motion parallax, the density of projectors in the projector array must be sufficiently high. With commercially available projectors, however, it is difficult to make a projector array in which the projectors are located very close to each other. One reason for this is that the distance between adjacent viewpoints is limited by the size of each projector. In addition, the system scale would increase and the large number of video outputs would increase the system's cost. A virtual high-density projector array has therefore been developed by arranging a single LCD display, a lens array, and a Fresnel concave lens. The distance between viewpoints can be diminished by making a virtual lens array of the real lens array by using the Fresnel concave lens. Because a single LCD display is used for the projector array, a single video output can be used as an image source, the cost of which is lower than that of using many image sources for multiple projectors.

Figure 6.24 shows the principle of such an arrangement. The system consists of a number of lenses, an LCD, a half-mirror, and a retroreflector that serves as the screen. The lenses are located at an appropriate distance from the imaging area of the LCD so that the projected areas of the projection lenses overlap. Shield plates are placed between the lenses to prevent light from other viewpoints from entering a lens. The luminance of the projected image depends on the LCD luminance, viewing angle, and retroreflector performance. The resolution of the image from each viewpoint depends on the LCD resolution. The number of viewpoints is equal to the number of projection lenses.

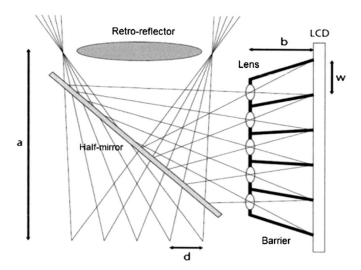

Fig. 6.24 RePro3D configuration

Fig. 6.25 Appearance of
RePro3D prototype

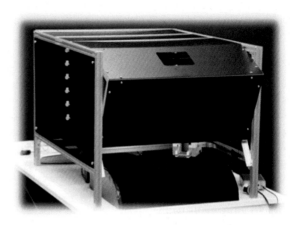

Figure 6.25 shows the prototype. We used 42 projection lenses, each 25 mm in diameter and having a focal length 25 mm. The Fresnel concave lens used in the prototype was 370 mm in diameter, and its focal length was 231 mm. We used a high-luminance LCD with a resolution of 1680 × 1050 pixels and a luminance of 1000 cd/m^2 and used Reflite 8301 retroreflector. The projection lenses were arranged in a matrix with 6 rows and 7 columns; therefore, the total number of viewpoints was 42. The resolution of the projected image seen from each viewpoint was 175 × 175 pixels. The distance between viewpoints was 16 mm. The device was able to project up to 400 mm from the user's viewpoint. The image was projected in a space of size 200 × 200 × 300 mm.

Figure 6.26 shows a 3D object that was projected onto the retroreflective screen and could be seen from several viewpoints. The positional relationship of each displayed object changed according to the change of viewpoint. This finding indicates that our

Fig. 6.26 Motion disparity

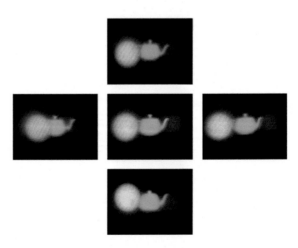

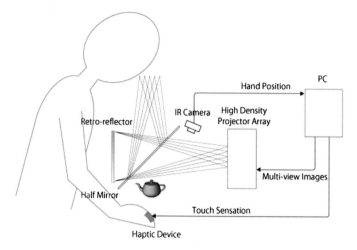

Fig. 6.27 Visuo-haptic system overview

proposed method can produce a stereoscopic image superimposed in real space with smooth motion parallax. We placed an infrared (IR) camera (Point Gray Research, Firefly MV) with an IR pass filter and IR LEDs above the projected area to capture the user's hand movements as shown in Fig. 6.27. Then we implemented the user input system, which recognizes the degree of contact between the user's hand and the displayed image. Using this function, we built an application that enables the user to touch a character floating in space. If the user touches the character, the character reacts to the user's touch, and the user can perceive this reaction by looking at the changes in the character's appearance and from sound cues.

Figure 6.28 shows a demonstration installation in which the character, an animated fairy floating in real space, reacts when touched by the user's finger. In addition, the user wears a haptic device on his/her finger. When the user touches the 3D image, he/she feels a tactile sensation generated by the haptic device. The mechanism that produces the sensation on the user's finger is based on the Gravity Grabber technology [8]. Gravity Grabber produces fingerpad deformation by using a pair of small motors and a belt as described in Sect. 6.4.1. To create a "pushing" sensation, the dual motors are driven in opposite directions so that they roll up the belt, thus delivering vertical

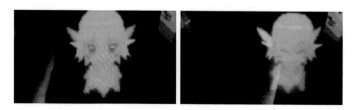

Fig. 6.28 Interaction with a virtual character

Fig. 6.29 Interaction with
haptic feedback via Gravity
Grabber

force to the user's fingerpad (see Fig. 6.29). The belt tension is determined by the degree of contact between the finger and the 3D image.

The results of tests using the RePro3D prototype confirmed that our proposed method produces autostereoscopic images superimposed in real space and does so with smooth motion parallax. In this prototype we also realized a user interface that enables users to interact physically with a virtual character floating in space. We thus demonstrated that RePro3D provides a visual and haptic interface that enables users to see and touch a virtual 3D object as if the object were real.

6.7 HaptoMIRAGE

HaptoMIRAGE is an autostereoscopic display for seamless interaction with real and virtual objects. This system can project the 3D image in mid-air with 180°–wide-angle of view based on our proposed ARIA technology described below, and up to three users can see the same object from different points of view. The 3D image can be superimposed on the real object so that the user can get natural interaction with the mixed reality environment. HaptoMirage not only superimposes 3D images on the real environment but also lets the user draw autostereoscopic 3D line drawings on the real object. So it enables us to interact with the mixed reality environment in a natural manner and to easily create and feel the mixed reality world. Our goal is to implement a mixed reality platform with natural 3D interaction for creative design, storytelling, entertainment, and remote collaboration by seamlessly mixing the "real" and "virtual" worlds.

6.7.1 Virtual Shutter Glasses Using ARIA (Active-shuttered Real Image Autostereoscopy)

As discussed in Sect. 6.6, integral photography and RPT-based autostereoscopy are two major methods to realize full-parallax autostereoscopy. In addition to the 3D image being displayed in full-parallax autostereoscopic 3D, it must be produced as

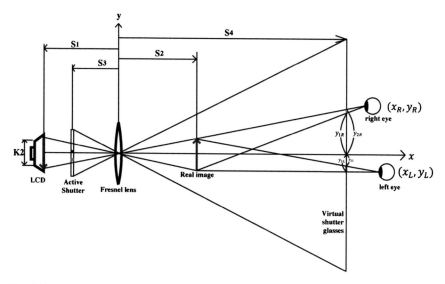

Fig. 6.30 Realization of virtual shutter glasses using ARIA optics

an image floating in the air. RePro3D, which is an RPT-based full-parallax autostereo-scopic 3D display, is capable of not only generating vertical and horizontal motion parallax but also producing a full-parallax autostereoscopic 3D image as an aerial image (i.e., floating in the air). However, RPT-based autostereoscopy has a drawback: its small area of observation. It is difficult to get a large area of observation without constructing a huge array of projectors.

On the other hand, the frame sequential method using shutter glasses (a time-division 3D method has an advantage for multiviewpoint stereoscopy. Because it measures the human user's position, it can present a 3D aerial image that can be observed in wide area of observation. Its drawbacks are that a user must wear shutter glasses and that it is not at all autostereoscopic.

We have proposed a new method of frame sequential stereoscopy that does not require the wearing of any special eyewear as shutter glasses; i.e., an autostereoscopic frame sequential method. It is based on active-shuttered real-image autostereoscopy (ARIA) [20]. Figure 6.30 shows how ARIA is used to realize virtual shutter glasses.

As is shown in Fig. 6.30, a liquid crystal display (LCD) and an active-shutter are placed at distances of S_1 and S_3, respectively, behind a Fresnel lens of focal length f. The real images of the LCD and the shutter are made by the lens at distances of S_2 and S_4, respectively.

$$\frac{1}{S_1} + \frac{1}{S_2} = \frac{1}{f}, \quad \frac{1}{S_3} + \frac{1}{S_4} = \frac{1}{f}$$

A human user observes the real image on LCD through the real image of the shutter. On the LCD, the image for the left eye and the image for the right eye are displayed frame by frame alternately. The user's right eye position (x_R, y_R) and left eye position (x_L, y_L) are measured by a motion-sensing device with eye recognition ability, such as Kinect for Windows. When the image for the left eye is presented as the real image, the corresponding part of the active-shutter in front of the left eye (i.e., between y_{1L} and y_{2L}) is open. When the image for the right eye is presented, the corresponding part of the active-shutter in front of the right eye (i.e., between y_{2R} and y_{1R}) is open. It is also possible to change the design so that the shutter in front of the right eye closes when the image for the left eye is displayed, and vice versa. Thus the active-shutter acts as virtual shutter glasses.

When the effective display size of the LCD is 2K, by putting $K' = \frac{S_2}{S_1} K$, we get the following equations.

$$y_{1R} = \frac{y_R(S_4 - S_2) - K'(x_R - S_4)}{x_R - S_2}$$

$$y_{2R} = \frac{y_R(S_4 - S_2) + K'(x_R - S_4)}{x_R - S_2}$$

$$y_{1L} = \frac{y_L(S_4 - S_2) - K'(x_L - S_4)}{x_L - S_2}$$

$$y_{2L} = \frac{y_L(S_4 - S_2) + K'(x_L - S_4)}{x_L - S_2}$$

Real coordinates on the LCD display can be obtained as follows:

$$y'_{1R} = -\frac{S_3}{S_4}y_{1R}, \quad y'_{2R} = -\frac{S_3}{S_4}y_{2R}, \quad y'_{1L} = -\frac{S_3}{S_4}y_{1L}, \quad y'_{2L} = -\frac{S_3}{S_4}y_{2L}.$$

For an interpupillary distance d, the 3D observable distance x is in the following range:

$$S_4 \le x \le S_4 + \frac{d}{2K} \cdot \frac{S_1}{S_2}(S_4 - S_2).$$

6.7.2 Prototype System

Figure 6.31 shows the prototype HaptoMIRAGE 180° 3D display system. In this system, the parameters are set as $S_1 = 0.4\,\text{m}$ ($S_2 = 0.4\,\text{m}$), $S_3 = 0.23\,\text{m}$ ($S_4 = 1.53\,\text{m}$), $2K = 0.2\,\text{m}$, and $f = 0.2\,\text{m}$. The system consists of three components, each having a 60° field of autostereoscopic view based on our technology called ARIA. The Fresnel lens makes the real image from the LCD display, the position of the user is measured by a camera-based motion capture system, and the active shutter using a transparent LCD panel provides the virtual shutter glasses. The shutter is switched at 60 Hz, the user can see the real image as a floating 3D image, and up to three users can see the autostereoscopic image from different viewpoints at the same time.

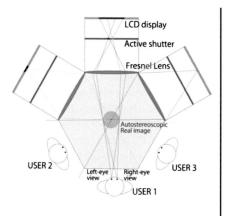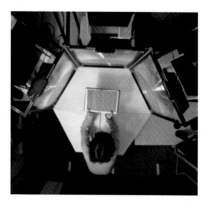

Fig. 6.31 Overall view of HaptoMIRAGE system

Fig. 6.32 Direct interaction with floating 3D object (*left*), drawing 3D object (*center*), and matching 3D virtual object with real objects (*right*)

Without wearing any special glasses, the users can see the 3D image floating in the real environment as in Fig. 6.32. When a user points a finger at certain area of the 3D image, the other users can easily find where it is. The users can use their fingers to make colorful line drawings on the real object. This is similar to light drawing, but the difference is that the users can see the 3D image of their finger's trajectory before their eyes and can interact with the drawings.

6.8 Summary

In this project, we are trying to construct an intelligent information environment, based on our proposed theory of haptic primary colors, that is both visible and tangible and is one where real-space communication, human-machine interfaces, and media processing are integrated. The goal is to create a human-harmonized "tangible information environment" that allows human beings to obtain and understand haptic information about the real space, to transmit the thus obtained haptic space, and to actively interact with other people using the transmitted haptic space. The tangible environment would enable telecommunication, tele-experience, and pseudo-experience with the sensation of working as though in a natural environment. It would also enable humans to engage in creative activities such as design and creation as though they were in the real environment.

We have succeeded in transmitting fine haptic sensations, such as material texture and temperature, from an avatar robot's fingers to a human user's fingers. The avatar robot is a telexistence anthropomorphic robot dubbed TELESAR V, with a body and limbs having 53 degrees of freedom. This robot can transmit not only visual and auditory sensations of presence to human users but also realistic haptic sensations. Other results of this research project include RePro3D, a full-parallax, autostereoscopic 3D (three-dimensional) display with haptic feedback using RPT (retroreflective projection technology); TECHTILE Toolkit, a prototyping tool for the design and improvement of haptic media; and HaptoMIRAGE, 180°-field-of-view autostereoscopic 3D display using ARIA (active-shuttered real image autostereoscopy) that up to three users can enjoy simultaneously.

Acknowledgments This project of Construction and Utilization of Human-harmonized "Tangible" Information Environment is supported by JST (Japan Science and Technology Agency)-CREST (Core Research for Evolutionary Science and Technology).This study has been conducted with the following members of Tachi Laboratory: Kouta Minamizawa, Masahiro Furukawa, Masano Nakayama, Charith Lasantha Fernando, Hideaki Nii, Katsunari Sato, Takumi Yoshida, Sho Kamuro, Keitaro Shimizu, Tadatoshi Kurogi, Yuta Ueda, Nobuhisa Hanamitsu, and MHD Yamen Saraiji.

References

1. S. Tachi, K. Minamizawa, M, Furukawa, C.L. Fernando, Haptic media: construction and utilization of human-harmonized "Tangible" information environment. *Proceedings of the 23rd International Conference on Artificial Reality and Telexistence (ICAT)* (Tokyo, Japan, 2013), pp. 145–150
2. S. Tachi, *Telexistence*, 2nd edn. (World Scientific, 2015). ISBN 978-981-4618-06-9
3. H. Kajimoto, N. Kawakami, T. Maeda, S. Tachi, Tactile feeling display using functional electrical stimulation. *Proceeding of the 9th International Conference on Artificial Reality and Telexistence (ICAT)* (Tokyo, Japan, 1999), pp. 107–114
4. K. Sato, K. Kamiyama, N. Kawakami, S. Tachi, Finger-shaped GelForce: sensor for measuring surface traction fields for robotic hand. IEEE Trans. Haptics 3(1), 37–47 (2010)
5. Y. Hirobe, T. Yoshida, S. Kuroki, K. Minamizawa, K. Sato, S. Tachi, *Colorful Touch Palette, ACM SIGGRAPH 2010* (Emerging Technologies, Los Angeles, CA, USA, 2010)
6. K. Sato, S. Tachi, Design of electrotactile stimulation to rep-resent distribution of force vectors. *Proceedings of IEEE Haptics Symposium 2010* (Waltham, Massachusetts, USA, 2010), pp. 121–128
7. K. Kamiyama, H. Kajimoto, N. Kawakami, S. Tachi, Evaluation of a vision-based tactile sensor. *Proceedings of IEEE International Conference on Robotics and Automation2*, 1542–1547 (2004)
8. K. Minamizawa, K. Tojo, H. Kajimoto, N. Kawakami, S. Tachi, Haptic interface for middle phalanx using dual motors. *Proceedings of EuroHaptics Conference 2006* (Paris, France, 2006), pp. 235–240
9. K. Minamizawa, Y. Kakehi, M. Nakatani, S. Mihara, S. Tachi, TECHTILE toolkit—A prototyping tool for design and education of haptic media. *Proceedings of Laval Virtual VRIC 2012* (Laval, France, 2012)

10. K. Sato, H. Shinoda, S. Tachi, Finger-shaped thermal sensor using thermo-sensitive paint and camera for telexistence. *Proceedings of 2011 IEEE International Conference on Robotics and Automation (ICRA2011)* (Shanghai, China, 2011), pp. 1120–1125
11. S. Tachi, K. Tanie, K. Komoriya, M. Kaneko, Tele-existence (I): design and evaluation of a visual display with sensation of presence. *Proceedings of the 5th Symposium on Theory and Practice of Robots and Manipulators (RoManSy' 84)* (Udine, Italy, 1984), pp. 245–254
12. S.Tachi, H. Arai, T. Maeda, Tele-existence master-slave system for remote manipulation. *Proceedings of the IEEE International Workshop on Intelligent Robots and Systems (IROS '90)* (Tsuchiura, Japan, 1990), pp. 343–348
13. C.L. Fernando, M. Furukawa, T. Kurogi, S. Kamuro, K. Sato, K. Minamizawa, S. Tachi, Design of TELESAR V for transferring bodily con-sciousness in telexistence. *Proceedings of IEEE/RSJ International Conference on Intelligent Robots and Systems*, pp. 5112–5118 (2012)
14. C.L. Fernando, M. Furukawa, K. Minamizawa, S. Tachi, Experiencing one's own hand in telexistence manipulation with a 15 DOF anthro-pomorphic robot hand and a flexible Master Glove. *Proceedings of the 23rd International Conference on Artificial Reality and Telexistence (ICAT)* (Tokyo, Japan, 2013), pp. 20–27
15. S. Tachi, K. Minamizawa, M. Furukawa, K. Sato, Study on telexistence lxv—telesar5: haptic telexistence robot system. *Proceedings of EC2011* (Tokyo, Japan, 2011) (in Japanese)
16. S. Tachi, From 3D to VR and further to telexistence. *Proceedings of the 23rd International Conference on Artificial Reality and Telexistence (ICAT)* (Tokyo, Japan, 2013), pp. 1–10
17. T. Kurogi, M. Nakayama, K. Sato, S. Kamuro, C.L. Fernando, M. Furukawa, K. Minamizawa, S. Tachi, Haptic transmission system to recognize differences in surface textures of objects for telexistence. *Proceedings of IEEE Virtual Reality*, pp. 137–138 (2013)
18. T. Yoshida, S. Kamuro, K. Minamizawa, H. Nii, S. Tachi, *RePro3D: Full-parallax 3D Display using Retro-reflective Projection Technology, ACM SIGGRAPH 2010* (Emerging Technologies, Los Angeles, CA, USA, 2010)
19. T. Yoshida, K. Shimizu, T. Kurogi, S. Kamuro, K. Minamizawa, H. Nii, S. Tachi, RePro3D: full-parallax 3D display with haptic feedback using retro-reflective projection technology. *Proceedings of IEEE International Symposium on Virtual Reality Innovations, 2011*, pp. 49–54 (2011)
20. H. Nii, K. Zhu, H. Yoshikawa, N.L. Htat, R. Aigner, R. Nakatsu: Fuwa-vision: an auto-stereoscopic floating-image display. *ACM SIGGRAPH Asia 2012 Emerging Technologies, SA '12*, 13:1–13:4 (2012)

Chapter 7
Perceptual Illusion and Development of a Sense-Centered Human Interface

Yasuharu Koike

Abstract Tele-existence is the replication of physically plausible information through the provision of real sensation of presence. Here, we sought to elucidate the mechanisms of perceptual illusion within the context of brain function. Improving our understanding of perceptual illusion will contribute to the realization of new and more efficient human interfaces.

Keywords Musculo-skeletal model · Stiffness · Equilibrium position · Pseudo-Haptics · Electromyogram

7.1 Introduction

Our bodies contain numerous and various sensors. Those sensors send signals to the cerebral cortex, and sensations are then perceived. Most sensations are identified with a specific type of stimulus. Furthermore, perception is not directly related to sensor activity. Most sensors receive signals passively. Muscles act as actuators to create the force for body motion, but the sensors also detect force and positioning of the body. Our hands have many tactile sensors and can be controlled voluntarily. So ours hands are active sensor for touch.

Computer input devices, such as mice and trackpads, measure hand position and translate it to cursor position on a screen. Recently, Apple® developed the Force Touch trackpad, adding a new dimension to touch interfaces. New multi-touch gestures with force are being developed and adopted in computer interaction. However, we control force in touching unconsciously, so gestures have to be developed with consideration to behavior in daily life. Muscle activity reflects changes in force and can be measured as electromyography (EMG) signals. Proposed here is a new interface which measures muscle activity and estimates not only position, but also force

Y. Koike (✉)
Solution Research Laboratory, Tokyo Institute of Technology,
4259-J3-10, Nagatsuta, Midori-ku, Yokohama 226-8503, Japan
e-mail: koike@pi.titech.ac.jp

© Springer Japan 2016
T. Nishida (ed.), *Human-Harmonized Information Technology, Volume 1*,
DOI 10.1007/978-4-431-55867-5_7

and stiffness simultaneously. To develop intuitive manipulation, muscle control for manipulation was also studied.

When we manipulate an object, its weight is important information in the production of joint torque, because the dynamics of the object are non-linear and complex. Also, the perception of heaviness is still an open problem, and the size-weight illusion, where small objects feel heavier than large objects of the same weight, is a well known phenomenon.

In this chapter, a sensor which detects weight is discussed, and a new illusion in perception is explained. The musculoskeletal model plays a crucial role in understanding the phenomenon. A new human interface based on the musculoskeletal model is also introduced.

7.2 Haptics and Force

Sensory systems measure various stimuli and perceive information from the environment. Table 7.1 shows the different types of sensory systems and their associated modalities of information [1]. Our sensory systems use four types of sensory receptors, mechanoreceptors, chemoreceptors, photoreceptors, and thermoreceptors. Chemoreceptors are related to olfaction, gustation, itch, and visceral sensations. Visual sensors detect light, with different visual sensors reacting to different wavelengths. The brain integrates the signals from receptors and extracts information, such as smell, color, or temperature.

As shown in Table 7.1, there is no sensor to directly measure weight. Somatosensory information is received at the hand by pressure, as well as at the arm by hand displacement, and captured by cutaneous mechanoreceptors (touch) or muscle and joint receptors (proprioception). Muscles have three kinds of mechanoreceptors, which respond to muscle length, contraction velocity, and muscle force.

Table 7.1 Sensory systems

Stimulus source	Sensory system	Modality	Receptor cell types
Exteroception	Visual	Vision	Rods, cones
Exteroception	Auditory	Hearing	Hair cells (cochlea)
Exteroception	Vestibular	Balance	Hair cells (vestibular labyrinth)
	Somatosensory	Somatic senses	Dorsal root ganglion neurons
Exteroception		Touch	Cutaneous mechanoreceptors
Proprioception		Tension, Motion	Muscle and joint receptors
Exteroception		Temperature sense	Cold and warm receptors
Exteroception	Gustatory	Taste	Taste buds
Exteroception	Olfactory	Smell	Olfactory sensory neurons

Modified from [1]

Proprioception refers to the sensing of information from muscle and joint receptors on the body's own motion. The sensing of one's own motion is called kinaesthesia, and the main receptor involved in kinaesthesia is the muscle spindle. Motor commands from the central nervous system (CNS) related to the perception of heaviness are sent to the muscles. The receptors also send afferent feedback signals back to the CNS. The CNS can estimate the result of the motor command using an efference copy and compare the estimate with the afferent feedback.

Exteroception refers to information from outside of the body, such as light, sound, and smell. Vision plays an important role in recognizing the world. When we grasp an object, its size, color, material, position, and other properties are recognized. For example, the relationship between size, material, and weight are trained by the experience of manipulation.

7.3 The System of Sense

Auditory sensors capture vibrations of the air. Visual sensors detect light. Molecules are detected by sensory cells in the nose and mouth, allowing us to smell and taste. Temperature, pain, and pressure are sensed on the skin by receptors such as Pacinian corpuscles, Ruffini's corpuscles, and Meissner's corpuscles. Sources of sensed sound and light can be distant, but smell comes from nearby. Arm length dictates distance for touch sensation, and the hand is an articulating sensor for capturing shape and hardness. Furthermore, there are other sensors that receive information passively.

When vibrations of the eardrum are passed on through the middle ear to the cochlea, sound is perceived. However, physical vibrations do not necessarily match the perception of the sound. The brain can pick out information from sensor signals (Fig. 7.1). For example, we can focus on a particular conversation in a noisy room. This phenomenon is explained by selective attention. This means that when we

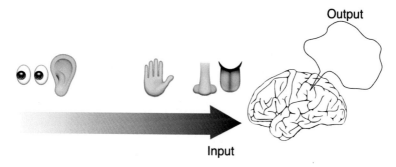

Fig. 7.1 The brain receives information from the sensors, but each sensor has a different delay, and different regions of the brain received their signals, so the brain has to integrate the information. Perception differs from real sensory information, because the brain compensates for the lack of information

receive a sensation, not only bottom-up sensory signals, but also top-down signals affect perception. The "McGurk Effect" [2] is a good example. When subjects hear the syllables /ba-ba/ while viewing the lip motion /ga-ga/, most subjects report that the sound is /da-da/. This example also demonstrates that perception is not directly connected to sensor signals.

Another example is pseudo-haptics [3], which is a technique for simulating haptic sensation using visual feedback. This phenomenon is caused by the difference between the user's displacement of the input device and the visual displacement of the object on the screen. This difference is known as the control/display (C/D) ratio (Eq. 7.1) in the human interface field.

$$\text{C/D ratio} = \frac{x_{hand}}{x_{display}} \tag{7.1}$$

One of the most popular human interfaces is the computer mouse. When we use a mouse, hand motion on the desk and cursor motion on the screen are not the same (Fig. 7.2). Forward and backward hand motions are translated respectively to upward and downward motions on the screen. We do not typically notice this translation.

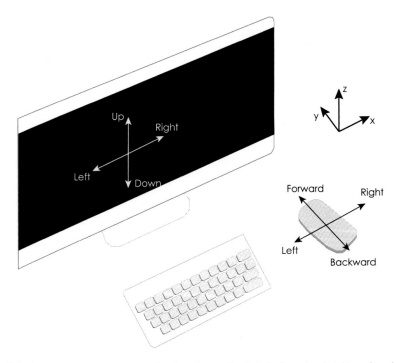

Fig. 7.2 A computer mouse measures hand motion on the desk. *Leftward* and *rightward* motion is reflected on the screen directly, but *forward* and *backward* motion is reflected indirectly as *upward* and *downward* motion. Still, we do not usually perceive this translation

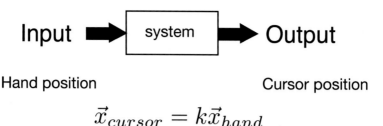

Fig. 7.3 Input and Output signals of computer mouse

However, if the motion is slower or faster than expected, it becomes bothersome. So we can adjust the speed of the cursor through the computer's settings. In Fig. 7.3, k is a parameter for position change. This is the same as the C/D ratio. Even though this ratio is not adjusted manually, we learn the relationship between our hand's motion and the cursor's motion. After learning or adjusting the C/D ratio, we cease to be aware of the transformation. Yet if this ratio is changed unexpectedly, we feel force. This phenomenon is the basis of pseudo-haptics.

Pseudo-haptic feedback of isometric input devices was also tested using virtual springs [4]. Spring force (F) is defined by the spring constant (K) and displacement (x) as:

$$F = Kx$$
$$x_{cursor} = F_{hand}/K_{virtual} \qquad (7.2)$$

When cursor motion (x_{cursor}) is controlled by force (F_{hand}), the spring constant ($K_{virtual}$) is a parameter to adjust the motion.

$$K_{virtual} = F_{hand}/x_{cursor} \qquad (7.3)$$

The displacement (x) is inversely proportional to the spring constant (K), and $K_{virtual}$ is similar to the C/D ratio in Eq. 7.1.

The hand is pulled by the equilibrium position x_{eq} with spring K and damper B (Fig. 7.4).

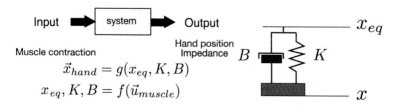

Fig. 7.4 Musculoskeletal system

Parameters K and B can also be defined as stiffness and viscosity, respectively. Along with equilibrium position, they are controlled by muscle contraction. The implications of these parameters are explained in later sections, but different combinations of these parameters can result in the same hand position. Conversely, C/D ratio is one parameter without redundancy. In this chapter, new human interface concept is proposed using these parameters.

7.4   Musculoskeletal Model

Hand force is produced by muscle tension. Skeletal muscle generates force in the pulling direction. For this reason, each joint has one or more pairs of muscles. The musculoskeletal model calculates joint torque from each muscle activation pattern.

7.4.1   Muscle Tension

The force that a muscle exerts depends on the muscle length and contractile velocity. Muscles have spring-like properties, with muscle force increasing as length increases. But when the length exceeds a threshold, force gradually decreases. Still, in daily life, muscle length does not typically go beyond this threshold, and also muscle tendons help to prevent this. Conversely, muscle force decreases as contractile velocity increases. But when muscle length increases, force is not affected by the velocity.

Each muscle is connected at a joint, and muscle length changes with the joint angle. For example, as the angle of the elbow joint increases, the length of the flexor muscle shortens while the opposing extensor muscle lengthens. This equates to a decrease in flexor tension and an increase in extensor tension.

7.4.2   Joint Torque

Net joint torque is calculated from the difference in flexor and extensor muscle tensions. This also means that each muscle tension is not directly related to joint torque.

Consider two examples, one where flexor muscle tension is 10 (arbitrary units) and extensor muscle tension is 7, resulting in a joint torque of 3, and another example where flexor muscle tension is 4, and extensor muscle tension is 1, again resulting in a joint torque of 3. What is the difference between these examples?

In Fig. 7.5, two conditions for muscle tension are plotted. When flexor and extensor muscle tensions are equal, joint torque becomes zero, and the arm is stable at some

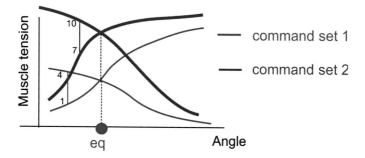

Fig. 7.5 Co-contraction

Fig. 7.6 Force generation

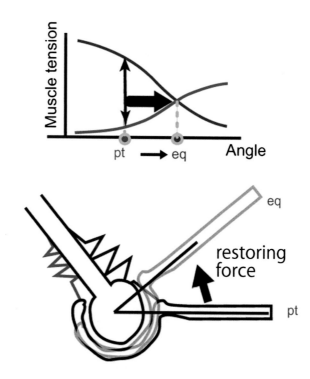

position (command set 1). At another strong contraction level, the same posture (command set 2) can also be obtained. We call this position equilibrium posture.

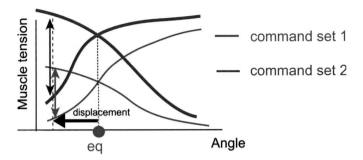

Fig. 7.7 Stiffness

7.4.3 Joint Stiffness

When joint position moves with the same contraction level, restoring force is generated (Fig. 7.6).

The magnitude of this force depends on each muscle's contraction level. At the same posture, stiffness depends on muscle activation level (Fig. 7.7). The ratio of this restoring force and displacement is called joint stiffness.

$$Jointstiffness = \frac{restoringforce}{displacement} \tag{7.4}$$

In Fig. 7.5, restoring force is equal, but displacement is different. In Fig. 7.7, displacement is equal, but restoring force is different. For both cases, joint stiffness of command set 1 is greater than that of command set 2.

7.4.4 Equilibrium Position Change

To produce a trajectory, it has been hypothesized that the CNS sends only final posture information, and muscle activities are generated such that the joint is stabilized at the equilibrium position [5] (Fig. 7.8).

To test this hypothesis, Bizzi and colleagues performed an experiment using a deafferent monkey [6]. If the hypothesis were correct, the hand position would move to the end point just before the motion. The hand would be there because the brain (in this hypothesis) sends commands to stabilize the hand at the end position. However, when they did the experiment, they obtained different results. The hand moved to the middle position and then to the end point. They concluded that the brain sends commands to gradually shift the hand to the end point. So it came to be thought that the brain plans trajectory. However, if the brain can estimate the sensor signals using the feedforward model of our arm, in which the efference copy is an input signal, the experimental result can be explained using a simple end-point control hypothesis.

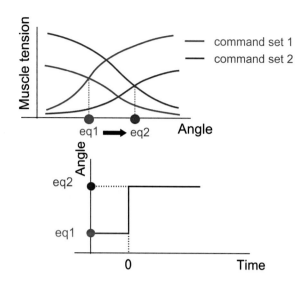

Fig. 7.8 Equilibrium control

7.4.5 Uniform Control Hypothesis

As mentioned in the previous section, we can change equilibrium position and stiffness independently. This means that we have a redundant control system. For example, in order to hold an object of weight m in hand, where the distance between the wrist joint and object position is d, and force F equals mg, the wrist must produce a torque of $mgd \cos \theta$ to compensate for the weight of the object. The brain changes the equilibrium position and stiffness to produce torque $\tau = K(\theta_{eq} - \theta)$, If the object's weight is known, it is easy to set the equilibrium position and stiffness. For familiar objects, stiffness is set to an appropriately low value, and the brain changes the equilibrium position depending on the object's weight. If the weight of the object is unknown, stiffness is controlled to the high value, and the difference between the equilibrium position and current position is small. High stiffness allows the hand to be stabilized even if the weight estimation is not completely accurate (Fig. 7.9).

7.4.6 Pseudo-haptic in 3D

The characteristics of pseudo-haptics have been tested for 2D motion on a frontal parallel screen. For virtual reality, binocular disparity is utilized by three dimensional displays. To determine the applicability of pseudo-haptics in virtual reality, the performance of pseudo-haptics in 3D space needed to be tested [7] (Fig. 7.10).

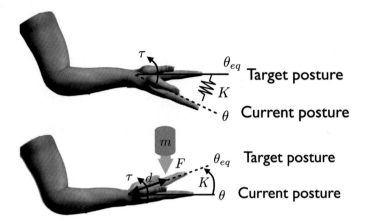

Fig. 7.9 Uniform control for motion and force

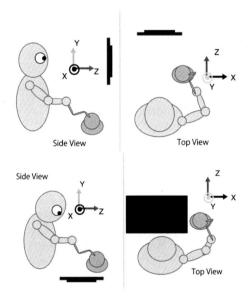

Fig. 7.10 Experimental setup

Results showed that the magnitude of pseudo-haptic sensation was reduced in the depth direction, compared to planar directions; i.e., discrimination of motion in the depth direction was decreased. This indicated that motion detection is important in perceiving pseudo-haptic sensation.

7.5 Pseudo-haptics by Stiffness

In Eq. 7.2, the spring constant is the ratio between force of hand and displacement on the screen, and it is similar to the C/D ratio. The stiffness of the musculoskeletal model can be estimated from EMG signals in real time and used to change weight perception. Co-contraction level can be modulated voluntarily, but it can also be non-voluntarily altered by environmental conditions. When we catch an object, stiffness level is dependent on the weight of the object [8]. Stiffness is low before contact, and increases just before contact onset. The maximum value of the stiffness is proportional to the weight of the object. If stiffness is related to weight perception, weight judgment would be different just before or after contact. To verify this hypothesis, we investigated the effect of temporal factors on weight perception [9]. We conducted ball-catching experiments in a virtual environment where the timing of load force exertion was shifted away from the visual contact timing (Fig. 7.11).

The perception of an object's heaviness is not only dependent on its weight. It is well known that spatial information of an object, such as size, can easily deceive our perception of its heaviness. To further understand neural mechanism underlying weight perception, we investigated effects of temporal information on the weight perception. We conducted experiments in which a falling ball is displayed on a screen and load force of the ball is exerted on the hand by a haptic device. By shifting the timing of load force exertion away from visual contact timing (i.e., time when the ball hit the hand in the display), we found that the ball was perceived heavier/lighter when force was applied earlier/later than visual contact. We also found that the illusion in perceived heaviness induced by the time offset between visual and haptic contact timing became smaller after participants had been conditioned to the time offset. These results suggest that the illusion found in our experiments was not caused by the physical time offset between force exertion and visual contact but by the perceived time offset between them and/or estimation error in force exertion timing.

7.5.1 Experimental Protocol

Six right-handed male adults (age: 21–39) took part in three experiments 1, 2, and 3, conducted on separate days. Experiment 1 was conducted to investigate how the time offset between load force exertion and visual contact affects perceived weight of the ball. In Experiments 2 and 3, we investigated how weight perception changes after participants were persistently exposed to constant time offsets. All participants performed Experiment 1 first. The order of Experiments 2 and 3 was randomized among all participants, with half performing Experiment 2 before 3 and the other half performing Experiment 2 after 3. Each experiment was organized into three sessions: "Conditioning", "Simultaneity Test", and "Weight Perception Test" sessions, presented in this order. Rest breaks of several minutes were taken between sessions.

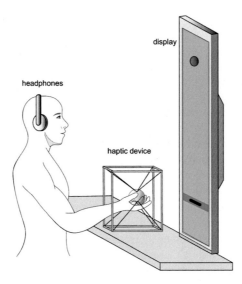

Fig. 7.11 Experiment system. A virtual *red ball* (radius = 2 cm) and a *black square cursor* (width = 10 cm, height = 2 cm) projecting the hand position in the vertical direction were displayed on a plasma display. Subjects held a ball-shaped plastic grip attached to a SPIDAR haptic device, which consisted of eight motors and strings. Load force was applied through tension in the strings by the motors. The grip position was calculated from angle encoders attached to the motors. Subjects wore a pair of noise-canceling headphones to reduce the sound generated by the motors of the haptic device

7.5.2 Conditioning Session

Participants performed 80 ball-catching trials in the Conditioning session. The inter-trial interval was 2 s. The sequence of events in a single trial is shown in Fig. 7.12. At the beginning of the trial, the ball appeared at 80 cm above the blue bar, accompanied with a beep sound, and started falling after a random delay. The ball load force was then applied with or without time offset from visual contact.

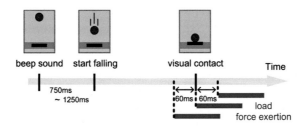

Fig. 7.12 The sequence of events in a single ball-catching trial during the Conditioning session. The load force is applied at the same time (Experiment 1), 60 ms before (Experiment 2), or 60 ms after (Experiment 3) the ball contacts the hand cursor in the display

In Experiment 1, the load force was synchronized with visual contact. In Experiment 2, the force was applied 60 ms before visual contact, and in Experiment 3, 60 ms after visual contact. The magnitude of load force was 3.92 N for all Conditioning sessions. This value was selected to simulate the feeling of catching a ball weighing 400 g. In accordance with the time offsets used in the three experiments, we denoted the Conditioning sessions as "sync" (Experiment1), "lead" (Experiment2), and "lag" (Experiment3).

7.5.3 Simultaneity Test Session

Each participant underwent 99 ball-catching trials in the Simultaneity Test session. The sequence of the events in a single trial was the same as that shown in Fig. 7.12, except for the time offset values. The offset for each trial was selected randomly from the list. The magnitude and the duration of load force in each trial were 3.92 N and 1 s. Just as in the Conditioning session, we asked the participants to counteract the load force to catch the virtual ball. The participants were instructed to make judgments about the temporal order of visual contact and force exertion. We asked them to report which event occurred first by pressing the left or right button of a computer mouse held in their left hands.

We instructed participants to counteract the load force so as to keep the black cursor within the blue bar as consistently as possible.

7.5.4 Weight Perception Test Session

In each of the three experiments, the Weight Perception Test session was organized into five sets. A single set was composed of 99 trials in Experiment 1, and 76 trials in Experiment 2 and 3. Rest breaks of several minutes were taken between sets. In

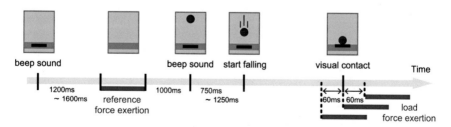

Fig. 7.13 The sequence of events in a single weight judgment trial during the Weight Perception Test session. After applying the constant magnitude reference force, participants performed ball-catching. The timing of load force exertion was chosen randomly from three candidates corresponding to the times simultaneous to (0 ms offset trials), 60 ms before (−60 ms offset trials), or 60 ms after (+60 ms offset trials) visual contact of the ball

Table 7.2 Load force values and frequencies in the Weight Perception Test session

Force magnitude [N] (appearance frequency for each time offset within a single set)								
2.94 (1)	3.185 (3)	3.43 (3)	3.675 (3)	3.92 (3)	4.165 (3)	4.41 (3)	4.655 (3)	4.9 (1)

each set, participants first performed 30 ball-catching trials without any perceptual judgment. The time offsets for the first 30 ball-catching trials were the same as those in the Conditioning session in each experiment. The rest of the trials were weight judgment trials in which participants were asked to compare the heaviness of the ball and a reference force. Figure 7.13 shows the time sequence of the events in a single weight judgment trial. At the beginning of the trial, the black cursor disappeared from the display, accompanied with a beep sound. After a random delay, a reference force with magnitude 3.92 N was applied for 1 s. After the 1 s time interval, the ball and the black cursor appeared with a second beep sound. Participants then performed the ball-catching task after a random delay ranging from 0.75 to 1.25 s. Time offset was again imposed between visual contact and load force exertion. Its value was selected randomly from one of the following values: −60, 0, or +60 ms in Experiment 1, −60 or 0 ms in Experiment 2, and 0 or +60 ms in Experiment 3. Here, negative or positive offset signs indicate that load force preceded or followed visual contact, respectively. Each offset appeared 23 times in every set. Magnitude of load force was also selected randomly. The magnitude values are listed in Table 7.2 with their appearance frequency for each time offset within a single set.

Participants were asked not to overcorrect for the reference force. The instructions for the ballcatching task were the same as those for the Conditioning session. After catching the ball, participants were required to judge the heaviness of the load force compared to the reference force. Participants reported which force they perceived as heavier by pressing the left or right button of a computer mouse.

After performing ball-catching trials with 60 ms advanced or delayed load force exertion, participants' subjective judgment on the simultaneity of visual contact and force exertion changed, reflecting a shift in perception of time offset. In addition, timing of catching motion initiation relative to visual contact changed, reflecting a shift in estimation of force timing. We also found that participants began to perceive the ball as lighter after conditioning to 60 ms advanced offset and heavier after the 60 ms delayed offset. These results suggest that perceived heaviness depends not on the actual time offset between force exertion and visual contact but on the subjectively perceived time offset between them and/or estimation error in force timing.

7.5.5 Perceptual Judgment Analysis

For the Simultaneity Test session, the judgment of participants was modeled to a psychometric curve. The probability of judging "load force preceding visual contact" was fitted with a sigmoid function,

$$prob(force\ first) = \frac{1}{1 + \exp(\theta_0 + \theta_1 \Delta t)}$$ (7.5)

where Δt is time offset, and θ_0 and θ_1 are the regression coefficients. A psychometric curve was made for each participant using their individual judgments. A group psychometric curve was also made from the judgments across all participants. The point of subjective simultaneity (PSS), where Δt gives $prob = 0.5$, can be calculated as PSS = $-\theta_0/\theta_1$.

For the Weight Perception Test session, the participants' judgments were again modeled to a psychometric curve. The probability of judging that "the ball was heavier than the reference force" was fitted with a sigmoid function,

$$prob(ball\ heavier) = \frac{1}{1 + \exp(\phi_0 + \phi_1 \Delta F)}$$ (7.6)

where ΔF is the percent difference in load force magnitude compared to that of the reference force and takes a negative value when the load force is comparatively smaller. Both individual and group psychometric curves were computed for each time offset used in each of the experiments. The point of subjective equality (PSE), where ΔF gives $prob = 0.5$, can be calculated as PSE = $-\phi_0/\phi_1$. The PSE indicates the magnitude of load force perceived to be the same as that of the reference force.

7.5.6 Result of Simultaneity

For the Simultaneity Test sessions, we analyzed how perception of the temporal order of the visual contact and load force events changed after three different types

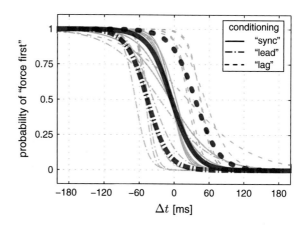

Fig. 7.14 Group-average psychometric curves after the three types of time offset conditioning. *Circles*, *squares*, and *triangles* represent the group-average probability for the "sync," "lead," and "lag" conditioning, respectively

of conditioning. Psychometric curves for each participant and each conditioning type are shown in Fig. 7.14. The subjective simultaneity of the two events was evaluated by the PSS of the psychometric curves (see Eq. 7.6). The average PSS across participants were −44.7 (SD: 14.0) ms, −4.5 (SD: 4.0) ms, and 36.5 (SD: 13.1) ms after the "lead", "sync", and "lag" conditionings, respectively. The group-average psychometric curves are also shown in Fig. 7.14. The curves for "lead" and "lag" conditioning were clearly shifted leftward and rightward, respectively, in comparison to "sync" conditioning. The PSS shifts for "lead" conditioning with respect to "sync" conditioning were −40.1 (SD: 15.2) ms averaged across participants. This was significantly less than zero according to a one-sided t-test. On the other hand, the PSS shifts for "lag" conditioning with respect to "sync" conditioning were 40.8 (SD: 15.4) ms averaged across participants. This was significantly greater than zero. Therefore, PSS shifted toward the direction of persistently exposed time offset during the Conditioning session.

Fig. 7.15 Weight judgment. **a** Psychometric curves for each participants after "sync" conditioning. *Line color* represents time offsets in weight judgment trials. **b** Group-average psychometric curves after "sync" (*solid lines*), "lead" (*dash-dotted lines*), and "lag" (*dotted lines*) conditionings

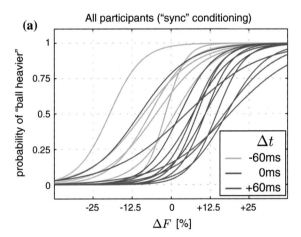

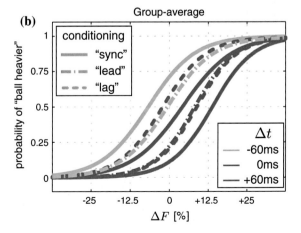

7.5.7 Result of Weight Perception

After "sync" conditioning.

Figure 7.15a shows each participant's psychometric curves of weight perception after "sync" conditioning. Although psychometric curves differed from participant to participant, they moved toward the right as offset increased from −60 ms to +60 ms. This tendency can be clearly seen in the plot of group-average psychometric curves (see solid lines in Fig. 7.15b). The psychometric curve shifts indicate that the same magnitude of load force was perceived differently as time offset changed. For example, when the load force magnitude was the same as that of the reference force ($\Delta F = 0\,\%$), the probability that participants perceived the ball heavier became larger as the offset became negative (i.e., the load force preceded).

The difference in perceived heaviness can also be evaluated by the difference in PSE of the psychometric curves (see Eq. 7.6). The average PSE across participants were $-6.9(SD : 7.2)\%$, $3.9(SD : 7.4)\%$, and $14.3(SD : 4.5)\%$ for −60, 0, +60 ms offset trials, respectively. Note that the smaller the PSE, the heavier the load force perceived. The average PSE shifts from 0 ms to −60 ms offset trials was $-10.7(SD : 3.5)\%$ and was significantly less than zero. The average PSE shifts from 0 ms to +60 ms offset trials was $10.4(SD : 9.7)\%$. This shift was significantly greater than zero. Therefore, load force exerted earlier than visual contact was perceived as heavier than that exerted at the same time as visual contact, and when the load force was exerted later than visual contact, it was perceived as lighter.

After "lead" and "lag" conditioning

Figure 7.15b shows group-average psychometric curves for the weight judgments in the three experiments. After "lead" conditioning, psychometric curves for both of −60 ms and 0 time offsets shifted toward the right compared for "sync" conditioning. The rightward shifts indicate that the participants perceived the ball's weight to be lighter. On the contrary, after "lad" conditioning, the curves for both of 0 ms and +60 ms time offsets shifted toward the left compared for "sync" conditioning. The leftward shifts indicate that the participants perceived the ball's weight to be heavier. Change in perceived weight was evaluated by PSE shifts averaged across participants. The average PSE shifts from "sync" to "lead" conditionings were $6.2(SD : 5.3)\%$ and $4.1(SD : 9.4)\%$ for −60 ms offset trials and 0 ms offset trials, respectively. The PSE shift for −60ms offset trials was significantly greater than zero ($t(5) = 2.84; P = 0.018$). Although the PSE shift for 0ms offset trials was not significantly greater than zero, it tended to shift rightward. The average PSE shifts from "sync" to "lag" conditionings were $-6.2(SD : 3.0)\%$ and $-5.2(SD : 3.9)\%$, for 0 ms and +60 ms offset trials, respectively. Those shifts were significantly less than zero. These results indicate that the participants' ball weight perception was changed by being conditioned to time offset between load force exertion and visual contact. The participants began to perceive the ball's weight as lighter after "lead" conditioning and heavier after "lag" conditioning.

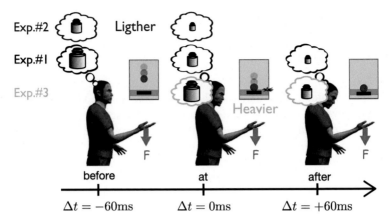

Fig. 7.16 Weight judgment results

We found that subjects weight perception changed after conditioning to time offset (Fig. 7.16). The weight was perceived lighter after conditioning to the −60 ms time offset, and perceived heavier after conditioning to the −60 ms time offset. Therefore, time offset itself was not the causal factor for the weight illusion.

7.5.8 Relationship Between PSE and PSS

The results of the weight judgment trials in Experiment 1 revealed that the weight of the falling ball was perceived differently by introducing time offsets between load force exertion and visual contact (Fig. 7.15). In Experiment 2 and 3, we also found that the weight of the ball was perceived differently after "lead" and "lag" conditioning, even though the time offsets were the same as those used in the weight judgment trials in Experiment 1 (Fig. 7.15). Therefore, the perceived weight illusion observed in Experiment 1 seems not to be related to actual physical time offset between visual contact and load force exertion. Rather, the illusion in weight perception seems to be connected to the participants' subjective perception of time offset. This subjective time offset is thought to be modified by shifts in PSS after "lead" and "lag" conditioning. To show how perceived weight is related to physical or subjective time offset, the PSEs of group-average psychometric curves shown in Fig. 7.15 are plotted with respect to their corresponding physical or subjective offsets (Fig. 7.17). Here the subjective time offsets were calculated by subtracting the PSS of the group-average psychometric curve in each experiment from the physical time offsets used in the Weight Perception Test session in each experiment. We can see that the same physical offset yielded different PSE values (black open marks). On the other hand, PSE values plotted with respect to subjective offset (gray filled marks) increased approximately linearly with subjective offset value. The correlation coefficient of PSS and subjective time lag was 0.98.

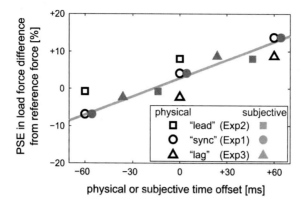

Fig. 7.17 PSEs of group-average psychometric curves for weight judgments in all experiments are plotted with respect to actual (physical) time offsets as black unfilled marks. PSEs are also plotted as gray filled marks with respect to subjective time offsets (physical offset minus PSS of group-average psychometric curves for temporal simultaneity). Shapes of the marks represent the Conditioning sessions. The *gray solid line* is a linear regression of the gray marks

7.5.9 Relationship Between PSE and Estimation of Error in Force Exertion Timing

In addition to the subjective perception of time offset, the estimation of force exertion timing in sensorimotor system also seems to be modified after "lead" and "lag" conditioning. Here we analyze the relationship between perceived weight and estimation error in force exertion timing. Although we cannot directly measure the estimation of force exertion timing, we can infer it from the motion initiation timing relative to visual contact. Let us assume that ball-catching motions are initiated some fixed second in advance of the estimated timing of force exertion. This assumption is supported by other experiments in which the timings of muscle activity and catching motion were found to be consistently initiated a few hundred millisecond before the ball contacts the hand [10–14]. We also assume that the margin between the motion initiation timing and the estimated timing varied among participants, but did not change within a single participant in the three experiments. According to these assumptions, we inferred changes in the estimation of force timing by analyzing changes in the motion initiation timing relative to visual contact. Figure 7.18 plots the PSEs of group-average psychometric curves shown in Fig. 7.15 against the estimation error in load force exertion timing. Note that we assumed that there was no estimation error in 0 ms offset trials after "sync" conditioning (Experiment 1). The estimation error was then calculated by subtracting group-average motion initiation timing in each experiment from the sum of time offset and group-average motion initiation timing in Experiment 1. For example, the estimation error in +60 ms off-

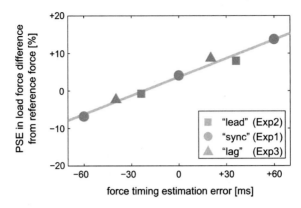

Fig. 7.18 PSEs of group-average psychometric curves for weight judgments in all experiments are plotted with respect to the estimation error in load force exertion timing. The estimation error for α ms offset trials in Experiment β was calculated by subtracting group-average motion initiation timing in Experiment β from the sum of α ms offset and group-average motion initiation timing in Experiment 1

set trials in Experiment 3 was 20.1 ($= 60 + (-75.3) - (-35.9)$), where the values of -75.3 and -35.9 ms correspond to group-average motion initiation timings in Experiment 1 and 3, respectively (values of group-average motion initiation timing in each experiment is described in Sect. 7.2). We can see that the PSE values increased almost linearly with the estimation error. The correlation coefficient of PSE and the estimation error was 0.99.

7.6 Representation of Motion in the Brain

Stiffness is closely related to weight perception (described in Sect. 7.5.9). But where is stiffness information represented in the brain? Muscle activations are represented in the primary motor cortex. But stiffness of the hand is related to either joint coordinates or environmental coordinates. Understanding the coordinate systems employed by the brain is crucial to uncovering the mechanisms of weight perception.

The brain allows skillful manipulation of the body to interact with the external environment. This sophisticated and flexible operation involves transformations between coordinate systems of the internal body and external environment, possibly computed in distributed brain regions. The internal coordinate system is body- and/or joint-centered, and may thus be represented intrinsically, whereas the external coordinate system refers to points outside the body.

The representation of intrinsic (i.e., joint) and extrinsic (i.e., movement) coordinate frames were analyzed using functional magnetic resonance imaging (fMRI). During fMRI acquisition, healthy human participants performed isometric flexion and extension tasks (Fig. 7.19) in different forearm postures. In a pronated posture

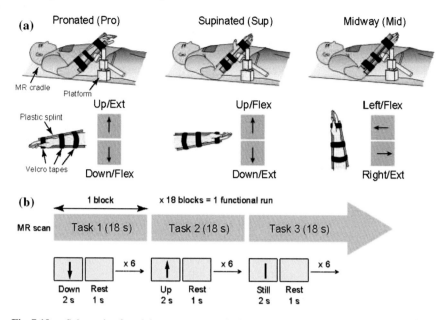

Fig. 7.19 **a** Schematic of participant postures and relation between movement directions and tasks according to visual instructions in three different wrist postures. **b** Block design for the fMRI experiment

(Pro), an upward force exertion was equivalent to an extension task and cued with an up arrow (Up/Ext), whereas a downward force exertion was equivalent to a flexion task and cued with a down arrow (Down/Flex) (Fig. 7.19a, left panel). In a supinated posture (Sup), an upward force exertion was equivalent to a flexion task and cued with an up arrow (Up/Flex), whereas a downward force exertion was equivalent to an extension task and cued with a down arrow (Down/Ext (Fig. 7.19a, center panel).

In a midway posture between Pro and Sup (Mid), a leftward force exertion was equivalent to a flexion task and cued with a left arrow (Left/Flex), whereas a rightward force exertion was equivalent to an extension task and cued with a right arrow (Right/Ext) (Fig. 7.19a, right panel).

Figure 7.19b shows the block design for the fMRI experiment. Execution tasks (Flex and Ext) were instructed with up and down arrows (in Pro and Sup) or left and right arrows (in Mid) inside a gray box, and a no-force task (Still) was instructed with a vertical bar (in Pro and Sup) or a horizontal bar (in Mid).

Figure 7.20a shows an accuracies for Flex versus Ext classification and Up versus Down classification using Pro and Sup data. Gray bars represent mean accuracies of 10 participants (Participant 1–10) calculated using 6-fold cross validation and black bars represent grand mean accuracies averaged across participants. Error bars denote standard deviation. There was no significant difference between the grand mean accuracies of the two classifications. The obtained classifiers were considered direction-specific (left group; Up vs. Down classification) and join-specific

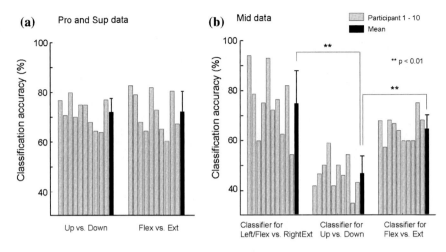

Fig. 7.20 **a** Accuracy for Flex versus Ext classification and up versus down classification using Pro and Sup data. **b** Classification accuracy using Mid data

(right group; Flex vs. Ext classification) classifiers. Figure 7.20b shows the classification accuracies using Mid data. Gray bars are accuracies of 10 participants (Participant 1–10) and black bars are grand mean accuracies averaged across participants. The trained classifier did not specifically discriminate joint action (Flex vs. Ext) or movement direction (Left vs. Right), but discriminated mixed joint action and movement direction features (Left/Flex vs. Right/Ext) since only Mid data was used for classifier training. Results using direction-specific (Up vs. Down) classifiers for each participant (gray bars) and grand mean accuracy averaged across participants (a black bar). The direction-specific classifier for each participant was the mean of 6 classifiers obtained from 6-fold cross validation using Pro and Sup data (Fig. 7.20a, left group). Results using joint-specific (Flex vs. Ext) classifiers for each participant (gray bars) and grand mean accuracy averaged across participants (a black bar). The joint-specific classifier for each participant was the mean of 6 classifiers obtained from 6-fold cross validation using Pro and Sup data (Fig. 7.20a, right group).

Mean contribution ratios of intrinsic and extrinsic coordination in four ROIs, primary motor cortex hand knob (M1), ventral premotor area (PMv), dorsal premotor area (PMd), and supplementary motor area (SMA), were calculated and averaged across participants.

The motor-related cortical regions identified in the current study match those of prior studies in this field. More specifically, our results revealed that intrinsic coordination was mainly associated with M1, while extrinsic coordination was mainly associated with PMv, PMd, and SMA. This is reasonable, considering the layered organization of the cerebral cortex and signal pathways to M1, PM and SMA. Since M1 transmits output signals to the muscles through a number of layers, the selection of flexion and extension tasks, which is associated with only internal body control, may be represented in M1. At the same time, the other layers of M1 receive input

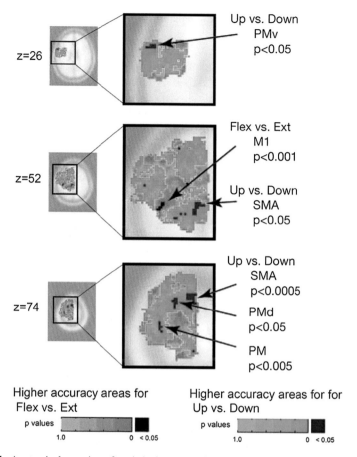

Fig. 7.21 Anatomical mapping of statistical group analysis results

from PM, SMA, and cingulate motor area, which may be the reason why direction of movement is encoded not only in PM regions but also in M1 [15, 16]. This in turn would explain why, in our analysis, 39 % of M1 voxels showed contribution to extrinsic coordination in Fig. 7.21. Prior studies have shown that PMv represents direction of action [15–17], but others suggest that premotor areas operate at a hierarchical level comparable to M1 since they appear to have direct connections with spinal motoneurons, particularly those innervating hand muscles [1, 18]. In this respect, our results replicated these findings, and we can explain why statistically significant clusters were not found in the PMv-ROI while a relatively high amount of PMv voxels (i.e., 42 %) contributed to intrinsic coordination (Fig. 7.21). PMv is considered to be involved in visuomotor transformations [19, 20], and we believe our results support this view. Tasks in our experiment were cued with graphical arrows. Thus, visuomotor transformations from direction information in the external world to action information in the internal body would be necessary. In addition, a path of visuo-motor transformations required for grasping connects the dorsal extrastriate cortex and PMv via the anterior intraparietal area [21]. Although our experimental tasks were not finger movements, similar information may be processed for wrist flexion and extension. PMv then outputs visuomotor transformed information to M1, which may also explain the 42 % contribution by PMv to intrinsic coordination. Rizzolatti and colleagues also showed that a path of visuomotor transformations required for reaching connects the parieto-occipital extrastriate area and PMd separately from the path required for grasping [21]. Since, in the current study, PMd showed a 70 % contribution to extrinsic coordination, reaching and wrist flexion and extension may also share similar information. Other studies have also revealed that PMd is associated with motor planning and initiation [22, 23] and action prediction [24]. Considering the experimental design of the current study, participants performed tasks according to periodic visual stimuli and had to memorize the relationship between each task and respective cue. Therefore, participants might have naturally predicted and prepared for the next task, which would attribute to PMd activation. Therefore, these brain activities might be necessary for both joint action and movement direction.

7.7 Applications of a Sense-Centered Human Interface

7.7.1 TCieX

We developed a sense-centered human interface named the Touch-Centric Interaction Embodiment Exploratorium (TCieX) [25]. This system uses visual interaction to communicate weight, stiffness, or viscosity by exploiting pseudo-haptics in human-computer interaction. TCieX is a collection of simple interaction test suites that allow experience of different combinations of multimodal interactions. This system measures the hand motion and pressure on a display and biological signals (e.g. EMG signals) simultaneously to control cursor position, velocity, and acceleration (Fig. 7.22).

An illusory sense of haptics also occurs with the combination of these signals.

Fig. 7.22 TCieX by iPad®

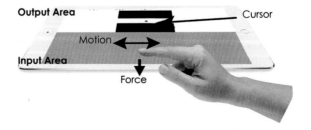

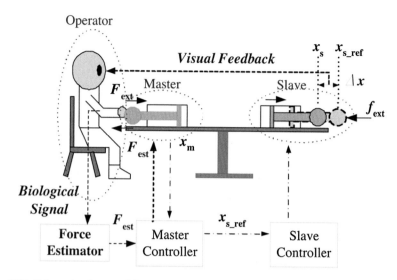

Fig. 7.23 Schematic of external force estimation by biological signals

7.7.2 Surgery Robot

The da Vinci Surgical System® (Intuitive Surgical, Sunnyvale, CA) is one of the most well-known robot surgery systems. A 3D high definition vision system provides a clear and magnified view for the surgeon. The surgeon manipulates a master robot to intuitively control a slave robot. The master-slave robot system translates hand motion into smaller, more precise motion without haptic information. It is technically feasible to add haptic sensation to the slave robot arm, but difficult to add force-torque sensors because the tip of the slave robot is disposable to maintain sterility. Force feedback is useful to prevent user fatigue. For this reason, force feedback without force sensors has been developed [26, 27].

Figure 7.23 shows a schematic for estimation of external force. The operator can see the motion of the slave arm, and the stiffness of the slave is constant (K_{slave}).

$$F_{hand} = \delta x_{slave} \times K_{slave} \tag{7.7}$$

This allows the operator to estimate the force of the slave robot. Our sense-centered human interface provides an alternative means of acquiring force sensation [28].

7.7.3 Power-Assist Robot

The conventional power-assist robot is controlled by torque, which is estimated from EMG signals. The power is proportional to the contraction level. However, this

Fig. 7.24 Power-assist robot
using equilibrium-based
control

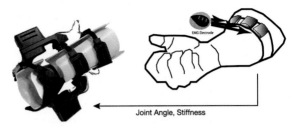

Fig. 7.25 Equilibrium-based
control is more stable than
the conventional
torque-based control

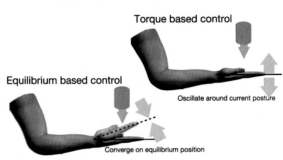

kind system is liable to become unstable particularly during posture control. Our
new control method based on equilibrium position (described in Sect. 7.4.3) offers
greater stability than conventional methods.

When holding an object, hand position is kept at the same position. The co-
contraction level can also change while keeping the same posture. This means that
the command scheme has redundancy, and another parameter exists for control.
Our arm can be modeled as a mass-spring-damper system using muscle spring-
like properties. Hand force can be defined as $Force = K_{springconstant} \times (x_0 - x) - B_{viscosity}\dot{x}$, where x_0 is the estimated position from EMG activity and represent
equilibrium position. Values x and $\dot{x}$ are current position and velocity measured by
the position sensor of the motor. Figure 7.24 shows a power-assist robot with position
and impedance controlled by EMG of the forearm.

The conventional method of control uses joint torque estimated from EMG. During
posture control, stabilization of posture is achieved by exerting joint torque. Power-
assist systems enhance this exertion, and this causes positional errors, which can
be observed as oscillatory motion. In our system, joint torque is exerted toward the
equilibrium position [14] (Fig. 7.25).

7.8 Conclusion

Sense-centered human interfaces have the potential to influence perception by
exploiting the intricacies of the brain's sensory systems. Yet further development

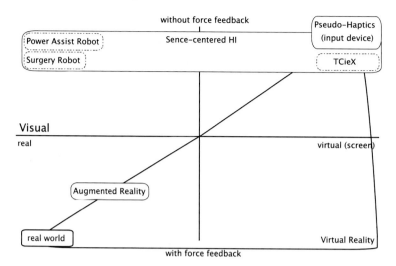

Fig. 7.26 Matrix map of virtual reality from the standpoint of force feedback

of body and brain models, sensor devices, and signal processing techniques, as well as more quantitative evaluations of the perception is needed.

The techniques described here offer a framework for new human-interfaces as well as new humanoid robots capable of detecting sensation as humans do, allowing them to work in environments meant for humans.

Figrue 7.26 shows a matrix map of virtual reality techniques from the standpoint of force feedback. The horizontal axis indicates visual information, real or virtual. The vertical axis indicates force feedback. Virtual reality (VR) replicates the real world by providing sensory and visual feedback using computer-simulated devices.

Tele-operation is a prime example of a VR system. Visual information from a camera is real, but we cannot touch what is displayed. So haptic devices reproduce force feedback, which is measured by a force-torque sensor. VR allows for the replication of a broad range of real-world sensations in a virtual world.

Pseudo-haptics is a technique for simulating haptic sensation using visual feedback without a haptic device. Our sense-centered human interface also provides haptic sensation without haptic device, but the difference between them is the type of input information. Pseudo-haptics uses input information which corresponds to the output signal. C/D ratio is a ratio of output to input. Our system also uses sensor signals, but the equilibrium position or stiffness does not directly correspond to the output information. Also these types of information are typically controlled unconsciously.

When we push a button, the force used depends on the person. The number of possible input key combinations of a 4-digit passcode is 10^4. If two different levels of force are added to the system, the number of possible combinations increases to 20^4 [29]. Applied force for pushing buttons is usually controlled unconsciously, is consistent over time, and differs between people, making it potentially useful in security applications. Force sensors are effective in measuring force for human interface applications. But EMG signals reflect not only force information, but also stiffness and equilibrium position. Sense-centered human interfaces based on EMG can be used to estimate subjective perception and enhance sensation.

Acknowledgments This research was supported by CREST Creation of Human-Harmonized Information Technology for Convivial Society. I thank my colleagues, Dr. Kumiyo Nakakoji, Dr. Masahiro Ishii, and Dr. Kenji Kawashima, for providing invaluable insight and expertise.

References

1. R.K. Eric, J.H. Schwartz, T.M. Jessell, *Principles of Neural Science*, vol. 4 (2000)
2. J. MacDonald, H. McGurk, Visual influences on speech perception processes. Percept. Psychophys. **24**(3), 253–257 (1978)
3. A. Lécuyer, Simulating haptic feedback using vision: a survey of research and applications of pseudo-haptic feedback. Presence: Teleoperators Virtual Environ. **18**(1), 39–53 (2009)
4. A. Lécuyer, S. Coquillart, A. Kheddar, P. Richard, P. Coiffet, Pseudo-haptic feedback: can isometric input devices simulate force feedback? in *Proceedings IEEE Virtual Reality 2000 (Cat. No.00CB37048)* (2000)
5. E. Bizzi, A. Polit, P. Morasso, Mechanisms underlying achievement of final head position. J. Neurophysiol. **39**(2), 435–444 (1976)
6. E. Bizzi, N. Accornero, W. Chapple, N. Hogan, Arm trajectory formation in monkeys. Experimental brain research. Experimentelle Hirnforschung. Experimentation Cerebrale **46**(1), 139–143 (1982)
7. M. Ishii, S. Sato, Pseudo-Haptics in three-dimensional space. ITE Trans. Media Technol. Appl. **66**(6), J188–J191 (2012)
8. Y. Koike, K. Jaehyo, D. Shin, Role of stiffness in weight perception. Jap. Psychol. Res. **48**(3), 174–187 (2006)
9. H. Kambara, D. Shin, T. Kawase, N. Yoshimura, K. Akahane, M. Sato, Y. Koike, The effect of temporal perception on weight perception. Frontiers Psychol. 4(FEB), 1–14 (2013)
10. F. Lacquaniti, C. Maioli, The role of preparation in tuning anticipatory and reflex responses during catching. J. Neurosci. Official J. Soc. Neurosci. **9**(1), 134–148 (1989)
11. M. Zago, G. Bosco, V. Maffei, M. Iosa, Y.P. Ivanenko, F. Lacquaniti, Internal models of target motion: expected dynamics overrides measured kinematics in timing manual interceptions. J. Neurophysiol. **91**(4), 1620–1634 (2004)
12. S. Hong, J. Kim, M. Sato, Y. Koike, A research of human s time-to-contact prediction model for ball catching task. (7), 1246–1256 (2005)
13. H. Kambara, K. Ohishi, Y. Koike, Learning strategy in time-to-contact estimation of falling objects. J. Adv. Comput. Intell. Intell. Inf. **15**(8), 972–979 (2011)
14. T. Kawase, H. Kambara, Y. Koike, A power assist device based on joint equilibrium point estimation from EMG signals. J. Robot. Mechatron. **24**(1), 205–218 (2012)
15. M. Eisenberg, L. Shmuelof, E. Vaadia, E. Zohary, Functional organization of human motor cortex: directional selectivity for movement. J. Neurosci. Official J. Soc. Neurosci. **30**(26), 8897–8905 (2010)
16. C.M. Toxopeus, B.M. de Jong, G. Valsan, B.A. Conway, K.L. Leenders, N.M. Maurits, Direction of movement is encoded in the human primary motor cortex. PLoS ONE **6**(11), (2011)
17. S. Kakei, D.S. Hoffman, P.L. Strick, Direction of action is represented in the ventral premotor cortex. Nat. Neurosci. **4**(10), 1020–1025 (2001)
18. R.P. Dum, P.L. Strick, Motor areas in the frontal lobe of the primate. Physiol. Behav. **77**(4–5), 677–682 (2002)

19. F. Lacquaniti, Visuo-motor transformations for arm reaching. Eur. J. Neurosci. **10**(1), 195–203 (1998)
20. N. Picard, P.L. Strick, *Imaging the Premotor Areas* (2001)
21. G. Rizzolatti, G. Luppino, M. Matelli, *The Organization of the Cortical Motor System: New Concepts* (1998)
22. J. Duque, L. Labruna, S. Verset, E. Olivier, R.B. Ivry, *Dissociating the Role of Prefrontal and Premotor Cortices in Controlling Inhibitory Mechanisms during Motor Preparation* (2012)
23. T. Hanakawa, M.A. Dimyan, M. Hallett, Motor planning, imagery, and execution in the distributed motor network: a time-course study with functional MRI. Cereb. Cortex **18**(12), 2775–2788 (2008)
24. W. Stadler, D.V.M. Ott, A. Springer, R.I. Schubotz, S. Schütz-Bosbach, W. Prinz, *Repetitive TMS Suggests a Role of the Human Dorsal Premotor Cortex in Action Prediction* (2012)
25. K. Nakakoji, TCieX : an environment for designing and experiencing a variety of visuo-haptic sensory conflicts, in *Proceedings of the 3rd IEEE VR2011 Workshop on PIVE 2011, number Pive* (2011), pp. 23–26
26. K. Tadano, K. Kawashima, *Development of a MasterSlave System with Force-Sensing Abilities using Pneumatic Actuators for Laparoscopic Surgery* (2010)
27. H. Li, K. Kawashima, K. Tadano, S. Ganguly, S. Nakano, Achieving haptic perception in forceps manipulator using pneumatic artificial muscle. IEEE/ASME Trans. Mechatron. **18**(1), 74–85 (2013)
28. Yu. Okamoto, K. Tadano, T. K. Kawashima, K. Words, A basic study on biological signal of master-salve system operator. J. Robot. Mechatron. **24**(5), 908–916 (2012)
29. K. Zintus-art, D. Shin, N. Yoshimura, H. Kambara, Advanced mobile security system operated by bioelectrical sensor. **8**(4), 139–150 (2014)

Chapter 8
Sensing and Controlling Human Gaze in Daily Living Space for Human-Harmonized Information Environments

Yoichi Sato, Yusuke Sugano, Akihiro Sugimoto, Yoshinori Kuno and Hideki Koike

Abstract This chapter introduces new techniques we developed for sensing and guiding human gaze non-invasively in daily living space. Such technologies are the key to realize human-harmonized information systems which can provide us various kinds of supports effectively without distracting our activities. Toward the goal of realizing non-invasive gaze sensing, we developed gaze estimation techniques, which requires very limited or no calibration effort by exploiting various cues such as spontaneous attraction of our visual attention to visual stimuli. For shifting our gaze to desired locations in a non-disturbing and natural way, we exploited two approaches for gaze control: subtle modulation of visual stimuli based on visual saliency models, and non-verbal gestures in human-robot interactions.

Keywords Appearance-based gaze sensing · Calibration-free gaze estimation · Visual saliency · Gaze guidance

Y. Sato (✉)
Institute of Industrial Science, The University of Tokyo, 4-6-1 Komaba,
Meguro-ku, Tokyo, Japan
e-mail: ysato@iis.u-tokyo.ac.jp

Y. Sugano
Max Planck Institute for Informatics, 66123 Saarbrücken, Germany
e-mail: sugano@mpi-inf.mpg.de

A. Sugimoto
National Institute of Informatics, 2-1-2 Hitotsubashi, Chiyoda-ku, Tokyo, Japan
e-mail: sugimoto@nii.ac.jp

Y. Kuno
Saitama University, 255 Shimo-Okubo, Sakura-ku, Saitama, Japan
e-mail: kuno@cv.ics.saitama-u.ac.jp

H. Koike
Tokyo Institute of Technology, 2-12-1 Ookayama, Meguro-ku, Tokyo, Japan
e-mail: koike@cs.titech.ac.jp

© Springer Japan 2016
T. Nishida (ed.), *Human-Harmonized Information Technology, Volume 1*,
DOI 10.1007/978-4-431-55867-5_8

199

8.1 Introduction

When we interact with other people to support or collaborate with them in various situations in our daily lives, we always pay close attention to what other people are attended to. With such awareness of other people's attention, we are able to decide when to interrupt and, if necessary, provide support to other people without distracting them. The awareness of attention is also expected to play a key role in realizing natural human-machine interactions. Therefore, a human-harmonized information system should be capable of sensing our attention in a non-invasive manner, so that the system can provide us various supports without distracting our activities. Moreover, we argue that, not only sensing human attention, human-harmonized information systems should be able to guide our attention naturally at appropriate timing to a desired location.

This motivated us to develop novel techniques for sensing and guiding human attention in a non-invasive manner. This chapter describes the outcome of our CREST project toward the goal, more specifically, remote gaze sensing methods that require less or no calibration effort (Sect. 8.2), gaze guidance based on visual saliency and its application (Sect. 8.3), and gaze guidance by a humanoid robot with non-verbal behaviors (Sect. 8.4).

8.2 Human Gaze Sensing in Daily-Life Environments

The goal of gaze estimation is to determine where a person is looking at. While we need to rely on head orientation as a rough indicator of human gaze in far-distance settings such as surveillance camera systems [5], observing eyes is the most direct way to infer the target person's gaze. Because of its wide variety of application fields ranging from scientific studies to practical applications, various eye gaze estimation techniques have been studied for many years [16]. However, existing techniques still have some critical limitations affecting the easiness of use, which is one of the most important properties required for a gaze estimation technique in daily-life environments.

In this section, we introduce our research attempts on appearance-based gaze estimation. In Sect. 8.2.1, we discuss the core technique of appearance-based method that require only a remote camera to estimate eye gaze directions. In Sect. 8.2.2, we further introduce approaches to make appearance-based methods *calibration-free*, working without any personal calibration actions.

8.2.1 Appearance-Based Gaze Estimation

In general, remote gaze estimation techniques have a great advantage that they do not require users to wear special devices. Existing remote gaze techniques can be mainly categorized into either model-based or appearance-based approaches. Model-based approaches estimate pose of a geometric eyeball model using high-resolution eye cameras and additional light sources. While they can achieve relatively higher accuracy and are taken in commercial eye trackers, it often requires specialized hardware such as high-resolution close-up cameras and additional light sources. In contrast, appearance-based approaches only require eye images and thus have an advantage when only low-resolution images are available as input.

The biggest limitation of appearance-based gaze estimation is that it requires relatively larger amount of calibration data to establish the estimation function. In this section, we introduce the adaptive linear regression (ALR) method to reduce the required number of training samples [30]. This can be realized by introducing more effective regression algorithms via ℓ^1-minimization that can work with sparse training samples.

8.2.1.1 Adaptive Linear Regression

Eye Feature Extraction

Existing appearance-based methods generate the eye image feature from a captured image by raster scanning all its pixels, thus the typical feature dimensionality reaches several thousand [46] or even higher (e.g. edge map is added in [51]). On one hand, a high-dimensional feature keeps all the information in the image. On the other hand, since gaze directions have only two degrees of freedom, such high-dimensional features are highly redundant. Moreover, actually captured eye regions can be of variant resolutions, and therefore, pixel-wise feature extraction faces the problem of inconsistent output dimensions.

We use a low-dimensional feature extraction method consisting of two steps: eye region alignment and feature generation. In the first step, the eye regions are accurately aligned for different eye images. The inner and outer eye corners from an anchor eye image are first detected by an edge filter. Then the eye corner regions are stored as image templates to match the eye corners of other eye images, and finally align the eye region.

In the feature generation step, once the aligned eye image region is obtained, it is further divided into 15 even subregions, as shown in Fig. 8.1. Then the feature vector

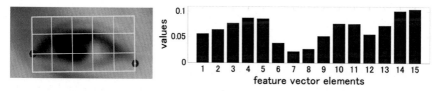

Fig. 8.1 Eye appearance feature extraction. *Left* Illustration of eye corner detection and 3×5 subregion division. *Right* Generated 15-D feature vector (Reproduced with permission of © 2014 IEEE [30].)

is generated by summarizing pixel values in each subregions and combining them to form a unique feature vector.

Eye Appearance Manifold

All the eye appearance features, which are extracted from the accurately aligned image regions, constitute a manifold in the high dimensional space. Since the eyeball movement has only two degrees of freedom, the manifold has an intrinsic dimensionality of close to two. To test this statement, we project all the features onto a 3-D space by PCA for visualization, as shown in Fig. 8.2. Several observations can be made here. First, the eye feature manifold can be approximated as a 2-D surface with most of its information accumulating inside the first two major dimensions. Second, the proposed 15-D feature well keeps more information in the first three major dimensions (Fig. 8.2c) than the pixel-wise extracted feature (Fig. 8.2b). Therefore, although the manifold in Fig. 8.2b seems smoother, the information can be hidden in other dimensions. Finally but most importantly, the projected features on the manifolds in Fig. 8.2b, c show a similar pattern to the gaze positions in Fig. 8.2a.

Local Regression via Interpolation

Following these observations, without any prior knowledge, unknown gaze positions can be found by using linear interpolation by assuming locality, i.e. limiting the interpolation within a sufficient small region centered by the unknown sample in the manifold. The existing methods [46] guarantee this locality assumption by obtaining dense training samples, from which they select some training samples with the smallest Euclidean distances from the unknown for interpolation. However, if the training samples are only sparsely collected, as shown in Fig. 8.2, the local linearity assumption cannot be satisfied. Therefore, problem with sparse training samples motivates our methods. Our idea is to adaptively find an optimal set of training samples that best reconstruct the test image linearly, and we show that by using the same

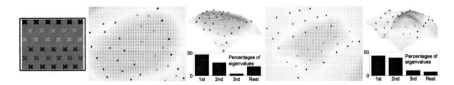

Fig. 8.2 2-D gaze space and eye appearance feature manifold. *Left* Illustration of 33 gaze positions on 2-D screen. *Middle* Projection of corresponding eye appearance manifold on 3-D space. The magnitudes of the eigenvalues are shown as percentages. *Right* Illustration of manifold projection for our proposed 15-D low dimensional feature. Notice the similarity between the gaze positions on the screen and the feature coordinates on the manifold (Reproduced with permission of © 2014 IEEE [30].)

linear combination, gaze estimation can be done accurately without requiring dense training data.

The idea is to take into consideration all the training samples at first, and then adaptively choose some of them in interpolation. The way to do the choosing is to use the ℓ^1-minimization. In particular, our interpolation can be written in a standard matrix multiplication form, where the weights tell how much each training sample contributes. If one weight is zero, it means the corresponding training sample is not selected, and vice versa. In addition, we put a constraint in our formulation so that the summation of all weights is always one, and we also have an ε to control the the interpolation error. These weights are optimized by using any of the efficient ℓ^1 solvers and then used to compute the unknown gaze position via interpolation.

ℓ^1-minimization has been used in previous vision-related researches, among which the works by Wright et al. [52], Wagner et al. [49] and Tan et al. [47] share similarities to ours. However, our work essentially differs in some aspects. First, they apply face recognition, which is a classification problem, while we handle a typical regression problem. In this sense, our focus is not discriminability but accurate estimation, and we newly show the effectiveness of ℓ^1-optimization-based method in handling a regression problem. Second, Wright et al. [52] also introduce an error term ε without mentioning how to determine its value. However, we find that the ε value is crucial to our solution and should be carefully chosen, while it is not the case for classification problems. As a result, we dynamically optimize ε by checking whether the ℓ^1 norm of our weights is equal to one. Another difference is that [52] assumes sparsity in reconstruction errors while we assume fewer supporting training samples for optimal representation for a query image.

Evaluation

We evaluate the estimation accuracy of the basic ALR method in this section. Details of the experimental setups and approaches include:

- **Training samples**. The training samples were sparsely collected in four sets with totals of 9, 18, 23, and 33.
- **Test samples**. For each training set, nearly 100 test samples were collected whose gaze positions were randomly chosen on the screen.
- **Dataset size**. The four sets of training/test samples were collected for each of the seven subjects.
- **Fixed head pose**. A chin rest was used to help stabilize the users' heads.
- **Eye image alignment**. With fixed head poses, the eye regions were directly cropped from the same region for all images.
- **Feature**. In our case, 15-D features were extracted with 3×5 subregions as described above. While for other methods in comparison, different features were generated and used as they proposed.

We compare the proposed ALR method with some latest appearance-based methods in terms of gaze position estimation accuracy. These methods were proposed by

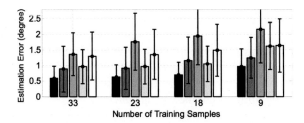

Fig. 8.3 Comparison of average gaze estimation results. For each number of training samples, results of ALR, local region [46], PCA+GPR [34], HOG+SVR [31], and CSLBP+GPR [28] are shown from *left* to *right* (Reproduced with permission of © 2014 IEEE [30].)

using different feature descriptors as and regression techniques [28, 31, 34, 46]. We use the same dataset to test their performances. As a result, their average estimation errors and their standard deviations are given in Fig. 8.3. The proposed method shows the highest estimation accuracy in different experimental conditions. In general, it achieved estimation accuracies of better than 1°. As for other methods, although they use more complex descriptors and different regression techniques, their accuracies are clearly not as good as ours in the conditions of sparse training samples.

8.2.1.2   Allowing Free Head Motion

Another major limitation of the appearance-based methods lies in that most of them assume a fixed head pose. This limitation is hard to remove because the head motion has 6 degrees of freedom which must be handled by more training data. Therefore directly solving the problem requires a prohibitively large number of training samples.

To effectively solve this problem while significantly reduce the training cost, we also proposed an approach extending the ALR method [29]. In this method, we initially estimate the gaze direction under the fixed head pose as introduced above, and then apply a series of rotations to the head coordinate system so that the gaze direction error caused by geometric head rotation can be compensated. We further investigate the relationship between the changes of head directions and the biases of gaze estimations caused by eye appearance distortions, and propose an additional calibration process using a 5 s video clip. This achieves the average estimation accuracy of 2.4° under free head motion without using complex devices such as infrared/stereo cameras/lights and pan-tilt units.

8.2.2   Calibration-Free Gaze Estimation

One of the biggest limitation of existing gaze estimation techniques is that they require person-specific calibration. As discussed in the previous section, the calibration is in general done by showing some gaze targets to the target user and acquiring eye images with ground-truth gaze directions. Since the calibration process requires an active participation of the user and makes natural gaze estimation impossible, it can bring a strong constraint on the application scenarios. Calibration drift is another issue that is shared among existing techniques, and their performances significantly decrease when the condition becomes different from the initial calibration setting. In this subsection, we introduce two different calibration-free gaze estimation approaches to address this problem.

8.2.2.1 Saliency-Based Auto Calibration

The key idea of the first approach [44] is to acquire ground-truth calibration information from the target user's natural behavior. This idea can be realized by using computational models of *visual saliency*.

It is known that humans can rapidly look at regions with high visual saliency, i.e., a region containing unique and distinctive visual features compared to the surrounding regions. Computational visual saliency models have been studied to mimic and understand this mechanism of visual attention, and can be used to estimate visual saliency maps in a bottom-up manner from images and videos (see [2] for a recent survey). The visual saliency maps computed from a video that the user is seeing tell us which region can attract more attention, and hence can be used as a probabilistic calibration data to learn the mapping from the eye images to the gaze points.

Our method takes a set of eye images recorded in synchronization with a video clip as the input, and automatically determines the relationship between the eye images and gaze directions. While existing methods require additional calibration data to estimate gaze positions of these eye images, in our method the input data can also serve as the calibration data.

The proposed method is illustrated in Fig. 8.4. Once the saliency maps are extracted from the input video frames, we aggregate the saliency maps based on the similarity of the eye images to produce more accurate gaze probability maps.

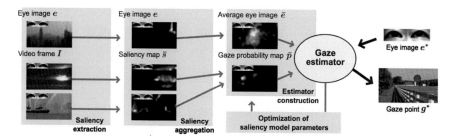

Fig. 8.4 Illustration of the saliency-based calibration approach. The method consists of mainly four steps: saliency extraction, saliency aggregation, estimator construction and saliency model optimization (Reproduced with permission of © 2013 IEEE [44])

The method then learns the relationship between the gaze probability maps and the eye images. In addition, a feedback scheme optimizes the feature weights used to compute the visual saliency maps. The feedback loop enables us to further strengthen the relationship between the gaze probability maps and the eye images.

Saliency Extraction

Our method adopts five low-level features and one high-level feature to compute the saliency maps. For low-level features, we use commonly-used feature channels, i.e., color, intensity, and orientations as the static features, and flicker and motion as dynamic features. Five saliency maps are computed from these features using the Graph-based Visual Saliency (GBVS) algorithm [17]. In addition to these low-level features, it is well known that humans tend to fixate on salient objects such as human faces. In order to capture this high-level saliency, we also compute a face channel-based saliency model [4] using a face detector. As a result, synchronized pairs of six saliency maps and eye images are produced. As can be seen in the examples shown in Fig. 8.4, saliency maps represent saliency values in the image space, and highly salient regions in the saliency map are likely to coincide with the actual gaze point.

Saliency Aggregation

Although the saliency maps can be correlated with gaze point distributions, their accuracy is insufficient for determining the exact gaze point locations on each map. We hence compute the probability distribution of the gaze point by aggregating the computed saliency maps. When we assume a fixed head position, there is a one-to-one correspondence between the ground-truth gaze points and the eye appearance. Therefore, by aggregating the saliency maps based on the similarity of the associated eye images, we can assume that the region around the actual gaze point has a sharp peak of saliency.

The eye images are first clustered according to their similarity scores, and then weighted means of the corresponding saliency maps are computed based on the similarity scores. The aggregated map can be used as the gaze probability map which represents the probability distribution of the gaze point more accurately.

Gaze Estimation

We then establish a mapping from the eye image to gaze points using the set of average eye images and corresponding gaze probability maps obtained in the previous step. Unlike standard calibration data, the gaze probability map only provides the probability distribution of the gaze point. Hence we approximate marginalization of the gaze probability with a Monte Carlo approximation, and apply a Gaussian process regression [37] to find the mapping function.

Fig. 8.5 Illustration of feature weight optimization. Feature weights are optimized by maximizing the similarity between estimated gaze positions and weighted sum maps (Reproduced with permission of © 2013 IEEE [44])

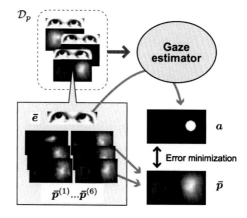

Feature Weight Optimization

In the first path, all six saliency features are independently aggregated, and the maps are linearly combined to produce the summed gaze probability map. In our method, the feature weights are further refined through an optimization loop as illustrated in Fig. 8.5. Once the gaze estimator is built, it can be used to estimate the gaze points from the average eye images. Using this data, our method optimizes the feature weights by minimizing the sum of the squared residuals between weighted sum maps and estimated gaze position maps. This maximizes the consistency between the gaze estimator and the saliency model.

Evaluation

In order to evaluate the performance of the proposed method, we used a set of 80 online video clips which include various types of video clips such as music videos and short films. We randomly extracted 30 s video sequences from each video source without an audio signal, and created four 10 min datasets A, B, C, D. Seven novice test persons are asked to watch all of them, and the estimation errors are evaluated using ground-truth positions obtained using a commercial gaze tracker. As a baseline, we also compare our method with a standard appearance-based gaze estimation method that uses an explicit calibration.

The estimation results are summarized in Table 8.1. Each row corresponds to the result using each dataset, where all 20 video clips are used for both the training and testing. The columns list the distance and angular errors of the proposed method and the calibrated appearance-based estimator. The overall average error was 39 mm ($\approx$3.5°), which is comparative to the calibrated estimator and sufficient for obtaining the regions of attention in images.

Table 8.1 Average error for each dataset

Dataset	Proposed method		Calibrated method	
	Error (mm)	Error (deg.)	Error (mm)	Error (deg.)
A	41 ± 26	3.7 ± 2.3	33 ± 15	3.0 ± 1.4
B	36 ± 23	3.3 ± 2.1	24 ± 13	2.2 ± 1.2
C	41 ± 25	3.7 ± 2.3	27 ± 15	2.5 ± 1.4
D	36 ± 25	3.3 ± 2.3	34 ± 16	3.1 ± 1.5
Average	$\mathbf{39 \pm 25}$	$\mathbf{3.5 \pm 2.3}$	30 ± 15	2.7 ± 1.4

The columns are the distance and angular estimation errors (average ± standard deviation) when using our method and the baseline method with an explicit calibration (Reproduced with permission of © 2013 IEEE [44])

8.2.2.2 Learning-Based Person-Independent Estimation

Another possible strategy for calibration-free gaze estimation is preliminary training a generic gaze estimator that can handle arbitrary users. If we have a large dataset that contains diverse people, head poses, and gaze directions, it is possible to train a person- and head pose-independent gaze estimation function. In this section, we introduce our method based on a multi-view gaze dataset [45].

In order to increase the head pose variation in the dataset, images are recorded by a multi-camera system and the view synthesis is performed via 3D reconstruction of eye regions. The gaze estimator is trained by an extension of random forests, and the best performance is achieved in person- and pose-independent, calibration-free gaze estimation from low-resolution images.

Dataset

For the purpose of learning a person- and pose-independent gaze estimation function, the training dataset must contain a dense samples in terms of persons, head poses, and gaze directions. In addition, accurate 3D positions of eyes and gaze targets in the camera coordinate system have to be provided as an annotation, and the coordinate system must be consistent across persons.

A total of 50 people participated in the data collection. As shown in Fig. 8.6 (left), eight cameras are attached to the frame of a monitor, and intrinsic and extrinsic camera parameters are calibrated beforehand. In order to obtain ground-truth gaze target positions displayed on the monitor, the 3D position of the monitor plane in the camera coordinate system is also calibrated. A chin rest was used to stabilize the head position located at 60 cm apart from the monitor, and participants were instructed to look at a visual target displayed on the monitor. The visual target were displayed at 160 regular grid positions in a random order. As a result, 160 (gaze directions) × 8 (cameras) × 50 (persons) images were recorded.

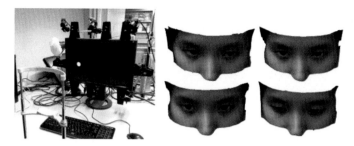

Fig. 8.6 Data collection. *Left* System configuration for data collection. *Right* Examples of recon-structed 3D eye region models (Reproduced with permission of © 2014 IEEE [45])

Data Annotation and 3D Reconstruction

The captured images are further annotated with facial landmarks. The locations of six facial landmarks are manually annotated on the first eight images for each person, and they are refined via a simple multi-view template matching on the rest of the images. These 3D landmark positions are further used to define head poses of the data.

We use a patch-based multi-view stereo algorithm [11] to reconstruct the 3D shapes from 8 multi-view images. The reconstructed 3D point cloud is further pre-processed by outlier removal and smoothing, and we then apply a Poisson recon-struction to obtain the 3D mesh of the eye region. The texture of the 3D mesh is computed using the mean of all source images. Figure 8.6 (right) shows examples of the reconstructed models.

Training Data Synthesis

Using the dataset, we take a learning-by-synthesis approach to person- and pose-independent gaze estimation. The purpose of the data synthesis is to increase the variation coverage of the head pose. The required training space can be reduced to 2D polar coordinates, i.e., positions of the virtual camera on a viewing sphere around the eye position. During test phase, the input head pose and eye image can be converted into an equivalent 2D polar coordinate representation and a corresponding eye image.

As shown in Fig. 8.7 (left), eye images are synthesized in the range of viewing angles around the eye position where the eye is observable. The range is divided into 6° intervals, and eye images are synthesized at a total of 144 head poses (=virtual camera positions). Figure 8.7 (right) shows examples of the synthesized eye images.

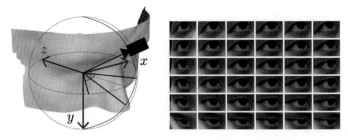

Fig. 8.7 Training data synthesis. *Left* Placement of the virtual cameras. *Right* Examples of synthesized eye images (Reproduced with permission of © 2014 IEEE [45])

Gaze Estimator Training

The training data described above consists of gaze direction vectors, head pose vectors and eye images. The gaze direction is defined as a 2D polar angle vector in the camera coordinate system, and the head pose vector is the rotation vector from the head coordinate system to the world coordinate system. Our goal is to learn a regression function that predicts a 3D gaze direction from the input feature (eye image and head pose).

We use a method based on random forests [3] to learn the regression function. In our problem setting, the input feature consists of multiple modalities, the appearance and the pose of an eye, which are both closely correlated with the output variable, 3D gaze direction. Therefore, we take an approach of learning random forests with some redundancy of head poses.

Figure 8.8 illustrates the structure of our redundant random forests. We cluster training samples into head pose clusters, where each cluster contains samples with

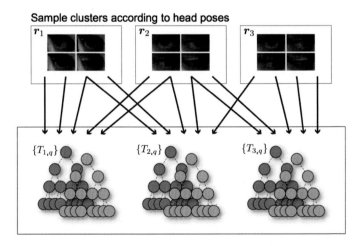

Fig. 8.8 Structure of the gaze estimation function. A set of regression trees with different but overlapping head pose ranges is trained (Reproduced with permission of © 2014 IEEE [45])

the same head pose. Instead of directly learning regression functions for each cluster, we create redundant subsets of the training data to jointly learn regression functions. Namely, to learn a regression function corresponding to the ith head pose, we randomly select training samples from each of the k-nearest sample clusters in the head pose space. A random regression forest is then built using the selected random samples. The test input is queried to its k-nearest regression forests in terms of the distance from the input head pose. Then, the output gaze direction is computed as a mean across all trees of the queried regression forests.

Evaluation

We compared our method with two baseline methods. The first method is the ALR method discussed in Sect. 8.2.1. k-nearest neighbor regression is selected as the second method because of its real-time estimation capability, which is crucial for various gaze applications.

From the dataset, we used 144 synthesized poses for training, and 8 recorded poses for testing. The input image size was set to 15×9 for both training and testing. Figure 8.9 (left) shows the mean estimation errors of all 50 participants for within-subject and cross-subject training. Within-subject errors are evaluated using the target person's own synthesized training data, and this indicates the upper limit of the performance of the proposed learning-by-synthesis approach. Cross-subject errors are evaluated using three-fold cross validation using synthesized training data of 33 different persons. Please note that the cross-subject setting is calibration-free, i.e., not using any training samples from the target person. The proposed method achieved the lowest error with both within-subject and cross-subject training, and the mean error of our method with cross-subject training was $6.5 \pm 1.5°$.

Figure 8.9 (right) shows mean accuracy with respect to the number of training subjects. In the figure, although the accuracy improvement becomes smaller at around 33 subjects, the case of three-fold cross validation discussed above, it does not

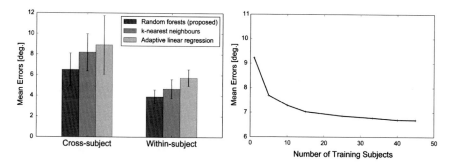

Fig. 8.9 Structure of the gaze estimation function. A set of regression trees with different but overlapping head pose ranges is trained (Reproduced with permission of © 2014 IEEE [45])

apparently converge even with 46 subjects. This result suggests the potential of achieving even greater accuracy by using a larger amount of training data.

8.2.3   Discussion

In Sect. 8.2.1.1, we first introduced a method to solve the core task of appearance-based gaze estimation. The key is the ALR method that optimally selects a sparse set of training samples for gaze estimation. With the proposed method, a gaze tracking system can be implemented that allows for quick calibration.

In Sect. 8.2.2.1, we discussed a method that automatically calibrates a gaze estimation function by using saliency maps. Our method automatically establishes the mapping from the eye image to the gaze point using video clips. Taking a synchronized set of eye images and video frames, our method trains the gaze estimator by regarding the saliency maps as the probabilistic distributions of the gaze points. In our experimental setting with fixed head positions, our method achieves an accuracy with about a 3.5° error.

In Sect. 8.2.2.2, we further discussed a purely learning-based, person- and head pose-independent gaze estimation method. In this method, the gaze estimator is learned using a large amount of synthesized training data. Owing to the synthesized dataset, the learned estimator can estimate gaze directions for arbitrary head poses that are not contained in the original data. The multi-view gaze dataset was made publicly available for future researches.

8.3   Visual Saliency for Subtle Gaze Guidance

8.3.1   Computational Models of Visual Saliency

A large amount of effort for developing computational models of human visual attention has ever been devoted to only *visual* processing. Human visual attention, however, can be easily modulated by other modalities. As an intuitive example, when we hear something interest or strange we tend to look at the direction of sounds even if that direction is not so visually salient. As such, sounds are often strongly related to events that draw human visual attention. We will be able to further augment computational models of human visual attention if we incorporate auditory information into them.

Based on the motivation above, our work [32] proposes a novel model of human visual attention driven by auditory cues. In our model, auditory information plays a supportive role in simulating visual attention, in contrast to standard multi-modal fusion approaches [10, 33, 39, 40]. More concretely, we take an approach that detects visual features in synchronization with surprising auditory events. Our model first detects *transient* events using the Bayesian surprise model in visual [20] and auditory [41] domains separately, and then looks for visual features in *synchronization* with detected auditory events. Surprise maps are then *modulated* by the selected features.

8.3.1.1   Framework of Our Proposed Model

Figure 8.10 depicts the framework of the proposed model. As shown in this figure, our proposed model consists of four main steps: our model detects transient auditory events, and then selects visual features in synchronization with detected auditory events to modulate the final saliency maps. Note that the proposed model is built on a two-pass algorithm, where the first 3 steps are devoted to selecting visual features that describe major audio-visual events in the input video to produce the final map in the last step.

Bayesian Surprise

The first step extracts surprising events in visual and auditory domains individually where image and audio signals are separately applied to the Bayesian surprise model.

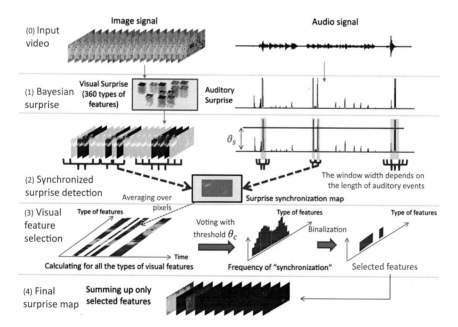

Fig. 8.10 Framework of the proposed model (Reproduced with permission of © 2015 Springer [32].)

For a given input video, 360 visual surprise maps[1] with different types of features and a single auditory surprise signal are extracted.

Synchronization Detector

The second step evaluates synchronization of each visual surprise map with the auditory surprise signal. For this purpose, synchronization detectors are attached to every location in each of the 360 visual surprise maps and the auditory surprise signals, resulting in 360 maps. Every map is averaged over pixels to create a sequence describing how synchronized the corresponding visual surprise map is with the auditory surprise.

A synchronization detector comprises the following three steps. Segments of surprising auditory events are first extracted from the auditory surprise signal using a predefined auditory surprise threshold. For every segment, normalized cross correlation (NCC) is calculated between the auditory surprise signal and visual surprises at every location in each of the 360 visual surprise maps. Every synchronization map is finally averaged over pixels to obtain a sequence that describes how synchronized the visual surprise map is with the auditory surprise.

Features Selection

The third step is devoted to selecting visual features that well synchronize with the auditory surprise. Counting the number of samples with a sufficient level of synchronization for every sequence (we use a predefined correlation threshold here), we obtain a histogram representing the degree of synchronization for every visual surprise map with the auditory surprise. Remembering that every visual surprise map corresponds to a specific type of features, feature selection based on audio-visual synchronization can be implemented by binarizing the histogram, where a threshold for the binarization is adaptively chosen so that its slight change significantly impacts on the number of selected features.

Final Surprise Map

The last step is for forming the final surprise map composed of visual surprise maps with the selected visual features. Only the visual surprise maps of the selected features (with active in the binarized histogram) are accumulated to form the final surprise map. In this way, our proposed model uses a smaller number of visual features than 360 for forming the final map.

---

[1]12 feature channels (intensity, 2 color opponents, 4 orientations, temporal onset and 4 directed motion energies) and 6 spatial scales, yielding $12 \times 6 = 72$ feature maps in total. In addition, 5 cascade detectors are implemented at every pixel in every feature map.

Table 8.2 Selected features using the optimal thresholds

	Baseline	Video 1	Video 2	Video 3	Video 4	Video 5	Video 6
Intensity	30	0	8	8	30	0	6
Color	60	4	17	27	60	8	23
Orientation	120	0	46	39	120	0	7
Onset	30	0	0	0	30	1	0
Motion	120	0	0	0	120	14	0
Total	360	4	71	74	360	23	36

Reproduced with permission of © 2015 Springer [32]

8.3.1.2 Evaluation

We experimentally evaluated our proposed model. We selected 6 video clips (advert_
bbc4_bees, advert_bbc4_library, sports_kendo, basketball_of_sports, documentary_
adrenaline, BBC_wildlife_eagle; we call video 1, 2, etc. in this order), all of which
are provided by the DIEM project.[2] We showed them to 15 human subjects. While the
subjects were watching the video clips, their eye movements were recorded using an
eye tracker Tobii TX300 and then gaze points were detected. As a metric to quantify
how well a model predicts actual human eye movements, we used the normalized
scan-path saliency (NSS) [20] calculated from the gaze points.

Table 8.2 shows the number of selected visual features by our model with the optimal threshold values for the auditory surprise threshold and the correlation threshold.
We can see that only a small fraction of 360 types of features were selected. We also
observe that categories such as intensity or color of selected features highly depend
on each input video. This is reasonable because what image features are closely
correlated with auditory events depends on the video. This also justifies our implementation with a two-pass algorithm.

We compared performances with the state-of-the-art models in addition to the
baseline model [20]. They are the saliency map model [21], and the audio-visual
attention model using the sound localization [33]. We also compared our model
with the model, hereafter called the random feature selection model, in which we
randomly selected a given number of image features among all image features used
in [20], where the number of features to be selected was set in accordance with the
number of image features determined by the optimal threshold values (see Table 8.2).

Figure 8.11 illustrates averages of NSS scores over frames for each video and for
each model. We see in Fig. 8.11 that our proposed model produced best NSS scores
for all the video, outperforming the other models. Interestingly, the random feature
selection model tends to outperform the baseline model. This indicates that using all
the image features does not necessarily perform better. Using a smaller number of
image features may be better.

---

[2]http://thediemproject.wordpress.com.

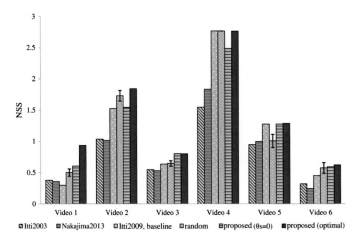

Fig. 8.11 Comparison of NSS averaged over frames for each video (Reproduced with permission of © 2015 Springer [32].)

8.3.1.3 Discussion

Our approach stands on using auditory features as a synchrony cue for selecting visual features. Differently from just fusing audio-visual information, our approach boosts the ability of visual information by selecting visual features synchronized with surprising auditory events.

We used correlation to evaluate synchronization between audio and visual surprises. Mutual information can be also used as an alternative measure for synchronization [38]. We can improve our model into several directions in future, e.g. the introduction to adaptive image feature selection depending on the auditory event or the location in the image and machine learning strategies for capturing generic structures of audio-visual events.

8.3.2 Saliency-Based Gaze Guidance

With the rapid progress of computer facilities, computer usage in every aspect of our daily life has become more and more popular. In fact, we have a drastically increased number of information systems such as the smartphone or the tablet PC. Moreover, electronic bulletin boards can be found everywhere and the electrical audio assistant is available in many cities. These information systems should be in good harmony with human beings and, thus, developing a technology for naturally guiding the human gaze is a key issue.

In order to develop such a technology, we put ourselves in the position of using visual saliency and directly modulate saliency for guiding human visual attention.

Namely, our work [13] proposes a method for modulating an image, for a given region in the image, to synthesize the image in which the region shows the highest saliency. Our method iteratively modulates the intensity and color so that the saliency inside the region increases while that outside the region decreases. This iteration is carried out until we obtain the image in which a given region is most salient over the entire image. With the image obtained in this way, we can smoothly attract human visual attention to the given region, without any interruption to the human gaze.

8.3.2.1 Saliency-Based Image Modulation

We assume that for an input image, we are given a region that should draw human visual attention. A given region is not always salient in an input image. We thus iteratively modulate the image so that the given region becomes most salient in the entire image. We note that our method is restricted to modulating only the intensity and color.

Control Saliency

In order to raise the saliency of a given region, we have to strengthen visual features inside the region. Furthermore, weakening the visual features outside the region also contributes to reducing the saliency outside the region; as a result, the saliency inside the region increases. The visual features mentioned here refer to the intensity and color.

Controlling the visual features depending on the location in the image is more effective than uniformly controlling them over the entire image. This is because saliency at a pixel is computed based on how discriminative the pixel is from its surroundings. Therefore, the relationship in visual features between a pixel of interest and its surroundings is a key in controlling saliency.

Image Modulation

We introduce two of parameters in our modulation: the saliency-based weight w_p and the ratio for saliency value $Q_p = (Q_p^R, Q_p^G, Q_p^B)$ where p denotes a pixel and R, G, B indicate red, green, blue channels respectively. The saliency-based weight adjusts the direction of change when taking into account whether the pixel of interest is inside or outside the region. The ratio for saliency value, on the other hand, determines the degree of change of visual features when taking into account difference from the surrounding area. We remark that the saliency-based weight depends on the pixel position while the ratio for saliency value depends on both the pixel position and RGB-channels.

At each iteration, RGB-values at each pixel are updated:

$$R'_p = R_p + w_p Q^R_p,$$
$$G'_p = G_p + w_p Q^G_p,$$
$$B'_p = B_p + w_p Q^B_p,$$

where R_p, G_p, B_p respectively denote red-, green-, blue-channel values of pixel p before the updating, and R'_p, G'_p, B'_p denote those after the updating.

The above updating may cause significant difference of the updated image in visual perception from the input image. To reduce such difference as much as possible, we introduce adjustment into RGB-channel values. Namely, for each channel, we introduce a bias and dynamic range adaptation so that the histogram of channel values over the image after the updating becomes as similar as possible to that before the updating. This can be formulated as the weighted least squares method where weights are determined by taking into account the saliency-based weight.

Using the obtained bias $\alpha = (\alpha^R, \alpha^G, \alpha^B)$ and dynamic range adaptation $\beta = (\beta^R, \beta^G, \beta^B)$, we adjust the updated image as follows.

$$\widetilde{R}'_p = \beta^R R'_p + \alpha^R,$$
$$\widetilde{G}'_p = \beta^G G'_p + \alpha^G,$$
$$\widetilde{B}'_p = \beta^B B'_p + \alpha^B.$$

We iterate the above pair of updating and adjustment until the given region becomes most salient in the entire image. In this way, our modulated image guarantees that a given region is most salient while minimizing visual perceptual difference of the modulated image from the input image.

Saliency-Based Weight

The saliency-based weight depends on not only the saliency value of a concerned pixel but also whether or not the pixel is inside the region. The saliency-based weight of a pixel inside the region should be positive while that outside the region should be negative. This is because we increase the saliency inside the region and decrease the saliency outside the region. The magnitude of the saliency-based weight of each pixel may be proportional to the saliency value of the pixel. We, however, smooth it over the entire image in order to avoid drastic impact caused by change in sign at the region boundary. Therefore, after attaching an appropriate sign to the saliency value of each pixel, we apply the Gaussian filter to have the saliency-based weight at the pixel.

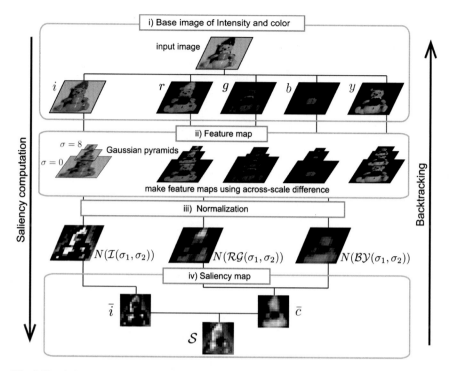

Fig. 8.12 Saliency computation and its backtracking

Ratio for Saliency Value

The ratio for saliency value reflects how much each feature influences the saliency of a concerned pixel. For example, if the red color heavily influences the saliency, we enlarge the red-channel ratio for saliency value (i.e., Q_p^K) of the pixel. We thus evaluate which color or intensity provides great impact on the saliency of a pixel. To compute the influence, we return to the procedures for computing the saliency map. We can identify how each visual feature influences on the saliency at a given pixel by backtracking one by one through the saliency-computation procedures (Fig. 8.12).

8.3.2.2 Evaluation

We experimentally evaluated our proposed modulation method. We prepared 40 different color input images of 512×256 pixels. We specify a region to each input image. Furthermore, we selected 10 input images and specify another region to each so that we have 50 modulated images in total. We note that we chose a less salient region in an input image to specify a region. For a pair of an input image and a specified region, we applied our modulation method. We also applied our method

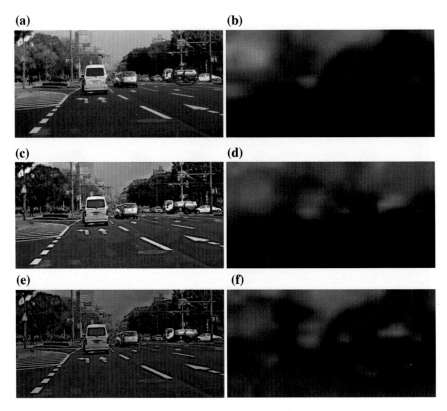

Fig. 8.13 Examples of input image and modulated images with and without adjustment. The *red circle* in (**a**) is a specified region to enhance saliency. **a** Input image. **b** Saliency map of input image. **c** Modulated image with adjustment. **d** Saliency map of the modulated image with adjustment. **e** Modulated image w/o adjustment. **f** Saliency map of the modulated image w/o adjustment

without adjustment (namely, without bias and dynamic range adaptation) to see how our adjustment is effective.

Figure 8.13 illustrates an example of our input images and modulated images together with corresponding saliency maps. As we see, our specified region becomes most salient over the image after the modulation. We can also observe that our adjustment contributes to keep visual perceptual similarity of the modulated image to the input image.

We also evaluated how modulated images draw gaze points to the specified regions. We randomly showed 90 images (40 input images and 50 modulated images) to 24 human subjects where each image was shown for three seconds. We remark that for the gaze point initialization, we displayed a white image with the cross located in the center between successive two images. While the subjects were looking at the images, their eye movements were recorded using an eye tracker Tobii TX300 and then gaze points were detected. We then evaluated whether or not the specified region of each image drew the gaze points.

Fig. 8.14 Average rates for drawing visual attention

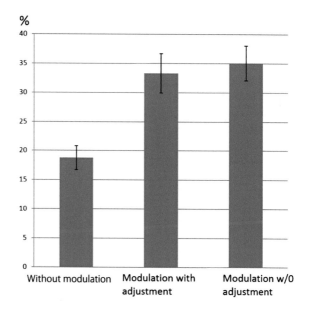

Figure 8.14 shows the average of ratios for drawing gaze points to a specified region. We see that modulated images significantly improved the ratio. Indeed, our hypothesis testing statistically confirms that the ratios before and after the modulation are significantly different from each other.

8.3.2.3 Discussion

We discussed an image modulation method for naturally guiding human visual attention. Our method is different from conventional methods [1, 26] in that our method is based on a fully bottom-up information gathering obtained from an image. Namely, we stood on the position of using visual saliency and presented iteratively modulating the intensity and color of an image until the saliency of a given region becomes highest over the entire image. Experimental results confirm that our image modulation method draws human visual attention toward our specified region.

The advantage of our method is that we do not need to present any visual stimulus to a subject in order to attract his visual attention. Incorporating human perceptual properties into our image modulation is left for future work.

8.3.3 Gaze Guidance for Interactive Systems

In most interactive systems, it is often the case that information contents providers want to guide viewers' attention to a particular location of the display. For example in digital signage, the contents providers want people to look at their products rather than models who are smiling on the display. On web pages, they want to guide people's attention to banner advertisements. In electronic markets, people's attention should be guided to today's campaign products.

There have been some approaches which guide people's attention to a particular location of the display. These approaches include changing the color of the object, flashing the object, vibrating the object, and so on to draw people's attention. Such "active" methods, however, are not appreciated by the people. For example, flashing or animation would interrupt the people's concentration to their main task. The web pages using such visual effect would become unpopular.

On the other hand, there are some studies to guide people's attention without making much modification to the display. Some of them can even move their focus without being recognized the modification by focusing on the characteristics of human's visual perception. Recent work [1, 14] uses saliency map by Itti et al. [22]. However, the approaches using the saliency map often changes the color and intensity of the image, and therefore the modified image often become unnatural.

We proposes a method to guide people's visual attention to the intended location without being recognized by the people using dynamic resolution control.

8.3.3.1 Visual Guidance Using Dynamic Resolution Control

The human visual system is always searching for something in the real world. When it finds something interesting, it would stay on the object a little longer (i.e. fixation) and then keep on moving. When the image is blurred, although it depends on the blur strength, the human visual system cannot obtain much information and it would change its focus to other objects. However, if it finds the object with high resolution, the visual system would stay on the object. Our attention control mechanism uses such characteristics of the human visual system. The whole image is blurred while the region to which we want to guide people's gaze is remained in high resolution.

By using this approach, we could move people's focus to our intended position. However, one problem of this approach is that people easily recognize the attention control when we use the strong blur. We do not want people to realize the blur.

Our solution to this problem is that we first show the original high resolution image to the people. Then the image is gradually blurred until they realize the blur. When the people's gaze is guided, the image is gradually recovered to its original resolution. This process is illustrated in Fig. 8.15.

In our experiment, the Gaussian filter was used. The Gaussian filter is one of the smoothing filters and it is calculated as $f(x, y) = \frac{1}{2\pi\sigma^2} e^{-\frac{x^2+y^2}{2\sigma^2}}$, where $x = y = 13$ in our study.

In order to confirm the effectiveness of our approach, it is necessary to show the following.

- Is it possible to move people's attention by using resolution control?
- Is there any threshold in blur level at which people are aware of the blur?

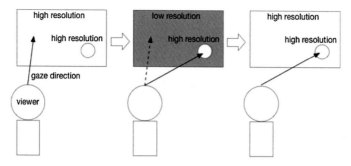

Fig. 8.15 A basic concept of navigating users' attention using resolution control

In the following sections, we describe two experiments which are conducted to answer the above questions.

8.3.3.2 Experiment 1

Figure 8.16 shows the set up of this experiment. There is a 23 inch LCD display (1920 × 1080 pixel) on the table with a Tobii TX300 eye tracker. In order to measure accurate gaze direction, a chin rest was used. The distance between the eye and the display is 60 cm. Subjects were allowed to see the image on the display freely.

Figure 8.17 shows the results of the experiment. By seeing the heat maps, it is understandable that users' gaze were statistically guided on the high resolution region. We did not tell the subjects before the experiment that there is a high resolution area in the image. When the experiments finished, the subjects were asked if they recognize that there is a high resolution region. They, however, answered that they did not recognize it.

Figure 8.18 (left) is a graph which shows a relation between the blur strength (σ) and the time to take until subjects' gaze first enter to the high resolution area. A horizontal axis shows the blur strength and a vertical axis shows the time. When $\sigma = 1$, it took 5.5 s in average. However, when $\sigma \geq 2$, it took 3 s in average. It is clear that the subjects' gaze was guided successfully.

Fig. 8.16 A set up of the experiments (Reproduced with permission of © 2015 IPSJ [15])

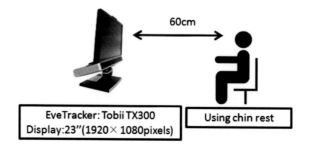

60cm

| EyeTracker: Tobii TX300 Display:23"(1920× 1080pixels) | Using chin rest |

(a)   **(b)**

(c)   **(d)**

Fig. 8.17 The images used in the first experiment and their heat maps (Reproduced with permission of © 2015 IPSJ [15]). **a** A presented image when $\sigma = 0$. **b** A heat map when $\sigma = 0$. **c** A blurred image when $\sigma = 5$. **d** A heat map when $\sigma = 5$. A white circle indicates the high resolution region

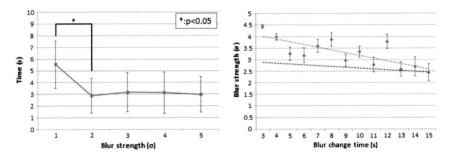

Fig. 8.18 Results of the experiment 1 (*left*) and experiment 2 (*right*)

8.3.3.3 Experiment 2

The purpose of this experiment is to investigate when people are aware of the guidance. In other words, we want to know σ at which people are aware of the resolution control. And if that $\sigma > 2$, it is said that we can guide people's gaze without being recognized.

We used the same hardware set up for the experiment as the experiment 1. The image was shown on the display and was gradually blurred from $\sigma = 0$ to $\sigma = 5$ within different transition time (3–15 s). Subjects were asked to click the mouse when they recognized the blur.

Figure 8.18 (right) shows the result of the experiment 2. This graph shows the relation between the time to be completely blurred (i.e. $\sigma = 5$) and the blur strength when the subjects clicked the mouse button. From this graph, it is understandable that there is a certain threshold at which the subjects recognize the blur. And the threshold depends on the transition time. The graph shows that the subjects were easier to recognize the blur if the transition time was long and were more difficult if the transition time was short. This is because if the transition time is long the subjects have enough time to find the area which is easier to recognize the blur.

8.3.3.4 Discussion

One of the advantages of our approach is that it can be used in multiple person's environment. Bailey's approach [1] tracks one person's gaze and make a flash while he/her is not seeing the intended position. In multiple person's environment, someone may see the flash. On the other hand, our approach can be applied to multiple person's environment. The resolution control is done below a threshold that people can recognize the blur. Even if multiple people see the different location simultaneously, it is hard to recognize the blur.

Subliminal stimuli [24, 43] are stimuli below a threshold for conscious perception. Its effectiveness has been under discussion in cognitive studies for long years. However, since there is a concern that it may force to embed information to people's brain without being recognized, its use has not been allowed on TV or movies. Since our method guides people's attention without being recognized, there might be the similar concern that our method is a kind of subliminal. The main issue of the subliminal is that it tries to send information which cannot be recognized by the user. On the other hand, our approach does not hide any information even though it navigates their attention without being recognized. At this point, our approach is essentially different with subliminal.

Here is the summary.

- People's attention is guided to the high resolution area.
- The effect of gaze guidance is obvious at $\sigma \geq 2$.
- People are not aware of the blur below a certain threshold.
- The longer the transition time is, the smaller the blur strength at which people become aware of the blur.

From above, we conclude that our method can guide people's visual attention without being noticed.

8.4 Human Gaze Control by Robots

Suppose we have the following situation: You would like to show a prototype of your new product to a colleague. He is working in an office shared by several other people. You enter the office and approach to his desk. You notice him reading some report. You do not want to disturb him, so you wait until he lifts his face from the report. Taking this opportunity, you look at his face, making eye contact. Then, you may say, "Hello," and turn your head to look at the prototype in your hand. He also looks at it. You turn your head toward his face again, saying, "What do you think?" He knows what you are talking about. Here, by looking at your colleague using the proper timing, you can attract his gaze and attention toward you, and by eye contact, you establish a communication channel with him. After that, you can expect to have established mutual gaze patterns with him. If you look at anything, he surely looks at the same object. In other words, you can control his gaze.

In this project, we propose a robot that can initiate interactions with a human in a socially acceptable manner, as described above. Most human-robot interaction studies consider cases where either robots and humans are already interacting, or where humans who require the robots' services call the robots by voice and/or nonverbal behaviors such as hand gestures to initiate interaction with the robots. However, there are cases where a robot needs to initiate interaction with a human being. The robot also needs to behave in a socially acceptable manner in such cases. To do so, we propose to consider the human's level of visual focus of attention. The Visual Focus Of Attention (VFOA) is the behavioral and cognitive process that indicates where and at what a person is looking, and in computer vision, it is mainly determined by eye gaze and head pose dynamics [42]. The Level of Visual Focus Of Attention (LVFOA) refers to how much concentration is given to a particular VFOA and is classified into discrete levels: low, high, or medium [8]. If the robot needs to start communication urgently such as during an emergency, it does not need to consider the current situation of the person. Otherwise, the robot should observe the person to know at what/who s/he is looking (VFOA) and how attentively s/he is doing so (LVFOA). Then, it should determine the proper timing to attract her/his attention so that it does not interfere with her/his current activities such as work. We propose a system in which the robot interacts with the target person intelligently and in a socially acceptable manner so that it can interact by considering her/his current VFOA as well as other people in the environment.

In Sect. 8.4.1, we describe how the robot can control a target person's gaze to attract her/his attention and establish mutual gaze based on the level of visual focus of attention (LVFOA). In Sect. 8.4.2, we describe our robot head with eyes designed for effective gaze communication as described in Sect. 8.4.1.

8.4.1 Initiating Interaction from a Robot Based on the Level of Visual Focus of Attention

The VFOA is an important cue for attracting attention and initiating interaction because—(i) it helps with understanding what the person is doing and (ii) it indicates addressee-hood (who is looking at whom). For instance, if the target person's VFOA is toward the robot, the robot can immediately establish a communication channel through eye contact. If the target person is involved in some task, the robot should wait to find the proper timing to attract her/his attention and establish a communication channel. In this research, the proper timing is determined by detecting the level of attention of the target person on her/his current task. In a scenario such as reading, writing, or browsing, the robot should initiate interaction with the target person when her/his level of attention is low. In other settings, such as at a museum, the robot may need to consider people's high level of attention towards exhibits to provide guidance on objects of interest.

8.4.1.1 Proposed Approach

The proposed approach is illustrated in Fig. 8.19a, b. In the *initiating interaction module* (Fig. 8.19a left), the robot recognizes and tracks the target person's VFOA. If they are initially face-to-face, the robot generates an awareness signal and makes eye contact with the target person. Otherwise, the robot tries to attract the target person's attention by recognizing her/his current task. The robot detects the level of the current VFOA until T_s (where T_s is the maximum span of sustained VFOA, which is explained in the next section). The robot uses either a low or high level of current VFOA (depending on the person's current task) at time t as its trigger to generate an attention attraction (AA) signal (weak or strong) depending on the viewing situation of her/his shifted VFOA. A person's field of view is divided into central and peripheral visions. We represent the viewing situation (relation between the target person's gaze (face) direction and the robot position) by where the robot is seen in the field of view of the target person. We classify it into the three regions: Central Field of View (CFV), Near Peripheral Field of View (NPFV (RNPFV: the right side, and LNPFV: the left side)), and Far Peripheral Field of View (FPFV (RFPFV: the right side, and LFPFV: the left side)) [18, 19, 50].

If the VFOA is detected in the CFV/LNPFV/RNPFV, then the robot generates a head turning action (weak signal). However, if the detected VFOA is in the LFPFV or RFPFV, then the robot generates a head shaking action (strong signal). Figrue 8.20 illustrates these classified regions when the camera is placed in the CFV region. We define the angular regions based on the detected frontal and profile faces. For example, in the CFV region, we detect frontal faces only. However, in the other regions, we may detect two face patterns such as a half-pose right profile face and a full-pose right profile face in the LFPFV region.

Once the robot succeeds in attracting the target person's attention toward it, the *communication channel establishment module* (right part of Fig. 8.19a) tries to establish a communication channel with her/him. For this purpose, the robot determines the level of shifted attention toward it. Based on the level of shifted attention, the robot generates an awareness signal toward the target person to indicate that it wants to communicate with her/him. Finally, the robot makes eye contact through eye blinking to establish a communication channel.

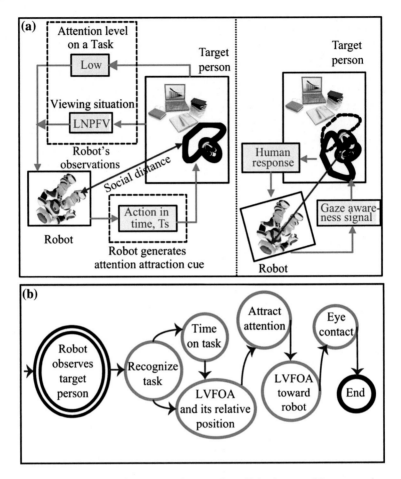

Fig. 8.19 **a** An abstract view of the proposed approach, and **b** basic steps of the proposed approach (Reproduced with permission of © 2015 IEEE [9])

8.4.1.2   Recognition of VFOA and Its Level

We are interested in detecting: *sustained attention* and *focused or shifted attention*. Focused or shifted attention is a short-term response to a stimulus or any other unexpected occurrence. The span or length of this attention is very brief [6] and after a few seconds, it is likely that the person will look away, return to the previous task, or think about something else. Sustained attention on the other hand is the level of attention that produces consistent results on a task over time. The duration of sustained attention also depends on the task. To learn about this, we observed humans working on various tasks and measured the duration. For our system, we use the maximum value for each task obtained in the observations as the maximum waiting

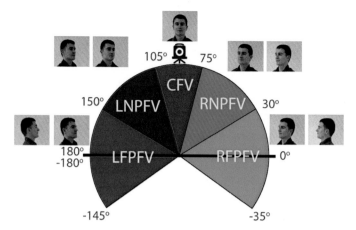

Fig. 8.20 Classification of head orientation into five angular regions. The faces shown from the GTAV face database [48] (Reproduced with permission of © 2015 IEEE [9])

time for the robot when it cannot find the proper timing for initiating interaction. We also use visual cues, gaze pattern, and task context to recognize VFOA and estimate its level.

Visual Cues

We detect and track the head to obtain the head pose. We also detect head movements, in particular, to find head movements toward the robot.

Gaze Pattern

A person's gaze pattern indicates her/his object of interest [12]. In general, human gaze patterns are classified into three viewing categories, distinguished by context: *spontaneous viewing, task or scene-relevant viewing,* and *orientation of thought viewing* [25]. *Spontaneous viewing* occurs when a person views the scene without any specific task in mind, i.e., when s/he is "just seeing" the scene. *Task or scene-relevant viewing* occurs when a person views the scene with a particular question or task in mind (e.g., s/he may be interested in a particular painting in the museum). *Orientation of thought viewing* occurs when the subject is not paying much attention to where she is looking, but is attending to some "inner thought". We consider the former two. In this research, we consider a gaze pattern as that which is constructed by considering the effects of both head movements and eye gaze. We classify gaze patterns using the support vector machine classifier [23]. Figure 8.21 shows examples of gaze pattern recognition.

(a)   **(b)**

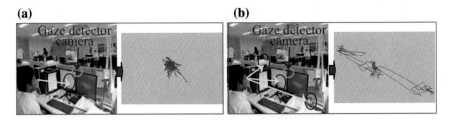

Fig. 8.21 Gaze pattern: **a** task or scene-relevant viewing, **b** spontaneous viewing (Reproduced with permission of © 2015 IEEE [9])

Task Context

Task context is determined by recognizing the task in which the target person is involved. For instance, if the target person is involved in a "reading" task, then the contextual cue such as "downward head" indicates that her/his attention is toward the book. However, the "page turn over", or "upward the head" behaviors indicate that the person loses her/his attention. We consider four tasks in this project: reading, writing, browsing, and viewing painting. We use the histogram of orientation gradient (HOG) feature [7] to train the SVM classifier to recognize tasks. For each task, we use the task related VFOA span, (T_s) to determine how long the robot should wait or within which period of time the robot interacts with the target person. We also define some task specific cues to determine the level of attention. For example, in the reading situation, we use the "page turn over" behavior and deviation in tilt angle cues to measure the LVFOA.

LVFOA Recognition

The level of VFOA is classified into two categories (low or high) based on the contextual cues, and gaze pattern. When the level of attention goes low, the system assumes that a loss of VFOA is detected. In any case, if spontaneous viewing is detected, then it is assumed that the person has no particular attention on a task. Thus, a low attention level is detected. In addition, we use the context cues for the current task. For example, in the case of reading and writing tasks, in addition to head pose changes, we also consider the "page turn over" and "stop writing" behaviors for detection of low attention level.

We tested the robot system in an office scenario and a museum scenario and confirmed that it works as expected. We compared our robot with one that does not consider the contextual situations of people. We found that our robot obtained a favorable impression from the participants. Details are found in [9].

8.4.2 Design of a Robot Head for Gaze Communication

Human eyes not only serve the function of enabling us "to see" something, but also performs the vital role of allowing us "to show" our gaze for non-verbal communication, such as through establishing eye contact and joint attention. The eyes of service robots should therefore also perform both of these functions. Moreover, they should be friendly in appearance so that humans would feel comfortable with the robots. Therefore we maintain that it is important to consider the capacity for gaze communication and friendliness in designing the appearance of robot eyes. In this project, we examined which shape for robot eyes is most suitable for gaze reading and gives the friendliest impression, through experiments where we altered the shape and iris size of robot eyes.

8.4.2.1 Eyes for Accurate Gaze Reading

Eyes and gaze have been examined in various fields. In biology, Kobayashi and Kohshima [27] found that among primates, only human eyes have no pigment in the sclera; moreover they also have the horizontally longest shape with the largest exposed area of sclera. Various explanations were offered as to why other primates have sclera colored in a similar fashion to their irises or the outside of their eyes. But all the explanations were based on the consensus that primates might be avoiding clearly showing their gaze. In contrast, human eyes have sclera with clearly different colors from those of the irises and the outside of the eyes. This enables human gaze to be readily comprehended by others. Kobayashi and Kohshima proposed the hypothesis of "gaze grooming" as the reason for why human eyes have this feature. From this study, we decided to focus in our own study, on whether the difference in the shape of the eyes, changes the ease of gaze reading.

Based on the eye parameters of pigments focused on by Kobayashi and Koshima [27], we changed the lid distance of the eyes when preparing design candidates. We prepared three types of outline shape for the eyes, specifically "round," "ellipse," and "squint." These three shapes were generated by setting the lid distance at 1.0, 0.5, and 0.25 times as long as the eye width, respectively. In the same manner, we changed the iris diameter to 0.75, 0.5, and 0.25 times as long as the eye width, and labeled them "large," "medium," and "small," respectively. Consequently, we had 9 types (the combination of 3 outline shapes and 3 iris sizes) of eye design, as shown in Fig. 8.22. A spherical shape and medium gray color were employed for the robot face in all instances to negate any effect of facial design. Notably, the eye employing the ellipse outline shape and the medium iris diameter (Fig. 8.22-E) is the most similar to the human eye in terms of the ratio of these parameters.

We developed a robot head as shown in Fig. 8.23 to examine which shape of robot eyes is most suitable for gaze reading. Each of the eyes consists of a projector, a mirror and a screen. The eye images, generated by CG, are projected onto the hemisphere screen via rear-projection. By using this projection mechanism, we can change the

Fig. 8.22 Candidate designs for robot eyes derived by varying lid distance and iridal diameter (Reproduced with permission of © 2013 John Benjamins Publishing Company [36].)

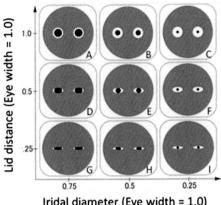

Fig. 8.23 **a** Overview of our proposed robot head. **b** The inside of the robot head consists of laser projectors, mirrors and screens (Reproduced with permission of © 2013 John Benjamins Publishing Company [36].)

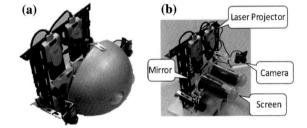

iris diameter. In addition, by replacing the mask, we can change the outline shape of the eyes.

We then conducted experiments to analyze the relationship between the accuracy of gaze reading and the shape of the robot eyes by using this robot head. We evaluated errors in gaze reading using the nine types of design candidates for robot eyes shown in Fig. 8.22. In the experiments, we lined up a series of markers between the participant and the robot head, as shown in Fig. 8.24. We asked the participant to stand in front of the robot head, face-to-face, with his/her head fixed on the mount. We then asked the participant to state at which marker the robot looked. Figure 8.25 shows the result. See details of the experiments in [36].

8.4.2.2 Friendly Eyes

We sought to examine the impression of friendliness by changing the outline shape of the eyes and the size of the iris, and seeing how participants responded. We conducted experiments to ascertain the apparent friendliness of the nine types of robot eyes shown in Fig. 8.22. We evaluated the degree of apparent friendliness by using Thurstone's method of paired comparison. We developed a web-based system

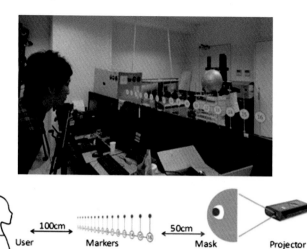

Fig. 8.24 Experimental scene of robot gaze reading (Reproduced with permission of © 2013 John Benjamins Publishing Company [36].)

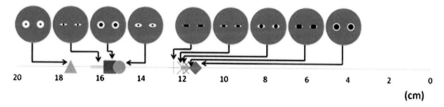

Fig. 8.25 Errors of gaze reading for each design candidate for robot eyes. The smaller value indicate smaller error and thus a more readable gaze (Reproduced with permission of © 2013 John Benjamins Publishing Company [36].)

for collecting answers from participants. Participants could choose one of the two images of a pair of robot eyes by tapping the iPad screen. We asked participants to answer the question, "These are robot faces. Which face do you think is friendlier?" for all 36 pairs of combinations of the nine types of robot eyes, which appeared in random order. We note that in actuality, the question was in Japanese. We used 105 participants: 60 males, 43 females, and 2 no-records. They were Japanese students of the school of liberal arts at Saitama University. We then analyzed the result by using Thurstone's method of paired comparison for scaling the impression of the robot eyes. Figure 8.26 shows the result.

8.4.2.3 Design Principles of Robot Eyes

From these experimental results, we have established the design principles of the robot eyes, and have developed a robot head based on the principles. We had expected

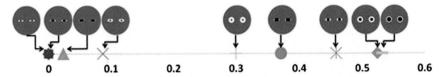

Fig. 8.26 Result of scaled experiment in impression of robot eyes by Thurstone's method of paired comparison, case III model by Japanese students. The graph was made by scaling it so that for Fig. 8.22-I, smallest value is 0. The more chosen a shape of eyes is by participants, the higher the scale value that shape of eyes gains (Reproduced with permission of © 2013 John Benjamins Publishing Company [36].)

that the human-like eye (F) would show the most accurate result in gaze reading as Kobayashi and Koshiba indicated [27]. However, the design with a round outline shape and a large iris (A) gave the best result. Although the differences from the most human-like eyes (E), D, H, and G are small. The results are not good if the iris is small compared to the eye's size (F, B, I, and C). Therefore, we can conclude that the iris should be large compared to the eye's size for accurate gaze reading. The impression of eyes may also depend on nationality, race, and other factors. Our participants (Japanese students) most preferred the design with a round outline shape and a large iris (Fig. 8.22-A). In addition to the experiments described above, we examined which head shape: a sphere, a flat plane, or a sphere with a nose could give the most accurate gaze reading result by a similar experiment described in Sect. 8.4.2.1 [35]. From these, we can conclude that a robot face with the eyes of a round outline shape and a large iris (Fig. 8.22-A) and with a nose is most suitable for gaze reading and conveying an impression of friendliness. We have developed such a robot head as shown in Fig. 8.27. This research provides the basic principles of robot eye design although we still need to consider various other factors in designing robot heads.

Fig. 8.27 Developed robot head with projection eyes

8.5 Conclusion

In this chapter, we presented techniques developed in our CREST project for sensing and guiding our gaze without distracting our activities. For remote gaze sensing with less or no calibration effort, we introduced three key ideas. Firstly, we proposed an appearance-based gaze sensing method with adaptive linear regression (ALR) that optimally selects a sparse set of training samples for gaze estimation. The method achieves higher accuracy of gaze estimation with significantly fewer training samples of low resolution eye images than existing appearance-based gaze estimation methods. Secondly, we exploited the new approach of carrying out auto calibration of gaze sensing from user fs natural viewing behavior predicted with a computational model of visual saliency. Lastly, we introduced a user-independent single-shot gaze estimation method. The key idea is to learn a generic gaze estimator by using a large dataset of eye images collected for different people, head poses, and gaze directions.

For guiding human gaze to desired locations in a non-disturbing way, we studied two approaches for gaze control. The first approach is subtle modulation of visual stimuli based on visual saliency models. We have shown that our gaze can be guided to a desired region in the visual stimuli (a given image) by modulating intensity or color contrast of the region, to the level just enough to make the region stand out. Related to the gaze guidance based on visual saliency, we also studied a new approach of enhancing visual saliency by integrating inputs from different modalities, more specifically, augmenting a visual saliency model by incorporating auditory information. The second approach for gaze guidance is to control human gaze by using robot's non-verbal behavior in human-robot interaction. To allow a robot to initiate interactions with a human in a socially acceptable manner, we introduced a model of human-robot interaction based on the level of visual focus of attention of a user. We also presented design principles of robot eyes in both their appearance and motion. Experiments carried out by using a prototype robot demonstrated the effectiveness of the proposed model of interaction and the eye design.

Acknowledgments The work presented in this chapter was supported by CREST, JST.

References

1. R. Bailey, A. McNamara, N. Sudarsanam, C. Grimm, Subtle gaze direction. ACM Trans. Graph. (TOG) **28**(4), 100 (2009)
2. A. Borji, L. Itti, State-of-the-art in visual attention modeling. IEEE Trans. Pattern Anal. Mach. Intell. **35**(1), 185–207 (2013)
3. L. Breiman, Random forests. Mach. Learn. **45**(1), 5–32 (2001)
4. M. Cerf, J. Harel, W. Einhäuser, C. Koch, Predicting human gaze using low-level saliency combined with face detection, in *Advances in Neural Information Processing Systems* (2008), pp. 241–248
5. I. Chamveha, Y. Sugano, D. Sugimura, T. Siriteerakul, T. Okabe, Y. Sato, A. Sugimoto, Head direction estimation from low resolution images with scene adaptation. Comput. Vis. Image Underst. **117**(10), 1502–1511 (2013)

6. D. Cornish, D. Dukette, *The Essential 20: Twenty Components of an Excellent Health Care Team* (Dorrance Publishing Co. Inc., 2010)
7. N. Dalal, B. Triggs, Histograms of oriented gradients for human detection, in *CVPR (1)* (IEEE Computer Society, 2005), pp. 886–893
8. D. Das, M.M. Hoque, T. Onuki, Y. Kobayashi, Y. Kuno, Vision-based attention control system for socially interactive robots, in: *IEEE International Symposium on Robot and Human Interactive Communication* (Paris, France, 2012), pp. 496–502
9. D. Das, M.G. Rashed, Y. Kobayashi, Y. Kuno, Supporting human-robot interaction based on the level of visual focus of attention, in *IEEE Transactions on Human-Machine Systems* (Accepted for Publication)
10. G. Evangelopoulos, A. Zlatintsi, A. Potamianos, P. Maragos, K. Rapantzikos, G. Skoumas, Y. Avrithis, Multimodal saliency and fusion for movie summarization based on aural, visual, and textual attention. IEEE Trans. Multimedia **15**(7), 1553–1568 (2013)
11. Y. Furukawa, J. Ponce, Accurate, dense, and robust multiview stereopsis. IEEE Trans. Pattern Anal. Mach. Intell. **32**(8), 1362–1376 (2010)
12. A.J. Glenstrup, T. Engell-Nielsen, Eye controlled media: present and future state. Ph.D. thesis, Information Psychology, University of Copenhagen, DIKU, DK-2100, Denmark, 1995
13. A. Hagiwara, A. Sugimoto, K. Kawamoto, Saliency-based image editing for guiding visual attention, in *Proceedings of the 1st International Workshop on Pervasive Eye Tracking and Mobile Eye-Based Interaction* (ACM, 2011), pp. 43–48
14. A. Hagiwara, A. Sugimoto, K. Kawamoto, Saliency-based image editing for guiding visual attention, in *Proceedings of the 1st International Workshop on Pervasive Eye Tracking & #38; Mobile Eye-based Interaction, PETMEI '11* (ACM, New York, 2011), pp. 43–48
15. Y.S. Hajime Hata Hideki Koike, Visual attention guidance using image resolution control. J. Inf. Proc. Soc. Jpn. **56**(4), 1142–1151 (2015)
16. D.W. Hansen, Q. Ji, In the eye of the beholder: a survey of models for eyes and gaze. IEEE Trans. Pattern Anal. Mach. Intell. **32**(3), 478–500 (2010)
17. J. Harel, C. Koch, P. Perona, Graph-based visual saliency, in *Advances in Neural Information Processing Systems* (2006), pp. 545–552
18. M.M. Hoque, D. Das, T. Onuki, Y. Kobayashi, Y. Kuno, An integrated approach of attention control of target human by nonverbal behaviors of robots in different viewing situations, in *IROS* (IEEE, 2012), pp. 1399–1406
19. M.M. Hoque, T. Onuki, Y. Kobayashi, Y. Kuno, Effect of robot's gaze behaviors for attracting and controlling human attention. Adv. Robot. **27**(11), 813–829 (2013)
20. L. Itti, P. Baldi, Bayesian surprise attracts human attention. Vis. Res. **49**(10), 1295–1306 (2009)
21. L. Itti, N. Dhavale, F. Pighin, Realistic avatar eye and head animation using a neurobiological model of visual attention, in *Optical Science and Technology, SPIE's 48th Annual Meeting* (International Society for Optics and Photonics, 2004), pp. 64–78
22. L. Itti, C. Koch, E. Niebur, A model of saliency-based visual attention for rapid scene analysis. IEEE Trans. Pattern Anal. Mach. Intell. **20**(11), 1254–1259 (1998)
23. T. Joachims, Making large-scale svm learning practical, in *Advances in Kernel Methods—Support Vector Learning* (1999)
24. J.C. Karremans, W. Stroebe, Beyond vicary's fantasies: the impact of subliminal priming and brand choice. J. Exp. Soc. Psychol. 792–798 (2006)
25. D. Kahneman, *Attention and Effort* (Prentice-Hall, 1973)
26. Y. Kim, A. Varshney, Persuading visual attention through geometry. IEEE Trans. Visual. Comput. Graph. **14**(4), 772–782 (2008)
27. H. Kobayashi, S. Kohshima, Unique morphology of the human eye and its adaptive meaning: comparative studies on external morphology of the primate eye. J. Hum. Evol. **40**, 419–435 (2001)
28. K. Liang, Y. Chahir, M. Molina, C. Tijus, F. Jouen, Appearance-based gaze tracking with spectral clustering and semi-supervised gaussian process regression, in *ETSA* (2013), pp. 17–23

29. F. Lu, T. Okabe, Y. Sugano, Y. Sato, Learning gaze biases with head motion for head pose-free gaze estimation. Image Vis. Comput. **32**(3), 169–179 (2014)
30. F. Lu, Y. Sugano, T. Okabe, Y. Sato, Adaptive linear regressionfor appearance-based gaze estimation. IEEE Trans. Pattern Anal. Mach. Intell. **10**, 2033–2046 (2014)
31. F. Martinez, A. Carbone, E. Pissaloux, Gaze estimation using local features and non-linear regression, in *ICIP* (2012), pp. 1961–1964
32. J. Nakajima, A. Kimura, A. Sugimoto, K. Kashino, Visual attention driven by auditory cues— selecting visual features in synchronization with attracting auditory events, in *MultiMedia Modeling—21st International Conference, MMM 2015* (Sydney, NSW, Australia, January 5– 7, 2015), *Proceedings, Part II* (2015), pp. 74–86
33. J. Nakajima, A. Sugimoto, K. Kawamoto, Incorporating audio signals into constructing a visual saliency map, in *Image and Video Technology* (Springer, 2014), pp. 468–480
34. B. Noris, K. Benmachiche, A. Billard, Calibration-free eye gaze direction detection with gaussian processes, in *VISAPP* (2008), pp. 611–616
35. T. Onuki, K. Ida, T. Ezure, T. Ishinoda, K. Sano, Y. Kobayashi, Y. Kuno, Designing robot eyes and head and their motions for gaze communication. Int. Conf. Intell. Comput. (ICIC2014) **LNCS8588**, 607–618 (2014)
36. T. Onuki, T. Ishinoda, E. Tsuburaya, Y. Miyata, Y. Kobayashi, Y. Kuno, Designing robot eyes for communicating gaze. Interact. Stud. **14**(3), 451–479 (2013)
37. C.E. Rasmussen, C.K.I. Williams, *Gaussian Processes for Machine Learning* (The MIT Press, 2006)
38. M. Rolf, M. Asada, Visual attention by audiovisual signal-level synchrony, in *Proceedings of the 9th ACM/IEEE International Conference on Human-Robot Interaction Workshop on Attention Models in Robotics: Visual Systems for Better HRI* (2014)
39. J. Ruesch, M. Lopes, A. Bernardino, J. Hornstein, J. Santos-Victor, R. Pfeifer, Multimodal saliency-based bottom-up attention a framework for the humanoid robot icub, in *Robotics and Automation, 2008. ICRA 2008. IEEE International Conference on* (IEEE, 2008), pp. 962–967
40. B. Schauerte, B. Kühn, K. Kroschel, R. Stiefelhagen, Multimodal saliency-based attention for object-based scene analysis, in *Intelligent Robots and Systems (IROS), 2011 IEEE/RSJ International Conference on* (IEEE, 2011), pp. 1173–1179
41. B. Schauerte, R. Stiefelhagen, "wow!" bayesian surprise for salient acoustic event detection, in *Acoustics, Speech and Signal Processing (ICASSP), 2013 IEEE International Conference on* (IEEE, 2013), pp. 6402–6406
42. R. Stiefelhagen, J. Yang, A. Waibel, Modeling focus of attention for meeting indexing based on multiple cues. IEEE Trans. Neural Netw. **13**(4), 928–938 (2002)
43. W. Stroebe, The subtle power of hidden messages. Sci. Am. Mind **23**, 46–51 (2012)
44. Y. Sugano, Y. Matsushita, Y. Sato, Appearance-based gaze estimation using visual saliency. IEEE Trans. Pattern Anal. Mach. Intell. **35**(2), 329–341 (2013)
45. Y. Sugano, Y. Matsushita, Y. Sato, Learning-by-synthesis for appearance-based 3d gaze estimation, in *Proceedings of the 2014 IEEE Conference on Computer Vision and Pattern Recognition (CVPR 2014)* (IEEE, 2014), pp. 1821–1828
46. K. Tan, D. Kriegman, N. Ahuja, Appearance-based eye gaze estimation, in *WACV* (2002), pp. 191–195
47. X. Tan, L. Qiao, W. Gao, J. Liu, Robust faces manifold modeling: most expressive versus most Sparse criterion, in *ICCV Workshops* (2010), pp. 139–146
48. F. Tarrés, Gtav face database, http://gps-tsc.upc.es/GTAV/ResearchAreas/UPCFaceDatabase/ GTAVFaceDatabase.htm
49. A. Wagner, J. Wright, A. Ganesh, Z. Zhou, Y. Ma, Towards a practical face recognition system: robust registration and illumination by sparse representation. CVPR **2009**, 597–604 (2009)
50. C. Ware, *Information Visulization: Perception for Design* (Morgan Kaufmann Publishers Inc., San Francisco, 2004)
51. O. Williams, A. Blake, R. Cipolla, Sparse and semi-supervised visual mapping with the S^{3}GP, in *CVPR* (2006), pp. 230–237
52. J. Wright, A. Yang, A. Ganesh, S. Sastry, Y. Ma, Robust face recognition via sparse representation. PAMI **31**(2), 210–227 (2008)

Chapter 9
Smart Posterboard: Multi-modal Sensing and Analysis of Poster Conversations

Tatsuya Kawahara

Abstract Conversations in poster sessions in academic events, referred to as poster conversations, pose interesting and challenging topics on multi-modal multi-party interactions. This article gives an overview of our CREST project on the smart posterboard for multi-modal conversation analysis. The smart posterboard has multiple sensing devices to record poster conversations, so we can review who came to the poster and what kind of questions or comments he/she made. The conversation analysis combines speech and image processing such as face and eye-gaze tracking, speech enhancement and speaker diarization. It is shown that eye-gaze information is useful for predicting turn-taking and also improving speaker diarization. Moreover, high-level indexing of interest and comprehension level of the audience is explored based on the multi-modal behaviors during the conversation. This is realized by predicting the audience's speech acts such as questions and reactive tokens.

Keywords Multi-modal · Conversation analysis · Speech processing · Posterboard

9.1 Introduction

Speech and image processing technologies have been improved so much that their target now includes natural human-human behaviors, which are made without being aware of interface devices. Examples of this kind of direction include meeting capturing [1] and conversation analysis [2]. We have conducted the CREST project, which focused on conversations in poster sessions, hereafter referred to as poster conversations [3, 4]. Poster sessions have become a norm in many academic conventions and open laboratories because of the flexible and interactive characteristics. In most cases, however, paper posters are still used even in the ICT areas. In some cases, digital devices such as LCD and PC projectors are used, but they do not have sensing devices. Currently, many lectures in academic events are recorded and distributed via Internet, but recording of poster sessions is never done or even tried.

T. Kawahara (✉)
Kyoto University, Sakyo-ku, Kyoto 606-8501, Japan
e-mail: kawahara@i.kyoto-u.ac.jp

© Springer Japan 2016
T. Nishida (ed.), *Human-Harmonized Information Technology, Volume 1*,
DOI 10.1007/978-4-431-55867-5_9

Poster conversations have a mixture characteristics of lectures and meetings; typically a presenter explains his/her work to a small audience using a poster, and the audience gives feedbacks in real time by nodding and verbal backchannels, and occasionally makes questions and comments. Conversations are interactive and also multi-modal because participants are standing and moving unlike in meetings. Another good point of poster conversations is that we can easily make a setting for data collection which is controlled in terms of familiarity with topics and other participants and yet is "natural and real".

The goal of the project is signal-level sensing and high-level analysis of human interactions. Specific tasks include face detection, eye-gaze detection, speech separation, and speaker diarization. These will realize a new indexing scheme of poster session archives. For example, after a long session of poster presentation, we often want to get a short review of the question-answers and feedbacks from the audience.

As opposed to the conventional "content-based" indexing approach which focuses on the presenter's speech by conducting speech recognition and natural language analysis, we adopt an "interaction-oriented" approach which looks into the audience's reaction. Specifically we focus on non-linguistic behaviors such as backchannel, nodding and eye-gaze information, because the audience better understands the key points of the presentation than the current machines. An overview of the proposed scheme is depicted in Fig. 9.1.

We have designed and implemented a research platform for multi-modal sensing and analysis of poster conversations. From the audio channel, utterances as well as laughter and backchannels are detected. Eye-gaze and nodding are also detected by using video and motion sensing devices. Special devices such as a motion-capturing system and eye-tracking recorders are used to make ground-truth annotation, but only video cameras and distant microphones are used in the practical system.

We also investigate high-level indexing of which segment was attractive and/or difficult for the audience to follow. This will be useful in speech archives because people would be interested in listening to the points other people liked. However, estimation of the interest and comprehension level is apparently difficult and largely subjective. Therefore, we turn to speech acts which are observable and presumably related with these mental states. One is prominent reactive tokens signaled by the

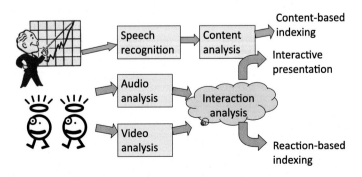

Fig. 9.1 Overview of multi-modal interaction analysis

Fig. 9.2 Proposed scheme of multi-modal sensing and analysis

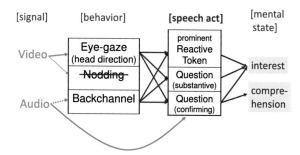

audience and the other is questions raised by them. Prediction of these speech acts from multi-modal behaviors is expected to approximate the estimation of the interest and comprehension level. The scheme is depicted in Fig. 9.2.

9.2 Overview of System and Corpus

9.2.1 Smart Posterboard System

We have designed and implemented a smart posterboard, which can record a poster session and sense human behaviors. Since it is not practical to ask every participant to wear special devices such as a head-set microphone and an eye-tracking recorder and also to set up any devices attached to a room, all sensing devices are attached to the posterboard, which is actually a 65-in. LCD screen. Specifically, the digital posterboard is equipped with a 19-channel microphone array on the top, and attached with six cameras and two Kinect sensors. An outlook of the smart posterboard is given in Fig. 9.3. A more lightweight and portable system is realized by only using the Kinect sensors, which captures audio and video signals.

9.2.2 Multi-modal Corpus of Poster Conversations

We have recorded a number of poster conversations for multi-modal interaction analysis [3, 5]. In each session, one presenter (labeled as "A") prepared a poster on his/her own academic research, and there was an audience of two persons (labeled as "B" and "C"), standing in front of the poster and listening to the presentation. Each poster was designed to introduce research topics of the presenter to researchers or students in other fields. The audience subjects were not familiar with the presenter and had not heard the presentation before. The duration of each session was 20–30 min. Some presenters made a presentation in two sessions, but to a different audience.

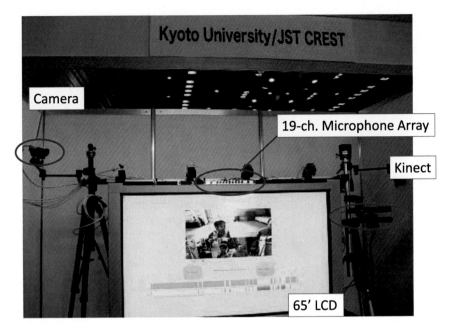

Fig. 9.3 Outlook of smart posterboard

All speech data were segmented into IPUs (Inter-Pausal Unit) and sentence units with time and speaker labels, and transcribed according to the guideline of the Corpus of Spontaneous Japanese (CSJ) [6]. Fillers, laughter and verbal backchannels were also manually annotated. While fillers are usually followed by utterances by the same speaker, backchannels are uttered by themselves.

For the ground-truth annotation, special multi-modal sensing devices such as a motion capturing system were used while every participant wore a wireless head-set microphone and an eye-tracking recorder or a magnetometric sensor. In the early phase of the project, eye-gaze information was derived from the eye-tracking recorder and the motion capturing system by matching the gaze vector against the position of the other participants and the poster. But their calibration and post-processing are very time-consuming. In the latter phase of the project, the magnetometric sensor were adopted to estimate head orientations instead of precise eye-gaze.

9.2.3 Detection of Participants' Eye-Gaze and Speech

Detection of participants and their multi-modal feedback behaviors such as eye-gaze and speech using the smart posterboard (green lines in Fig. 9.2) is explained. It is realized with multi-modal information processing, as shown in Fig. 9.4, and briefly explained in the following subsections.

Fig. 9.4 Process flow of multi-modal sensing

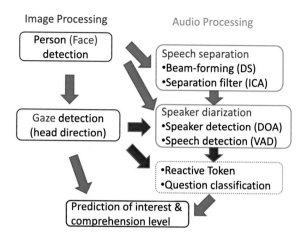

9.2.3.1   Face and Eye-Gaze Detection

Kinect sensors are used to detect the participants' face and their eye-gaze. As it is difficult to detect the eye-ball with the Kinect's resolution, the eye-gaze is approximated with the head orientation. A preliminary analysis using the eye-tracking recorder showed that the difference between the actual eye-gaze and the head orientation is 10° on average, but it is much smaller when the participants look at the poster. The process of the face and the head orientation detection is as follows [7]:

1. Face detection
   Haar-like features are extracted from the color and ToF (Time-of-Flight) images to detect the face of the participants. Multiple persons can be detected simultaneously even if they move around.
2. Head model estimation
   For each detected participant, a three-dimensional shape and colors of the head are extracted from the ToF image and the color image, respectively. Then, a head model is defined with the polygon and texture information.
3. Head tracking
   Head tracking is realized by fitting the video image into the head model. A particle filter is adopted to track the three-dimensional position of the head and its three-dimensional orientation.
4. Identification of eye-gaze object
   From the six-dimensional parameters, an eye-gaze vector is computed in the three-dimensional space. The object of the eye-gaze is determined by this vector and the position of the objects. In this study, the eye-gaze object is limited to the poster and other participants.

The entire process mentioned above can be run in real time by using a GPU for tracking each person.

9.2.3.2 Detection of Nodding

Nodding can be detected as a movement of the head, whose position is estimated in the above process. However, discrimination against noisy or unconscious movements is still difficult. Therefore, nodding is not used in most of this study.

9.2.3.3 Speech Separation and Speaker Diarization

Speech separation and enhancement are realized with the blind spatial subtraction array (BSSA), which consists of the delay-and-sum (DS) beamformer and a noise estimator based on independent component analysis (ICA) [8]. Here, the position information of the participants estimated by the image processing is used for beamforming and initialization of the ICA filter estimation. This is one of the advantages of multi-modal signal processing. While the participants move around, the filter estimation is updated online.

When the 19-channel microphone array is used, speech separation and enhancement can be performed with a high SNR, but not in real time. Using the Kinect sensor realizes real-time processing, but degrades the quality of speech.

By this process, the audio input is separated to the presenter and the audience. Although discrimination among the audience is not done, DoA (Direction of Arrival) estimation can be used for identifying the speaker among the audience. In a baseline system, simple voice activity detection (VAD) is conducted on each of the two channels by using power and spectrum information in order to make speaker diarization. We can use highly-enhanced but distorted speech for VAD, but still keeps moderately-enhanced and intelligible speech for re-playing.

In Sect. 9.4, a more elaborate speaker diarization method is addressed by combining multi-channel audio input and eye-gaze information of the participants.

9.3 Prediction of Turn-Taking from Multi-modal Behaviors

Turn-taking in conversations is a natural behavior in human activities. Studies on turn-taking have been conventionally focused on dyadic conversations between two persons. While there are a number of studies conducting analysis on the turn-taking patterns [9–12], some studies investigated a prediction mechanism for a dialogue system to take or yield turns based on machine learning [13–16]. Some studies even attempt to evaluate the synchrony of dialogue [17, 18].

Recently, conversational analysis and modeling have been extended to multi-party interactions such as meetings and free conversations by more than two persons. Turn-taking in multi-party interactions is more complicated than that in the dyadic dialogue case, in which a long pause suggests yielding turns to the (only one) partner. Predicting whom the turn is yielded to or who will take the turn is significant for an intelligent conversational agent handling multiple partners [19, 20] as well as an automated system to beamform microphones or zoom in cameras on the speakers.

Studies on computational modeling on turn-taking in multi-party interactions are very limited so far. Laskowski et al. [21] presented a stochastic turn-taking model based on N-gram for the ICSI meeting corpus. Jokinen et al. [22] investigated the use of eye-gaze information for predicting turn-holding or giving in three-party conversations.

This section deals with turn-taking behaviors in poster sessions. Conversations in poster sessions are different from those in meetings and free conversations addressed in the previous works, in that presenters hold most of turns and thus the amount of utterances is very unbalanced. However, the segments of audiences' questions and comments are more informative and should not be missed, and thus prediction of such events is important in online applications such as automated recording control and a conversational agent. Therefore, the goal of this work is to predict turn-taking by the audience in poster conversations, and, if that happens, which person in the audience will take the turn to speak.

We approach this problem by combining multi-modal information sources. While most of the aforementioned previous studies focused on prosodic features of the current speakers, it is widely-known that eye-gaze information plays a significant role in turn-taking [23], and the works by Jokinen [22] and by Bohus [19] exploited that information in their modeling. The existence of posters, however, requires different modeling in poster conversations as the eye-gaze of the participants are focused on the poster in most of the time. This is true to other kinds of interactions using some materials such as maps and computers. Several kinds of parameterization of eye-gaze patterns including the poster object are investigated for effective features related with turn-taking. Moreover, backchannel information such as nodding and verbal reactions by the audience is also incorporated

In this study, four poster sessions are used. In majority of utterances (IPUs) of the presenter ("A"), the turn was held by himself/herself. The ratio of turn-taking by the audience (either "B" or "C") is only 11.9%. In this work, therefore, prediction of turn-taking is formulated as a detection problem rather than a classification problem. The evaluation measure should be recall and precision of turn-taking by the audience, not the classification accuracy of turn-holding and yielding by the presenter. This is consistent with the goal of the study.

9.3.1 Analysis on Eye-Gaze and Backchannel Features in Turn-Taking

First, statistics of eye-gaze and backchannel events are investigated on their relationship with turn-taking by the audience.

9.3.1.1 Distribution of Eye-Gaze

The object of the eye-gaze of all participants is identified at the end of the presenter's utterances. The target object can be either the poster or other participants. The

Fig. 9.5 Statistics of
eye-gaze and its relationship
with turn-taking (ratio)

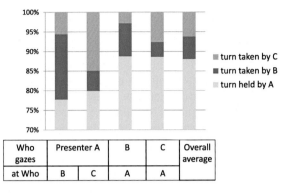

Who gazes	Presenter A	B	C	Overall average
at Who	B	C	A	A	

Table 9.1 Duration of eye-gaze and its relationship with turn-taking (s)

	Turn held by presenter	Turn taken by audience	
	A	B	C
A gazed at B	0.220	**0.589**	0.299
A gazed at C	0.387	0.391	**0.791**
B gazed at A	0.161	0.205	0.078
C gazed at A	0.308	0.215	0.355

statistics are shown in Fig. 9.5 in relation with the turn-taking events. It is observed that the presenter is more likely to gaze at the person in the audience right before yielding the turn to him/her. We can also see that the person who takes the turn is more likely to gaze at the presenter, but the ratio of the turn-yielding by the presenter is not higher than the average over the entire data set.

The duration of the eye-gaze is also measured. It is measured within the segment of 2.5 s before the end of the presenter's utterances because the majority of the IPUs are less than 2.5 s. It is listed in Table 9.1 in relation with the turn-taking events. We can see the presenter gazed at the person right before yielding the turn to him/her significantly longer than other cases. However, there is no significant difference in the duration of the eye-gaze by the audience according to the turn-taking events.

9.3.1.2 Joint Eye-Gaze Events

Next, joint eye-gaze events by the presenter and the audience are defined as shown in Table 9.2. In this table, notation of "audience" is used, but actually these events are defined for each person in the audience. Thus, "Ii" means the mutual gaze by the presenter and a particular person in the audience, and "Pp" means the joint attention to the poster object.

Table 9.2 Definition of joint eye-gaze events by presenter and audience

Who	Presenter		
	Gazes at	Audience (**I**)	Poster (**P**)
Audience	Presenter (**i**)	**Ii**	**Pi**
	Poster (**p**)	**Ip**	**Pp**

Table 9.3 Statistics of joint eye-gaze events by presenter and audience in relation with turn-taking (ratio of occurrence frequency)

	#Turn held by presenter A (%)	#Turn taken by audience		Total (%)
		(Self) (%)	(Other) (%)	
Ii	3.1	0.4	0.1	3.6
Ip	7.9	**1.8**	0.6	10.3
Pi	4.7	0.3	0.2	5.2
Pp	73.7	3.6	3.6	80.9

Statistics of these events at the end of the presenter's utterances are summarized in Table 9.3. Here, the counts of the events are summed over the two persons in the audience. They are classified according to the turn-taking events, and turn-taking by the audience is classified into two cases: the person involved in the eye-gaze event actually took the turn (self), and the other person took the turn (other). It is confirmed that the joint gaze at the poster is most dominant (around 80 %) in the poster conversations. The mutual gaze ("Ii") is expected to be related with turn-taking, but its frequency is not so high. The frequency of "Pi" is not high, either. The most potentially useful event is "Ip", in which the presenter gazes at the person in the audience before giving the turn. This is consistent with the observation in the previous subsection.

9.3.1.3 Dynamics of Eye-Gaze

In the analysis of the previous subsections, gazing information by the audience is not so clearly related with turn-taking. The audience might have sent a signal to the presenter by gazing that he would like to take a turn, but turn-taking actually happens when the presenter looks back to him/her. To confirm this, the dynamic patterns of the eye-gaze events are investigated by a window of 2.5 s over 10 s before the end of the presenter's utterances. As a result, we observe a tendency that the frequency and duration of "Ii" and "Ip" are increasing toward the end of the utterances, while "Pi" appeared relatively longer in the segment of 5 s before the end of the utterances. This indicates that "Pi" is followed by "Ii" or "Ip". This suggests that bigram information of the eye-gaze events may be useful when we have a larger amount of data.

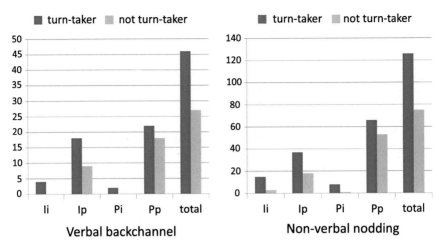

Fig. 9.6 Statistics of backchannels and their relationship with turn-taking (occurrence frequency)

9.3.1.4 Backchannels

Verbal backchannels, typically "*hai*" in Japanese and "yeah" or "okay" in English, indicate that the listener is understanding what is being said. Nodding is regarded as a non-verbal backchannel, and it is more frequently observed in poster conversations than in simple spoken dialogue.

The occurrence frequencies of these events are counted within the segment of 2.5 s before the end of the presenter's utterances. They are shown in Fig. 9.6 according to the joint eye-gaze events. It is observed that the person in the audience who takes the turn (=turn-taker) made more backchannels both in verbal and non-verbal manners, and the tendency is more apparent in the particular eye-gaze events of "Ii" and "Ip" which are closely related with the turn-taking events.

9.3.2 Prediction of Turn-Taking by Audience

Based on the analysis in the previous subsection, features for predicting turn-taking by the audience are parameterized. The prediction task is divided into two sub-tasks: detection of speaker change and identification of the next speaker. In the first sub-task, we predict whether the turn is yielded from the presenter to (someone in) the audience, and if that happens, then we predict who in the audience takes the turn in the second sub-task. Note that these predictions are done at every end-point of the presenter's utterance (IPU) using the information prior to the speaker change or the utterance by the new speaker.

Prediction experiments were conducted based on machine learning using the data set in a cross-validation manner; one session is tested using the classifier trained with the other sessions, and this process is repeated by changing the training and testing set.

9.3.2.1 Prediction of Speaker Change

For the first sub-task, prosodic features are adopted as a baseline based on the previous works (e.g. [16, 22]). Specifically, F0 (mean, max, min, and range) and power (mean and max) of the presenter's utterance is computed prior to the prediction point. Each feature is normalized by the speaker by taking the z-score; it is subtracted by the mean and then divided by the variance for the corresponding speaker.

Backchannel features are defined by taking occurrence counts prior to the prediction point for each type (verbal backchannel and non-verbal nodding).

Eye-gaze features are defined as below:

1. Eye-gaze object
   For the presenter, (P) poster or (I) audience;
   For (anybody in) the audience, (p) poster, (i) presenter, or (o) other person in the audience.
2. Joint eye-gaze event: "Ii", "Ip", "Pi", "Pp"
   These can happen simultaneously for multiple persons in the audience, but only one is chosen by the priority order listed above.
3. Duration of the above 1. ((I) and (i))
   A maximum is taken over persons in the audience.
4. Duration of the above 2. (except "Pp")

Note that these parameters can be extended to any number of the persons in the audience, although only two persons were present in this data set.

Support vector machines (SVM) and logistic regression (MaxEnt) model are used for machine learning, but they show comparable performance. The result with SVM is listed in Table 9.4. Here, recall, precision and F-measure are computed for speaker change, or turn-taking by the audience. This case accounts for only 11.9 % and its prediction is a very challenging task, while we can easily get an accuracy of over 90 % for prediction of turn-holding by the presenter. We are particularly concerned on the recall of speaker change, considering the nature of the task and application scenarios.

Among the individual features, as shown in Table 9.4, the prosodic features obtain the best recall while the eye-gaze features achieve the best precision and F-measure. In the table, combination of all four kinds of the eye-gaze parameterization listed above is adopted, however, using one of them is sufficient and there is not a significant difference in performance among them. Combination of the prosodic features and

Table 9.4 Prediction result of speaker change

Feature	Recall	Precision	F-measure
Prosody	0.667	0.178	0.280
Backchannel (BC)	0.459	0.113	0.179
Eye-gaze (gaze)	0.461	0.216	0.290
Prosody+BC	0.668	0.165	0.263
Prosody+gaze	**0.706**	0.209	0.319
Prosody+BC+gaze	0.678	0.189	0.294

Table 9.5 Prediction result of the next speaker

	Feature	Accuracy (%)
1.	Eye-gaze object	53.8
2.	Joint eye-gaze event	53.8
	1.+2.	55.8
3.	1.+2. + duration	66.4
BC	Backchannel	52.6
	Combination of above all (3.+BC)	**69.7**

eye-gaze features is effective in improving both recall and precision. On the other hand, the backchannel features get the lowest performance, and its combination with the other features is not effective, resulting in degradation of the performance.

9.3.2.2 Prediction of Next Speaker

Predicting the next speaker in a multi-party conversation (before he/she actually speaks) is also a challenging task, and has not been addressed in the previous work. For this sub-task, the prosodic features of the current speaker are not usable because it does not have information suggesting who the turn will be yielded to. Therefore, the backchannel features and eye-gaze features described in the previous subsection are adopted, but they are computed for individual persons in the audience, instead of taking the maximum or selecting among them.

In this experiment, SVM performs slightly better than logistic regression model, thus the prediction accuracy obtained with SVM is listed in Table 9.5. As there are only two persons in the audience, random selection would give an accuracy of 50 %.

The simple eye-gaze features focused on the prediction point (1 and 2) obtains an accuracy slightly better than the chance rate, but incorporating duration information (3) significantly improves the accuracy. In this experiment, the backchannel features have some effect; the person who made more backchannels is more likely to take the turn. By combining all features, the accuracy reaches almost 70 %.

9.4 Speaker Diarization with Backchannel Detection Using Eye-Gaze Information

In the previous section, it is shown that eye-gaze information is useful for predicting turn-taking. Based on this finding, we investigate a new scheme of speaker diarization. Speaker diarization is a process to identify "who spoke when" in multi-party conversations. A number of diarization methods [24, 25] have been investigated based on acoustic information. In real multi-party conversations, the diarization performance is degraded by adversary acoustic conditions such as background noise and distant talking. To solve the problem, some studies tried to incorporate multi-modal information such as motion and gesture [12, 25].

Although it is known that eye-gaze information can be used to predict participants' utterances, it has not been integrated in speaker diarization tasks. This section addresses a multi-modal diarization method which integrates eye-gaze information with acoustic information. The proposed method extracts acoustic and eye-gaze features, which are integrated in a stochastic manner to detect utterances.

Furthermore, the diarization results are enhanced by detecting audience's backchannels. Backchannels are frequently observed in poster conversations and involve different eye-gaze behaviors since they indicate that the listener does not take a turn. Detection of backchannels is also realized by using the same multi-modal scheme but training a different model. By eliminating the detected backchannels and noise from the diarization result, we can easily access to meaningful utterances such as questions and comments, while backchannels show interaction level of the conversation.

In this study, eight poster sessions are used. Since utterances by the audience are not frequent, it is difficult to detect these utterances accurately. Moreover, the audience's backchannels account for about 40 % of their utterance duration.

9.4.1 Multi-modal Speaker Diarization

9.4.1.1 MUSIC Method Using Microphone Array

Conventional speaker diarization methods have used Mel-Frequency Cepstral Coefficients (MFCCs) and Directions Of Arrival (DOA) of sound sources [24]. An acoustic baseline method in this study is based on sound source localization using DOAs derived from the microphone array.

To estimate a DOA, we adopt the MUltiple SIgnal Classification (MUSIC) method [26], which can detect multiple DOAs simultaneously. The MUSIC spectrum $M_t(\theta)$ is calculated based on the orthogonal property between an input acoustic signal and a noise subspace. Note that θ is an angle between the microphone array and the target of estimation, and t represents a time frame. The MUSIC spectrum represents DOA likelihoods, and the large spectrum suggests that the participant makes an utterance from that angle. To calculate the spectrum, it is needed to determine the number of sound sources. In this study, the number of sound sources is predicted with SVM using the eigenvalue distribution of a spatial correlation matrix [27].

The proposed method incorporates eye-gaze information to speaker diarization. The method first extracts acoustic and eye-gaze features to compute a probability of speech activity respectively, then it combines the two probabilities for the frame-wise decision. The process is conducted independently on every time frame t and for each participant i.

The acoustic features are calculated based on the MUSIC spectrum. We can use the ith participant's head location $\theta_{i,t}$ tracked by the Kinect sensors. The possible location of the participant is constrained within a certain range $(\pm\theta_B)$ from the detected location $\theta_{i,t}$. The acoustic features of the ith participant in the time frame t consist of the MUSIC spectrum in the range:

$$\mathbf{a}_{i,t} = \left[M_t \left(\theta_{i,t} - \theta_B \right), \cdots, M_t \left(\theta_{i,t} \right), \cdots, M_t \left(\theta_{i,t} + \theta_B \right) \right]^T \quad (9.1)$$

9.4.1.2   Eye-Gaze Features

The eye-gaze features for the ith participant $\mathbf{g}_{i,t}$ are same as those used in Sect. 9.3.2.1, except that unigram and bigram of the eye-gaze objects and the joint eye-gaze events are added.

9.4.1.3   Integration of Acoustic and Eye-Gaze Information

The acoustic features $\mathbf{a}_{i,t}$ are integrated with the eye-gaze features $\mathbf{g}_{i,t}$ to detect the ith participant's speech activity $v_{i,t}$ in the time frame t. Note that the speech activity $v_{i,t}$ is binary: speaking ($v_{i,t} = 1$) or not-speaking ($v_{i,t} = 0$). Here, a linear interpolation is adopted to combine probabilities independently computed by the two feature sets [25]:

$$f_{i,t}(\mathbf{a}_{i,t}, \mathbf{g}_{i,t}) = \alpha \, p(v_{i,t} = 1 | \mathbf{a}_{i,t}) + (1 - \alpha) \, p(v_{i,t} = 1 | \mathbf{g}_{i,t}) \quad (9.2)$$

Here $\alpha \in [0, 1]$ is a weight coefficient. Each probability is computed by a logistic regression model. It is also possible to combine the two feature sets in the feature domain and directly compute a posterior probability $p(v_{i,t} | \mathbf{a}_{i,t}, \mathbf{g}_{i,t})$. Compared with this joint model, the linear interpolation model has a merit that training data does not have to be aligned between the acoustic and eye-gaze features because of independency of the two discriminative models. Furthermore, the weight coefficient α can be appropriately determined based on the acoustic environments such as Signal-to-Noise Ratio (SNR). Here, it is estimated using an entropy h of the acoustic posterior probability $p(v_{i,t} | \mathbf{a}_{i,t})$ [28] as

$$\alpha = \alpha_c \cdot \frac{1-h}{1-h_c} , \tag{9.3}$$

where h_c and α_c are an entropy and an ideal weight coefficient in a clean acoustic environment, respectively. When the estimated weight coefficient is larger than one or less than zero, the coefficient is set to one or zero, respectively. For online processing, the coefficient is updated periodically.

9.4.1.4 Speaker Diarization Experiment

Logistic regression models were trained separately for the presenter and the audience by cross-validation of the eight sessions. In order to evaluate performance under ambient noise, audio data was prepared by superimposing a diffusive noise recorded in a crowded place. SNRs were set to 20, 15, 10, 5 and 0 dB. In real poster conversations carried out in academic conventions, the SNRs are expected to be around 0 to 5 dB.

The multi-modal method is compared with other methods listed below:

1. *baseline MUSIC* [29]
   This method conducts peak tracking of the MUSIC spectrum and GMM-based clustering in the angle domain. Each cluster corresponds to each participant. This method does not use any cue from visual information.
2. *baseline + location constraint* [30]
   This method also performs peak tracking of the MUSIC spectrum, and compares the detected peak with the estimated head location within the $\pm \theta_B$ range. If this constraint is not met, the hypothesis is discarded.
3. *acoustic-only model*
   This method fixes the weight coefficient α to 1 in Eq. (9.2), and uses only the acoustic information.

For an evaluation measure, Diarization Error Rate (DER) [31] is used in this experiment. DER consists of False Acceptance (FA), False Rejection (FR), and Speaker Error (SE) as below:

$$DER = \frac{\#FA + \#FR + \#SE}{\#S} , \tag{9.4}$$

where $\#S$ is the number of speech frames in the reference data.

Table 9.6 lists DERs for each SNR. The two baseline methods (*baseline MUSIC* and *baseline + location constraint*) showed lower accuracy because they are rule-based and not robust against dynamic changes of the MUSIC spectrum and participants' locations. Compared with the acoustic-only model, the proposed multi-modal model achieves higher performance under noisy environments (SNR = 5, 0 dB). Thus, we can see the effect of the eye-gaze information under noisy environments expected in real poster sessions.

Table 9.6 Evaluation of speaker diarization (DER [%])

Method		SNR (dB)						
		∞	20	15	10	5	0	Average
Baseline MUSIC	[29]	16.94	23.14	31.66	47.92	67.03	88.80	45.92
Baseline + location constraint	[30]	8.34	14.45	22.31	36.09	55.80	78.05	35.84
Acoustic-only model	Eq. (9.2) w/o $g_{i,t}$	**6.16**	**7.28**	**9.36**	14.20	22.94	35.89	15.97
Multi-modal model	Eq. (9.2)	6.27	7.81	9.96	**13.69**	**18.18**	**21.61**	**12.92**

The weight coefficient α in Eq. (9.2) was also manually tuned where the stepping size was 0.1. In the clean environment (SNR = ∞ dB), the optimal weight was 1.0. On the other hand, in the noisy environments (SNR = 5 and 0 dB), the optimal weights were 0.6 or 0.5. These results suggest that the weight of eye-gaze features is appropriately increased in noisy environments. The average DER by the manual tuning is 11.78 %, which is slightly better than the result (12.92 %) by the automatic weight estimation (Eq. 9.3). Therefore, the automatic weight estimation works reasonably according to the acoustic environment.

9.4.2 Detection of Backchannels

The diarization result includes backchannels and also falsely accepted noise especially for audience's utterances. A post-processing model is introduced to detect and eliminate them and highlight questions and comments by the audience, which are important for efficient review of poster conversations. There have been few works on detection of backchannels while many studies have been conducted to predict appropriate timing of backchannels [32–35].

Backchannels suggest that the current speaker can hold the turn, and the listener does not take a turn. In that sense, the eye-gaze behaviors are different from those of turn-taking. Thus, a different model is trained using the eye-gaze behaviors to predict backchannels. Here, the multi-modal scheme formalized in the previous subsection is modified. The eye-gaze features and the multi-modal integration model are same, but here the acoustic features are re-designed. Multi-channel acoustic signals are enhanced for each participant by delay-and-sum beamforming. The enhanced signal is used to calculate the acoustic features as follows:

1. the number of time frames of the utterance segment calculated from the diarization result
2. MFCC parameters (12-MFCCs and 12-ΔMFCCs)
3. Power (and ΔPower)
4. Regression coefficients of fundamental frequency (F0) and power at the end of the preceding utterance [34]

Logistic regression models are trained to predict three events: backchannels, utterances other than backchannels, and noise. For each utterance segment as a result of speaker diarization, cumulative likelihoods are calculated by the three models, and they are normalized so that the sum of the three is one. The eliminated utterance segments are determined by the thresholding operation with a sum of the posterior probabilities on backchannels and noise.

The diarization result is post-processed by another model for elimination of backchannels and noise. The reference labels in this experiment regard backchannels as non-speech events.

The following methods are compared. They were applied after the multi-modal speaker diarization (last row of Table 9.6).

1. *thresholding with utterance duration*
   A threshold in this method is the duration of each utterance section since the duration of backchannels is usually shorter than others. This corresponds to using only the first feature listed above.
2. *acoustic-only model*
   This method uses the acoustic features listed above.
3. *multi-modal model*
   This method also uses the eye-gaze features in addition to the acoustic features.

Here, we focus on substantial utterances by the audience for efficient access to the recordings. Since there are rarely overlapping utterances other than backchannels, we measured Equal Error Rate (EER) where False Acceptance Rate (FAR) equals to False Rejection Rate (FRR). FAR and FRR are defined as:

$$FAR = \frac{\#FA}{\#NS}, \quad FRR = \frac{\#FR}{\#S}, \tag{9.5}$$

where $\#NS$ is the number of non-speech frames in the reference. EER is calculated by varying the threshold in speaker diarization.

Table 9.7 lists EERs for each SNR. Compared to the case without post-processing (*no post-processing*), the proposed multi-modal model significantly reduces EERs. This shows the effectiveness of elimination of backchannels and noise after speaker diarization. The simple thresholding method (*thresholding with utterance duration*) reduces EERs in noisy conditions, but degrades in clean conditions. It is difficult to detect backchannels only with the utterance duration. The effect of the eye-gaze features is also confirmed under noisy environments (SNR = 5.0 dB).

Table 9.7 Evaluation of audience's speech detection (EER [%])

Method		SNR (dB)						
		∞	20	15	10	5	0	Average
No post-processing		13.37	15.80	17.86	20.86	25.77	31.80	20.91
Thresholding with utterance duration		15.95	17.60	18.64	20.38	24.74	30.81	21.35
Acoustic-only model	Eq. (9.2) w/o $g_{i,t}$	**12.14**	**13.98**	15.47	**18.19**	23.34	30.20	18.89
Multi-modal model	Eq. (9.2)	12.23	14.11	**15.42**	18.29	**23.07**	**29.72**	**18.80**

9.5 Detection of Hot Spots via Prominent Reactive Tokens of Audience

This section addresses high-level indexing of poster conversations based on the interactive characteristics. As opposed to the conventional content-based approach which focuses on the presenter's speech, we focus on the audience's reaction, specifically the audience's reactive tokens and laughter. By reactive tokens (*Aizuchi* in Japanese), we mean the listener's verbal short response, which expresses his/her state of the mind during the conversation. We particularly focus on prominent non-lexical reactive tokens, such as "*hu:n*", "*he:*" in Japanese and "wow", "gosh" in English, which are not used for simple acknowledgment and presumably related with the state of the mind of the listener. These can be articulated with a variety of prosodic patterns; they can be prolonged to an arbitrary length.

It is assumed that the audience signals their interest level with this kinds of non-lexical reactive tokens, and that detection of the audience's interest level is useful for indexing the speech archives, because people would be interested in listening to the points other people were interested in. It is also presumed that people would be interested in the funny spots where laughter was made. In this work, those spots which induced (or elicited) laughter and non-lexical reactive tokens are defined as hot spots, and their automatic detection is investigated.

In this study, eight poster sessions are used.

9.5.1 Detection of Laughter and Reactive Tokens

Detection of laughter has been addressed by several studies [36–38]. Typically, a dedicated classifier such as GMM and SVM is prepared for discriminating laughter against speech. On the other hand, studies on detecting reactive tokens is limited. Ward [39] investigated prosodic patterns of reactive tokens, but did not conduct automatic detection. Other works [40, 41] focused on distinction of affirmative answers "yes" and tokens used in backchannels. In Japanese, there are a variety of syllabic patterns in reactive tokens, including both lexical and non-lexical tokens.

A framework for acoustic event detection in audio recordings of conversations is designed based on a combination of BIC-based segmentation and GMM-based classification [42]. For each segment, classification based on GMM is applied. GMMs are prepared for five classes of male speech, female speech, noise, laughter and reactive tokens. Laughter is detected with this GMM-based classification.

Reactive tokens are more difficult to detect, because they are much similar to normal speech in terms of acoustic characteristics. Thus, we incorporate two additional processes to verify the candidates of reactive tokens hypothesized by GMM-based classification. One is the filled pause detector which considers monotonousness of spectral and pitch patterns [43]. The other is a speech recognition system, which is used to filter out filled pauses included in its lexicon. In summary, reactive tokens are detected only when supported by the following three classifiers.

- dedicated GMM
- filled pause detector (to reject normal speech)
- speech recognizer (to reject fillers)

Detection accuracy of laughter and reactive tokens is shown in Table 9.8 with evaluation measures of recall, precision and F-measure. Here, F-measure is defined with a double weight on precision, because there are a number of indistinct laughter and reactive tokens, which are hard to recall and not useful for indexing.

As shown in Table 9.8, overall recall is not high, but we can detect most of the distinct events such as loud laughter and long reactive tokens. These distinct events are more related with the hot spots than subtle events. The frame-wise classification accuracy among five GMM classes is 82.3 %.

9.5.2 Subjective Evaluation of Detected Hot Spots

Based on the detected laughter and reactive tokens, hot spots are defined to correspond to these two kinds of events. Specifically, hot spots are labeled for utterances which induce (or elicit) the events. The segments are defined by utterance units, i.e. made of a couple of utterances, with a maximum duration determined by a threshold.

Table 9.8 Detection accuracy of laughter and reactive tokens

	Recall	Precision	F-measure
Laughter	0.419	0.750	0.648
Reactive token	0.439	0.707	0.630

Table 9.9 Ratio of appropriate hot spots among detected spots ("precision")

	Precision (oracle)
Spots accompanying laughter	74.7 % (89.2 %)
Spots accompanying reactive token	86.5 % (95.2 %)

Subjective evaluations were conducted on the hot spots indexed in this manner. Four subjects, who had not attended the presentation nor listened to the recorded audio content, were asked to listen to each of the segmented hot spots in the original time sequence, and to make evaluations on the questionnaire, as below.

Q1: Do you understand the reason why the reactive token/laughter occurred?
Q2: Do you find this segment interesting/funny?
Q3: Do you think this segment is necessary or useful for listening to the content?

The result of Question 1 (percentage of "yes"), summarized in Table 9.9, suggests the ratio of appropriate hot spots or "precision" among the detected hot spots, because the third person verified the spots were naturally inducing laughter or reactive tokens. The figures labeled "(oracle)" in Table 9.9 show the result when limited to the segments where laughter or reactive tokens were correctly detected. It is confirmed that a large majority of the detected spots are appropriate. There are more "false" detections for the segments accompanying laughter; laughter is socially made to relax the participants in the poster conversations.

The answers to Questions 2 and 3 are more subjective, but suggest the usefulness of the hot spots. Only a half of the spots associated with laughter are funny for the subjects (Q2), and they found 35 % of the spots not funny. The result suggests that feeling funny largely depends on the person. And we should note that there are not many funny parts in the poster sessions by nature.

On the other hand, more than 90 % of the spots associated with reactive tokens are interesting (Q2), and useful or necessary (Q3) for the subjects. The result supports the effectiveness of the hot spots extracted based on the reaction of the audience.

9.5.3 Prosodic Analysis of Reactive Tokens

In the system described above, all non-lexical reactive tokens are detected without considering their syllabic and prosodic patterns. In this subsection, syllabic and prosodic patterns of reactive tokens related with the interest level are investigated Generally, prosodic features play an important role in conveying para-linguistic and non-verbal information. In previous works [40, 41], it was reported that prosodic features are useful in identifying reactive tokens. Ward [39] made an analysis of pragmatic functions conveyed by the prosodic features in English non-lexical tokens.

An experiment was designed to identify the syllabic and prosodic patterns closely related with the interest level for detection of hot spots. For this investigation, three

Table 9.10 Significant combinations of syllabic and prosodic patterns of reactive tokens

		Interest	Surprise
hu:N	Duration	*	*
	F0 max		
	F0 range		
	Power		
he:	Duration	*	*
	F0 max	*	*
	F0 range		*
	Power	*	*
a:	Duration		
	F0 max	*	
	F0 range		
	Power	*	

syllabic patterns of "*hu:N*", "*he:*" and "*a:*" were selected. They are presumably related with the interest level and also most frequently observed in the corpus, except lexical tokens.

Duration, F0 (maximum and range) and power (maximum) are computed for each reactive token, and they are normalized for every person; for each feature, we compute the mean, and this mean is subtracted from the feature values.

For each syllabic kind of reactive token and for each prosodic feature, top-ten and bottom-ten samples, i.e. samples that have largest/smallest values of the prosodic feature, were selected. For each of them, an audio segment was extracted to cover the reactive token and its preceding utterances. This process is similar to the hot spot detection described in the previous subsection, but was done manually according to the criteria.

Then, five subjects listened to the audio segments and evaluated the audience's state of the mind. Twelve items were evaluated in a scale of four ("strongly feel" to "do not feel"). Among them two items are related to the interest level and other two items are related to the surprise level.[1] Table 9.10 lists the results (marked by "*") that have a statistically significant ($p < 0.05$) difference between top-ten and bottom-ten samples. It is observed that prolonged "*hu:N*" means interest and surprise while "*a:*" with higher pitch or larger power means interest. On the other hand, "*he:*" can be emphasized in all prosodic features to express interest and surprise.

Using this prosodic information will enhance the precision of the hot spot detection. The tokens with larger power and/or a longer duration is apparently easier to detect than indistinct tokens, and they are more related with the hot spot. This simple principle is consistent with the proposed scheme.

---

[1] We used different Japanese wording for interest and for surprise to enhance the reliability of the evaluation; we adopt the result if the two matches.

9.6 Prediction of Interest and Comprehension Level via Audience's Questions from Multi-modal Behaviors

Feedback behaviors of an audience are important cues in analyzing presentation-style conversations. We can guess whether the audience is attracted to the presentation by observing their feedback behaviors. This characteristic is more prominent when the audience is smaller; the audience can make not only non-verbal feedbacks such as nodding, but also verbal backchannels. Eye-gaze behaviors also becomes more observable. In poster conversations, moreover, the audience can ask questions even during the presentation. By observing their reactions, particularly the quantity and quality of their questions and comments, we can guess whether the presentation is understood or liked by the audience.

In the previous section, it is shown that non-lexical reactive tokens are a good indicator of the audience's interest level. The relationship between the audience's turn-taking and feedback behaviors including backchannels and eye-gaze patterns is also confirmed.

This section addresses estimation of the interest and comprehension level of the audience based on the multi-modal behaviors. As annotation of the interest and comprehension level is apparently difficult and largely subjective, we turn to speech acts which are observable and presumably related with these mental states. One is prominent reactive tokens signaled by the audience and the other is questions raised by them. Moreover, questions are classified into confirming questions and substantive questions. Prediction of these speech acts from the multi-modal behaviors is expected to approximate the estimation of the interest and comprehension level.

In this study, ten poster sessions are used. Each poster was designed to introduce research topics of the presenter to researchers or students in other fields. It consists of four or eight components (hereafter called "slide topics") of rather independent topics. This design is a bit different from typical posters presented in academic conferences, but makes it straightforward to assess the interest and comprehension level of the audience for each slide topic. Usually, a poster conversation proceeds with an explanation of slide topics one by one, and is followed by an overall QA and discussion phase. In the QA/discussion phase, it is difficult to annotate which topic they refer. Therefore, the conversation segments of the explanation on the slide topics are used.

In the ten sessions used in this study, there are 58 slide topics in total. Since two persons participated as an audience in each session, there are 116 slots (hereafter called "topic segments") for which the interest and comprehension level should be estimated.

9.6.1 Definition of Interest and Comprehension Level

In order to get a gold-standard annotation, it would be a natural way to ask every participant of the poster conversations on the interest and comprehension level on each slide topic after the session. However, this is not possible in a large scale and also for the previously recorded sessions. The questionnaire results may also be subjective and difficult to assess the reliability.

Therefore, we focus on observable speech acts which are closely related with the interest and comprehension level. In the previous section, we identified particular syllabic and prosodic patterns of reactive tokens ("*he:*", "*a:*", "*fu:N*" in Japanese, corresponding to "wow" in English) signal interest of the audience [44]. We refer to them as prominent reactive tokens.

We also empirically know that questions raised by the audience signal their interest; the audience ask more questions to know more and better when they are more attracted to the presentation. Furthermore, we can judge the comprehension level by examining the kind of questions; when the audience asks something already explained, they must have a difficulty in understanding it.

9.6.1.1 Annotation of Question Type

Questions are classified into two types: confirming questions and substantive questions. The confirming questions are asked to make sure of the understanding of the current explanation, thus they can be answered simply by "Yes" or "No". [2] The substantive questions, on the other hand, are asking about what was not explained by the presenter, thus they cannot be answered by "Yes" or "No" only; an additional explanation is needed. Substantial questions are occasionally comments even in a question form.

9.6.1.2 Relationship Between Question Type and Interest and Comprehension Level

In four sessions, audience subjects were asked to answer their interest and comprehension level on each slide topic after the session. These are used for analysis on the relationship between these gold-standard annotations and observed questions.

Figure 9.7 shows distributions of the interest and comprehension level for each question type. The interest level is quantized into five levels from 1 (not interested) to 5 (very interested), and the comprehension level is marked from 1 (did not understand) to 5 (fully understood). In the graph, a majority of confirming questions (86%) indicate a low comprehension level (level 1 and 2). We also see a general tendency that occurrence of questions of either types is correlated with a higher interest level (level 4&5).

---

[2]This does not mean the presenter actually answered simply by "Yes" or "No".

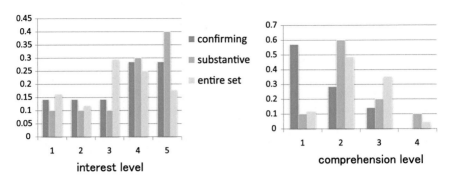

Fig. 9.7 Distribution of interest and comprehension level according to question type

From these observations and the previous finding, the following annotation scheme is adopted.

- high interest level ← questions of any types and/or prominent reactive tokens.
- low comprehension level ← confirming questions.

Detection of these states would be particularly useful in reviewing the poster sessions or improving the presentations.

9.6.2 Relationship Between Multi-modal Behaviors and Questions

Next, statistics of backchannel and eye-gaze behaviors of the audience are investigated on their relationship with questions asked by them.

9.6.2.1 Backchannels

It is assumed that the listener tends to make backchannels more frequently when they are attracted. In this analysis, non-lexical reactive tokens (e.g. "wow") are excluded since the prominent part of them are used for the annotation, though their occurrence frequency is much smaller (less than 20 % of all) than that of the lexical tokens (e.g. "yeah" and "okay").

Nodding is regarded as a non-verbal backchannel, and it is more frequently observed in poster conversations than in daily conversations. Our preliminary analysis showed, however, that there is not a distinct tendency in the occurrence frequency of non-verbal noddings, thus they are not used.

The occurrence frequency of the verbal backchannels normalized by the presenter's utterance (sentence unit) is counted within the topic segments. The statistics are listed according to the question type in Table 9.11. In the table, "entire" means

Table 9.11 Relationship of audience's backchannel (count/utterance) and questions (by type)

	Confirming	Substantive	Entire
Backchannel	0.42	0.52	0.34

Table 9.12 Relationship of audience's eye-gaze at the presenter (count/utterance and duration ratio) and questions (by type)

	Confirming	Substantive	Entire
Gaze occurrence	**0.38**	**1.02**	0.64
Gaze duration	0.05	**0.15**	0.07

the overall average computed for the entire topic segments of the data set. Since no questions were made in more than a half topic segments, the entire average is lower than the values in the other two columns. It is observed that the audience make more backchannels when asking questions, especially substantive questions.

9.6.2.2 Eye-Gaze at Presenter

The object and the duration of the eye-gaze of all participants during the topic segments are identified prior to the audiences' questions. The target object can be either the poster or other participants. In poster conversations, unlike daily conversations, participants look at the poster in most of the time. Therefore, eye-gaze at other participants has a reason and effect. The analysis in Sect. 9.3 showed that eye-gaze information is related with turn-taking events; specifically, the eye-gaze by the presenter mostly controls the turn-taking.

In this work, the eye-gaze by the audience is investigated on its relationship with the questions they ask. In particular, the eye-gaze of each person of the audience at the presenter is counted. The average occurrence count (per presenter's utterance) and the total duration (normalized per second) within the topic segments are measured. Their statistics are listed in Table 9.12. We can see a significant decrease and increase when asking confirming questions and substantive questions, respectively. It is reasoned that the audience is more focused on the poster trying to understand the content before asking confirming questions, while they want to attract the presenter's attention before asking substantive questions.

In a more detailed analysis done sentence by sentence, a gradual increase of the eye-gaze at the presenter is observed prior to substantive questions, while there is no such dynamic changes in the case of confirming questions.

The results suggest that eye-gaze information is potentially useful for identifying the question type and also estimating the interest and comprehension level.

9.6.3   Prediction of Interest and Comprehension Level

Based on the analysis in the previous subsection, we have implemented and evaluated classifiers to predict the interest and comprehension level of the audience in each topic segment.

First, each of audience behaviors needs to be parameterized. The features described in the previous subsection are used. An average count of backchannels per the presenter's utterance is computed. Eye-gaze at the presenter is parameterized into an occurrence count per the presenter's utterance and the duration ratio within the topic segment.

Then, regarding the machine learning method for classification, a naive Bayes classifier is adopted, as the data size is not so large to estimate extra parameters such as weights of the features. For a given feature vector $F = \{f_1, \ldots, f_d\}$, a naive Bayes classification is done by

$$p(c|F) = p(c) * \prod_i p(f_i|c)$$

where c is a considered class ("high interest level or not" and "low comprehension level or not"). For computation of $p(f_i|c)$, we adopt a simple histogram quantization, in which feature values are classified into one of bins, instead of assuming a probabilistic density function. This also circumvents estimation of any model parameters. The feature bins are defined by simply splitting a histogram into 3 or 4. Then, the relative occurrence frequency in each bin is transformed into the probability form.

Experimental evaluations were done by cross-validation.

9.6.3.1   Prediction of Questions and Reactive Tokens for Interest Level Estimation

First, an experiment of estimating the interest level of the audience was conducted. This problem is formulated by predicting the topic segment in which questions and/or prominent reactive tokens are made by the audience. These topic segments are regarded as "interesting" to the person who made such speech acts.

The results with different sets of features are listed in Table 9.13. F-measure is a harmonic mean of recall and precision of "interesting" segments, though recall and precision are almost same in this experiment. Accuracy is a ratio of correct output among all 116 topic segments. The chance-rate baseline when we count all segments as "interesting" is 49.1 %.

Incorporation of the backchannel and eye-gaze features significantly improves the accuracy, and the combination of both features results in the best accuracy of over 70 %. It turned out that the two kinds of parameterization of the eye-gaze feature (occurrence count and duration ratio) are redundant because dropping one of them

Table 9.13 Prediction result of topic segments involving questions and/or reactive tokens

	F-measure	Accuracy (%)
Baseline (chance rate)	0.49	49.1
(1) Backchannel	0.59	55.2
(2) Gaze occurrence	0.63	61.2
(3) Gaze duration	0.65	57.8
Combination of (1)–(3)	0.70	70.7

Table 9.14 Identification result of confirming or substantive questions

	Accuracy (%)
Baseline (chance rate)	51.3
(1) Backchannel	56.8
(2) Gaze occurrence	75.7
(3) Gaze duration	67.6
Combination of (1)–(3)	75.7

does not degrade the performance. However, we confirm the multi-modal synergetic effect of the backchannel and eye-gaze information.

9.6.3.2 Identification of Question Type for Comprehension Level Estimation

Next, an experiment of estimating the comprehension level of the audience was conducted. This problem is formulated by identifying the confirming question given a question, which signals that the person does not understand the topic segment. Namely, these topic segments are regarded as "low comprehension (difficult to understand)" for the person who made the confirming questions.

The classification results of confirming questions versus substantive questions are listed in Table 9.14. In this task, the chance-rate baseline based on the prior statistic $p(c)$ is 51.3 %.

All features have some effects in improving the accuracy, but the eye-gaze occurrence count alone achieves the best performance and combining it with other features does not give an additional gain. This is explained by a large difference in its value among the question types as shown in Table 9.12.

As the simple occurrence frequency of backchannels is not useful for this task, the syllabic or prosodic patterns of the backchannels [45] should be investigated in the future.

9.7   Poster Session Browser

Based on the result and findings of this study, a poster session browser is designed and developed, as shown in Fig. 9.8. The browser visualizes activities during the poster session including speech utterances and eye-gaze at other participants for each person. It also plays the recorded audio and video based on the indices.

Along the timeline, utterance segments of each participant are marked as a result of speaker diarization and backchannel detection. We can easily access to substantial utterances from the audience such as questions and comments. Moreover, eye-gaze events are also visualized so we can estimate the interaction level of the conversation. For each person in the audience, the marked segments represent when the person gave his/her eye-gaze to the presenter.

Under the timeline, a scale-downed timeline overview is shown to allow users to outlook the entire session. By clicking a segment on the timeline overview, users can directly move to the area and see the conversation segment in the area. Poster sessions generally last very long and presenters need to explain the same content repeatedly while substantial utterances such as questions and comments by an audience is occasional but important. The above functions allow the users to efficiently access to the substantial utterances without watching the entire video.

The browser will be helpful for the presenter to review the session afterwards, since the presenter can hardly memorize the audience's questions and comments during the long session. The browser will also be useful for the colleagues or supervisor of the presenter to see how many people came to the poster and if they were interested in the presentation. It is also possible to quickly view what the audience said and how the presenter responded to them. In the future, the browser may be used in public, so viewers see the other participants' comments. But this needs to obtain a permission from the participants as well as the session organizer.

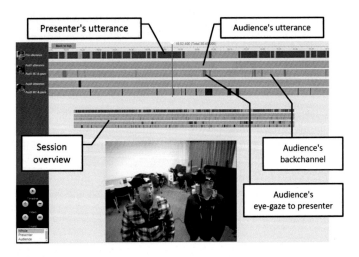

Fig. 9.8 Poster conversation browser

Table 9.15 Browsing time to complete quizzes; "reduction ratio" is measured against the session duration

Subject	Time	Reduction ratio (%)
A	9 m 50 s	33.3
B	8 m 11 s	27.7
C	8 m 13 s	27.8
D	6 m 58 s	23.6
Average	8 m 18 s	28.1

Since the system is independent of conversational content (e.g. audio, video, utterance segment), users can easily customize this tool to other conversational forms such as meetings and discussions. Detailed information of the visualized data is described in a configuration csv file. Various types of time-series multi-modal data can be displayed on the timeline by editing the csv file. The csv file also describes the display format of the browser: colors of segments on the timeline and display positions of the visualized data. The system is designed as a Web application where the backend is implemented in Java, and the interface is implemented in HTML, CSS, and Javascript. Playing videos and audios is realized by HTML5. The browser is lightweight and OS-independent.

A simple evaluation of the browser interface was conducted by measuring the time needed for reviewing substantial exchanges in a poster session. One session was chosen from our corpus and four subjects were engaged in this experiment. They were asked to answer twelve quizzes by browsing the recorded session. The quizzes were chosen from the questions uttered by the audience and the two possible answers were prepared. The subjects were asked to select one of them which was actually given by the presenter. The questions were sorted in a time-wise random manner.

Table 9.15 shows the time the subjects expended to complete all quizzes. All subjects were able to correctly answer all quizzes in less than ten minutes, whereas the session actually lasted 29 min. On average, reviewing time is approximately 28.1 % of the duration of the session. The browser with the speaker diarization result provides an effective interface to efficiently search substantial utterances in the session.

9.8 Conclusions

We have conducted multi-modal conversation analysis focused on poster sessions. Poster conversations are interactive, but often long and redundant. Therefore, simple recording of the session is not so useful.

The primary goal of the study was robust signal-level sensing of participants, i.e. who came to the poster, and their verbal feedbacks, i.e. what they said. This is still challenging given distant and low-resolution sensing devices. Combination of multi-modal information sources was investigated to enhance the performance.

First, multi-modal behaviors prior to turn-taking events were investigated. For prediction of speaker change or turn-taking by the audience, both prosodic features of the presenter and eye-gaze features of all participants are useful. The most relevant among the eye-gaze information is the presenter's gazing at the speaker to whom the turn is to be yielded.

Based on this finding, a multi-modal speaker diarization method was realized by integrating eye-gaze information with acoustic information. Moreover, the diarization result was enhanced by eliminating backchannels and falsely accepted noise. The stochastic multi-modal scheme improved the performance of speaker diarization and the effect of eye-gaze information was confirmed under noisy environments.

The next step was high-level indexing of interest and comprehension level of the audience. The problem was formulated via relevant speech acts using non-verbal feedback behaviors of the audience. Two approaches were presented in this work.

One is indexing of hot spots based on the reaction of the audience, specifically, laughter and non-lexical reactive tokens. Detection of laughter is relatively easier, but the detected spots are not necessarily funny or useful, because the evaluation is largely affected by subjects. On the other hand, the spots associated with reactive tokens are consistently interesting and meaningful. Furthermore, the specific prosodic patterns closely related with the interest level were identified.

The other approach is estimation of interest and comprehension level based on the audience's feedback behaviors and speech acts such as questions and prominent reactive tokens. Specifically, estimation of the interest level was reduced to prediction of occurrence of questions and prominent reactive tokens, and estimation of comprehension level was realized by classification of the question type.

To visualize these detected events and indices, a poster session browser has been developed. The browser will be useful for assessing the effect of the processes and further improving them.

Acknowledgments This work was conducted by the members of the CREST project including Hiromasa Yoshimoto, Tony Tung, Yukoh Wakabayashi, Kouhei Sumi, Zhi-Qiang Chang, Takuma Iwatate, Soichiro Hayashi, Koji Inoue, Katsuya Takanashi (Kyoto University) and Yuji Onuma, Shunsuke Nakai, Ryoichi Miyazaki, Hiroshi Saruwatari (Nara Institute of Science and Technology).

References

1. S. Renals, T. Hain, H. Bourlard, Recognition and understanding of meetings: The AMI and AMIDA projects. *Proceedings of IEEE Workshop Automatic Speech Recognition & Understanding* (2007)
2. K. Ohtsuka, Conversation scene analysis. Signal Process. Magaz. **28**(4), 127–131 (2011)
3. T. Kawahara, Multi-modal sensing and analysis of poster conversations toward smart posterboard. In *Proceedings of SIGdial Meeting Discourse and Dialogue*, pp. 1–9 (keynote speech) (2012)
4. T. Kawahara, Smart posterboard: Multi-modal sensing and analysis of poster conversations. In *Proceedings of APSIPA ASC*, page (plenary overview talk) (2013)

5. T. Kawahara, H.Setoguchi, K. Takanashi, K.Ishizuka, S. Araki, Multi-modal recording, analysis and indexing of poster sessions. *Proceedings of INTERSPEECH*, pp. 1622–1625 (2008)
6. K. Maekawa, Corpus of spontaneous Japanese: its design and evaluation. *Proceedings of ISCA and IEEE Workshop on Spontaneous Speech Processing and Recognition*, pp. 7–12 (2003)
7. H. Yoshimoto, Y. Nakamura, Cubistic representation for real-time 3D shape and pose estimation of unknown rigid object. *Proceedings ICCV, Workshop*, pp. 522–529 (2013)
8. Y. Takahashi, T. Takatani, K. Osako, H. Saruwatari, K. Shikano, Blind spatial subtraction array for speech enhancement in noisy environment. IEEE Trans. Audio, Speech Language Process. **17**(4), 650–664 (2009)
9. T. Ohsuga, M. Nishida, Y. Horiuchi, A. Ichikawa, Investigation of the relationship between turn-taking and prosodic features in spontaneous dialogue. *Proceedings INTERSPEECH*, pp. 33–36 (2005)
10. C.T. Ishi, H. Ishiguro, N. Hagita, Analysis of prosodic and linguistic cues of phrase finals for turn-taking and dialog acts. *Proceedings of INTERSPEECH*, pp. 2006–2009 (2006)
11. N.G. Ward, Y.A. Bayyari, A case study in the identification of prosodic cues to turn-taking: back-channeling in Arabic. *Proceedings of INTERSPEECH*, pp. 2018–2021 (2006)
12. B. Xiao, V. Rozgic, A. Katsamanis, B.R. Baucom, P.G. Georgiou, S. Narayanan, Acoustic and visual cues of turn-taking dynamics in dyadic interactions. *Proceedings of INTERSPEECH*, pp. 2441–2444 (2011)
13. R. Sato, R. Higashinaka, M. Tamoto, M. Nakano, K. Aikawa, Learning decision trees to determine turn-taking by spoken dialogue systems. *Proceedings of ICSLP*, pp. 861–864 (2002)
14. D. Schlangen, From reaction to prediction: experiments with computational models of turn-taking. *Proceedings INTERSPEECH*, pp. 2010–2013 (2006)
15. A. Raux, M. Eskenazi, A finite-state turn-taking model for spoken dialog systems. *Proceedings of HLT/NAACL* (2009)
16. N.G. Ward, O. Fuentes, A. Vega, Dialog prediction for a general model of turn-taking. *Proceedings of INTERSPEECH*, pp. 2662–2665 (2010)
17. S. Benus, Are we 'in sync': turn-taking in collaborative dialogues. *Proceedings of INTERSPEECH*, pp. 2167–2170 (2009)
18. N. Campbell, S. Scherer, Comparing measures of synchrony and alignment in dialogue speech timing with respect to turn-taking activity. *Proceedings of INTERSPEECH*, pp. 2546–2549 (2010)
19. D. Bohus, E. Horvitz, Models for multiparty engagement in open-world dialog. *Proceedings of SIGdial* (2009)
20. S. Fujie, Y. Matsuyama, H. Taniyama, T. Kobayashi, Conversation robot participating in and activating a group communication. *Proceedings of INTERSPEECH*, pp. 264–267 (2009)
21. K. Laskowski, J. Edlund, M. Heldner, A single-port non-parametric model of turn-taking in multi-party conversation. *Proceedings of ICASSP*, pp. 5600–5603 (2011)
22. K. Jokinen, K. Harada, M. Nishida, S. Yamamoto, Turn-alignment using eye-gaze and speech in conversational interaction. *Proceedings of InterSpeech*, pp. 2018–2021 (2011)
23. A. Kendon, Some functions of gaze direction in social interaction. Acta Psychol. **26**, 22–63 (1967)
24. S.E. Tranter, D.A. Reynolds, An overview of automatic speaker diarization systems. IEEE Trans. ASLP **14**(5), 1557–1565 (2006)
25. G. Friedland, A. Janin, D. Imseng, X. Anguera Miro, L. Gottlieb, M. Huijbregts, M.T. Knox, O. Vinyals, The ICSI RT-09 speaker diarization system. IEEE Trans. ASLP **20**(2), 371–381 (2012)
26. R. Schmidt, Multiple emitter location and signal parameter estimation. IEEE Trans. Antennas Propag. **34**(3), 276–280 (1986)
27. K. Yamamoto, F. Asano, T. Yamada, N. Kitawaki, Detection of overlapping speech in meetings using support vector machines and support vector regression. IEICE Trans. **E89-A**(8), 2158–2165 (2006)
28. H. Misra, H. Bourlard, V. Tyagi, New entropy based combination rules in hmm/ann multi-stream asr. Proc. ICASSP **2**, 741–744 (2003)

29. S. Araki, M. Fujimoto, K. Ishizuka, H. Sawada, S. Makino, A DOA based speaker diarization system for real meetings. *Prooceedings of HSCMA*, pp. 29–32 (2008)
30. Y. Wakabayashi, K. Inoue, H. Yoshimoto, T. Kawahara, Speaker diarization based on audio-visual integration for smart posterboard. *Proceedings of APSIPA ASC* (2014)
31. J.G. Fiscus, J. Ajot, M. Michel, J.S. Garofolo, *The Rich Transcription 2006 Spring Meeting Recognition Evaluation* (Springer, 2006)
32. H. Koiso, Y. Horiuchi, S. Tutiya, A. Ichikawa, Y. Den, An analysis of turn-taking and backchannels based on prosodic and syntactic features in Japanese map task dialogs. Language & Speech **41**(3–4), 295–321 (1998)
33. N. Ward, W. Tsukahara, Prosodic features which cue back-channel responses in English and Japanese. J. Pragmatics **32**(8), 1177–1207 (2000)
34. N. Kitaoka, M. Takeuchi, R. Nishimura, S. Nakagawa, Response timing detection using prosodic and linguistic information for human-friendly spoken dialog systems. J. Japn. Soc. Artific. Intell. **20**(3), 220–228 (2005)
35. D. Ozkan, L.-P. Morency, Modeling wisdom of crowds using latent mixture of discriminative experts. *Proceedings of ACL/HLT* (2011)
36. L.S.Kennedy, D.P.W. Ellis, Laughter detection in meetings. *NIST Meeting Recognition Workshop* (2004)
37. K.P. Truong, D.A. van Leeuwen, Automatic detection of laughter. *Proceedings InterSpeech*, pp. 485–488 (2005)
38. K.Laskowski, Contrasting emotion-bearing laughter types in multiparticipant vocal activity detection for meetings. *Proceedings of IEEE-ICASSP*, pp. 4765–4768 (2009)
39. N. Ward, Pragmatic functions of prosodic features in non-lexical utterances. *Speech Prosody*, pp. 325–328 (2004)
40. F. Yang, G. Tur, E. Shriberg, Exploiting dialog act tagging and prosodic information for action item identification. *Proceedings of IEEE-ICASSP*, pp. 4941–4944 (2008)
41. A. Gravano, S. Benus, J. Hirschberg, S. Mitchell, I. Vovsha, Classification of discourse functions of affirmative words in spoken dialogue. *Proceedings of InterSpeech*, pp. 1613–1616 (2007)
42. K. Sumi, T. Kawahara, J. Ogata, M. Goto, Acoustic event detection for spotting hot spots in podcasts. *Proceedings of INTERSPEECH*, pp. 1143–1146 (2009)
43. M. Goto, K. Itou, S. Hayamizu, A real-time filled pause detection system for spontaneous speech recognition research. *Proceedings of EuroSpeech*, pp. 227–230 (1999)
44. T. Kawahara, Z.Q. Chang, K. Takanashi, Analysis on prosodic features of Japanese reactive tokens in poster conversations. *Proceedings Int'l Conference Speech Prosody* (2010)
45. S. Strombergsson, J. Edlund, D. House, Prosodic measurements and question types in the spontal corpus of Swedish dialogues. *Proceedings of InterSpeech* (2012)

Chapter 10
Critical Roles of Implicit Interpersonal Information in Communication

Makio Kashino, Shinsuke Shimojo and Katsumi Watanabe

Abstract Recent studies of cognitive science have convincingly demonstrated that human behavior, decision making and emotion depend heavily on "implicit mind," that is, automatic, involuntary mental processes even the person herself/himself is not aware of. Such implicit processes may interact between partners, producing a kind of "resonance," in which two or more bodies and brains, coupled via sensorimotor systems, act nearly as a single system. The basic concept of this project is that such "implicit interpersonal information (IIPI)" provides the basis for smooth and effective communication. We have been developing new methods to decode IIPI from brain activities, physiological responses, and body movements, and to control IIPI by sensorimotor stimulation and non-invasive brain stimulation. Here, we detail on two topics from the project, namely, interpersonal synchronization of involuntary body movements as IIPI, and autism as an impairment of IIPI. The findings of the project would provide guidelines for developing human-harmonized information systems.

Keywords Implicit interpersonal information (IIPI) · Interpersonal synchronization · Body movement · Hyperscanning electroencephalogram (EEG) · Eye movement · Pupil diameter · Autonomic nervous system · Oxytocin · Autism spectrum disorder · Sensorimotor specificity

M. Kashino (✉)
NTT Communication Science Laboratories, NTT Corporation, Kanagawa, Japan
e-mail: kashino.makio@lab.ntt.co.jp

S. Shimojo
California Institute of Technology, California, USA
e-mail: sshimojo@caltech.edu

K. Watanabe
Waseda University, Tokyo, Japan
e-mail: katz@waseda.jp

© Springer Japan 2016
T. Nishida (ed.), *Human-Harmonized Information Technology, Volume 1*,
DOI 10.1007/978-4-431-55867-5_10

271

10.1 Introduction

Various kinds of telecommunication systems, such as smart phones, chat, and video conference systems, are widely used in the modern world. These systems enable us to communicate with others conveniently beyond the restriction of the physical space. Compared to face-to-face communication, however, it is often difficult to transmit subtle nuances and "atmosphere" with those systems. As a consequence, it typically leads to inefficient discussions, misunderstandings, and conflicts, which would be largely avoided in face-to-face communication.

The conventional approach to solve such problems is to improve the physical performance of the system (by increasing the size and resolution of a visual display, the number of channels of the audio signal, and the frequency band, and so on). Such technical improvements bring about certain improvements, but not sufficient. As far as the user is a human, any technological improvements can not be effective unless it is expedient to human characteristics and mechanisms. Moreover, communication may be rather disturbed by adding unnecessary information. Thus, conversation over the conventional telephone can be less stressful than that by using video conference system with high-definition screen.

We approach the problem from the other side, namely, a human-centered viewpoint. In the first place, what are the critical factors that determine the quality of human communication? Once such factors are identified, it is possible to establish the design principles for securing face-to-face communication quality even via remote communication systems. In addition, by controlling the critical information appropriately, it may be possible to implement communication systems with enhanced nuances and reduced disturbance comparing to face-to-face interaction. Also, the systematic knowledge of factors that determine the quality of communication will be applicable not only to the interaction of human-to-human, but also to the interaction of the human-to-computer systems, which will become quite common in the near future. Having these things in mind, we started this project in 2010 to identify factors that determine the quality of communication, and their neural basis.

The fundamental assumption of our project is that consciousness (or explicit mind) is only a fraction of the whole "mind" [1]. Recent findings of cognitive science convincingly demonstrated that human behavior, decision making and emotion depend not only on conscious deliberation, but heavily on "implicit mind," that is, automatic, fast, involuntary mental processes even the person herself/himself is not aware of [2, 3]. Then, it would be natural that such implicit processes also play critical roles in human-to-human communication. In daily communication, needless to say, explicit information such as language and symbolic gestures is indispensable. At the same time, the internal state of a person can be represented by implicit information, such as subtle, unintended body movements and various physiological changes reflecting the activities of the autonomic and endocrine systems. Such implicit information can be thought of as rather "honest" information because it cannot be controlled voluntarily as in telling a lie using language. Even though the recipients are not aware of such implicit information, their feelings and decisions may be affected faithfully by

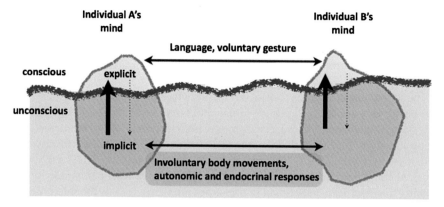

Fig. 10.1 Concept of IIPI [1]. Human behavior, decision making and emotion depend not only on conscious deliberation, but heavily on "implicit mind," that is, automatic, fast, involuntary mental processes even the person herself/himself is not aware of. In interpersonal communication, unconscious body movements of partners interact with one another, creating a kind of resonance. The resonance, or "implicit interpersonal information (IIPI)," may provide basis for understanding and sharing emotions, in addition to explicit language and gesture

the stimulus and the context. Such implicit processes may interact between partners, producing a kind of "resonance," in which two or more bodies and brains, coupled via sensorimotor systems, act nearly as a single system. The general aim of this project is to test the general hypothesis that such "implicit interpersonal information (IIPI)" provides the basis for smooth communication (Fig. 10.1).

To this end, we have been conducting several lines of research in parallel. The first is to identify and to decode IIPI. As the saying goes, "the eyes are more eloquent than the mouth." In the context of decoding mental states from the eyes, gaze direction has been used extensively as an index of visual attention or interest. However, what is reflected on the eyes is not limited to mental states directed to or evoked by visual objects. We have been studying how to decode mental states such as saliency, familiarity, and preference not only for visual objects but also for sounds based on the information obtained from the eyes. Such information includes a kind of eye movement called microsaccade (small, rapid, involuntary eye movements, which typically occur once in a second or two during visual fixation) [4] and changes in pupil diameter (controlled by the balance of sympathetic and parasympathetic nervous systems, and reflects, to some extent, the level of neurotransmitters that control cognitive processing in the brain) [5, 6].

We have also been studying the responses of the brain and autonomic nervous systems, hormone secretion, and body movements. In one of such studies, we have developed a method to measure the concentration of oxytocin (a hormone considered to promote trust and attachment to others) in human saliva with the highest accuracy at present. This enabled us to identify a physiological mechanism underlying relaxation induced by music listening. Listening to music with a slow tempo promotes the secretion of oxytocin, which activates the parasympathetic nervous system, resulting in relaxation [7].

While above mentioned methods are for decoding the information about the implicit mental states of an individual, we have further proceeded to study the interpersonal interaction of such information. As an example, in Sect. 10.2, we will introduce in some detail the study on the interpersonal synchronization of implicit body actions.

The second line of research focuses on patients with communication disorders. We have been trying to identify the cause of impaired communication in high-functioning (i.e., without intellectual disorder) autism spectrum disorder (ASD). We found that the basic sensory functions of ASD individuals often show specific patterns distinct from those of neurotypical (NT) individuals. The findings provide a fresh view that impaired communication in high-functioning ASD may, at least partly, due to the inability to detect IIPI, rather than higher-order problems such as the inference of other's intention ("theory of mind" [8, 9]). We will cover this topic in some detail in Sect. 10.3.

The third line of research is the development of the methods to improve the quality of communication by controlling IIPI and/or neural processes involved in the processing of IIPI. We have identified factors that could occur in communication systems and hamper IIPI, such as transmission delay, asynchrony between sensory modalities, transmission loss of information about subtle facial expressions and body movements. Then we examined their impact on the quality of communication, tolerance and adaptability of users. These studies provide guidelines for achieving the same communication quality as face-to-face. Moreover, we have developed techniques to overcome the physical limitations of communication systems such as delay or asynchrony by controlling sensory information [10]. We have also been studying the method of non-invasive brain stimulation on neural sites involved in the processing of IIPI, such as the reward system deep inside the brain [11–13].

The fourth is the elucidation of neural mechanisms involved in the processing of IIPI. We conducted simultaneous measurement of brain activities of two parties performing a coordination task to identify relevant brain sites and to analyze the interaction of those sites across brains [14] (Sect. 10.2). Further, we established animal models (rats) of communication to study neural mechanisms underlying social facilitation and mirroring using invasive brain measurements and stimulation [15].

In the following sections, we will pick up a few among those research results.

10.2 Interpersonal Synchronization as IIPI

Social communication has been considered one of the most complex cognitive functions, partly due to its close relationship to language, and other explicit mental processes such as top-down executive control, inference and decision making. On the other hand, the recent discovery of the mirror neuron and the mirror system [16] point to somewhat different direction, i.e. a more automatic and spontaneous nature of social communication. So after all, is social communication at a higher cognitive, or a lower biological level of mental processing? – Both, obviously, but what is relatively neglected is the latter. Bodily synchrony in various species may be interpreted as a primitive biological basis of social behavior. Synchronization phenomena in croaking of frogs, glimmer of firefly, alarming call of birds, are just to name a few examples.

This line of consideration immediately raises a question as to whether synchrony provides a somatic basis of sociality in the human, and what underlying neural mechanisms makes it possible. In the following, we will provide one of the earliest evidence for such, and the tight link between behavioral and social synchrony.

Synchronization is, in a broad physical sense, coordination of rhythmic oscillators due to their interaction. Interpersonal body movement synchronization has been widely observed. A person's footsteps unconsciously synchronize with those of a partner when two people are walking together, even though their foot lengths, and thus their intrinsic cycles, are different [17–19]. The phenomenon has been thought of as social self-organizing process [20]. Previous studies found that the degree of interpersonal body movement synchrony, such as finger tapping and drumming, predicted subsequent social ratings [21, 22]. The findings indicate a close relationship between social interface and body movement synchronization [23]. However, the mechanism of body movement synchrony and its relationship to implicit interpersonal interaction remain vague.

We thus aimed to evaluate unconscious body movement synchrony and implicit interpersonal interactions between two participants [14]. We also aimed to assess the underlying neural correlates and functional connectivity within and among the brain regions of two participants.

We measured unconscious fingertip movements between the two participants while simultaneously recording electroencephalogram (EEG) in a face-to-face setting (Fig. 10.2a, b). Participants were asked to straighten their arms, point and hold their index fingers toward each other, and look at the other participant's fingertip. Face-to-face interactions simplify yet closely approximate real-life situations and reinforce the social nature of interpersonal interactions [24].

We believe that our implicit fingertip synchrony task, as well as unconscious footstep synchrony, interpersonal finger tapping and drumming synchrony, are all forms of social synchronization and our task is the simplest form of such. Thus, we hypothesized that interpersonal interaction between two participants would increase body movement synchronization and the interaction would be correlated with social traits of personality. The traits in turn would possibly be reflected in within- and among-brain synchronizations. More specifically, we expected experience-based changes of synchrony in sensorimotor as well as in theory-of-mind related networks, including the precuneus, inferior parietal and posterior temporal cortex [25, 26]. The parietal cortex is especially expected to be involved, given that implicit processing of emotional stimuli, as compared to explicit emotional processing, is associated with theta synchronization in the right parietal cortex [27]. Previous EEG simultaneous recording studies (i.e., hyperscanning EEG) also showed that the right parietal area played a key role in non-verbal social coordination and movement synchrony [28, 29].

(a)

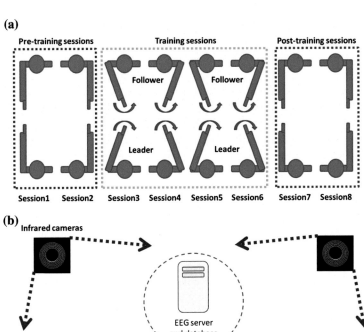

(b)

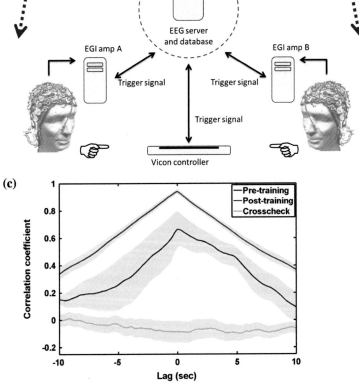

(c)

◀ **Fig. 10.2** Experimental setup and behavioral results [14]. **a** *Session 1* Participants were asked to straighten their arms, point and hold their index fingers toward each other, and look at the other participant's fingertip. They were instructed to look at the other participant's finger while holding their own finger as stationary as possible. One participant was instructed to use left arm and the other was instructed to use right arm. *Session 2* Same as the session 1, except participants changed the arm from left to right and from right to left respectively. *Session 3* One participant (leader, who was randomly selected from the naïve participant pair) was instructed to randomly move his finger (in the approximate area of 20 × 20 cm square) and the other (follower) was instructed to follow. *Session 4* Same as the session 3, except participants changed the arm from left to right and from right to left respectively. *Session 5 and 6* Same as the session 3 and 4, *Session 7 and 8* Same as the session 1 and 2. We call sessions 1–2 the pre-training sessions, the sessions 3–6 the training sessions, and the 7–8 the post-training sessions. **b** Hyperscanning-EEG setup. The EEG data was passed through a client to a EEG server and database, which was regulated by an experiment controller. Client computers received fingertip movement information from the two participants. Two EEG recording systems were synchronized using a pulse signal from the control server computer delivered to both EEG recording systems. **c** Average cross correlation coefficients of fingertip movements in each condition (pre-training, post-training, and crosscheck validation) with its standard errors (*gray*). The training significantly increased finger movement correlation between the two participants ($p < 0.03$). No significant correlation was found in crosscheck condition (i.e. cross correlation results after random shuffling of participants, $p = 0.62$). Results are shown as means s.e.m. Statistical analyses performed using a two-tailed student's t-test

Simultaneous functional magnetic resonance imaging (fMRI) of two participants, called hyperscanning, has been used to assess brain activity while participants can interact with each other [30, 31]. However, due to some technical limitations in fMRI, we believe that "hyperscanning EEG" of two participants may open new vistas on the neural mechanisms underlying social relationships and decision making [28, 29, 32, 33] by providing a tool for quantifying neural synchronization in face-to-face interactions with high temporal resolution [28, 34, 35].

Local neural synchronization can be detected by measuring frequency-specific power changes of each electrode component of the EEG. However, local power changes alone cannot provide evidence of large-scale network formation because it depends on oscillatory interactions between spatially distant cortical regions [36, 37], which may be critical for understanding neural mechanisms during interpersonal interaction. To address this issue, we used phase synchrony to quantify long-range functional connectivity; this would allow us to detect not only intra-brain, but also inter-brain connectivity.

Thus in short, we devised the novel combination of hyperscanning EEG and motion tracking with the implicit body movement synchronization paradigm [38]. The advantage of this experimental paradigm is twofold. First, we were able to detect an implicit-level interaction that is interpersonal and real time in nature (due to the instruction to the participant to keep its finger as stable as possible, neglecting the partner's). Unlike previous studies mainly concentrated on explicit social interactions, we specifically aimed to identify an implicit process by minimizing explicit interaction. "Social yet implicit" is the key word. Despite the instruction, the partner's finger movement turned out not to be entirely neglected at the implicit level, thus the participants tended to unconsciously synchronize each other.

The second advantage of the paradigm rests on the fact that since the instructions in our experimental paradigm were to stay stationary, movement artifacts were minimized in the EEG data. Robustness to noise during face-to-face interaction makes our experimental paradigm optimally sensitive to the underlying EEG dynamics and the functional connectivity of implicit interpersonal interaction.

We used such finger-to-finger task as an implicit synchrony measure in the pre- and the post-tests. Between them, was a training session where the two participants (the "leader" and the "follower") need to move their fingers cooperatively. There was a control training session where the follower was asked to move his/her finger not cooperatively (as different as possible) with the leader's movements.

We hypothesize that the cooperative training will increase both bodily and neural synchrony between the participants. We also hypothesize that such synchrony would be correlated with social trait of personality (measured by Leary's scales for social anxiety [39].

Summary of the results are as follows:

First, finger movement correlation between two participants was significantly higher in the post-training, in comparison to the pre-training sessions (Fig. 10.2c). The maximum correlation coefficients occurred at the zero time lag. However, the non-social or the non-responsive training did not increase synchrony.

Second, we found significant negative correlations of the fingertip synchrony increase with each pair's averaged scores of 'Fear of Negative Evaluation' and 'Blushing Propensity', indicating that the more the person has social anxiety, the less the fingertip synchrony increases.

Third, performing EEG-based source localization, we observed that theta (4–7.5 Hz) frequency activity in the precuneus (PrC) and beta (12–30 Hz) frequency activity in the right posterior middle temporal gyrus (MTG) increased significantly (Fig. 10.3a, b). The right inferior parietal and posterior temporal cortices have been suggested to play a critical role in various aspects of social cognition, such as theory of mind and empathy [25].

We also found a significant positive correlation between the fingertip synchrony changes from post- to pre-training sessions and the ventromedial prefrontal cortex (VMPFC) theta frequency activity (Fig. 10.3c). The VMPFC has been indicated as a shared circuit for reflective representations of both self (i.e., introspection) and others (i.e., theory of mind) [9].

Finally and most critically, the functional connectivity analysis found that the overall number of significant phase synchrony in inter-brain connections increased after training, but not in intra-brain connections (Fig. 10.4a). Thus, the cooperative training increased synchrony not only between fingertip movements of the two participants but also between cortical regions across the two brains. Inter-brain connections were found mainly in the inferior frontal gyrus (IFG), anterior cingulate (AC), parahippocampal gyrus (PHG), and postcentral gyrus (PoCG) (phase randomization surrogate statistics, $p < 0.000001$) (Fig. 10.4b, c), overall consistent with our hypotheses above.

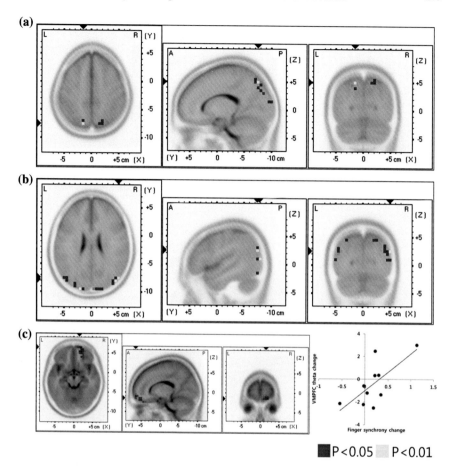

Fig. 10.3 sLORETA source localization [14]. Source localization contrasting between the post- and pre-training in **a** theta (4–7.5 Hz) and **b** beta (12–30 Hz) frequency range. The training significantly increased the theta (4–7.5 Hz) activity in the precuneus (PrC) (BA7, $X = -15, Y = -75, Z = 50$; MNI coordinates; corrected for multiple comparisons using nonparametric permutation test, *red* $p < 0.01, yellow$ $p < 0.001$) and the beta (12–30 Hz) activity in the posterior middle temporal gyrus (MTG) (BA39, $X = 50, Y = -74, Z = 24$; MNI coordinates; corrected for multiple comparisons using nonparametric permutation test, *red* $p < 0.05$, *yellow* $p < 0.01$). **c** Regression analysis. Significant positive correlation between the fingertip synchrony change and ventromedial prefrontal cortex beta frequency power change between post- and pre-training sessions (BA11, $X = 15, Y = 65, Z = -15$; MNI coordinates; regression with nonparametric permutation test, $p < 0.05, n = 20$)

The increase of fingertip synchrony after the training session indicates that the large, voluntary, and intentional mimicry affects the small, involuntary, and unintentional body movement synchronization afterwards. Two participants seem to build their own rhythmic structure during the intentional mimicry training, resulting in increased unintentional synchronization. It is consistent with, and extending the previous studies showing that motor mimicry increased implicit social interaction

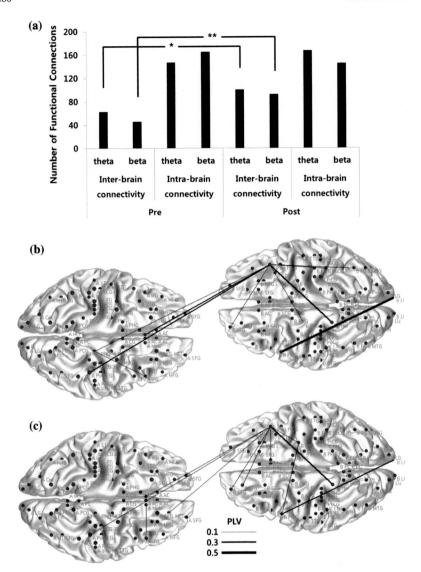

Fig. 10.4 Inter- and intra-brain phase synchrony [14]. **a** The total number of functional connections that showed significant phase synchrony (phase randomization surrogate statistics, $p < 0.000001$) of inter- and intra-brain in theta (4–7.5 Hz) and beta (12–30 Hz) frequency range (chi-square test, $^*p < 0.005$, $^{**}p < 0.0001$). The overall number of significant phase synchrony increased after training in inter-brain connections, but not in intra. **b** Topography of the phase synchrony connections between all 168 cortical ROIs of the two participants (*Left brain* leader, *right brain* follower) when contrasting post- against pre-training (phase randomization surrogate statistics, $p < 0.000001$) in theta (4–7.5 Hz) and **c** beta (12–30 Hz). Inter-brain connections were found mainly in the inferior frontal gyrus (IFG), anterior cingulate (AC), parahippocampal gyrus (PHG), and postcentral gyrus (PoCG)

between two interacting participants [40], and that the spontaneous bi-directional improvisation (i.e. implicit synchronization) increased motor synchrony compared with the uni-directional imitation (i.e. explicit following) [41]. Correlations between the fingertip synchrony increase and the social anxiety scales further support that the increased fingertip synchrony could be a marker of implicit social interaction.

The significant increase of phase synchrony in inter-brain connections after the cooperative interaction (training) is theoretically informative, especially since the increase did not occur in several control conditions, including (1) mere repetition of the test session (thus not mere learning), (2) single subject interacting with a dot moving on the screen which was based on the recorded finger movement and (3) with a recorded video of another subject. Also, it should be noted that the phase synchrony increased only inter-brain, not intra-brain (Fig. 10.4).

In a big picture, the current findings argue against the commonsense modern view of the brain and the society—i.e., a very tight unity of a single brain, and very sparse and remote, interpersonal communication among them. Instead, the brain regions are connected inter-brain via bodily interactions, thus to form a loose dynamic coupling possibly in the daily natural interactions.

10.3 Autism as an Impairment of IIPI

Autism spectrum disorder (ASD) is a kind of developmental disorder (the course of development is non-typical due to the functional impairment of certain parts of the brain). The core syndromes of ASD are (1) disorder in mutual interpersonal relationship, (2) communication disorder, and (3) restricted interests and repetitive behavior, which usually become apparent around the ages of 1–3. Not a few individuals with high-functioning ASD notice their disorder when they grow up, facing with troubles in interpersonal relationship and inadaptability to school or work. In the scientific and clinical fields of ASD, the focus is usually on the disorders of interpersonal relationship and communication. For example, an influential theory of ASD claims that the core disorder of ASD is the lack of "theory of mind" (the ability to infer other's intention, knowledge, and belief) [8, 9], and has been examined both from behavioral and neural viewpoints. We have a different view, putting more emphasis on the reception and production of IIPI, which are assumed to support smooth communication. Based on this view, we have been studying basic functions in vision and hearing, which play essential roles in the reception of IIPI.

10.3.1 Basic Auditory Processing in ASD

Individuals with ASD often have difficulty listening to a partner's voice in the environment where multiple sounds coexist, such as a cafeteria, despite the fact that they are not diagnosed as hearing-impaired with a standard audiometric test. To figure out the cause of this difficulty, we performed a series of experiments evaluating basic auditory functions [42]. No ASD ($N = 26$) and NT ($N = 28$) participants were diagnosed as hearing impaired in pure-tone audiometry. Additionally, no significant difference was found between the two groups in an auditory mono-syllable identification test. However, when background noise was superimposed on the mono-syllables, ASDs required significantly lower noise level to obtain the same performance level as NTs. Their complaint was thus supported by objective measurements.

To further explore the cause of the difficulty in selective listening in ASD, we examined various auditory functions including frequency resolution, temporal resolution, sensitivities to interaural time and level differences (ITD and ILD, respectively), pitch discrimination, and so on, and found a characteristic pattern of results for ASD. First, ASDs showed significantly lower sensitivity to ITD and ILD, which are major cues for sound direction in the horizontal plane. Second, a population of ASDs showed significantly lower sensitivity to the temporal fine structure (TFS) of sound waveforms. TFS is one of the cues for pitch [43]. Sound direction and pitch play essential roles in separating sound sources and directing attention to a specific sound source among multiple sound sources presented concurrently. It is quite natural that the impairment in the detection of those cues would cause difficulty in selective listening.

The finding also provides insights about the biological basis of ASD. The sounds received by the ears are first undergone frequency analysis in the cochlea, then transmitted via the brainstem nuclei and thalamus to the auditory cortex in the brain, where auditory perception takes place. ITD, ILD and TFS are detected at the brainstem nuclei [43, 44], suggesting that a population of ASD may have impairment in the brainstem. This is consistent with anatomical findings obtained from postmortal brains [45]. One should note that not all ASD individuals have the brainstem impairment, and those who have the brainstem impairment do not have impairment in other sites of the brain. What is important here is that a significant proportion of ASD individuals has subcortical impairment distinct from cortical ones usually related to interpersonal relationship and communication.

This finding also provides the possibility of objective diagnosis of ASD based on auditory experiments. If we select three critical items (mono-syllable identification under noise, detection of ITD, and detection of TFS) as axes and plot individual data of ASD and NT participants, a certain area in the three-dimensional space exclusively contained ASDs (Fig. 10.5). However, there is also a population of ASDs that cannot be distinguished from NTs with the three items. ASD may consist of separate subgroups, each of which has different biological bases.

We further compared the ability of grouping frequency components between ASD and NT [46]. This is a critical auditory function in multi-source environments, because when acoustic signals from different sound sources are mixed upon arrival at the ears, the auditory system has to organize (or, group) their frequency components by their features [47]. We showed that individuals with ASD performed, counterintuitively, better in terms of hearing a target sequence among distractors that had similar spectral uncertainties (Fig. 10.6). Their superior performance in this task indicates an enhanced discrimination between auditory streams with the same spec-

Fig. 10.5 Objective screening of ASD based on auditory sensitivities [42]. Three critical items of basic auditory functions (mono-syllable identification under noise, detection of interaural time difference, and detection of TFS) are selected as axes and individual data of ASD and NT participants are plotted. The pink-colored area in the three-dimensional space contained ASDs exclusively

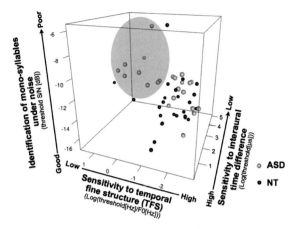

tral uncertainties but different spectro-temporal details. The enhanced discrimination of acoustic components may be related to the absence of the automatic grouping of acoustic components with the same features, which results in difficulties in speech perception in a noisy environment.

An essential question here is whether such specificity of auditory functions in ASD is among the causes of the core syndromes of ASD, namely, disorders in interpersonal relationship and communication, or, simply coexists without causal relationship. It is premature to conclude, but the former possibility seems promising. If an infant cannot turn his/her head towards the direction of a calling voice in dairy situations where multiple sounds often coexist, and the specific auditory impairment is unnoticed by the surrounding people, interpersonal interactions would be severely limited, which may result in problems in the development of social abilities. Further studies are awaited to clarify this point.

10.3.2   Gaze of ASD

In the visual domain, as well as in the auditory (as indicated in the previous section), individuals with ASD may have some abnormality even at the sensory sampling level. For example, a general tendency among them to avoid gazing at the eyes has been reported. However, psychophysical tests conducted in lab settings often fail to show expected differences between ASD and neurotypical (NT) participants.

One reason is that general intelligence is not impaired in high-functioning ASD. ASD participants often employ cognitive strategies to mimic normal behavior. To assess spontaneous tendencies of ASD free from such cognitive strategies, we applied "Don't look" paradigm to participants with varying Autism Quotient (AQ) scores [48, 49]. We presented face images to participants and measured their eye movements under the instruction not to look at the mouth. We predicted that high AQ participants

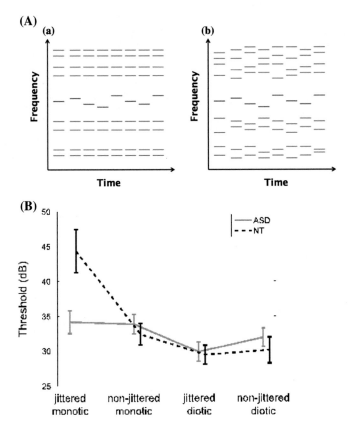

Fig. 10.6 Segregation of concurrent sounds with similar spectral uncertainties [46]. **A** The auditory stimuli contained one target sequence (*red lines*) and eight masker sequences (*blue lines*). The target sequence always had jittered frequencies within a fixed protected region. **a** The masker sequences had fixed frequencies outside the protected region for the non-jittered conditions. **b** The masker sequences had jittered frequencies outside the protected region for the jittered conditions. **B** Target detection thresholds in the ASD and control groups for the four conditions, indicated as mean standard error. The maskers were sent to the right ear for the monotonic conditions or to both ears for the diotic conditions. Both the ASD group and the control group were capable of segregating the target and the masker that carried different spatial information. On the other hand, for the monotic conditions, the significant difference between the jittered and non-jittered thresholds was observed in the control group, but this difference was not observed in the ASD group

may reveal their intrinsic eye-avoidance tendency in this condition, because their cognitive control would be "misdirected" and compensation strategies would not work. Consistent with the prediction, the AQ score was correlated with eye-avoidance tendency (Fig. 10.7).

We further extend this paradigm to a situation where participants viewed paired face and flower images and have to avoid looking at either one [50]. It was found that ASDs had less difficulty suppressing orienting to faces. ASDs (or high AQ) and NTs

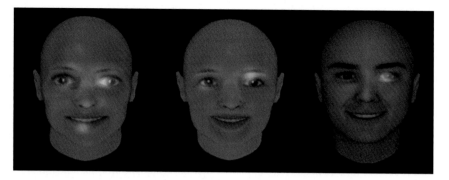

Fig. 10.7 Examples of gaze patterns in "Don't look at the mouth" paradigm [49]. Thirty college students (undiagnosed, AQ average 24.4 ($N = 30$); Male AQ average 25.5 ($N = 20$), Female AQ average 22.4 ($N = 10$)) viewed face images, while their gaze was monitored. The participants were asked to avoid looking at the eyes (not shown here) or the mouth. Gaze patterns were compared across High AQ ($N = 11$, AQ score 27–40, average 32.3) and Low AQ ($N = 13$, AQ score 10–21, average 18.2) groups. The green (red) blobs represent the gaze distribution of low (high) AQ participants, respectively. Low AQ participants tend to look at eyes, whereas high AQ participants tend to avoid the eyes

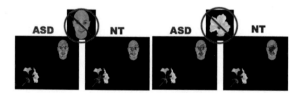

Fig. 10.8 Gaze patterns in "Don't look" paradigm [50]. NT participants ($N = 12$, Male 7, Female 5; AQ 11–39) and diagnosed ASD participants ($N = 9$, Male 5, Female 4; AQ 25–46) viewed paired face and flower images, while their gaze was monitored. The image pairs were arranged diagonally *upper-right* to *lower-left*, to minimize generic spatial biases. The participants were asked to avoid looking at the face or the flower in a 2-alternative forced-choice task. The *red (blue) points* represent the gaze distribution of ASD (NT) participants, respectively. ASDs looked less at face ($p < 0.04$; less at eyes) and more at blank, in "Don't look at the flower" condition (*right*) ($p < 0.03$)

(or low AQ) showed different gaze patterns across social (e.g., eyes) and non-social regions in a face (Fig. 10.8). The "Don't Look" paradigm would provide an objective and effective method for screening ASDs from NTs.

10.4   Future Directions of IIPI Research

In order to achieve human-harmonized information systems, scientific knowledge and technologies of measuring, decoding, and controlling human behaviors are vital. As to this goal, our findings on implicit interpersonal information are of importance, and our project has been based on, and points toward, the research agenda that smooth and effective interpersonal communication depends strongly on implicit, non-symbolic information that emerges from dynamic interactions among agents. The examples shown in this chapter clearly illustrate this and provide the scientific ground for future research and technological development, including the delay compensation by using implicit visual-motor responses [10], diagnosis procedures for autistic spectrum disorders based on auditory [42, 46] and gaze processing [48–50]. We have also developed a marketing method based on leaky attractiveness [51] and objective measurements of immersiveness by using autonomic nervous and hormonal responses [52].

Among possible fields of applications, most prospective fields are learning, teaching [53], collaborations in working, physical, art, and cultural activities. Most of collaborative (or collective) behaviors occur in dynamic, reciprocal interactions. This is particularly true when such activities involve many pieces of implicit agreement or tacit knowledge [54]. Recent advancements of neuroscience and cognitive sciences have examined the multifaceted and dynamic processes in explicit and implicit interpersonal interactions [14, 18, 29, 31, 41, 55–58]. However, how such interactions are manifested and regulated in everyday life is largely unknown. Furthermore, technological developments based on implicit interpersonal communications have yet to be seen.

We have hypothesized that there might be two potential barriers to further advance our knowledge and technologies of implicit interpersonal information. First, many researches have been focused on "reading the mind from the brain." This is mainly because recent advances in brain imaging have been capturing interests of researchers. However, over the decade of our research projects on implicit interpersonal information, it has gradually become clear that there exists unnoticed (and therefore implicit) information among agents on surfaces of the agents' bodies and even in the space between the body surfaces. Moreover, reading the body surfaces would lead to more knowledge and technological advances in implicit interpersonal information.

For example, think about in-person interactions between an athlete and a coach. There are many potential channels though which information are conveyed: direct conversations, explicit and implicit feedback from the coach by observing the athlete's movement, explicit and implicit bodily feedback from the athlete's own actions, explicit and implicit feedback from observations of his/her own performance, social encouragement and discouragement, life patterns of the athlete, etc. Patterns appearing on the "surfaces" of the athlete's body (skin, perspiration, breathing pattern, movement patterns, etc.) would tell a lot of states of the athlete. In addition, we would know that there are atmospheres that lead to either good or bad performance, often consequential and sometimes independent of the consequence of interactions among agents. This may appear to transpire from nowhere yet can be felt by those involved in the interaction. However, it is rather difficult to describe what they actually are and even more difficult to implement processes that mediate such contexts. This is mainly because the agents are unaware of it when they are highly involved in activities. Therefore, "truly wearable" devices that do not interfere with users activities are highly desired in the near future.

Based on these ideas in minds and a recent advance in a performance material capable of measuring biometric information [59], we have started up a new project "Information Processing Systems based on Implicit Ambient Surface Information." In this project, we apply the knowledge and technologies assimilated in the pas research projects and extend to understand of information that exists on the surfaces of human body and machines but are largely ignored ("Implicit Ambient Surface Information"). We utilize it to establish intelligent information processing systems for creative human-machine collaboration. Especially, we aim at developing technologies that recode and decode implicit body movements and physiological responses without disrupting natural behaviors. Additionally, we accumulate scientific knowledge for theoretical advances. In order to achieve this, we plan to set practical fields (e.g., sports) and to test the developed technologies, propose theories, and accomplish the higher quality of activities by humans with collaborations with machines.

As stated in [53], explicit representations of "minds" are consequence of implicit and reciprocal processes between two agents. Thus, the networks of "minds" (or societies) are not necessarily based on explicit knowledge and concepts but entangled with complex implicit interactions at myriad levels ("rhizome" [60]) Then, an important question is how to measure, decode, and even control such implicit interactions.

One way to do this, among others, is to have users (e.g., athletes) be aware of implicit processes by explicit or implicit feedback and let them think (or even not think) about how they might impact such implicit interaction. Conversely, to understand their performing context, coaches would also have to have metacognition and emotion regulations. Knowledge and technologies to be developed by the new project "Information Processing Systems based on Implicit Ambient Surface Information" will help explicit and implicit collaborations between humans, between humans and machines, between humans though machines, and possibly between machines.

References

1. M. Kashino, M. Yoneya, H.-I. Liao, S. Furukawa, Reading the implicit mind from the body. NTT Tech. Rev. **12**(11) (2014)
2. A.R. Damasio, *The Feeling of What Happens: Body and Emotion in the Making of Consciousness* (Mariner Books, 2000)
3. D. Kahneman, *Thinking* (Fast and Slow, Farrar, Straus and Giroux, 2011)
4. M. Yoneya, H.-I. Liao, S. Kidani, S. Furukawa, M. Kashino. Sounds in sequence modulate dynamic characteristics of microsaccades. *Association for Research in Otolaryngology Mid-Winter Meeting* (2014)
5. H.-I. Liao, S. Kidani, M. Yoneya, M. Kashino, S. Furukawa. Correspondences among pupillary dilation response, subjective salience of sounds, and loudness. Psychonomic Bulletin and Review (in press)
6. S. Yoshimoto, H. Imai, M. Kashino, T. Takeuchi, Pupil response and the subliminal mere exposure effect. PLoS One **9**(2), e90670 (2014)

7. Y. Ooishi, H. Mukai, K. Watanabe, S. Kawato, M. Kashino. The effect of the tempo of music on the secretion of steroid and peptide hormones into human saliva. *The 35th Annual Meeting of the Japan Neuroscience Society* (2012)

8. S. Baron-Cohen, A.M. Leslie, U. Frith, Does the autistic child have a 'theory of mind'? Cognition **21**(1), 37–46 (1985)

9. C. Keysers, V. Gazzola, Integrating simulation and theory of mind: from self to social cognition. Trends Cogn. Sci. **11**, 194–196 (2007)

10. S. Takamuku, H. Gomi, in *34th European Conference on Visual Perception*. Background visual motion reduces pseudo-haptic sensation caused by delayed visual feedback during letter writing (2011)

11. V.S. Chib, K. Yun, H. Takahashi, S. Shimojo, Noninvasive remote activation of the ventral midbrain by transcranial direct current stimulation of prefrontal cortex. Transl. Psychiatry **3**, e268,44, (2013)

12. Y. Takano, T. Yokawa, A. Masuda, J. Niimi, S. Tanaka, N. Hironaka, A rat model for measuring the effectiveness of transcranial direct current stimulation using fMRI. Neurosci. Lett. **491**, 40–43 (2011)

13. T. Tanaka, Y. Takano, S. Tanaka, N. Hironaka, T. Hanakawa, K. Watanabe, M. Honda, Transcranial direct-current stimulation increases extracellular dopamine levels in the rat striatum. Frontiers Syst. Neurosci. **7**(6) (2013)

14. K. Yun, K. Watanabe, S. Shimojo, Interpersonal body and neural synchronization as a marker of implicit social interaction. Sci. Rep. **2**, 959 (2012)

15. Y. Takano, M. Ukezono, An experimental task to examine the mirror system in rats. Sci. Rep. **4**, 6652 (2014)

16. G. Rizzolatti, L. Craighero, The mirror-neuron system. Annu. Rev. Neurosci. **27**, 169–192 (2004)

17. F.J. Bernieri, R. Rosenthal, *Fundamentals of Nonverbal Behavior*. (Cambridge University Press, Cambridge, 1991)

18. J.K. Burgoon, L. A. Stern, L. Dillman, *Interpersonal adaptation: dyadic interaction patterns* (Cambridge University Press, Cambridge, 1995)

19. R. Schmidt, M. Richardson. *Coordination: Neural, behavioral and social dynamics*. (Springer, New York, 2008)

20. Z. Neda, E. Ravasz, Y. Brechet, T. Vicsek, A.L. Barabasi, Self-organizing processes: the sound of many hands clapping. Nature **403**, 849–850 (2000)

21. M.J. Hove, J.L. Risen, It's all in the timing: Interpersonal synchrony increases affiliation. Soc. Cogn. **27**, 949–961 (2009)

22. S. Kirschner, M. Tomasello, Joint drumming: social context facilitates synchronization in preschool children. J. Exp. Child Psychol. **102**, 299–314 (2009)

23. A.R. Damasio, *Descartes' Error: Emotion, reason, and the human brain*. (Grosset/Putnam, 1994)

24. U. Bronfenbrenner, *The ecology of human development: Experiments by nature and design* (Harvard University Press, Cambridge, 1979)

25. J. Decety, C. Lamm, The role of the right temporoparietal junction in social interaction: how low-level computational processes contribute to meta-cognition. Neuroscientist **13**, 580–593 (2007)

26. M. Iacoboni, M.D. Lieberman, B.J. Knowlton, I. Molnar-Szakacs, M. Moritz, C.J. Throop, A.P. Fiske, Watching social interactions produces dorsomedial prefrontal and medial parietal BOLD fMRI signal increases compared to a resting baseline. NeuroImage **21**, 1167–1173 (2004)

27. G.G. Knyazev, J.Y. Slobodskoj-Plusnin, A.V. Bocharov, Event-related delta and theta synchronization during explicit and implicit emotion processing. Neuroscience **164**, 1588–1600 (2009)

28. G. Dumas, J. Nadel, B. Soussignan, J. Martinerie, L. Garnero, Inter-brain synchronization during social interaction. PLoS One **5**, e12166 (2010)

29. E. Tognoli, J. Lagarde, G.C. DeGuzman, J.A. Kelso, The phi complex as a neuromarker of human social coordination. Proc. Natl Acad. Sci. **104**, 8190 (2007)

30. B. King-Casas, D. Tomlin, C. Anen, C.F. Camerer, S.R. Quartz, P.R. Montague, Getting to know you: reputation and trust in a two-person economic exchange. Science **308**, 78–83 (2005)
31. P.R. Montague, G.S. Berns, J.D. Cohen, S.M. McClure, G. Pagnoni, M. Dhamala, M.C. Wiest, I. Karpov, R.D. King, N. Apple, R.E. Fisher, Hyperscanning: simultaneous fMRI during linked social interactions. Neuroimage **16**(4), 1159–1164 (2002)
32. F. de Vico Fallani, V. Nicosia, R. Sinatra, L. Astolfi, F. Cincotti, D. Mattia, C. Wilke, A. Doud, V. Latora, B. He, F. Babiloni. Defecting or Not Defecting: How to "Read" Human Behavior during Cooperative Games by EEG Measurements. PLoS One **5**, e14187 (2010)
33. K. Yun, D. Chung, J. Jeong, in *Proceedings of the 6th International Conference on Cognitive Science*. Emotional Interactions in Human Decision Making using EEG Hyperscanning, pp. 327–330 (2008)
34. U. Lindenberger, S.C. Li, W. Gruber, V. Müller, Brains swinging in concert: cortical phase synchronization while playing guitar. BMC Neurosci. **10**, 22 (2009)
35. G. Pfurtscheller, F.H. Lopes da Silva, Event-related EEG/MEG synchronization and desynchronization: basic principles. Clin. Neurophysiol. **110**, 1842–1857 (1999)
36. S.L. Bressler, J.A.S. Kelso, Cortical coordination dynamics and cognition. Trends Cognitive Sci. **5**, 26–36 (2001)
37. P. Fries, A mechanism for cognitive dynamics: neuronal communication through neuronal coherence. Trends Cogn. Sci. **9**, 474–480 (2005)
38. K. Watanabe, M.O. Abe, K. Takahashi, S. Shimojo. Short-term active interactions enhance implicit behavioral mirroring. Soc. Neurosci. **832**(20) (2011)
39. M.R. Leary, Social anxiousness: the construct and its measurement. J. Pers. Assess. **47**, 66–75 (1983)
40. T.L. Chartrand, J.A. Bargh, The chameleon effect: the perception-behavior link and social interaction. J. Pers. Soc. Psychol. **76**, 893–910 (1999)
41. L. Noy, E. Dekel, U. Alon, The mirror game as a paradigm for studying the dynamics of two people improvising motion together. Proc. Natl Acad. Sci. **108**, 20947–20952 (2011)
42. M. Kashino, S. Furukawa, T. Nakano, S. Washizawa, S. Yamagishi, A. Ochi, A. Nagaike, S. Kitazawa, N. Kato, in *Association for Research in Otolaryngology MidWinter Meeting*. Specific deficits of basic auditory processing in high-functioning pervasive developmental disorders (2013)
43. H.E. Gockel, R.P. Carlyon, A. Mehta, C.J. Plack, The frequency following response (FFR) may reflect pitch-bearing information but is not a direct representation of pitch. J. Assoc. Res. Otolaryngol. **12**(6), 767–782 (2011)
44. Y.E. Cohen, E.I. Knudsen, Maps versus clusters: different representations of auditory space in the midbrain and forebrain. Trends Neurosci. **22**(3), 128–135 (1999)
45. R.J. Kulesza Jr, R. Lukose, L.V. Stevens, Malformation of the human superior olive in autistic spectrum disorders. Brain Res. **1367**, 360–371 (2011)
46. I.-F. Lin, T. Yamada, Y. Komine, N. Kato, M. Kashino, The absence of automatic grouping processes in individuals with autism spectrum disorder. Sci. Rep. **22**(5), 10524 (2015)
47. B.C. Moore, H.E. Gockel, Properties of auditory stream formation. Philos. Trans. R. Soc. Lond. B: Biol. Sci. **367**(1591), 919–931 (2012)
48. E. Shimojo, D.-A. Wu, S. Shimojo, Don't look at the mouth, but then where? – Orthogonal task reveals latent eye avoidance behavior in subjects with high Autism Quotient scores. *Annual Meeting of the Vision Sciences Society* (2012)
49. E. Shimojo, D.-A. Wu, S. Shimojo, Don't look at the face—social inhibition task reveals latent avoidance of social stimuli in gaze orientation in subjects with high Autism Quotient scores. Annual Meeting of the Vision Sciences Society (2013)
50. C. Wang, E. Shimojo, D.-A. Wu, S. Shimojo, Don't look at the mouth, but then where?— Orthogonal task reveals latent eye avoidance behavior in subjects with diagnosed ASDs: a movie version. J. Vision **14**(10), 682 (2014)
51. C. Saegusa, J. Intoy, S. Shimojo, Visual attractiveness is leaky: the asymmetrical relationship between face and hair. Frontiers Psychol. **6**, 377 (2015)

52. Y. Ooishi, M. Kobayashi, N. Kitagawa, K. Ueno, S. Ise, M. Kashino. Effects of speakers' unconscious subtle movemens on listener's autonomic nerve activity, *The 37th Annual Meeting of the Japan Neuroscience Society* (2014)
53. K. Watanabe, Teaching as a dynamic phenomenon with interpersonal interactions. Mind, Brain and Education **7**(2), 91–100 (2013)
54. M. Polanyi, *The Tacit Dimension* (University of Chicago Press, Chicago, 1966)
55. J. Decety, J.A. Sommerville, Shared representations between self and other: a social cognitive neuroscience view. Trends Cogn. Sci. **7**(12), 527–533 (2003)
56. G. Knoblich, N. Sebanz, The social nature of perception and action. Curr. Dir. Psychol. Sci. **15**(3), 99–104 (2006)
57. I. Konvalnika, A. Roepstroff, The two-brain approach: how can mutually interacting brains teach us something about social interaction? Frontiers Hum. Neurosci. **6**(215), 1–9 (2012)
58. N. Sebanz, H. Bekkering, G. Knoblich, Joint action: bodies and minds moving together. Trends Cogn. Sci. **10**(2), 70–76 (2006)
59. S. Tsukada, H. Nakashima, K. Torimitsu, Conductive polymer combined silk fiber bundle for bioelectrical signal recording. PLoS One **7**(4), e33689 (2012)
60. G. Deleuze, F. Guattari, *A Thousand Plateaus*. Minuit, 1980. (English translation: University of Minnesota Press, 1987)

Index

© Springer Japan 2016
T. Nishida (ed.), *Human-Harmonized Information Technology, Volume 1*,
DOI 10.1007/978-4-431-55867-5

Printed in the United States
By Bookmasters